INSIDE FALLUJAH

INSIDE FALLUJAH
THE UNEMBEDDED STORY

AHMED MANSOUR

OLIVE
BRANCH
PRESS

This book is dedicated to

The memory of the countless innocent Iraqi lives wasted during the bloody quest for oil domination.

The American servicemen and servicewomen, who represent the best and brightest of the United States, and to the memory of those who lost their lives in this unnecessary and unjust war.

Providing the world with an honest depiction of the terror that is war, in the hopes of avoiding it in the future.

First published in 2009 by

OLIVE BRANCH BOOKS
An imprint of Interlink Publishing Group, Inc.
46 Crosby Street, Northampton MA 01060
www.interlinkbooks.com

Text copyright © Ahmed Mansour, 2009

Library of Congress Cataloging-in-Publication Data
Mansour, Ahmed.
Inside Fallujah : the unembedded story / by Ahmed Mansour.
    p. cm.
ISBN 978-1-56656-778-7 (pbk.)
1. Fallujah, Battle of, Fallujah, Iraq, 2004--Personal narratives, Qatarian. 2. Iraq War, 2003—Personal narratives, Qatarian. 3. Mansour, Ahmed. 4. Al Jazeera (Television network) I. Title.
DS79.766.F3M366 2008
956.7044'342—dc22
                          2009000311

Cover image © AP Photos

Index by Sara C. Rauch

Printed and bound in the United States of America

To request our 48-page full-color catalog, please visit our website at: www.interlinkbooks.com, call us toll-free at: 1-800-238-LINK, or write to us at: Interlink Publishing, 46 Crosby Street, Northampton, MA 01060

CONTENTS

Preface vii
Acknowledgments ix
Prologue xi

I   BEFORE THE BATTLES OF FALLUJAH 1
        1   Iraq after a Year of Occupation 3
        2   The City of Fallujah 19
        3   Mercenaries in the Iraqi–American Conflict 30
        4   Rumblings of Revenge 42
        5   The Road to Samarra 54

II   APRIL 2004: THE FIRST BATTLE 67
        6   Dawn: A City Encircled 69
        7   Day One: Operation Vigilant Resolve Begins 86
        8   Day Two: US Forces Feel the First Sting of Defeat 99
        9   Day Three: Funeral Processions and Snipers 126
        10   Day Four: Iraqis Unite 154
        11   Day Five: A Deadly Rumor 166
        12   The Final Day of the Siege 198

III   POLITICAL BATTLES 215
        13   Bush's War on al-Jazeera 217
        14   A Confrontation of Words: My Interview with
                General Kimmitt 239
        15   Besieging the Besieger 251

IV   NOVEMBER 2004: FALLUJAH DESTROYED 273
        16   Is the Battle Over? 275
        17   Preparating for Annihilation 290
        18   Operation Phantom Fury 297
        19   "Cleaning Up": War Crimes, Mass Graves, and an
                Empty City 316

                                        Afterword 340
                                          Notes 342
                                          Index 348

PREFACE

The story of President George W. Bush's war on Iraq likely needs no introduction, but it is still worth recalling from the start that the President based his case for war against Iraq on three major points: nuclear proliferation, Iraq's possession of Weapons of Mass Destruction (WMDs), and Iraq's support of al-Qaeda or other foreign Islamic extremist militant organizations. The world eventually found that all three claims were made entirely without evidence, and their falsity was even verified by several reports released from within the Bush administration later in the war.

The discovery that the impetus for such a large-scale military attack was intentionally fabricated should have been enough to end the career of any politician. Yet this scandal made little, if any, difference to George W. Bush. Making his footprint on the path of human history was secured with this war, and any mayhem caused by it appears to be simply the cost of doing business.

During the course of this war against a country that posed no viable threat to America, many crimes against humanity were perpetrated. In the early part of April 2004, I witnessed a military operation that was called "heroic," but in truth was the stage for countless war crimes. I was assigned by al-Jazeera satellite channel to provide news coverage for Operation Vigilant Resolve, which took place in Fallujah as a response to the heinous mutilation and murder of private Blackwater USA security guards working in Iraq on behalf of the United States. We were a crew of only a few people, and we were the only televised media outlet that was able to infiltrate the siege on Fallujah and cover the operation as it unfolded. This book is an account of what I witnessed during the siege and an analysis of the events that came both before and after.

Because of the exclusive access I had during Operation Vigilant Resolve, I want to document what we witnessed there for the sake of humanity and history. As other reports have already exposed Bush for having had no case to start the war, I intend to report on the less-than-heroic nature of the so-called "heroic" military operations that comprised the war. It is of utmost importance, I believe, that the world witness all versions of this story in order to better discern the truth of what happened—and may still be happening, because American troops still have not left Iraq.

The documentation of this particular operation is crucial because of its significance for each of the warring parties. For the United States, the battle for Fallujah was likened to the battle for the city of Hue during the Tet Offensive, and prompted discussions of parallels between the war in Iraq and the Vietnam War. For Iraqi insurgents, militants, and other resistance groups and their sympathizers, Fallujah was a rallying point that looked for a time to have dealt a serious blow to American resolve.

Operation Vigilant Resolve is informally known as the first battle of Fallujah. It was halted with serious defeat to the American forces. But the end of this operation was merely a pause in the larger battle for control of the city of Fallujah. In November of the same year, American forces waged a second attack on Fallujah called Operation Phantom Fury. In reality, the second battle was merely a continuation of the first, and an act of bitter revenge for the defeat suffered by American forces the first time around. This book covers both operations.

ACKNOWLEDGMENTS

Before the reader gets on board for a journey through my experience of these battles, I would like to extend my sincere gratitude to all those who made this work possible. At the top of the list comes the people of Fallujah, whose lives constitute the substance of this book. In particular, I would like to thank the al-Saad and Hadeed families. Both showed my crew and me unending kindness during our entire stay in Fallujah, and humbled us with their immense generosity and hospitality. I must also thank my wife and children, because our lives together were put on hold while I was either away on travel or unavailable at home, writing this book.

I want to express my great gratitude to Minnesota State University, Mankato, for introducing me to the translator and the editor who labored for a year on this material. These individuals refused to simply directly translate this book into English; they believe that translated works often do not convey the author's main idea as well as they might. While translated works do cross language barriers, they don't necessarily cross cultural barriers, and sometimes the author's meaning is lost. All three of us wanted this version of the book to be written for the English-speaking reader so that the message of the book would not be hindered. So they stripped the Arabic book down to its foundations and built it back up in English. In essence, they didn't translate the Arabic book; they produced an English edition of it. This work required a lot of attention to the main ideas of the book, and a lot of time to find a way to maintain its message that would engage the audience and satisfy the author.

I would also like to thank all my colleagues and friends who invested a great deal in this book, and answered everything I asked of them. In particular, I would like to thank the crew members who covered the battle of Fallujah: Hamed Hadeed, Abdulazeem Muhammad, Layth Mushtaq, and Hussain Deli.

I want to make it clear that this book expresses my personal opinions. The writing here portrays a view of parts of this war through the lens of my exclusive, individual experience in this conflict. Al-Jazeera and its administration are in no way responsible for anything in this book and I am in no way acting as a spokesperson for that organization or any other organization.

Still, members of al-Jazeera's administration were helpful to me in the process of writing this book, because they are my co-workers. I would like to thank the person who has been a friend and a brother to me throughout this entire process: Sheikh Hamad bin Thamer al-Thani. I would also like to extend a thank you to Wadah Khanfar, my friend and colleague, and also the director general at al-Jazeera. These two gentlemen played a huge role in lifting the morale of our crew throughout its work covering the battle of Fallujah, a difficult time for us all.

I am responsible for any shortcomings in this book. Despite repeated revisions (it has gone through more than five), I still find myself writing the book almost from scratch every time it comes back to my desk. Every rewrite reveals room for improvement. At its best, this book is a small attempt to render the truth of this event as I witnessed it. I hope that it will be only the beginning of other, more extensive efforts to explain this event—efforts made by witnesses in Iraq who want to document what took place in Fallujah. My wish is that the battles of Fallujah do not become just another footnote in history, but instead are remembered as pivotal points in our human timeline, points that changed the direction of our global future.

—Doha, December 6, 2008

PROLOGUE

"In the general course of human nature, a power of a man's subsistence amounts to a power of his will."
          —Alexander Hamilton, article 79 of *The Federalist Papers*

It was just past midnight on April 4, 2004. I was working in our recently renovated newsroom in the Swan Lake Hotel, overlooking Sahat Kahramana (Amber Square) in Karradah, a suburb of Baghdad. On this particular night, I was immersed in reviewing my report on a recent visit to the city of Samarra. I was sharing the office with my colleague Hamed Hadeed. I heard the phone ring, and Hamed picked it up.

It didn't take long for my interest to be piqued by the urgent questions Hamed asked the person on the other end of the line. After a few moments, it became clear that it was al-Jazeera's director general, Wadah Khanfar, phoning from our headquarters in Doha. From what I could overhear, I understood only that something unusual was happening in or near the city of Fallujah.

As soon as he hung up, Hamed turned to me and said, "Wadah says he's got information that massive numbers of American troops have encircled Fallujah. The city is supposedly completely surrounded. He asked me to see what's going on."

"But it's past midnight," I said, "How are you going to get any kind of information?"

After a moment of thought, he said, "Let's call Hussain." Hussain Deli was our resident correspondent in Fallujah.

Over the course of Hamed's conversation with Hussain, it became clear that Hussain had no idea what, if anything, was transpiring just outside his city limits. He asked for some time to take a spin around the city. He wanted to check out the town squares, talk to some people, and maybe look outside the city limits for any suspicious activity. He promised to look for American troops, and in particular to see if any appeared to be approaching the entrances to the city.

An hour later, Hussain called to inform us that he had toured Fallujah and the surrounding neighborhoods, and found everything to be peaceful. Nothing appeared out of the ordinary within or outside city limits. There was nothing visible that would suggest a massive presence of American troops or an immediate threat of encirclement. We thanked him for his information and hung up.

Hamed and I speculated about several possible scenarios given the two conflicting stories we had received. We knew that tension in Fallujah had been alarmingly high since March 31, when a band of insurgents had launched an assault on a car driven by four mercenaries working for the US Army. The mercenaries' car was set ablaze, and eventually the four men died in the fire. Following this, a mob of locals dragged the charred corpses from the vehicle and paraded them along the city streets. This hideous attack had been filmed by a number of journalists and broadcast by news agencies across the globe, including al-Jazeera. Hussain Deli was among those who were able to capture noteworthy images of the incident. Following the attack, US officials, including President Bush, promised that the perpetrators would be brought to justice.

We took all of this into serious consideration after we received the news from Wadah that American troops were waiting to surround Fallujah the next day—Sunday, April 4, under the cover of night. Tense, difficult moments passed as we waited by the phone for more news and more instructions.

Prior to Wadah's phone call, al-Jazeera had already instructed us to make arrangements to provide news coverage in Fallujah from April 5–9, for the first anniversary of the US occupation of Iraq. We had formed four television crews to be sent to four major areas of Iraq, including Fallujah, and each crew was to be headed by one of al-Jazeera's distinguished news program presenters or show hosts. The first crew, stationed in Baghdad, was headed by my colleague Muhammad Kraishan. The second crew was to be sent to Arbeel, in northern Iraq, and headed by my colleague Ghassan bin Jeddo. Incidentally, that crew's mission was never completed. Ghassan never reported for his duty, for reasons I never knew nor asked about. The third crew was set to be stationed in Najaf and Karbala and was to be headed by my colleague Abdulqader Ayadh. I was to head the fourth crew in Fallujah, in addition to my other assignments.

While covering the anniversary of American occupation in Fallujah, I was also expected to record some episodes of my show, *Without Limits*. For these episodes I hoped to interview some former Iraqi military leaders who served in the last battle for Baghdad before the capital fell in 2003. I wanted to shed some light on some of the hidden aspects of that battle and I also wanted to investigate some of its secrets.[1] It wasn't going to be easy to be granted an interview, considering that the occupation authorities and the Iraqi Governing Council[2] had incriminated most Iraqis who were employed by the toppled regime. I also had to search for potential guests for my other show, *A Witness for an Era*. For this show, I primarily attempted to interview former Iraqi officials or decision makers.

All of which is to say that when Wadah Khanfar called the office around midnight on April 4 to tell us that troops were surrounding Fallujah, we were still working—discussing our plan for getting to Fallujah the next day. Our initial timeline had us in Fallujah for just five days, and this short stay seemed feasible at the time, because the bigger picture of the conflict wasn't yet clear. We had no idea that the city had already been surrounded by troops at the very moment we sat in the office, and that all roads leading in and out of the city were already blocked. We didn't know then that even the narrow dirt roads were closed, and that the entire city was already left with virtually no entrances or exits. We had no idea how grave the situation truly was, because Hussain's call had indicated that everything appeared peaceful within the city limits and nearby. Later, we would figure out that the troops were still a bit far from the city limits when Hussain toured the city in response to our phone call—and any soldiers near enough to spot were hidden by the cover of night. In any case, after Hussain's report on the calm, the circle of troops around Fallujah began to tighten, and the city was very quickly thrown in grave danger.

After all the phone calls, analysis, and speculation, eventually exhaustion got the better of us. It was 2:30 in the morning by the time we decided to get some rest. We knew we had to prepare for the tough task ahead in Fallujah, the details of which were unknown.

But before I take you along to Fallujah and the unfolding of the situation that Wadah had warned us about that fateful night, let's look at the situation in Iraq prior to the battle of Fallujah. What was happening in Iraq one year after the start of the American occupation, in the days before the first battle of Fallujah occurred?

PART I

BEFORE THE BATTLES OF FALLUJAH

1. IRAQ AFTER A YEAR OF OCCUPATION

On April 2, almost exactly one year into the American occupation of Iraq and two days before the news that American troops were encircling Fallujah, I was wandering the old markets of the city of Samarra, one of Mesopotamia's most ancient cities. I enjoy wandering the narrow alleyways of old Iraqi cities, despite the often deplorable security. I attempted to avoid the curiosity of those who might recognize me from al-Jazeera by wearing a hat and dark sunglasses, but an elderly Iraqi gentleman still managed to identify my face from the news. He grasped my hand, and looked searchingly into my face.

"Aren't you Ahmed Mansour?" he asked.

I said yes and smiled.

He said, urgently, "I want you to tell the world about what America has done to Iraq. I want you to tell the world that the destruction that has taken place during this one year of occupation surpasses everything Saddam Hussein did to Iraq in his 35-year rule. We never liked Saddam, but Americans are far worse than him. A thousand times worse." The man continued to talk for a few minutes, using this opportunity to vent his anger and pain. I listened to him out of respect, and then said my goodbyes and left.

The words of this man stuck with me as I wandered through the marketplace and echoed in my head later that day when I was a guest at Sheikh Nahedh Samarray's home. There I met with both common people and dignitaries of Samarra, and the group had a multitude of stories to share about what the American troops had done to the city of Samarra and its people during the first year of occupation. These stories, often heartbreaking, will be narrated later. By this point, it was becoming very clear to me why the anniversary coverage would be so immensely important to Iraqis and to the world.

The following day I met with Dr. Ali Mash-hadany, president of the Iraqi Union of Oil Experts, in Baghdad. He was one of the guests who agreed to an interview for the April 9 special coverage of Fallujah. His statements mirrored those of the elderly Samaritan who had cornered me in the market. Mash-hadany supplemented his concerns with numbers and statistics and gave me the scientific perspective one would expect from an oil and economy expert. Through talking with Mash-hadany, I began to learn the extent to which the American occupation was pillaging the scant resources still available in Iraq.

Mash-hadany estimated that Iraq's losses during one year of American occupation had reached $475 billion.

"How did you come up with this astronomical figure?" I asked during the interview.

He replied, "I didn't calculate or estimate these numbers by myself. My colleagues and I are a group of Iraqi experts in oil and economy. We reached this figure through calculations done on government properties and assets. Financial losses aren't calculated just by tallying up what's lost or damaged. They're calculated in a different way. Before Saddam was ousted, his regime used to appropriate ninety percent of Iraq's oil revenue to armaments. Now, all government property of arms, equipment, arms manufacturing plants, airports, and military constructions are destroyed."

Mash-hadany went on to explain that the majority of Iraqi warplanes had been well preserved and fully operational before the American occupation, and many were well taken care of while being stored on Iraqi farms. After the occupation, these warplanes were sawed up, salvaged, and sold by American occupation authorities as scrap metal. These warplanes were once worth millions of dollars and were originally paid for by Iraqi taxpayers, but were now being sold by contractors as scrap metal worth a few hundred dollars per ton. This process also meant that each operational T-72 tank, which weighed more than forty tons and cost more than $1 million to build, was now worth only about $1,000. The worst thing about this situation, Mash-hadany said, was that the Iraqi people were not aware of what was being done with the resources of their homeland.

"We conducted very thorough research to discover the extent of Iraq's resources—be it military equipment, arms manufacturing plants, military constructions, or camps," Mash-hadany continued. "We found out that Iraq had about 250 million dollars worth of resources, all of which is gone now. Don't forget that the Iraqi army, established after 1921, has been dissolved now, which means that not only were military resources such as warplanes reduced to rubble, but our more than 80 years of military strength and experience has been eliminated. The emotional loss of this experience is impossible to put a price tag on."

As for the funds spent on training military cadres and civilian personnel, Mash-hadany reported that the price tag on these lost funds was simply unfathomable. These funds were sent abroad for specialized training scholarships, and over the span of the past thirty years had reached over 250,000 people, each costing no less than $500,000 to be trained. The total cost of training Iraqi military personnel soared over 125 billion dollars, a number he claims is undeniably accurate. With the loss of the Iraqi military comes the loss of all this invested money.

Mash-hadany spoke of another $50 billion of the Oil for Food revenue that was appropriated by the toppled regime for the purpose of purchasing equipment for civilian use. Although most of that equipment was still in its original packaging, some of it was assembled but never used, and the rest was assembled and used very briefly. The US occupation, according to many witnesses, sent all that equipment out of Iraq, and no one knows how it was sold. Mash-hadany said, "Some of the equipment was given by Americans to American allies. We don't know who gave Americans the right to appropriate Iraq's resources however they wish."

"All of these damages are in addition to the destruction that fell upon many aspects of the country's natural resources. Farming comes to mind as an example. Oil institutions and oil wells are being damaged the most. Iraqi oil experts have been subjected to enough assassination threats to make them leave the country. There are organized liquidation operations launched against Iraqi experts in all areas, and there are daily assassinations and liquidations under many claims, all of which stem from one purpose: evacuating Iraq of all of its intellectuals, professionals, and experts, and leaving it only with those who can't build a state."

I was shocked by Mash-hadany's words because most of us outside Iraq, including me, were completely oblivious to these claims. Many people, one year into the occupation, were still talking about the catastrophic looting of the Iraqi National Museum. It seemed like what had been looted and stolen from this country was even bigger and grander than most have imagined—certainly bigger and grander than what one could take from a museum.

During the month that I stayed in Iraq prior to the start of the first battle of Fallujah, I visited most major cities in Iraq. During this year, I was shocked by what had come to pass in Iraq during only one year of occupation. Figures and numbers are the language I usually speak when I refer to such facts, but the truly exact figures and numbers are known only to two entities involved in this situation: the occupation authorities and their hired contractors, who disassembled factories, dismantled institutions, emptied warehouses, and shipped everything out of Iraq. Anyone wandering by the highways that connect Iraq to neighboring countries could easily see the massive numbers of trailers, all loaded with incalculable goods. These loads were always covered by a huge tarp or concealed by some other method, so it was not obvious to passersby that stolen goods were inside.

I had seen one of these incidents at first hand in March 2004, on a return trip to Baghdad from Tikrit, Saddam Hussein's birthplace and the administrative center of the district of Saladin. Along the way (it's about an 87-mile trip), I encountered a traffic accident where a semi-trailer had been overturned. Iraqi police and American troops surrounded the scene. The damaged semi-trailer was one among an entire caravan of other massive trucks, and all were guarded by American troops and Iraqi police. I asked the driver to pull over so I could find out what was going on. Usually, the Iraqi police know nothing about the incidents they participate in guarding. I presented my journalist ID to the Iraqi police anyway, and asked them to let me get closer to the scene. The Iraqis said that the American troops had ordered everyone away from the accident site. I tried to get some information about the nature of the accident and what had happened, but the Iraqi police told me nothing of any real value.

After several lengthy arguments with the Iraqi police, one of their officers recognized me from television and introduced himself. He allowed me to get a little closer to the overturned semi to further investigate its load. I saw a huge piece of equipment protruding from the wreck. I asked the officer what it was. He said it was something disassembled from an oil refinery in Tikrit. When I asked him where that piece was heading now, he said he had no idea. I was then spotted by an American soldier, so I presented my journalist ID to him. I told him I wanted to learn about the nature of the accident, and about the contents of the truck. I asked if he could tell me where all the trucks were heading. He didn't answer my question, and instead demanded I leave the scene immediately. He refused to give me any information and did not allow me to take any photos. All of this happened on the road from Tikrit to Baghdad, which is also the interstate that leads to Turkey through the city of Mosul.[3] The suspicion that these trucks were on their way out of the country is hard to escape.

I got even more striking data on the pillaging of Iraqi resources by American troops when I visited Samarra, the heart of the so-called Sunni Triangle. Samarra, 78 miles north of Baghdad, is the largest city in the Saladin province and home to a wealth of history and culture. This area is where the island of Buhayrat al-Tharthar (Lake Chatterbox) is located. The lake holds more than 21 trillion gallons of water and supplies the

Tigris and Euphrates with water during the dry seasons. Iraqi government warehouses that stored everything from food to military hardware were located here. A few weeks into the occupation, ownership of the warehouses was unofficially transferred to the American forces, along with the bounty stored inside their walls.

About this scandal, an Iraqi Governing Council official in Samarra said to me, "A few months into the occupation, Iraqis were surprised to find contractors moving the contents of these warehouses, a colossal operation that would require an enormous squadron of trailers and many years of labor to achieve. The contractors were emptying the warehouses and shipping the contents elsewhere. Iraqis discovered that it was the Americans who were running this process of selling the contents of all the warehouses."

The Governing Council official continued, "Iraqis found out that these contractors were under agreement to move and sell the warehouses that contained massive amounts of Iraqi resources, including brand new military hardware, army equipment, food supplies, equipment for civilian use, and computers, all of which had never been used. These are the sorts of resources the country needs to keep running.

"The area also has an industrial production plant called 'Saladin Industrial Installation.' The former regime, with help from the French, had equipped the plant with massive computer mainframes capable of running production operations for manufacturing sophisticated digital equipment, including commercial satellites and equipment for factories. The plant was new and hadn't even had an official christening. When we discovered that there were contractors disassembling this state-of-the-art plant in order to move it, we called the Iraqi police and the governor, and they responded and came to the scene. But at this point, no one, and I mean *no one*, was able to halt this grand act of vandalism and looting, not even the governor. We found out that the contractors had a sales contract... signed by a US army corporal. I am ashamed to tell you that the authority of an American corporal far surpasses that of the Iraqi governor and even the Iraqi Governing Council members.

"For the past year, since the start of the occupation, I have been trying, along with a great many good citizens of Iraq, to save what's left of our country's resources, but we've failed miserably. Our resources are being disassembled and sold, and some of them are even being given away for free as gifts to countries that aided the occupation—you know, the kind of countries that call themselves 'allies.' We're totally incapable of protecting our resources. I guarantee you that the National Museum is not the only thing that was reduced to ashes in this past year. During one year of occupation, the destruction and looting that our resources have been subjected to is far more hideous than what people saw on TV. Everything that's being propagated now is no more than a cover-up for the systematic looting of what's left of the country's properties, plants, installations, warehouses, and other resources that could've lasted Iraq for years to come. Yet, no one is speaking out because hardly anyone knows what's going on. No one listens to us when we speak out because everyone is stricken with grief because a loved one has been killed or detained by the Americans. As for satellite manufacturing equipment and other Iraqi resources, they're being auctioned off by an American soldier… that's where Iraq stands a year into the occupation."

No Jobs and No Money

The rise in unemployment in Iraq one year after the occupation was another frightening side effect of this conflict. Prior to the occupation, the Iraqi army employed more than half a million soldiers and professionals, and the Iraqi government employed more than seven million people. Since the occupation dissolved the Iraqi government and armed forces, most of those people were abruptly rendered unemployed. During my journey across Iraq in the first year of occupation, I met many former officers and former senior officials suffering from miserable living conditions. For example, in the northern province of Saladin, the majority of people I met were once employed by the Iraqi army, special security forces, the Republican Guard, or the state. After the occupation, some of them changed careers to become drivers, while others roamed the streets selling basic goods just to support their families. Some who were fortunate enough to own a piece of land went back to farming. The majority of displaced people were just plain jobless.

One of these displaced men told me, as he turned his face away in pain, "I have five girls, and some of them are in college. I was a major general, and I used to be a professor in the Supreme Defense Academy, Iraq's most prestigious military academy. I hold three doctorates in Military Science. But I am unemployed now. How am I to put food on the table? How are we going to survive?"

As for the institutions run by the new local administration, those offered little relief for the jobless Iraqis. The Iraqis who signed up with the police department or National Defense Agency were generally viewed as traitors because of their willingness to cooperate with occupation authorities. Consequently, targeting these workers became fair practice for the insurgents. At best, the workers of the new local administration were looked at with disgust by the general public. Just as did Saddam's Ba'ath Party,[4] the American occupation forces managed to recruit seven million employees, most of whom were simply looking for a job. Once recruited, they had to pay the price of being hated and distrusted by their fellow countrymen.

This chaos and joblessness wasn't only evident in large cities like Baghdad; this was the standard situation throughout Iraq, save in the few communities where the primary source of income had been established as trade or farming for many years. I visited a former military commander working the tiny farm he had inherited from his father. The farm was located in his hometown, about 124 miles from Baghdad. He couldn't afford a phone, and so when I reached his home unannounced, I was asked to wait until he came in from the farm. Eventually, he came to greet me, with his hands soiled with mud. He was wearing his farming clothes—he had been in the field irrigating his crops.

Embarrassed, he said, "Sorry, I'll wash up and get right back to you." When he came back, he was still looking embarrassed. "After the destruction of our army and the occupation of our country, I found nothing except this small piece of land my old man had left me. So, I came back to farming, and I hope to provide my family with some sustenance." It hurt me to see how such an accomplished man could be embarrassed about his place in life. I told him not to worry about his new employment, and that he was pursuing one of the noblest professions in the world.

Journalistic Chaos

When I used to visit Iraq during Saddam's reign, the only newspapers published in Iraq were sponsored by his official ruling party. For 35 years those newspapers had Saddam Hussein's portrait plastered on the front page. The articles in these publications took special care to speak of Saddam's achievements as if Iraqis were living through a special and noteworthy era: the age of Saddam Hussein. On every visit during that time period, I had the feeling that the newspapers I read were so similar to the ones I had read on previous visits that they might have been reprints of the same edition. I had to double-check the date to believe that the paper was current. This strange similarity between newspapers was a testament to Saddam's hold over the press throughout his reign.

One year into the American occupation, the world of printed media in Iraq had become utterly different. Every morning in Baghdad, I awoke to an enormous and varied pile of Iraqi newspapers outside my door. But only one or two of them were actually suitable for reading. The rest of the newspapers belonged to wayward political parties, former politicians, agents of other regimes vying for power, or private individuals. Gossip-based newspapers were also published and included in this pile. These magazines specialized in printing unfounded scandals or republishing scandals that had run in other Arab newspapers years earlier. The difference was that the new versions of these scandals were poorly paraphrased and cheaply produced. I remember reading a story about the divorce of an actress that I'd read in an Egyptian newspaper years before. The actress may have very possibly divorced and remarried several times since the release of the old story, but this latest release was definitely narrated with a special Iraqi touch of fabrication and falsification.

A member of the board of directors of the Association of Iraqi Journalists said that the number of newspapers published in Baghdad one year after the occupation had reached 235, some of which released no more than one edition. Some groups published more than one newspaper. The majority of these papers were distributed free of charge on the streets, in offices, and at hotels. It became a familiar morning sight to see Iraqi men handing out free publications to acquaintances and strangers alike. There are so many publications that some are not read by anyone except those who write for them! This was the overwhelming journalistic mess that had spread throughout Iraq after the American occupation—and I'm only describing what I saw in Baghdad. In other districts and cities, apparently hundreds of other newspapers were published and distributed that I never had the chance to see.

On December 9, 2005, the New York Times exposed that the funding for many of these newspapers was coming from American occupation sources. The Times reported that the writers for these papers were bribed to write articles that moved forward the US agenda. These revelations came as part of an entire season of newspaper-related scandals that later plagued the Bush administration after its failure to achieve any of its military and political goals in Iraq. The publishing of ideas propagated by the CIA in Iraqi newspaper articles bearing the names of Iraqi journalists should have been scandal enough to tarnish the reputation of any political regime in the world. Surprisingly, however, a senior official at the Pentagon issued a fatwa to the contrary. This "fatwa" of December 30, 2005, claimed that Pentagon-funded publications written by journalists promoting an American agenda in different parts of the world is not illegal. The Department of Defense inspector general also ruled that Pentagon-funded publications were also in accordance with US law.

The revealing article in the *Times* mentioned that the number of articles written by American soldiers and published in Iraqi newspapers under the names of Iraqi journalists had reached a thousand, and that the cost of publishing each article was about $1,500. The newspaper scandal exposed that what was happening in Iraq was merely an extension of what had happened in the Balkans, Afghanistan, and other political hotspots. The *Times* also revealed that the Pentagon had allotted hundreds of millions of dollars to advertising agencies, which then created propaganda campaigns to help the US succeed in its political plans for the Middle East. Creating this type of propaganda is possible through the internet, radio stations, TV channels, and newspapers. American forces involved in this process bought off the names of local journalists as well as the integrity behind them. They continued, as well, to promote their agenda either directly through occupation officials or indirectly through advertisement firms ran by former intelligence officers.

Contributing to this propaganda campaign were well-known advertising agencies such as AD Rendón and Advertising Federation of Lincoln, as well as the National Institute for Democracy, the International Republican Institute, and the US Army Psychological Warfare Unit, which is headquartered at Fort Bragg. The US claims that this propaganda campaign was trying to send an honest message of support for the efforts of the US government in Iraq, but even a former employee of the Advertising Federation of Lincoln described the advertising agenda as a "misleading web of lies."

Many new newspapers that popped up during this time in other Arab countries including Egypt, Jordan, and Lebanon were questioned as possibly being part of the American propaganda operation in the region. It was no longer sufficient to bribe a journalist on an individual level, or to publish fraudulent articles in a scattering of Iraqi publications. This propaganda operation entailed taking over entire newspapers to serve as forums for public figures who would promote the American point of view. The *New York Times* published a statement released by a Pentagon official in the Psychological Warfare Unit, which claimed that the Pentagon didn't want the public to get a hint of who might be behind the articles that were being published. This is why the Pentagon contracted journalists who were already working in these newspapers to allow the use of their names.

The newspaper and journalist scandal exposed only the first few Iraqi newspapers dedicated to promoting misleading US propaganda. These newspapers overwhelmed the public in every way, and Iraq was suddenly awash in a scandal that would have amazed even Joseph Goebbels.

An Explosion of New Political Parties

Along with the journalistic chaos that swept through Iraq during the first year of the occupation, the establishment of new political parties brought a parallel kind of upheaval. The count of new political parties that were officially declared within the first year of occupation reached somewhere close to 200. An Iraqi politician told me that the count actually reached 237 by the beginning of 2004, less than eight months into the occupation. These counts don't even include the minor parties that emerged and were limited to neighborhoods, districts, and cities; those parties were also estimated to be in the hundreds. As soon as the Iraqi regime fell, these newly established parties exploded onto Ba'ath headquarters and sites, claiming them as their own. Groups set up headquarters in former state institutions, VIP residences, government residential compounds, government military barracks, and even movie theaters and bars. In an internationally broadcast incident on March 29, 2004, the world witnessed a fistfight between members of the Party of God's Revenge—a small Shia party in Basra—and British troops. The troops had demanded the group vacate the Basra Chapter of the Iraqi Women's Association, which the new party had seized in order to exact "God's revenge." The building had then been turned into headquarters for the party from which it could exact some more of "God's revenge" on something else.

Residences of former regime officials were also hastily turned into operation headquarters for new parties. These former residences frequently became residences to new officials, who felt no shame in unceremoniously taking over their predecessor's homes. During my stay in Baghdad in March 2004, I also learned that the Iraqi Broadcast & Television building had been taken over by some Iraqi families. When I asked about what had become of the studio units inside, I was told that every spacious studio was occupied by several families.

During this confusing time, I went to visit Saladin Baha al-Din, a member of the Iraqi Governing Council, to arrange to have him as a guest on *Without Limits*. I found him living in the ministers' compound in al-Qadisya, in the heart of Baghdad. The compound was surrounded by a massive concrete wall rising to a height of twelve feet or so, not unlike the wall erected by Ariel Sharon around the West Bank. Al-Qadisya's wall, however, was heavily guarded by American tanks and Iraqi civil defense soldiers. These soldiers were in place to subdue the fear of explosives, which seemed to threaten every place occupation forces could be found. So many of these concrete walls were built that they eventually encircled all the buildings and hotels used by occupation authorities, including the residences once inhabited by Ba'ath party members. In this way, the occupying authority slowly occupied the city in the same way as the forces they had driven from power.

The Death of Security

Here's a sample of some of the headlines I woke up to throughout my journey around Iraq in March and April of 2004:

Former Interior Ministry Officer Assassinated and Daughter Injured.

Al-Mahmoodya's Police Department Sheriff Assassinated.

Booby-Trapped Vehicle Targets the Diyala Province.

Unidentified Attackers Kidnap Dr. Walid al-Khal.

Doctor Killed inside His Own Clinic.

As one Iraqi politician explained to me, murders, kidnappings, booby-trapped vehicles, rounds of gunfire, explosions, shells, and missiles were such common occurrences that everyone in Iraq under the US occupation lost any sense of security.

Even the former civil governor of Iraq, Paul Bremer, mentions in the Arab edition of his memoirs[5] that a total of seven failed assassination attempts were made on his life by the end of his term. General John Abizaid, who was in charge of the US Central Command for much of the war (he retired in May 2007), also escaped a rocket attack by the insurgents. On February 12, 2004, CNN's Lou Dobbs spoke of the attack, saying, "Today, gunmen in Fallujah launched a brazen attack against General John Abizaid, the commander of US forces. Insurgents attacked the general and other Americans as they visited the Fallujah headquarters of the Iraqi Civil Defense Corps. US troops responded with machine gunfire. There were no injuries to American troops." General Mark Kimmitt held a press conference later that evening in Baghdad. About the assassination attempt, he remarked, "Today at 1330 in Fallujah, General Abizaid and General Swannack were visiting the local Iraqi Civil Defense Corps battalion headquarters compound when three rocket-propelled grenades were fired at their convoy from rooftops in the vicinity." Certainly, the lives of all parties involved in this conflict were at risk.

So, if that was the security situation facing the American governor of Iraq and the commander of US forces, despite the protection of concrete walls and tens of thousands American soldiers, what would one speculate the security situation was for the common Iraqi citizen? Despite the fact that according to international law, providing security in an occupied territory is the responsibility of the occupying force, Donald Rumsfeld repeatedly made statements indicating that Iraqi security was an Iraqi responsibility, not an American responsibility. He said, "It's their country... They're going to have to govern it, and they're going to have to provide security for it." This statement undoubtedly violates all international conventions and laws for a country occupied by foreign forces.

This chaotic security situation, or more accurately, this *lack* of security, encouraged other mayhem in addition to insurgent attacks. The chaos led to the rise of organized, armed gangs who specialized in kidnapping wealthy citizens and members of the occupation forces, and these gangs demanded ransom in exchange for the release of their prisoners. Other gangs specialized in armed robberies, while a third kind of gangs focused on resolving internal feuds between gangs via liquidations and assassinations.

In March of 2004, Dr. Harith Aldhary, the secretary general of the Association of Muslim Scholars in Iraq (AMSI),[6] told me in an interview, "The number of Sunni religious scholars that were assassinated within one month is over fifty, including my own brother." Aldhary describes his brother as "a peaceable meek gentleman who was one of the most revered Sunni scholars in Baghdad." To his comments about the violence, he added, "There are lists of names issued by some parties supposedly for liquidating former Ba'athists; in reality, the lists aim at assassinating all distinguished experts, scholars, and academics among Sunnis, and they aim at ridding Iraq of all of its qualified citizens and experts under the excuse and claim that they are Ba'athists. This is dangerous and trespasses on all norms." Aldhary's comments demonstrate how dire this situation was for Iraqis and the future of their country—a country that now faced the possibility of no resources to sustain life, and no qualified citizens to maintain order and command respect.

The Legitimization of Conquest

After its initial occupation of Iraq, the United States established the Interim Governing Council. This council consisted of 25 Iraqis who represented a diverse spectrum of the Iraqi population. The formation of this council signaled the first time sectarianism had been used to shape an Iraqi government in hundreds of years. On top of that, many of the representatives had no popular support among the Iraqi people. More specifically, those members who traveled to Iraq via tanks and planes owned by the occupation obviously had no emotional connection to the country of Iraq. But this made no difference, since one year into the occupation the Governing Council had been given no real authority and was essentially useless. Only those members of the council who were favored by the United States had any real authority to make changes.

The homes allocated for members of the Iraqi Governing Council were located in al-Qadisya, in the heart of Baghdad. This area was called the Ministers' Compound and had at one time been Saddam's ministers' residential area. When I went to visit Saladin Baha al-Din there, I found the area to be basically an enormous military fort. It was surrounded by a massive twelve-foot concrete wall and very heavily guarded by the Iraqi police, Kurdish forces, and American troops. It was the American troops who issued orders and gave commands to all the protecting forces. While these soldiers stood still and dignified, it was the Iraqi policemen who did the dirty work: conducting the search of anyone who wished to enter, and carrying out the orders of the US soldiers. When I went to visit Baha al-Din, I was subjected to a very thorough and serious search by the Iraqi policemen. These policemen recognized me from my show and were deeply apologetic for the scrutiny. They said they were being watched by the US officers.

I asked my escort about the names of all the residents of this compound. I found out that most of them had come from overseas with the Americans in order to join the American forces in ruling Iraq. This process was similar to what had happened in the American conflict in Vietnam, and with many other countries once occupied by the United States. As in other situations, many of the people the US brought aboard its fleet of invading tanks and warplanes to serve in newly established governments returned to where they came from after their purpose was served. Some of the imported politicians in this particular conflict remained in Iraq after the council was disbanded because they had other roles to play in occupation endeavors, but many did not. Many of these newcomers furnished the residences they had just confiscated from former Ba'athist ministers with imported furniture because the furniture in those residences had been looted upon the fall of Saddam's regime. These politicians built what they believed would be permanent homes because they thought they would be ruling Iraq for years to come. They had no idea they were there on a very temporary basis, and would be disposed of rather quickly.

As one of the council members described to me, the council members not favored by the US occupation were barely able even to meet with a US official. Dr. Mohsen Abdul Hameed, a member of the Governing Council, was the chairman of the Islamic Party[7] when he was appointed head of the Governing Council. He requested a meeting with Lt. General Ricardo Sanchez for approval to visit the Abu Ghraib prison to check on the conditions of the detainees. The prisoners' families had been putting immense pressure on Abdul Hameed, since the arrests had often been random and arbitrary. In reference to this problem with the prisons, the chief policy officer and deputy administrator for the Coalition Provisional Authority, Richard Jones, acknowledged in a Baghdad press conference in March 2004 that the number of Iraqi detainees in prisons had soared above 12,000. A former detainee told me about the horrors he witnessed during his time in captivity at an occupation prison—a place no one is allowed but the prisoners and wardens. This former detainee told me he lost 88 pounds during seven months in detention. His family did not recognize him when he was finally released. Families of captives were not allowed information on the whereabouts of their detained loved ones, so these families often roamed about the general area of prisons hoping to find out where their relatives were being detained.

General Sanchez put off Abdul Hameed's request for a meeting about the prison situation for two weeks, and when he finally met with him, he did not allow him to visit Abu Ghraib. This was the common experience of council members who were not favored by the Americans. The occupation was the one real authority in Iraq; all other political bodies and councils were merely there to bestow legitimacy on the occupation and strengthen its stand. To understand how little authority the Governing Council Chairperson had during this time, it is enough to remember that Hameed had to wait for General Sanchez's permission to meet him for two weeks, after which he was denied his request for a prison visit and any consideration of releasing the detainees.

The Governing Council's role as a legitimizing mechanism of the occupation is no more evident than when you look at the age of the outfit. The council lasted for only a few days beyond the anniversary of the first year of occupation. After the council served the purpose of making the occupation legitimate, its members were forgotten in less than a month. Out of the 25 council members appointed by Americans, 2 were killed: Aqila Hashimi and Ezzedine Salim. Only 4 members of the Governing Council were selected to serve in the government headed by Ayad Allawi, which replaced it. Other members of this new government were leaders of political parties such as Ahmad Chalabi, Saladin Baha al-Din, and Mohsen Abdul Hameed. The remaining members of the council simply returned to where they had come from before the occupation. They became dissidents in exile, just as they had been during Saddam's rule. They left because the council had no base of support and had failed to create one, despite a year's worth of work with the occupation authorities. These exiles were risking their lives if they stayed in Iraq, because they had lost the little, if any, public support they might have had prior to their arrival on American tanks and planes.

US-appointed Minister of the Interior Sameer Sumidaee was living in London prior to his appointment to the Iraqi Governing Council. After the council dissolved, he said, "I had a life before I came to Baghdad, and I want to go back and resume that life."

As for what happened to Bahr al-Ulum (who was frequently seen bowing to Paul Bremer), one of his closest aides said, "the weather is pretty hot in Iraq now, and it is summer time… he might leave to go on vacation." Bahr al-Ulum was like many other council members who were living in London prior to their appointment, in that he returned to England after the purpose of the council was served. Others who followed this road include Mahmood Othman, the council member who verbally attacked the United States when the new Iraqi government did not have a post for him.

Among all original Governing Council members, Adnan Pachachi was the strongest competitor for the presidency seat and the candidate most likely to win. When Ghazi al-Yawar was appointed president and Pachachi realized that he had lost his chance of becoming president, Pachachi opted to go back to one of the Gulf States, where he had been living before he was brought to Iraq to become a council member.

The remaining members of the council, people who were selected from within Iraq and whose lavish convoys often took joyrides around

Baghdad, ended up losing their false dignified appearance once the council was dissolved and the members had to return to their normal lives in their average homes. Then they feared retaliation, especially since some of them had already been targeted by assassination attempts. But in some ways the people who were hurt most by the temporary nature of the council were the drivers, the escorts, and the bodyguards. These people had jobs with very handsome salaries, and they suddenly lost them.

Although the Iraqi Governing Council was eliminated by the beginning of the second year of occupation, the US-planted politicians in Iraq still had big roles to play. The Governing Council, as some observers note, was replaced by the new cabinet headed by Ayad Allawi. American newspapers, such as the *New York Times*, quoted former CIA officials saying that Allawi "used to be a CIA agent." Perhaps this is why Sheikh Ahmad Samarray, the cleric at the Abu Hanifa Mosque, the largest in Baghdad, declared in his sermon on May 7, 2004 that the new prime minister of Iraq was "no more than a spy." Agence France-Presse also quoted Sheikh Samarray as saying, "The UN Security Council comes here and certifies the members of the Iraqi Governing Council that are agents, who have been trained by the American Departments of Defense and State." Ultimately, Ayad Allawi and his cabinet suffered the same end that the Iraqi Governing Council faced earlier and the same fate suffered by US puppets in Vietnam, Somalia, Lebanon, and South America. If anyone wants to see the likely destiny of men chosen to work for US forces, one would only have to browse a few history books to read about the liquidations and assassinations.

Such was the situation in Iraq one year into the American occupation, just before the siege and battle of Fallujah in April 2004.

2. THE CITY OF FALLUJAH

"But man is not made for defeat. A man can be destroyed but not defeated."
—Ernest Hemingway, *The Old Man and the Sea*

What was it about Fallujah that provoked the highest echelons of US power to order the siege of the city, an unprecedented action in Iraq? What made the US government issue an order for a battalion of 10,000 soldiers to encircle such a large and heavily populated city? What made them block all entrances and exits?

Among the city of Fallujah's defining characteristics is its historically strong resistance to invasion. Fallujah's fierce opposition to foreign occupation wasn't born in 2003. Fallujah's defiance of the British occupation in the 1920s was equally impressive. In 1941, the Iraqi poet Marouf Alrassafi[8] spoke in praise of Fallujah's resistance against the British occupation in one of his longer poems, "The Day of Fallujah." The poem begins, "Beware Englishmen, for we won't allow ourselves to forget your desecration of the homes of Fallujah." The poem then moves to illuminate the aggression and savagery of the British occupation, contrasted with the bravery of the Fallujans. The poem concludes with, "So, praise goes to Mesopotamia, and may peace be upon Fallujah."

Situated some 35 miles west of Baghdad on the Euphrates River, Fallujah sits close to Lake Habbaniya, once a British resort. Fallujah is located along the freeway that runs between Baghdad, Syria, and Jordan, and it is the largest district within the Anbar province.[9] Strategically speaking, Fallujah is close to the Royal Air Force (RAF) Station at Habbaniya. This massive military base was established by the British in the 1920s, and has played a significant role in most of the military coups that took place in Iraq between 1958 and 1968. Habbaniya is considered one of the most important military bases in all of Iraq due to its close proximity to Baghdad.

Throughout the Saddam Hussein era, Fallujah was the only city that had a zero-tolerance policy for alcohol. During this time, Fallujah did not have a single operating bar, pub, tavern, saloon, distillery, brewery, or other alcohol manufacturing facility. Iraqis call Fallujah the "City of Mosques and Minarets"; it is home to over a hundred mosques, most of which have minarets. Or used to, before the US forces destroyed many of them during altercations with the citizens of the city. The most devastating desecration occurred during the second battle of Fallujah in November 2004—but more about that later.

Because of the strong religious devotion that characterizes the people of Fallujah, the residents were not saved from the torture of Saddam Hussein's tyrannical reign. During his rule, Hussein executed many Fallujans who were suspected of belonging to certain organized Islamic parties and movements that opposed the Ba'ath movement. During my interviews and coverage in this historic city, Fallujans shared many horrific stories with me. Many of these stories told of fellow townspeople being assassinated by Saddam's men. One of those stories described an ominous night in 1992, when Saddam executed 91 young men before dawn's light. Among these men were representatives from almost every single tribe in Fallujah. Nearly all the tribes in Fallujah lost a young man to Saddam's tyranny in a single night, and Saddam won the hatred of the entire city.

These executions demonstrate that Fallujans are innocent of the accusation of being Ba'athists, a label the Bush administration was ready to apply in a smear campaign against the Fallujans during the conflicts of 2004. Since so much of their own blood was shed at the hands of Saddam Hussein and the Ba'athists, "Ba'athist" is a term that cannot logically be applied to the Fallujans. Finally, these executions also illustrate that Fallujans are a people who endured grief, hardship, and oppression during Saddam's era, and as a result of their history, this city is built of tough, proud fighters with resolve made of steel.

Fallujah Reacts to the US Occupation

Since the beginning of the US occupation of Iraq in April 2003, Fallujah has maintained its reputation as a mutinous city, and its residents have refused to bend to US forces. Many battles and armed confrontations took place in Fallujah during the early stages of the occupation, but the confrontation that first attracted world attention (and the attention of US forces) took place on May 27, 2003, less than a month after Bush's infamous "Mission Accomplished" proclamation from the deck of the USS Abraham Lincoln saying that "major combat operations in Iraq have ended… in the battle of Iraq, the United States and our allies have prevailed."

In truth, combat operations were far from over. On the same day as George W. Bush's speech, a battle erupted in Fallujah. This conflict occurred between a brigade of American forces and a cell of insurgents led by Noor al-Deen al-Zawba'ie.[10] The violence broke out on the upper bridge that connects Fallujah to the freeway and passes over the Euphrates River. The battle raged for several hours and cost the American brigade a significant number of casualties—soldiers were injured, soldiers were killed, and an American military chopper was destroyed. It was a deadly battle for the Americans. This event is narrated in detail in my book *The Story of Baghdad's Fall*.[11]

Paul Bremer also speaks of the situation in Fallujah in his memoir, noting Fallujah's infamous past:

> Fallujah had a well-earned reputation as a tough town. A city of 300,000, Fallujah sprawled across a bend in the Euphrates, the crossroads of several traditional caravan trails west through the desert to Syria, which became useful smugglers' routes after the Gulf War when Saddam bypassed UN sanctions. When the British had taken over Mesopotamia from the Ottomans after World War I, the city was the center of a bloody rebellion.

Clearly, Bremer was also concerned about the potential for loss of life in Fallujah, and during the harsh battles of 2003 and 2004 was inclined to remember Fallujah's violent past.

In a report published by both the *New York Times* and Saudi newspaper *al-Sharq al-Awsat* three days after the attack, Michael Gordon wrote that US Army leaders deployed the Third Infantry Division to Fallujah following this violent and highly publicized confrontation. This division, according to these reports, had been eager to return home after a nine-month stay in Kuwait prior to the battle for Baghdad, but found out that the homecoming would be postponed because they were given the responsibility of securing the situation in Fallujah. The US Army also acknowledged the killing of two soldiers and the wounding of nine others.

This first confrontation in Fallujah was merely the spark that set aflame a cycle of violence. From that point forward, insurgent operations against American forces escalated, and the American forces in turn began treating the people of Fallujah with excessive force and complete disrespect. Fallujans began to protest that American forces were firing arbitrarily at citizens without cause. Occupation sources reportedly degraded tribal chieftains and violated the sanctity of the homes of civilian locals. Many Fallujans told me horrific stories of how the American troops behaved, as if no violation against Fallujans was beyond human decency.

Perhaps the strongest evidence of this mistreatment comes from the example of private security contractors—workers who were called mercenaries in more honest days, before commercial legal lingo invaded the world. In this particular conflict, these mercenaries had a reputation for disregarding Iraqi lives. When mercenaries went on what they called "high-profile tours," in private armored vehicles with foreign license plates and rear gunners stationed in the back, they couldn't afford to be caught in a traffic jam for fear of being ambushed by insurgents. In such cases, they didn't hesitate to plow past a crowd of civilian cars just to get out of the traffic jam. In the worst of circumstances, they even resorted to shooting those in the cars blocking the road, or running over civilians standing in the blockade. During high-profile tours, mercenaries were determined to keep up the pace of their driving, even if that required firing at Iraqis or otherwise disposing of them. Mercenaries also believed that anything with a button and a signal could detonate a bomb, and therefore cell phones qualified as potentially destructive equipment. So, even on a low-profile mission (in which they were traveling in a seemingly regular car, attempting to blend in), if mercenaries saw a civilian standing on the sidewalk doing something as benign as taking his cell phone out of his pocket, they didn't hesitate to shoot him.

Fallujan residents also reported that when mercenaries searched a house, they often destroyed the furniture and were disrespectful to women, children, and the elderly. They didn't hesitate to pull headscarves and veils off women's heads, frisk them with their hands, or tear off pieces of clothing to reveal a woman's undergarments. All of these actions are very offensive to women in Iraqi culture. Fallujans also reported that the mercenaries often groped Iraqi women in a way that would seriously offend any woman, regardless of nationality or cultural affiliation. It wasn't uncommon for the search of an Iraqi woman to be tantamount to sexual molestation, right before the eyes of the woman's husband and father.

A Fallujah resident told me, "They have gone too far in degrading us and humiliating us. I am to the point where I am ready to kill any American soldier if I get the chance. What's left for us? They are robbers. They steal money, jewelry, and even personal items. They steal anything and everything they can lay their hands on. Saddam's men were awful, but we're a proud Bedouin people with a common code of honor that stood strong even with Saddam's men. His men never dared enter a home to search it until we made sure everyone was decent and our girls had a chance to properly veil themselves. Only then would we let them in to do their search. But those Americans are low-life rogues."

In response to this treatment by American occupation forces, the desperate desire for revenge began to fester in Fallujans. The anger that the behavior of American troops cultivated among the Fallujans (and Iraqis in general) increased more with each passing day, and revenge operations against Americans began to expand and take on many different forms as the poor treatment of Fallujans continued. Revenge sometimes took the form of operations launched in haste by tribesmen and infuriated citizens, while other operations were carefully orchestrated and executed with precision by the insurgents.

One of the biggest revenge operations against Americans in Fallujah was masterminded and executed by al-Zawba'ie on July 10, 2003. In this operation, the insurgents managed to destroy the Fallujah police department, which the American troops were using as their command center in Fallujah. I visited the city a week after the attack, and saw the incredible level of destruction the insurgents managed to inflict on the police department building. One of the city residents who witnessed the attack told me that American casualties were at least twenty dead and many more injured. The Americans, however, never admitted that this attack was a heavy loss and this incident didn't get any serious attention in the media.

Another attack in the city, however, did receive a lot of attention. According to the US military spokesperson, Colonel William Darley, at 9AM on November 2, 2003, 16 soldiers were killed and 20 soldiers injured when an SA-7 shoulder-fired missile struck an engine on a Chinook transport helicopter[12] in Albo Eesa, a suburb of Fallujah. The doomed Chinook was en route home for leave, and carried 36 soldiers and a flight crew. The passengers had been heading for the airport in Baghdad, then were to proceed to Germany, and on to the US for a two-week vacation. At the time, American troops considered the losses in this attack to be the heaviest they had endured in a single day since the start of the war.

In an interview on Fox News, Secretary of Defense Donald Rumsfeld said, "It was a bad day. A bad day. A tragic day for those people. In a war, there are going to be days like that. And it is necessary that we recognize that." Despite his attempt to play down the critical danger that comes from an organized insurgency that can plan and synchronize such massive attacks, on other interviews broadcast that same day by NBC, ABC, and other news agencies, Rumsfeld admitted that this incident wasn't just a "bad day." In a follow-up interview with NBC, he added, "In a long, hard war, we're going to have tragic days," and then commented, "But they're necessary. They're part of a war that's difficult and complicated." Indeed, the insurgent revenge operations were indicators that the war was going to be long and tough, and would ultimately cost Americans much more than just a "bad day."

After this attack, the insurgents' operations escalated throughout the rest of 2003 and into 2004. On January 8, 2004, insurgents were able to shoot down a Black Hawk helicopter,[13] killing all 9 people on board, a loss that American officials did not deny. Five days later, the American military announced that one of its attack helicopters was shot down by enemy fire west of Baghdad. Witnesses, however, reported that the helicopter was shot down near Fallujah, where American troops were in the process of attacking a crowd of hundreds of civilians protesting the practices of occupation authorities, including their recent arrest of a young woman from Fallujah, whose only crime had been marrying a man the Americans accused of being a Saddam loyalist. The American attack on the protestors resulted in the killing of 3 civilians and the wounding of 5 others.

Repeated confrontations pushed American soldiers to commit further human rights violations and to continue to infringe on the basic rights of the city's residents. Fallujans themselves were pushed to launch more revenge-driven operations on American forces. Throughout my many visits to Fallujah, I don't recall meeting a single person who had not seen a fellow Fallujan being arrested, harassed, humiliated, or violated at the hand of American troops. The lucky ones who weren't violated themselves still had witnessed the violation of their fellow Fallujans. All of this was more than enough to put Fallujah on the American and global media map early in the war, and the Western press started giving Fallujah extra attention by providing special coverage reports on this city alone. Writers began to flock to Fallujah to witness firsthand the city that had become the Iraqi symbol of defiance against American occupation.

An April 30, 2003 article in the *Times* of London said that shortly after American troops arrived in the city, they took over a children's school, and turned it into a base, an act that resulted in deadly consequences. About this incident, Catherine Philip of the *Times* wrote, "While US commanders insisted that they had received a warm welcome, infantrymen said that they had been met with widespread hostility and been fired on repeatedly in the past three days." The Americans then started shooting at the protestors, claiming that they were defending themselves from Fallujan bullets.

During this confrontation, a citizen named Muthanna Saleh was standing by his front gate opposite the children's school, which had been overtaken by American forces, and he was shot in the leg. The *Times* quoted Mr. Saleh as saying, "I was shot and my brother, Walid, came to help me and then he was shot dead. Then I was shouting to my wife to come and help me and she came out and was shot in the leg." Then, when Saleh's brother-in-law tried to back a car out of the garage to help the family escape, he was shot, too. When Saleh finally made it to the Fallujah hospital, he found another 14 or more people killed and over 100 wounded in that same incident.

The *Times* reports that when asked about why his men fired at civilian protestors in this incident, Lt. Colonel Eric Nantz responded, "There was fire directly over the heads of soldiers on the roof. They returned fire in order to protect the lives of our soldiers."

An article published in the *Oakland Tribune* on the same date quoted Saleh as saying, "The Americans are lying. Nobody had any guns. If only they had shot into the air, nothing would have happened. They shot at us for no reason. They're criminals." The *Times* article emphasizes that American forces, as Fallujans claimed, routinely stole money and property, damaged furniture, humiliated men and violated women as they performed their searches of Fallujan homes. This intentionally degrading and humiliating treatment strongly encouraged Fallujan resistance to the presence of American troops. Thus, the US suddenly faced a growing insurgency problem.

Despite the heavy casualty count, Americans couldn't avoid traveling through Fallujah. Fallujah was the link between roads that connected American military bases and other necessary US facilities, such as RAF Habbaniya. Because of this heavy traffic, the chances of American forces being targeted by insurgents were very high. The world saw those possibilities realized in a massive attack, deadly enough to shake the White House and the entire Bush administration on March 31, 2004.

Four Mercenaries Meet Their Doom

That night, I was at our Baghdad bureau, consumed with preparations for a live airing of my show, *Without Limits*. My guest was supposed to be Governing Council member Saladin Baha al-Din. Suddenly, my preparations were interrupted by loud arguments and noise outside the studio. I peeked out to see what was going on with my colleagues, and I found them debating how fast they could send images they had just received from Fallujah to al-Jazeera's headquarters in Doha. My colleagues wanted to guarantee that al-Jazeera would be the first network to air the images in question because there were cameramen present at the incident from other global news networks.

"What happened in Fallujah?" I asked.

They told me I could watch the tape for myself as they sent the broadcast to Doha. As the images rolled across the screen, I immediately realized that what had happened in Fallujah was something big enough to send fear to the very core of the Bush administration.

The official narrative of "what happened in Fallujah" as circulated by press agencies and reported by a senior official in the Iraqi police is that a "group of gunmen at 10AM intercepted two white cars that were passing through the center of Fallujah and started firing at the people inside the cars, which led to their deaths. The people inside the car were believed to be foreigners. The attackers then set the two cars ablaze and fled the scene."

Paul Bremer recounts a different version of this incident in his memoir:

> The Fallujah crisis broke into the open on the morning of Wednesday, March 31. A small convoy of SUVs carrying Blackwater USA security guards was ambushed in the center of Fallujah. The gunmen raked the Americans' car with AK-47s. Then the vehicle was set alight. Dancing in a frenzy, a mob of townsmen dragged the smoldering corpses from the wreckage and ripped at the charred flesh with shovels. Then two blackened, dismembered bodies were strung from the girders of the city's main bridge across the river.

As Bremer's account describes, it was a desperate scene indeed, and one that was seized immediately by the media and noticed without delay by the American government.

Incidents of equal brutality and hideousness were taking place all over Iraq. But what was unusual in Fallujah was that there were so many cameramen from press agencies and television news networks filming the entire incident—every gruesome and gory detail. The attack was also unusual in that it seemed to have been brought about by common Fallujans. Citizens took to the streets to release the rage that had built up against the American troops throughout the year of military occupation. Teenagers and children participated. People desecrated the incinerated corpses and violated the sanctity of the dead. The corpses were dragged out into the open, and the angry mob hung the bodies from a bridge—coincidentally, a bridge that remained from British occupation. Worst of all, these commoners begged the world media to film their activities.

They wanted the world to be aware of what kind of behavior was being inspired by the presence of American troops in their city. They welcomed the presence of media in their city during the mob scene, and encouraged the cameramen to film all of their actions.

Paul Bremer's memoir speaks of how the media crews captured these horrifying images:

> Television crews taped this grisly scene, and by afternoon the horrible images appeared on Arab satellite television. An edited tape was shown later that day on American networks. The images immediately became icons of the brutal reality of the insurgency, and underscored the fact that the coalition military did not control Fallujah.

Al-Jazeera's correspondent in Fallujah, my colleague Hussain Deli, was one of those who captured the images that became the definition of insurgent brutality in Iraq. Once he captured his film, he immediately delivered the tape to al-Jazeera's Baghdad bureau to be broadcast to the headquarters in Doha. This was no al-Jazeera exclusive, however. Most other major international news networks aired the images they got from their correspondents and cameramen who were also present at the time of the incident. The images circulated widely across the world. The first reaction most viewers had to the images was to compare what they saw to images released just after the Somali-led revolt against American occupation in 1993.[14] Both sets of images showed viewers a world that was at the hands of an unleashed demon.

The morning following the attack, I traveled to Fallujah with my colleague Abdulazeem Muhammad, a Fallujah native, and cameraman, Layth Mushtaq. Along with us was a crew of technicians and engineers, who carried with them a load of mobile broadcast equipment. We were prepared to broadcast live from Fallujah should any sudden eruption of fighting take place. For me, this trip was also a trip of exploration—I wanted to find out more about the city so I could better prepare myself and my crew for the planned coverage of the first anniversary of the American occupation scheduled for April 9. Many questions ran through my mind that morning. Why would people do such a thing? Wasn't it enough to kill the mercenaries? What could possibly entice common people, including children, to drag the remains of the corpses through the street and leave them dangling from a bridge?

When I met with the elders of the city and spoke with them about the incident, one of them told me, "We don't condone what was done by the street people, but the insurgents are certainly not responsible for this act. The insurgents simply plotted an ambush attack against the mercenaries. The plan of that attack is part of their right to resist the occupation, a right conferred upon us and guaranteed by all international laws, codes, and conventions. The Americans, through their daily practices and treatment, have managed to create an indescribable kind of hatred in the hearts of the Iraqi general public. This hatred is what generated the heinous crime done by the street people."

Another tribal chieftain stepped forward and said, "We're tribesmen—a people of tradition who stand by a code of honor. During Saddam's rule, despite his arrogance and tyranny, none of his intelligence officers ever dared to arrest any of us without the presence of the town's mayor. They'd send a few policemen to ask for permission to enter the house first. Then, we could tidy the house, wake up the kids and gather them in a single room, and the women could veil themselves. Then the officers would enter and search as they wish without touching a single child or woman. But now, we find the American soldiers storming into our homes and standing over our heads while we're still in our bedrooms. Then they hustle us away after they've frightened our kids. People see scenes like these play out on the news day and night."

The chieftain continued, "The soldiers degrade us even though we are chieftains, tribesmen, and dignitaries. They put bags over our heads in front of the young, the old, the men, and the women. They even arrest our women sometimes. We can't face anyone after such indignation. There was one time when they invaded the entire city, house by house. After they searched and violated the sanctity of every single home in the city, they left without finding the target they claimed they were looking for."

He went on to explain the roots of the hatred his people now feel for American soldiers. "Add to this humiliation the fact that many families have been harmed by these soldiers, hundreds of people have been arrested, and even more have died. Consequently, there isn't a single home in the city that doesn't have some score or another to settle with the Americans. For the past year, the American soldiers have been manufacturing hatred for the occupation in the hearts of Iraqi people—from young to old. After all of this, what sort of behavior do you expect?"

It was clear that residents who had been witness to Fallujah's recent history blamed the Americans for the violence.

The demon released in Fallujah was upsetting enough to send a very real chill down the spine of George W. Bush and everyone involved in his administration. Aside from the other scandals that this incident exposed—that the US was not in control of the operations in Fallujah and that its troops were not welcomed by the Iraqi people as the Bush administration had claimed—the biggest one was that the corpses that had been inhumanely mutilated did not even belong to official US soldiers. They were bodies of private mercenaries the US military had hired to participate in many of the American army's operations. When it came to critical matters and risky endeavors requiring some disposable humans, the US Army did not take those jobs on themselves. They gave the dirty work to mercenaries.

3. MERCENARIES IN THE IRAQI–AMERICAN CONFLICT

U ntil this incident, not much was known about the presence of mercenaries and private armies hired to assist the US Army in Iraq. Personally, I had heard only scattered references in the media and countless stories from Iraqi civilians about their presence. On many occasions throughout my travels in Iraq, I had noticed civilian SUVs driven by men wearing black sunglasses with very round lenses and semi-military clothing. All of those civilians were remarkably well-built, their bodies rippling with distinctive muscle.

At the sight of these men, my colleagues, who were residing in Iraq, would declare simultaneously, "Mercenaries."

But I never fully understood the role of mercenaries in the war until after the four Blackwater USA employees met their demise in Fallujah. "Contractors" is the term officially used by the US government in reference to mercenaries. On December 5, 2006, the *Washington Post* confirmed the role of these "contractors" to be the same as "mercenaries" by saying that their responsibilities included: "providing security, interrogating prisoners, cooking meals, fixing equipment and constructing bases that were once reserved for soldiers." This list of responsibilities makes clear that these mercenaries weren't simply providing support services to soldiers; they were acting as replacements for soldiers and sharing the same duties.

Once conversational references to "mercenaries" were on my personal radar, I started noticing the telltale mercenary SUVs much more frequently, and disconcerting thoughts about their job in Iraq often occupied my mind during my travels. Occasionally I tried to follow these SUVs, in an attempt to observe their presence and activities. Keeping up with a single unit proved to be too difficult, however, because they were everywhere—in towns, on inter-city roads, on highways—there were countless numbers of them and they all looked the same. Tracking these vehicles was also difficult because they were usually escorting military convoys and shipping trailers. It was even more difficult following them while they were doing their primary job: guarding and securing top American officials in Iraq, especially the American civil governor of Iraq, Paul Bremer.

It was quite obvious that the mercenaries had earned hatred from the Iraqis. They made no attempt whatsoever to make any connection to the Iraqis. Uniformed American troops, despite the overall brutality of their performance, still made individual kind gestures once in a while. It wasn't uncommon for an American soldier, or even an entire company, to develop a very friendly relationship with an Iraqi community. It didn't happen every day, but it wasn't unheard of. It was also definitely not uncommon to see American troops high-fiving Iraqi teenagers, holding the arm of an elderly woman to help her cross a street, or helping someone out of a difficult situation. American soldiers were a mixed bag, and individually they ranged from the amiable assistant to the ruthless killer. This was not the case with mercenaries. They knew they were viewed as evil thugs, and they wanted it to keep it that way.

For the most part, mercenaries were viewed as monsters, primarily because they behaved monstrously. They never spoke to anyone using words—they only used the language of fire, bullets, and absolute lethal force. It was fairly common to see a mercenary crush a small civilian Iraqi car with passengers inside just because the mercenaries happened to be stuck in a traffic jam.

In one incident, I saw a mercenary almost kill an Iraqi storekeeper who was trying to tidy up his shop. The front side of his store was littered with wires and disposed electrical appliances. A leading vehicle in the mercenary convoy drove by the store as the man was picking up the electrical appliances and throwing them in a dumpster next to the store. The rear-gunner in the mercenary's vehicle aimed his weapon at the man and yelled, "Move it or lose it!"

Apparently, the mercenaries feared the electrical appliances were booby-trapped and thought the wires sticking out could be connected to a bomb. The Iraqi storekeeper did not know English and thus had no understanding of what the mercenaries were shouting at him, so he simply froze. The mercenary shouted at him to drop the appliance he was holding. When he stood there trying to tell the convoy he didn't understand English, they started firing. The man of course dropped what was in his hands and ran into his store for safety. When the appliance didn't blow up upon being dropped, the mercenaries realized it was just a piece of junk, not a bomb. But this is how they spoke to people: with bullets, not with words.

Because of the widespread hatred toward these mercenaries, a group of young Iraqi men put together an organization called Supporters of

Truth. The group published a report in mid-January of 2004 going into detail about the mercenaries in Iraq. Among the many things narrated in that report was a deeply disturbing story told by several shepherds and fishermen working in the near-deserted Diyala River along the Iraq–Iran border, a region characterized by extremely rough terrain and very sparse settlement. The shepherds and fishermen told of their experience encountering several dead bodies that were supposedly dropped from low-flying American choppers into the river. The report said that American authorities got rid of the mercenaries' bodies using this method because there were no legally-binding articles in their contracts that would compel US forces to transport the dead mercenaries back to their countries for proper burial. Apparently nothing compelled US forces to treat the mercenaries' corpses with the respect any dead are due.

I had previously visited the Diyala River region in July of 2003 and observed its rough terrain. The areas next to the Iranian border were sealed off to the general Iraqi public during Saddam's rule. It was a restricted area reserved for the Iraqi Army and the Republican Guard. The area was the staging ground for many military operations during the Iraq–Iran war. It was also home for the most critical military equipment warehouses and armament manufacturing facilities during the Saddam era. And near one of the river's dams was a secluded retreat used by Saddam Hussein during his rule.

During my July visit, I met with a few of the rare inhabitants of that intolerable terrain, and they told stories not unlike the ones told by the shepherds and fishermen in the report compiled by the Supporters of Truth. The locals hosted me for lunch at the retreat off the river dam, which the locals said Saddam had only visited once. I recall the frightening height and freakish steepness of the banks on both sides of the river. Even the flow of the water had a chilling quality. Past the dam the water flow was very heavy, and the water gushed down abysmal, ghostly ravines.

I learned much more about these mercenaries as the war raged on. In an interview aired by al-Jazeera on April 11, 2007, my guest was Dr. Ibrahim al-Shimari, the official spokesperson for one of the most prominent insurgent and organized resistance groups in Iraq. Over the course of our interview, al-Shimari said that his group, the Islamic Army of Iraq, had uncovered mass graves for mercenaries who worked for the US forces. His organization filmed the mass graves and distributed the footage inside Iraq and across the world by posting them on the internet. He said that uncovering mass graves of mercenaries had become common in Iraq, especially in areas where the terrain was rough and ravines were steep—areas much like the Diyala River region, the Jarf al-Sakhr area, and the Hiran Valley.

One of the first journalistic reports on these and other activities associated with mercenaries in Iraq was published by the *Guardian* on March 5, 2004. The report was highly controversial, since it confirmed that the Pentagon had to look for help from mercenaries for its effort in Iraq because it couldn't secure an adequate number of voluntary recruits. The report said that the Pentagon subcontracted the company known as Blackwater USA to recruit mercenaries with former experience in the marines or commandos. Blackwater USA was also to recruit members from outside the US, especially from South America. The *Guardian* mentioned that Blackwater USA did indeed recruit 60 former Chilean commandos who were trained by and served in the military government run by the former dictator Augusto Pinochet. Despite their extensive experience, when the commandos where transported from Santiago, they were retrained on a 2,400-acre training camp in North Carolina. They were soon sent to Iraq to replace US soldiers.

The source of this information was the president of Blackwater USA himself, Gary Jackson. In a phone interview published in the *Guardian* 26 days prior to the incident with the four Blackwater security guards in Fallujah, Jackson said, "We scour the ends of the earth to find professionals—the Chilean commandos are very, very professional and they fit within the Blackwater system." He emphasized the fact that 95 percent of his work came from government contracts, and also mentioned that his business was booming. The *Guardian* quoted Jackson as saying, "We have grown 300 percent over each of the past three years and we are small compared to the big organizations." This means that although Blackwater USA was the most well-known mercenary supplier after the attacks in Fallujah, there were many other major organizations staffing the US army with private contractors.

The article in the *Guardian* also said that salaries for mercenaries can range from $4,000 a month to $1,000 a day, depending on former experience and the tasks and responsibilities of the new position. Those who were hired to guard Paul Bremer, for example, were paid very differently from those who guarded oil installations and pipelines.

Other journalistic reports appeared around the same time as initial reports printed in the *Guardian*. In early March of 2004, Agence France-Presse published an interview with a 28-year-old former US army sergeant working in Iraq as a mercenary. This man, "Erwin," was quoted as saying, "This place is a gold mine. All you need is five years in the military and you can come here and make a good bundle." In this statement, Erwin hints at the fact that many US marines and commandos returned to Iraq after their official duty was over to work as mercenaries for handsome salaries.

Because of this generous compensation, the number of mercenaries in Iraq continued to grow. The aforementioned *Guardian* article also stated, "At the end of last year [2003] there were ten thousand hired security personnel in Iraq." That was the official count that was given to the media in 2003. However, as late as December 5, 2006, Renae Merle of the *Washington Post* reported that, "There are about 100,000 government contractors operating in Iraq, not counting subcontractors. This total is approaching the size of the US military force in Iraq, according to the military's first census of the growing population of civilians operating in the battlefield." In May 2007, *Middle East* magazine also mentioned that the number of mercenaries nearly matched the numbers of official US Army soldiers present in Iraq. The magazine cited a census that set the mercenaries' count at 120,000 while the count of US Army soldiers sat at about 135,000. Other sources indicate that this number might have been inaccurate—that the number of mercenaries might have been higher than this number if the tally took into consideration those assigned to menial tasks and minor support services, which are still part of the duty of any soldier. Taking these additional individuals into account, the numbers would more accurately have reached around 200,000.

This same message about high numbers of mercenaries was reiterated by John Hilary, director of campaigns and policy at War on Want.[15] When I interviewed him on May 9, 2007, Hilary stressed the point that this number of mercenaries accounts for the total of private contractors serving the US forces in all areas of work; he thought that those assigned to combat operations numbered about 48,000.

In October of 2006, War on Want released a detailed research report entitled *Corporate Mercenaries: The Threat of Private Military and Security Companies*. This report explained that there were 182 companies that managed individuals who acted as corporate mercenaries in Iraq. These companies provided a whole host of services for the United States, including performing combat operations. The total revenue these companies generated from their work in Iraq reached £320,000,000 in British currency (over $636,000,000 USD) in the year 2003. Their revenue in

2004, however, skyrocketed to £1,800,000,000 in British currency, which amounts to about $3,573,924,670 USD! Some published reports, including those developed by War on Want, indicate that that number met the 100 billion dollar mark by 2007—a very significant growth from the figure published in 2006.

What this information means is that there is a new lobby in action in the United States. Forget the age of lobbies that represented the interests of the retired, factory workers, farmers, teachers, the National Cable Television Association, the National Association of Broadcasters, the National Rifle Association, the tobacco industry, the retail food industry, the alcohol manufacturers, the Cuban Americans, the Jewish Americans. These are all powerful lobbies, but in some ways they represent the interests of Americans who are only simple ordinary people seeking to advance their cause in a system that allows for lobbies to sprout. This new lobby is different from the lobbies that have been present in the past because of the sheer amount of power it holds. This new lobby deals directly with ruthless professional killers ready to dispense their services to the highest bidder. When dealing with mercenaries, the determining factor in accepting or refusing a job is the wage, not the cause—the thought of killing or hurting other human beings is not a deterrent for these workers. Low morale is also not a problem because money—the magic green paper—elevates the morale of mercenary groups regardless of the type of trauma they might be experiencing while going through the job.

The report published by War on Want reveals that some of the biggest companies that directly participate in the fighting in Iraq are Blackwater USA, Hart Group, Control Risks, and Triple Canopy. The report stresses that the greatest danger in using mercenaries is that the organizations that employ them do not operate under any laws other than the articles of their commercial agreement with the US government. Those legally-uninhibited mercenaries played an important role in the second battle of Fallujah in November of 2004.

In the Middle East, the issue of mercenaries was largely unknown to people outside Iraq until the last few years. On my Wednesday show, *Without Limits*, I taped the first show on an Arab satellite channel to focus on this issue on May 9, 2007. The response from the audience was overwhelming. People were outraged by the mere idea that a political superpower like the United States would hire mercenaries to do the unpleasant work instead of employing soldiers who believe in their country and its mission. Viewers were also obviously outraged over the horrendous war crimes committed by the mercenaries. Finally, they were furious that the Arab media had done such a poor job covering the issue. The viewers' reactions were much stronger than I had expected, especially considering that my show was merely a brief introduction to a very complicated and murky issue.

Sadly, no matter what public awareness messages were aired and how much negative press surrounded the mercenaries, ex-soldiers under financial stress still signed up to devalue their lives in exchange for financial reward. They should have stayed home and taken on a respectable job—this would have ensured that they remain honorable soldiers. When confronted with high-paying job offers from corporations seeking to make a profit out of war, someone should have reminded them of the dust bowl farmers forced out by large farming corporations in John Steinbeck's *The Grapes of Wrath*. They should have stood up, proud, and said, "This here is my country. I b'long here. An' I don't give a goddamn if they's oil barrels an' dollar bills crowdin' a fella outa bed even. I ain't a-goin."

Fallujah and Mogadishu: The Specter of American Defeat

The shocking demise of the four mercenaries could have been swept under the rug like many similar incidents that occurred in Iraq during the early days of the war, but the presence of world media prevented the Bush administration from having the luxury of denial.

Because media from all over the world covered the incident, the American media could not ignore or downplay it—nor did they want to. There was global outrage over the incident for very viable and obvious reasons. It was clear that the people caught on the film had no respect for the lives they had taken or the corpses they desecrated, and that lack of respect was evidence of an unacceptable inhumanity. The mercenaries had once been alive and perhaps reprehensible, but death is the great equalizer. No matter how awful these mercenaries were, once they died, they were simply corpses, and they should not have been mutilated in the way that they were. Besides, what further revenge could possibly be exacted on a corpse? Regardless of how much anger and desire for revenge had been pent up in the oppressed, it should have been enough that the oppressor, a once living human being, had been killed. This is just a sampling of the many reactions viewers had to the scenes broadcast around the world.

The American media recognized these reactions, and jumped on the chance to give the incident plenty of attention. It was major headline news in all American television arenas—entertainment, headline news, and otherwise. The networks varied, however, on their approach to showing the graphic images. NBC, for example, avoided showing any actual corpses. CNN and Fox News showed the operation's aftermath and the attacks by the crowds, but also edited out the scenes with corpses, so the public didn't really get to see the true hideousness of what was done to the dead. ABC and CBS may have been the only American TV networks to get as close as possible to showing the whole truth of what actually occurred. These networks showed the operation's aftermath and the crowd riot scenes, but on top of that footage they also showed the insane mob prying charred corpses out of the vehicles and beating the corpses with shovels. When it came to the corpses being dragged through the street and hung from the bridge, the two networks opted to blur the images by using pixilation. International news networks chose to show the whole incident in raw detail, and omitted nothing. Alternative media in America, such Yahoo and other internet news sources, tried to follow suit by showing unedited versions of the incident, but these images only lasted for a short period of time before being pulled offline.

These images were certainly disturbing to the ordinary person, but they were undoubtedly more disturbing to the White House because almost all official analysts and independent observers linked the incident to a similar disturbance that took place in Somalia in 1993. In the Somali incident, the corpses of two American pilots were dragged across the streets of Mogadishu by angry mobs. That incident expedited the full unilateral withdrawal of US troops from Somalia. The Fallujah event took place at a point where the US forces had spent an amount of time in Iraq roughly equivalent to the time spent in Somalia when the Mogadishu incident happened. These similarities certainly alarmed the Bush administration.

Indeed, the days following the incident, newspapers published in the United States and around the world dedicated front page spreads to comparisons between the Somali incident and the conflict in Fallujah. On April 1, 2004, the *Times* reported, "These were scenes reminiscent of Somalia in 1993, when the body of a US soldier was dragged through the streets of Mogadishu by a chanting mob. The scenes prompted a hasty US withdrawal from Somalia and tamed its foreign policy for the rest of the decade."

American newspapers reported on the shock that the sight of the Fallujah scenes sent through the American general public. The *New York Times* published a report that demonstrated high numbers of Americans likening the Fallujah scenes to the 1993 Mogadishu scenes, and this opinion reflected what was reported in international papers as well. Rory McCarthy of the *Guardian* wrote an extensive report from Fallujah on April 2 describing the city as "the graveyard of Americans." Many of those Americans who recognized a similarity between the events, according to the *New York Times*, demanded an immediate withdrawal of US forces from Iraq. One citizen was quoted as saying, "Let's leave and let [the Iraqis] to manage their own affairs themselves." McCarthy's article from the *Guardian* also articulated that Americans living in the United States were particularly horrified and shaken by the attacks because the illusion of safety in the so-called "green zone," with its highly secured massive walls, was exposed for what it was: an illusion.

Because comparing the Fallujah incident to the Mogadishu incident brought back the demons of failure from the Somalia experience, there were fears among the Bush administration that it might also ultimately build overwhelming public support for a full withdrawal of American troops from Iraq—much like what happened in 1993. The American government knew that the discontent lingering from troubles in Somalia needed to be kept at bay. Statements from most American officials rejected any comparison between the two incidents in order to prevent the public from advocating withdrawal of US troops. One of the officials that objected to the comparison to the Somali revolt was Adam Ereli, the State Department deputy spokesperson. When asked by reporters about a comparison between the two incidents during the daily press briefing on April 1, Ereli responded: "The Mogadishu precedent was that, following attacks, we left. And that's not going to be—that's not going to happen here, I can tell you right now, number one. Number two, I think the parallel to Mogadishu is a little bit—is erroneous for the major reason that we are working in Iraq. The coalition is working in Iraq with the partnership of the Iraqi people." Scott McClellan, the White House press secretary, released a statement that described the mercenary killings as "despicable horrific attacks" and called the celebrating mobs "thugs and terrorists who seek to derail the transition to democracy for the Iraqi people." But he made no comparison to the 1993 incident with the Somalis.

Despite the differing reports released by the media and the US government, the attacks represented an undeniably serious defeat for Paul Bremer and the American mission in Iraq. In a graduation ceremony for American-trained Iraqi police academy students the day after the attack on the mercenaries, Bremer commented, "Yesterday's events in Fallujah are a dramatic example of the ongoing struggle between human dignity and barbarism." In regard to the four Blackwater USA mercenaries, he stressed that, "Their deaths [would] not go unpunished." He then added, "The cowards and ghouls who acted yesterday represent the worst of society." Bremer clearly showed concern over the severity of these attacks and the worldwide reaction.

Anxiety over reactions to these attacks did not stop at American officials in lower reaches of the government. President Bush, in a statement released on April 2, emphatically stated that the US would not pull out of Iraq despite the ferocity of the Fallujah attacks. This statement reiterated the American government's stance that this incident was unlike 1993's incident in Mogadishu, and therefore would not result in a total withdrawal of US forces. These statements expressed how shaken the Bush administration was over the incident at Fallujah, but also how this administration refused to lessen the effects of their presence in the region based solely on this incident.

The magnitude of the problems the Fallujah attacks caused for the Bush administration became further evident in the statement issued by Secretary of State Colin Powell just after the incident. In this statement, Powell asked NATO to assume a "new collective role" in Iraq for the first time since the occupation started, following an established US pattern of unilateral performance in Iraqi operations. On April 3, Judy Dempsey of the *Financial Times* summarized Powell's statement by saying, "NATO should consider a 'new collective role' in Iraq after the transfer of power to a new Iraqi government in July, Colin Powell, the US secretary of state, said on Friday." Dempsey then stressed the point that Powell's statement was indeed the first time the United States asked for help from NATO: "The unexpected request was the first time Washington has officially called on NATO to become actively involved in Iraq." Powell's statement was a clear, definite cry for assistance. This call for help showed that the Bush administration was suffering from very desperate anxiety following the attacks.

In the aftermath of the attacks, speculation ran rampant about the identity and work of the four unfortunate people whose corpses were desecrated. General Mark Kimmitt claimed some of the deceased were Iraqi civilians. In the Coalition Provisional Authority briefing held on April 1, General Kimmitt started with an opening statement in which he offered condolences. He said, "On behalf of the coalition military, let me also echo the condolences, as stated by Ambassador Bremer, on the deaths of the four soldiers and—the five soldiers and the four civilians." So, according to the general, some of those killed in this incident were defined as "civilians." Soon thereafter, however, Blackwater USA Security Consulting identified the corpses involved in the incident as Blackwater employees. In a statement issued by Blackwater USA, the company explained that the four security guards were escorting an American convoy delivering food supplies to one of the American bases near Fallujah when the attack occurred.

The first Blackwater USA employee killed in the attack was identified as Scott Helvenston, a 38-year-old former Navy SEAL who went to Iraq to "earn money," according to one of his friends who was interviewed afterwards by a Florida newspaper. The second employee was Jerry Zovko, nicknamed Jerko, a 32-year-old of Croatian heritage more recently from Cleveland, Ohio. He was 19 when he joined the US Army in 1991 and ended up serving with the 82nd Airborne Division. According to his brother Tom, Jerko spoke five languages fluently—English, Croatian, Spanish, Russian, and Arabic—and his fluency in so many languages demonstrated his impressive intellect. He left the army in 2001 and returned later as a mercenary in Iraq. The third employee was Michael Teague of Clarksville, Tennessee, another remarkable person who was a 12-year Army veteran and a bearer of a Bronze Star for service in Afghanistan. He had also served in Panama and Grenada.

The fourth employee's identity wasn't announced to the public at the time but was already known to his employer. His name was Wesley John Kealoha Batalona, and he was the luckiest of his three colleagues—until their demise—because he was born in the finest place of all. Wesley John Kealoha Batalona, or "Bata" as his military friends called him, was born on the rainy Hamakua Coast of Hawaii, a place associated with beautiful, tropical wilderness, and world-class tourism. Bata joined the army in 1974. He later joined the special school for Rangers, the Army's best-trained light infantry unit. Rangers train for a variety of combat conditions. Subordinates in his squad spoke of how tough and demanding Bata was in his training regiment. He was deployed in conflict three times. In 1989, Bata was sent to Panama, where he made a parachute assault on an airfield. The following year he participated in the Gulf War, and in 1993 he was deployed in Somalia. In 1994, he left the Rangers and the armed services altogether.

Bata worked at a pawnshop in the state of Georgia for several years, and then returned to his native Hawaii. The only job he could find with his skills was the position of night security guard at a hotel. After twenty years of service to his country, this decorated combat veteran was reduced from a dignified soldier to a man in a security uniform chasing after local Hawaiian kids who snuck into the hotel to swim in the fancy pool only tourists could afford. Of course that job wasn't emotionally or financially rewarding. His father was sick and needed money, and Bata was also trying to start up a program for counseling troubled local teenagers. Both reasons pushed him to take a job with Blackwater USA, which ultimately brought him to the city of Fallujah.

A man must be very special in order to look past his own financial hardship and think first of helping troubled teenagers and a relative struggling with sickness. This was the fourth man who was treated by Blackwater USA as just a number, just another casualty.

It was clear from Blackwater USA's statement that the four people killed in the attack were hardened professional fighters. But it's also important to note that these men were people once of valor and high intellect who were turned into mercenaries for one reason or another, and in the end gave their lives in nothing more than a senseless act of violence. All of these mercenaries carried a long list of military service in their background. These workers went on military missions armed with military weapons, and could not be classified as civilian workers, as General Mark Kimmitt had claimed earlier.

4. RUMBLINGS OF REVENGE

When we arrived in Fallujah after the killing of the four mercenaries, the first place I visited was the ambush site. The ashes
smeared on the ground were still fresh, even though the vehicles involved in the incident had been towed away. I spent the whole day
talking with and listening to the locals—I was anxious to get their reactions and views on the insurgents' ambush attack and the criminal deeds
of the civilian mobs. I also collected data about the city—its population,
its geography, and its resources. At the end of the day, I analyzed the survey
results I had collected from all the Fallujans I talked with about the city
and its recent activity.

Later that day, my colleague Saeed Alshoely and our director general
Wadah Khanfar arranged for me to do a report to be broadcast later on
the *Day's Harvest*, al-Jazeera's live news bulletin. Saeed asked me to cover
the Blackwater USA guards incident, its consequences, and its projected
ramifications. He wanted the report to be very brief but comprehensive
because the incident had already created a big stir in the Bush administration. The threats being released from American officials in response to
the incident were growing in intensity with each passing hour. I told
Alshoely and Khanfar that I wasn't a news anchor or a correspondent—
I was a talk-show host—so this coverage would be difficult. I wasn't used
to sound bites and video clips. Saeed reassured me that it would be fine,
and then gave me four minutes for my report—the maximum allowable
time for live correspondent input on a live news bulletin.

When the *Day's Harvest* started airing live, the host was my colleague
Jumana Nammour. She asked me only one question: "How is the situation
in Fallujah one day after the killing and mutilation of the four guards?"

In precisely four minutes, I condensed my full analysis of the situation.
I reported what I had seen in the city and heard from the Fallujans,
provided data about the city's geography and demographics, and informed
the audience of possible future developments. I concluded with my
opinion that things didn't look very good for anyone in the city of Fallujah, and that at this point any American military operation against Fallujah
would be difficult to say the very least.

After our work was done for the day, I left Fallujah with Abdulazeem
Muhammad and spent the night at his parents' house. We chose to spend
the night with Abdulazeem's family because there were no decent hotels

or motels in the city of Fallujah, and more importantly because it would have been offensive to him and his family for us to stay somewhere other than their home while visiting the city. Fallujans are a very proud and generous people. To stay at a hotel in a town where Abdulazeem's family lives would be tantamount to telling him that his family wasn't good enough to host me, especially since their house was large enough to accommodate an extra person.

Some of Fallujah's dignitaries, along with Abdulazeem's friends and extended family members, knew I was in town because they had seen me on the *Day's Harvest* earlier that afternoon. Those who had seen the report flocked to Abdulazeem's home to greet me. I stayed up late into the night talking with these townspeople. We discussed the city, the insurgents, the organized resistance, the American forces, and the future of the occupation in Iraq. The townspeople showed grave concern over the actions of the insurgents and the civilian mobs, as well as grave concern for their own safety and future.

The following Friday we arrived in Samarra and al-Jazeera (along with a scattering of other world news agencies and networks) broadcast Friday sermons from several different Fallujan mosques. Preachers and clergymen fumed in anger, condemning the mutilation of the mercenaries' corpses by civilian mobs. The mercenary killings were profoundly disturbing to all Iraqis, and for obvious reasons, to Fallujans in particular. The incident with the mercenaries brought back horrific memories of a very black chapter in the history of the Iraqi people. The Iraqi people were working fiercely against memories from the year 1958—the year of the coup against the monarchy. In this bloody coup, members of the royal family were ruthlessly murdered by angry mobs. These murders included the slaughter of women and children. The corpses of those murdered were mutilated and dragged across the streets of Baghdad, just like the mercenaries in Fallujah during the attack of 2004. In 1958, however, the atrocities didn't stop with desecration of the living. Even those already deceased weren't spared from the blinding anger of the Iraqis. The late Prime Minister Nuri al-Said was already dead and buried when the coup took place, but his corpse was dug out of its grave and dragged across the streets along with that of Crown Prince Abd Alilah. These corpses were hung by the Ministry of Defense of Iraq after they had been taken through the streets of Baghdad. The corpses remained hanging for several days.

Clearly Bush and his administration were not the only people working to keep the past behind them as this conflict continued. The flashback to these images of the 1958 coup deeply frightened religious leaders throughout Iraq, and for obvious reasons frightened leaders of Fallujah in particular. These leaders knew that the hatred demonstrated in the mercenary killings was the kind of hatred that, if let loose, could completely strip the Iraqi people of their humanity.

In the Friday sermon at Fallujah's main mosque, Imam Sheikh Khaled Ahmad said, "The mutilation that was done by those ignorant mobs is appalling and repulsive. No religious scholar can condone this. These actions are inexcusable regardless of the situation. Those who engaged in this act represent only themselves, and they have committed a very grave crime. I don't believe that the resistance commits egregious acts of this kind because there is no possible way to find any justification for this in Islamic law. We don't accept this, and neither do the people engaged in jihad and resistance. If you're engaged in jihad, your struggle needs to be completely for the sake of Allah, and therefore, your jihad needs to be in conformance with the orders of Allah, and with Islam."

Al-Jazeera also aired excerpts from the Friday sermon held at Abdulaziz Samarray Mosque. The preacher was Sheikh Makky Kubaisy, the representative of the Association of Muslim Scholars inside Fallujah. Sheikh Kubaisy clearly stated the Islamic ruling on the incident and then responded to the American threats to Fallujah. He said, "Resistance is the legitimate right of every occupied people according to every scripture revealed by God, every law made by man, and every law set by international standards and agreements. However, the mutilation that was done to the corpses is absolutely condemned by our religion's teachings. But what pushed people off the edge of humanity and toward committing such acts was the excessive oppression of the occupation. They didn't spare the sanctity of a single child or woman or elder from being violated. We don't know the names of the people who committed this act, so why should the entire city be held responsible for the actions of the unknown few? We are forewarning the American forces that Fallujah will not be an easy bite to swallow. If they try to invade us, they will definitely see violence escalating until it reaches every inch of Iraq."

It was clear that although religious leaders throughout Iraq responded to the civilian mobs with an overwhelming message of condemnation, they held the US responsible for forcing the Iraqis to engage in such brutal behavior. The voices of preachers stating opinions similar to those of Sheikh Kubaisy were sounded in the sermons of a multitude of Fallujan mosques that Friday afternoon following the attacks.

Bush's Personal Battle against Fallujah

Despite the strong condemnation by religious leaders in Fallujah, I knew the Fallujan people were not going to be subdued easily, considering Fallujah's history of resistance and its recent operations against the American troops. Looking at the severity of threats made by American officials and observing the rapid escalation of developments after the incident, it was also all too clear to me that the Bush administration wasn't going to let the mercenary incident pass without severe retaliation. The people of Fallujah had the misfortune of having a video-documented attack take place within their city limits, and the broadcast of those video images severely crippled the morale of the American forces and weakened support the American public gave to the war effort. The other issue was that the news of the mercenary role in the war was leaked to the public because of the killings. So, not only did Bush's army suffer damage to its morale after these attacks, but the entire nation was now revealed for what it was: a nation that didn't have the integrity to send its own sons and daughters to fight for a cause it supposedly believed in; a nation that hired disposable mercenaries because it lacked the courage to confront the opposition on its own. With all of these secrets exposed to the public, Bush was determined to exact revenge on the city of Fallujah in order to clean up America's global image.

Bush's domestic opponents, namely the Democrats, also did not let the mercenary incident pass without taking advantage of the chance for political leverage. Congresswoman Nancy Pelosi of San Francisco, who was the House Minority Leader in 2004, demanded a review of America's strategy in Iraq following these attacks. She said that the US troops had failed to keep Fallujah under control and that such failure prompted questions about the feasibility of the transfer of formal sovereignty to the Iraqis as soon as June 30, 2004. Pelosi also said that if the US forces were to abide by the proposed timeline, then Bush would have to come up with something better than the current plan. Yet, this statement wasn't her strongest condemnation of Bush's policies in Iraq. A few weeks later, in an interview published by the *San Francisco Chronicle* on May 20, she described Bush as "…an incompetent leader. In fact, he's not a leader. He's a person who has no judgment, no experience and no knowledge of the subjects that he has to decide upon." She then added, "He has on his shoulders the deaths of many more troops, because he would not heed the advice of his own State Department of what to expect after May 1…The shallowness that he has brought to the office has not changed since he got there."

I am not an American. I have never lived in the United States, and don't claim to be an authority on American politics. But even I know that when members of your cabinet and Congress, especially remarkable thinkers like Pelosi who have been elected by your own people, give such a poor characterization of your leadership, you must not be performing your duties the way you should be. Any president who receives such inflammatory criticism from his subordinates must be seriously mismanaging the affairs of his country.

Pelosi's sentiments were echoed by Democrats all over the United States after the mercenary attacks. On April 2, New Jersey Senator Frank Lautenberg, a Democrat, sent a letter to Paul Bremer telling him that the United States must leave Iraq as soon as possible but not before ensuring that Iraq would remain secure, united, and governed by the rule of law. Massachusetts Senator John Kerry, also a Democrat, said that the Fallujah attacks reflected the failure of the Bush policy on unilateral action. He also said that the administration's policies were still unbalanced, and had been since the start of the American occupation. (Though I have to say that I later heard Senator Kerry make statements that negated this belief; it seems to me that John Kerry's statements always go in one direction, make a U-turn, and come back in a different form.)

Regardless, the harsh statements unleashed by Bush opponents as well as the constant affirmation of Fallujah's image as a city of defiance kept Bush in a difficult situation after the mercenary killings. These inflammatory statements made by members of the US Congress also further complicated the transfer of formal sovereignty to the Iraqi people and the end of Paul Bremer's term in Iraq. With this heavy Democratic criticism and Fallujah's resistance inflecting serious damage on US morale, Bush and his administration became obsessed with fixing the problem that was festering in Fallujah, and unanimously agreed that the problems in the city must be taken care of swiftly and forcefully. On the tail of this decision, Paul Bremer wasted no time in vowing that the death of the mercenaries would not go unpunished.

Scott McClellan had his share of problems as press secretary after the Fallujah story broke. Journalists fired one difficult question after another to McClellan during a press conference on April 1. When reporters demanded to know whether US forces had arrested, or had any plans to arrest, any of the people involved in the mercenary killings, he responded angrily, "I'm not going to get into discussion of any military operations or planning from this podium. I will say that I'm confident those individuals will be brought to justice for these horrific, despicable attacks." When McClellan was asked if the president had seen the horrific images from the attack in Fallujah, he informed the press that the president had seen them, and that the images had only strengthened his resolve to bring stability and security to Iraq. McClellan added that the images did not scare the president, and that he intended to stay the course in Iraq.

Similar threats came from both top administration officials and from the US military itself. In a press conference held the same day, General Mark Kimmitt vowed a "deliberate" and "overwhelming" response to the mercenary attacks. He said that "[this response] will be at the time and the place of our choosing. We will hunt down the criminals. We will kill them or we will capture them."

Although Kimmitt so boldly vowed retaliation in this press conference one day after the attacks, he hadn't been so eager or so ready for retaliation in the hours just after the attacks. In a lengthy report of an interview with General Kimmitt compiled by John F. Burns of the *New York Times* on April 1, Burns writes, "Hours after the deaths of the four American civilians who were dragged from their vehicle and mutilated in Fallujah on Wednesday, an American general went before reporters in Baghdad with the air of measured assurance that has characterized every daily briefing on the military situation across Iraq. 'Despite an uptick in local engagements, the overall area of operations remains relatively stable with negligible impact on the coalition's ability to continue progress in governance, economic development, and restoration of essential services,' said Brig. General Mark Kimmitt, 51, the former paratrooper who is chief spokesman for the United States military command."

The discrepancy between this first statement and his threats the next day cannot be explained except by the fact that General Kimmitt was quite simply falsifying the reality of the situation when he claimed that the impact of the attacks was "negligible." The first statement was simply inaccurate. On the contrary, the mercenary attacks had major ramifications for all parties involved. After these attacks, General Kimmitt, like the rest of the US military, felt his morale drop to the lowest point since the war began. Perhaps Kimmitt was trying to downplay the incident so that he could encourage the possibility that he wouldn't have to lead an army of discouraged forces into a nasty battle. When Kimmitt realized that the entire United States was up in arms over the incident the day after it happened, he responded to the US reaction by agreeing wholeheartedly—by puffing and fuming, beating his chest, and making very public and very aggressive statements vowing total revenge.

Confusion over the exact circumstances of the event was echoed in the American media as well. After the scandalous news that the Bush administration was using mercenaries to serve its cause broke in the international media, and Blackwater USA identified the deceased mercenaries as professional fighters who had been on an armed military escort mission, the *Washington Post* still came out with an April 2 headline claiming that the four people killed were only civilians: "US Vows to Find Civilians' Killers." If we can call hardened professional soldiers armed with dangerous weapons and performing the duties of combat soldiers "civilians," then is everyone a civilian? This headline begs the question: are there any combatants left in this world, if we are to accept the definition offered by the *Washington Post*?

After the mercenary attack, an American official who wished to remain anonymous gave this statement to Reuters on April 2: "If this incident is allowed to pass without retaliation or investigation, and if it was accepted as the cost of doing business in dealing with Fallujah, that would give a very negative indication, a bad sign for us. Without retaliation, we will end up seeing many of those youth who were in the mob hanging dead bodies join the real insurgency and start firing at us and setting up explosives."

The heavily charged reaction to these mercenary attacks and the cries for revenge from the US public made it seem, at least for a brief period, that the incident with the mercenaries could possibly threaten the entire plan the Bush administration had in mind for Iraq. Both political and civilian voices began to clamor louder in the United States, demanding a withdrawal of occupation forces from Iraq. In many ways, it appeared Bush was losing control of his political strength at home and abroad. At a time when the Bush administration was supposed to be near the realization of their dreams of "transfer of formal sovereignty," "peace and security," and other wonderful and unrealistic ideals, the administration was instead developing plans for revenge and fighting off domestic and international opposition to the US war effort in Iraq.

Paul Bremer's mission was scheduled to end by June 30th, only 90 days from the date of the attacks on the mercenaries. On this date, Bremer was supposed to transfer sovereignty over to Ayad Allawi and then return to the United States. But how could he transfer that sovereignty in any meaningful way if the situation was as bad as it was in Fallujah?

Because Fallujah jeopardized all of the notions of stability and peace in Iraq and nearly brought his plans to a halt, Bush decided to take revenge in order to return the United States to its former image as a superpower in control of its plans for the country of Iraq. This revenge would be exacted not only on the insurgents who murdered the mercenaries, not only on the mobs of teenagers who mutilated the corpses, but also on the 300,000 civilian residents of Fallujah.

Entrapment and Escalated Violence

The American forces did not take long to prepare the "overwhelming" response to the mercenary attacks that was called for by General Kimmitt. Deputy Secretary of Defense Paul Wolfowitz (who, incidentally, later served as president of the World Bank and was forced to resign after he was discovered giving a pay raise to his mistress, an employee of the same organization), General Peter Pace,[16] and the House Armed Services Committee convened for a closed-door discussion of "potential American reactions" shortly after Kimmitt called for an American response to the attacks. Duncan Lee Hunter (R, CA), the chairman of the committee, told reporters after the meeting, "I think that history will prove that the folks that have taken actions against Americans have underestimated our capabilities to, number one, identify those people; and, number two, to eliminate them."

On April 3, India's *Tribune* reported, "US officials have identified several people involved in Wednesday's fatal attack on four US contractors in Fallujah. *ABC News* reported [on the attack], quoting intelligence sources as saying they included former members of Iraq's paramilitary forces and 'non-Iraqi Arabs.' Yesterday, ABC said US forces were expected to take decisive action against the attackers within the next several days, and intelligence sources knew who they were going after." On the same day as this report, CNN released a statement saying that US military officials were investigating whether or not the attack in Fallujah was planned. The CNN report commented that officials had told them, "The normally busy streets in the city about 30 miles west of Baghdad were empty and shops were closed at the time of the attack. Also, a number of local Iraqi media were in the area. Officials said there is no indication that residents of Fallujah knew what was being planned, but there was talk on the street that trouble might erupt."

Certainly the attack was planned and premeditated by the insurgents. What the military officials were alluding to in this report was that the residents of the city appeared to be planning for the attack even though they didn't quite know the target was going to be mercenaries. This news item on CNN was a hint that the US forces were planning to kill indiscriminately in their revenge, since they clearly considered common people corroborators if not collaborators in this attack.

More reports were released that indicated the US stand on bringing the perpetrators of the crimes in Fallujah to justice. On April 4, the Saudi newspaper *al-Sharq al-Awsat* published an interview with a spokesperson for US forces in Baghdad. The spokesperson said, "It's true, we have video tapes, and we'd be very interested in talking with the people who appear in them. However, we don't know how far along our intelligence has come in the process of identifying which people are behind this. Our forces will enter Fallujah to pursue those who ambushed the four Americans and then mutilated their bodies. We will enter Fallujah and make a presence there. We'll distinguish civilians from the enemy and then destroy the enemy."

For political-correctness purposes in this statement, the official claimed US forces would distinguish residents from insurgents. For the real military plan, he spelled out that Fallujan teenagers were considered to be enemy insurgents as far as the United States was concerned, and the United States was determined to "destroy the enemy." The teenagers were certainly not innocent—but just as certainly, they weren't insurgents! This plan was presumptuous, and undoubtedly led to the unfair treatment of many Fallujan teenagers during the first battle of Fallujah.

These reports of American statements represent only a sampling of the deep anxiety the Fallujah incident caused in the White House, the US Department of State, Congress, and military at home and abroad. It was clear to many outside viewers around the world that the American forces were letting blind anger get the best of them in their reactions to this attack. I remember vividly the deep discontent on the faces of the American officials when their statements about this conflict were broadcast on television. When I saw that anger, I knew it did not bode well for the future of Iraq. I realized that Americans were about to succumb to a level of incivility no more commendable than what was demonstrated when the Fallujan mobs committed their atrocities against the mercenary corpses. Even then I had an undeniable fear that the American forces were planning to take indiscriminating, collective revenge on the entire city for the crimes committed only by a certain group of people. The official announced plan, though, was that the American forces would demand that the city hand over the criminals, and only the criminals would be punished. The "criminals," incidentally, were defined as the teenagers, who did not in fact plot or execute the ambush.

The Yasin Brigades Take Responsibility for "Gift"

What made it even clearer that Fallujan teenagers were not responsible for planning the attacks on the mercenaries was the fact that a newly established resistance group claimed responsibility for the ambush a couple of days after it happened, before the siege started. The Sheikh Ahmad Yasin Brigades, named for the godfather of the Hamas Islamic Resistance Movement in Palestine, was only a few days old. A week prior to the incident in Fallujah, Sheikh Ahmad Yasin had been assassinated by Israeli forces as he left dawn prayer at his local mosque in his wheelchair. The resistance group called the 1920 Revolution Brigades considered Yasin a martyr, and decided to honor him as a regional revolutionary leader by naming a new division of brigades after him. The unrest in Fallujah gave the Brigades an opportunity for their first "job": an ambush attack on mercenaries working on behalf of the United States.

During my visit to Fallujah just after the ambush, flyers were being distributed by the Yasin Brigades claiming responsibility for the attack. Plastered across the fliers was the phrase, "Fallujah is the graveyard of the Americans." The statement below, which was re-broadcast worldwide by international media, read, "This [ambush attack] is a gift from us, the people of Fallujah, to the people of Palestine and to the family of our hero Sheikh Ahmad Yasin, the prince of all Mujahideen and resistance people, the wheel-chaired man who was butchered by the inhumane and immoral Zionist criminals."

The statement then went on to say, "After closely following several CIA and Israeli Mossad agents, our members were able to successfully execute the ambush and assassination operation on Wednesday, March 31, 2004. Then [after our withdrawal], angry Fallujah crowds burned the two vehicles, dragged the charred corpses, and mutilated them because of the growing hatred for the Americans. This was the Fallujans' response to the repeated violations and indignation done by American forces against mosques and homes, the degradation and insult directed to religious scholars and the elderly, the violation they've done to the women, and their terrorization of the children." The statement concluded with, "We advise the American forces to withdraw from Iraq, and we advise the families of American soldiers particularly and the owners of private companies not to ever come to Iraq."

After the Brigades took the blame for the incident, it stands to reason that the world had someone to hold as responsible. The world waited, then, to see if US forces were going to go after those who claimed responsibility, and whether they intended to bring the criminals to justice as promised.

Fallujah: An American Household Name

Most American television channels presented the public with investigations into some aspect of the incident in Fallujah and its consequences during this time period, whether it was through reports, discussions, debates, interviews, or conversation-style analysis. Perhaps the most outstanding coverage of the issue was provided by the distinguished award-winning journalist and superb author, Amy Goodman. Goodman and her colleague Juan Gonzales are co-hosts of *Democracy Now!*— America's leading pro-peace news forum. This show, along with the demonstrations of anti-war activist Cindy Sheehan, must have also (at least during the high pressure time of the Fallujah incident) been the leading cause of many sleepless nights for President Bush. I know Goodman because in April 2006, she invited me to be a guest on her show commemorating the third anniversary of the American occupation of Iraq. We talked about my coverage of the first battle of Fallujah for twenty minutes. She then dedicated another entire episode to an interview with me and my colleague Layth Mushtaq, the Fallujan cameraman who accompanied me throughout my entire coverage of the first battle of Fallujah.

On April 1, 2004, Goodman's show was naturally centered on the four unfortunate Blackwater USA mercenaries who were killed during the mob riots. On this episode, she hosted Ghazwan al-Mukhtar, a retired Iraqi engineer, and Noam Chomsky, one of America's leading intellectuals.

When asked about the behavior of the civilian mobs, al-Mukhtar explained their inhumane reactions in this way: "This incident happened in Fallujah where two days previous, the American army shot many people—even women and children—on the streets. [It had been] a bizarre shooting spree that was unjustified, killing many people. Fallujah has been a place where the US Army has actually used brutal force to suppress the people there, including using the F-15s and F-16s to attack villages where they think the resistance is. It is unjustified to use high explosives against individuals. This resulted in many, many casualties in the province. To add to this, the forces have detained, for fifty or sixty days, hundreds of people on and off. These actions alienated the people against the American forces and the American security contractors, which are really a private army, uncontrollable by the United States. This is part of the privatization of the war."

Al-Mukhtar stressed that these gruesome incidents were not limited to the city of Fallujah: "Two days ago, three days ago, there was a similar incident in Mosul, where two contractors were killed under electricity. These contractors were going to the electricity generating plant. The important—the thing that I know the media says is that the contractors were involved in protecting the food supply. This is the food supply for the US Army, not to be confused with providing help to the local population or anything. It's just a routine US convoy that may have food and may have on other occasions, armaments or anything. So, the resentments of the people of Fallujah are justified. What happens to them is—it's a sad thing, but you know, brutality breeds brutality, and violence breeds violence, and he who started first should take the responsibility, and I think the US army has used unjustified force against the people of Fallujah, and they have brutalized the people of Fallujah to the point where they had to respond with the same brutality."

Although al-Mukhtar's statements on this episode are quite lengthy, looking at his words in their entirety is crucial for the sake of registering and documenting the truth of this event as I see it. I'm not alone in this regard. An American writer, Abu Spinoza, included al-Mukhtar's statements in their entirety in his article posted on April 3, 2004 on Press Action.[17] I feel that it is my responsibility to help the American public realize that although the attack on the mercenaries was inhumane, it was a natural result of the brutality the US forces had used when working with the people of Fallujah after the fall of Baghdad in 2003.

The Fallujah incident was covered by many other news correspondents besides Amy Goodman, Abu Spinoza, or my colleagues and me at al-Jazeera. The incident completely saturated American media. This high amount of coverage undoubtedly put greater pressure on Bush, sharpened his desire for revenge, and deepened his anxiety about how to resolve the problems in Iraq. Eventually, the time came to release that painful pressure. After enduring a steady flow of bad press and criticism from Americans and foreigners alike, Bush decided it was time to avenge Fallujah's deeds against the American forces, and time to implement the grand plan for the "overwhelming" response that was called for by General Kimmitt just days after the attacks had occurred. Once the decision to draw up a plan for revenge was made, there was no going back.

5. THE ROAD TO SAMARRA

The next day, I headed to Samarra, where I found the talk of the town to be centered on some 800 residents who had recently been arrested by American troops. The townspeople were preparing for a convention in the city in order to demand the release of the prisoners from the occupation forces. Days later, I saw similar scenes in Tikrit, Ramadi,[18] Balad, Baqubah, Muqdadiyah, and other cities in the Diyala province.[19] In every city I visited on this short tour, American troops had managed to encourage so much hatred against the occupation because of their inhumane treatment of civilians that the Iraqis were constantly engaged in some stage of revolt.

Many eyewitnesses also confirmed that what happened to the four mercenaries in Fallujah was not unique. This type of activity had occurred in many other Iraqi cities, with only one difference: in those other cities, there had been no media present to broadcast the incidents across international lines. In other cities where media was not present, there was in many cases more drastic and more destructive types of revenge exacted on occupation forces.

Samarra was also a focal city in the conflict that required extra attention and news coverage, even with the media attention now focused on what was happening in Fallujah and the surrounding areas. The purpose behind visiting Samarra two days after the mercenary attacks was to do preliminary research and gather data needed for my part in the special coverage of the occupation anniversary.

Samarra is a town similar to Fallujah in tenacity—during this American occupation, the city stood so fiercely in defiance of occupying forces that it was subjected to a very tight, two-week siege by American forces in May 2007. During this conflict, a nearly unbreakable hold was placed on the city, a curfew was enforced, and a crushing battle broke out between Samarra's people and the American troops. That battle wasn't Samarra's first, but it would be the battle that most closely resembled the infamous first battle of Fallujah.

By the time I left for Samarra to continue my investigative journey, I had spent one day and one night in Fallujah. I spent that time collecting information and data, and surveying people for the anniversary news coverage. During my conversations with Fallujans, I tried to get the fullest possible picture of what was going on in their minds as civilians, and hear what they thought the future held. Almost everyone I talked with was worried. Fallujans asked me if *I* had any idea what might happen, and in turn, I'd ask what they expected to happen. We shared a mutual concerned curiosity about the future.

The speculations were unsettling. After all, Fallujah is not a military base. It is a normal city like any other crowded city anywhere else in the world. Its 300,000 civilian inhabitants share the same concerns that pepper the lives of other people in cities all over the world: managing work and making money, getting the children to school, finding jobs, getting married or dealing with divorce, having children, burying the dead, and trying to stave off hunger and poverty. The streets of Fallujah are lined with houses, not army barracks. It is simply a residential city and as such has no army to defend it. The resistance represents a very small portion of the city population. These insurgents had no stationary bases at the time of the mercenary attacks—no known locations, and no public banners that read "Wanna terrorize American forces? Come join the Insurgents!" or "Hate Americans? Call 1-900-KILL-USA."

Who were the Americans planning to wage a combat operation against if the enemy was unknown? Because small groups of insurgents were untraceable in Fallujah, it was undeniable that the Americans had to plan an attack on the entire city if they were going to exact revenge. Unfortunately, this type of massive, indiscriminate attack also constitutes an inarguable crime against humanity.

I headed from Fallujah to Samarra on April 2. I was informed of a shortcut road that would take me directly there, bypassing Baghdad. While traveling this road, I saw many charred and destroyed American vehicles littering the sides of the road—remnants of ambush attacks that American forces weren't able to remove for one reason or another. The protocol after an attack was usually that American forces would immediately close the road to the general public, remove the dead, rescue the injured American troops by chopper, and finally remove the damaged vehicles and equipment with large trucks and trailers. This way, no outsiders could tally the American losses. From the evidence on the sides of the road I was traveling, it seemed like the operations waged by the insurgents had risen so dramatically that American forces couldn't keep up, and hadn't had the time to remove everything. Most of these vehicles appeared to have been damaged by hidden explosives, not ambush attacks.

My visit to Samarra came as part of a series of visits to other cities and towns where insurgency was at its strongest and confrontations with US forces were the fiercest. Prior to Samarra, I had visited Ramadi, Fallujah, and Tikrit, and before that I visited many cities in the Diyala province. I had also paid visits to towns that were small in size, but had become infamous for the high levels of insurgent activity—towns such as Taji, Tarmeya, Dhloeya, and Balad. These towns were also often highlighted in international media. My goal in this trip was to get the fullest picture possible of the situation in Iraq as a whole, and also to be able to comprehend the condition of the hotspots in the country that might shape the future of its relationship with the American occupation. Trying to see the "larger picture" is something I have been attempting since the start of my career and my beginnings as a wartime correspondent. You must be sure not to focus on one particular aspect of a conflict, but the conflict as a whole. A visit to Samarra was an absolutely critical last piece in the puzzling picture of the cities where insurgents appeared to be in control.

Suhayb Samarray's Time at Abu Ghraib

Accompanying me on my travel to Samarra was my colleague Suhayb Albaaz Samarray, whose last name gives him away as a native of Samarra. He told me an interesting story during our travels together, which I believe illuminates the complex nature of the conflict I dissect in this book.

Before joining al-Jazeera's Baghdad bureau team as a cameraman, Suhayb was a paparazzo—a cameraman who chased celebrities. When a cameraman works as a paparazzo in a war-plagued country, he doesn't have the luxury of snapping unflattering pictures of Oprah Winfrey or shots of Michael Jackson suggestively handing a candy bar to a minor at his Neverland Ranch. Instead, these cameramen snap potentially scandalous pictures of occupation forces or combat operations, and these are the shots that could be worth money.

When these cameramen work in Iraq, the clients are not *Star* or other gossip magazines, but world news agencies, networks, and satellite television stations that have offices all over Baghdad, but are too short-staffed to have cameramen everywhere something noteworthy might be happening. The Iraqi paparazzi roam the streets of Baghdad holding mini quarter-cams and regular still-photography cameras, looking for occupation forces in any compromising situation. Suhayb had sold images a couple of times to al-Jazeera's Baghdad Bureau while working as a paparazzo. Because he is very active and restless by nature and therefore caught a lot of photos, the Baghdad bureau saw potential in him. After buying a few of his images, they offered him a job on a piece-by-piece basis.

Once he was employed by al-Jazeera and knew he had a guaranteed customer for his shots, Suhayb started roaming the streets of Baghdad even more frequently than he had. The Baghdad–Samarra freeway was so heavily littered with hidden explosives and so frequently the site of ambush operations that it was nicknamed "Ambush Street," a very tantalizing name for someone in search of telling wartime images. Suhayb decided he'd drive up and down that freeway for most of his day, like a fisherman trolling for a big catch. He knew sooner or later he'd capture an image worth something—it was more likely along this street than in the streets of Baghdad proper. The better the picture quality and the more unique the subject matter was, the higher he was paid. He was often without luck. There were days when he found remnants of an explosive that blew up an American vehicle, but most days he found nothing worth wasting film on.

One day, though, he stumbled on a battle site where a group of insurgents had ambushed some American troops. He arrived too late to take pictures of the battle itself, but not too late to take pictures of the American troops collecting their dead and rescuing their wounded. Without thinking about the consequences of taking pictures of American soldiers collecting their dead, Suhayb started snapping photographs and dreaming about what kind of money he was going to demand from al-Jazeera for the exclusive, high-quality pictures. Unfortunately, while he had been trying so hard to make his big catch, he had in fact become the big catch for the Americans, who spotted him almost immediately. Naturally, the American troops arrested him. They also accused him of cooperating with the insurgents. Otherwise, how could he explain his arrival precisely at the time the battle ended? When he told the Americans that the images were for al-Jazeera, they accused al-Jazeera of having advance knowledge of the attacks, and therefore sending its photographers at the right time. Several American officials repeated this senseless accusation. Lt. General Ricardo Sanchez and his boss General John Abizaid repeatedly, and mindlessly, spewed out direct accusations that al-Jazeera had collaborated with the insurgents and sent Suhayb to capture images of the aftermath of this battle.

The reality, however, was that al-Jazeera never needed advanced knowledge of an attack. It was guaranteed that al-Jazeera would be privy to images of any given battle. First of all, al-Jazeera had the foresight of hiring a good number of piece-by-piece paparazzi cameramen like

Suhayb. This didn't cost al-Jazeera much money, because the paparazzi didn't get paid unless they took pictures of something worth selling. So, the company had many paparazzi roaming the streets simultaneously, which increased its chances of having hired photographers at the right time and place, and explains its ability to present exclusive, high quality images for printing.

Secondly, and more importantly, al-Jazeera has far more viewers than any other news network in the Middle East. The insurgents, who are interested in advancing their own cause and want a forum to deliver their message to the public, very frequently submitted pictures taken by their supporters after battles had ended. The insurgents hoped al-Jazeera would air all the footage of the conflicts, including their cheaply-produced propaganda, and that hundreds of millions of viewers would be exposed to their message. That kind of publicity was worth any risk, including the possibility of not receiving payment for your work. Al-Jazeera always edited the footage, according to its editorial policy, and took out anything that could give support to the insurgents or was not considered newsworthy. But the images were still always available. The insurgents were chasing after al-Jazeera with the images, not the other way around. Al-Jazeera was not to blame for photographers being on the scene after battles had ended.

After he was captured by the American forces, Suhayb was taken to the infamous Abu Ghraib prison. After a series of lengthy and grueling interrogations, no formal charges were brought against him. Nevertheless, he was kept in detention, just like thousands of other Iraqis who were detained without charges.

While he was in prison, Suhayb recited the Quran every night. He is a man gifted with a loud and distinctive voice, so the inmates in the adjacent cells who didn't have a copy of the Quran enjoyed listening to him. One day, one of the senior interrogation officers confronted him about his recitations: "I heard you chanting some beautiful, soothing hymns the other night. Would you let me hear some of that again?"

Suhayb responded, "Those sounds you heard were not hymns. I wasn't singing. I was simply reciting the Quran."

The officer paused for a long time. He then asked, "Is this what the Quran is?" Suhayb replied, "Yes, that's all it is."

The officer requested, "Can you recite some more of it please?" After this request, Suhayb started reciting the Quran. He continued with his recitations until he noticed the officer had tears in his eyes. Suhayb was perplexed by this reaction because the officer wasn't a Muslim, he hadn't heard the verses of the Quran before, and he certainly didn't speak a word of Arabic. If the officer didn't understand what was being recited to him, why were the words having such a dramatic effect on him? Suhayb stopped his recitations because he didn't know what to make of the officer's reaction. The officer signaled to him to keep reciting, so he did. After a while, Suhayb finished the recitation. The officer stopped crying when the recitations stopped.

The officer asked, "Why are you here? What could a gentle man like you have done to get yourself in here?"

Suhayb told him his story. The officer told him, "I'll try my best to get you out of here, but that'll take time. Until that happens, I want you to do me a favor. Please let me come to you every night to hear you recite some of the Quran for me."

The scene from the first night was repeated every time the officer visited Suhayb. The officer would listen to the recitations as if he understood what was being said, and then he would react in a rush of tears until the recitation was finished.

After 77 days of this life at the Abu Ghraib prison, the officer came and told Suhayb, "You're getting out of here. I was finally able to settle your case and close your file." Suhayb was finally getting the chance to go home.

No one knows the details of what went on in that officer's mind, and why he was urged to help a man who recited religious verses he didn't understand let alone believe in. Perhaps Suhayb's rhythmic recitation of the Quran reminded him of hymns he sang in church in his hometown with family and neighbors. Maybe those recitations made him feel that Suhayb too was a human being who deserved to live a free life and worship freely like the officer's hometown people. This is just one of a million other possible speculations. What is certain is that the officer viewed Suhayb as a fellow human being; an equal entitled to the same rights as him.

The place where this story happened is of some significance. Over the course of the war, Abu Ghraib became infamous for the most widely circulated, most repulsive, and most shocking images of poorly-treated Iraqi prisoners. Despite the presence of some decent and humane soldiers like the officer who released Suhayb, Abu Ghraib's overall image is still one that would turn the stomach of any civilized human being.

The story of Suhayb is significant for a few reasons. The first is that the

Bush administration's attempt to blame war crimes on a "few bad apples" is false. War crimes were, and still are, committed because the war itself is immoral, not because of a few immoral people. As noted earlier, American soldiers are like any other group of people: a mixed bag of good and bad. Some are mentally corrupt human beings; others are decent people who don't have to tell you that they come from a solid family background because their behavior speaks for them. But even good human beings can do horrible things under certain circumstances. When your commander-in-chief wages an immoral war and violates Geneva Conventions and basic human rights, what's to hold you from immoral behavior as a private soldier? Certainly not every soldier at Abu Ghraib was mentally ill, but in the end Abu Ghraib will keep that reputation, because even decent people can do some pretty sick things when ordered to. The Bush administration's attempt to scapegoat a few lower-ranking soldiers was obviously a low-level effort to shift the blame of war crimes away from the administration as a whole.

The second way in which this story is significant is because it demonstrates the clear difference between uniformed American soldiers and mercenaries. Of all the stories I heard about the behavior of mercenaries, none recounted their behaving humanely, as some uniformed US soldiers did. This was precisely why private contractors were far more hated by Iraqis than US soldiers, and largely responsible for the reprehensible actions of the Fallujan mobs.

Majesty Turned to Mayhem

The name "Samarra" is a shortening of "sar man raa," which translates loosely to "eye candy." Indeed, the city's stunning architecture and impressive artwork pleased everyone who visited. As Suhayb and I approached Samarra, I thought of how we were getting closer to the presence of the Abbasids,[20] to the heart of a once massive and mighty empire. I was heading toward the city of Caliph al-Mu'tasim, who sent a huge army to Europe following the cry of a single oppressed woman.[21] Samarra was the hub of Iraq's historic might and pride. I was looking forward to seeing the architecture and taking in some of the important historic sights.

When we got to Samarra, the city I saw before me looked more like ancient ruins. There was no evidence of a civilization of high culture ever having lived within city limits, and certainly no evidence of happiness or prestige. The city was occupied by American forces; some parts were entirely destroyed and it was obvious that no attention was being paid to the infrastructure needed to support basic life for its residents. Only one decent looking piece of architecture caught my attention—a mosque with a spiral staircase swirling from the ground all the way to the top of the minaret. This was the Caliph al-Mu'tasim Mosque, built between the years 836 and 842, when the ruler was building his capital in the area that would eventually become modern-day Samarra.

Samarra is also home to one of the biggest shrines of the Shia sect—the tomb of Imam Ali al-Hadi, the Tenth Imam in the series of twelve infallible imams in which Shiites believe. But there are no practicing Shiites in the city of Samarra; the population of Samarra is about 285,000, and most are Sunnis or from indigenous Arab tribes. Sunnis believe there was no designated series of imams to begin with, and that no imams are infallible. As far as the Sunni belief is concerned, infallibility is a trait shared only by prophets and messengers of God. On the other hand, Shiites believe very strongly in the infallibility of imams.

Because all Samaritans follow the Sunni tradition, the caretaking of the Shia shrine in Samarra must be done entirely by local Sunni Samaritans. This has been the custom for hundreds of years. Religious Shia pilgrims visit the shrine from Iran, Iraq, Bahrain, Lebanon, and other countries with Shia populations. To the Sunnis, the rituals involved in such a pilgrimage qualify as borderline blasphemy. In fact, the whole idea of making a pilgrimage for the purpose of receiving blessings or guidance from a dead human being is considered a grave form of blasphemy among the Sunnis. If you asked many Sunnis their honest opinions about the Shiites and the shrine, the politically correct Sunnis would probably note that traditions are different, while the not-so-politically-correct Sunnis would simply say that the Shiites were weird and disgusting. Yet, despite this fundamental conflict, the Sunnis in Samarra have never denied visiting Shiites access to the shrine, or neglected the shrine—not even during Saddam's tyrannical rule.

This peaceful truce between the Sunni Samaritans and the visiting Shiites had been shaken by recent history, however. When the American occupation came to Iraq, promising religious tolerance, cultural diversity, social equality, and ethnic harmony, those promises eventually translated into the creation of a sectarian Sunni–Shia conflict. On February 22, 2006, the Shia shrine was rocked by a massive explosion, which severely damaged the dome. Because the bombing didn't completely destroy the monument, the criminals made another attempt to destroy the mosque on June 13, 2007. This bombing eliminated what was left of the two minarets of the shrine. It seems odd that such desperate attempts at stirring sectarian violence took place after the occupation forces supposedly began to spread values that advocated tolerance and diversity, and after such a long, unbroken period of peace between the two sects regarding the use of the shrine.

This violence had other deadly ramifications aside from the destruction of the Shia shrine. It was rumored around Samarra that my late colleague Atwar Bahjat was killed because she got fatally close to exposing the culprits behind the explosion.[22] Atwar, who had a Sunni father and a Shia mother, was naturally religiously diverse and tolerant. She was well-liked by both sects, and her promotion of religious tolerance was one of the things that made her killers dislike her. Her death remains mysterious to this day, as no one claimed responsibility, and it is not immediately obvious who would benefit from targeting a popular news correspondent. Samaritans believe that whoever blew up the Shia shrine is also responsible for killing Bahjat, and that this criminal would be very interested in the outbreak of sectarian violence in Samarra.

This was the Samarra that greeted us—a city a world away from the dazzling vision described in the history books.

In Samarra we were hosted by Sheikh Nahedh Samarray, one of Samarra's dignitaries and a well-respected religious scholar. He is an absolute pleasure to speak with because of his warmth and friendliness. I was first introduced to him at al-Jazeera's Baghdad bureau during an earlier visit to Iraq in 2003, when Wadah Khanfar was still the Baghdad bureau chief.

Along with Sheikh Nahedh Samarray, a group of Samaritan dignitaries and public figures met with us to discuss the situation in the city. They invited me to come see the famous Samaritan "eye candy" and to get to know the city, its heritage, and its people. These men said that perhaps the remnants of the regal history of Samarra would make it easier to tolerate the sight of Iraqi ruins. The remnants of Samarra's past offered promise that this country, someday, might be revitalized and rise again to a level of respect and power.

As we went through our tour, however, the historic city seemed neglected to me. On top of the negligence, there was the constant presence of the occupation, something the Samaritans were unable and unwilling to tolerate. Samaritans take great pride in the fact that they are descendants of important Arab tribes. Many descend from the tribes of the companions of Prophet Muhammad, while some Samaritans even descend from the tribe of the Prophet himself. When a population takes such great pride in its lineage and its long history, it is particularly difficult to accept the authority of an occupation. The Samaritans were strongly opposed to the occupation, and viewed those Iraqis willing to cooperate with the Americans as ruthless nomads with no honorable lineage to give them the pride to resist. To Samaritans, the physical reality of an occupation did not necessarily dictate a change in allegiance. They simply acknowledged that Iraqis had a weaker military than the occupation forces, which is why they were in control. But that control didn't mean that the Iraqis should be morally defeated. To the Samaritans, there was no excuse for moral defeat unless you had no pride in your bloodline.

This great sense of pride in Samarra was the primary catalyst for the constant confrontations between the occupation forces and the city residents. The tension between the forces translated into very high percentages of dead and imprisoned Samaritans during and after the fall of Baghdad. During my stay in the city, I tried to visit as many Samaritan homes as time and circumstance would permit. There wasn't a single family I met during my visits that didn't have a son who was wounded, imprisoned, or killed. One year into the American occupation, the number of Samaritans apprehended and kept in prison by US forces had reached 850 individuals, and that number multiplied very quickly in the years following. Samarra repeatedly rebelled against the occupation. The city was placed under siege and given a tight curfew after each rebellion. No amount of punishment the occupation placed on the rebels was enough to subdue the high morale of Samaritans.

After our tour of the city, we attended the Friday sermon at the mosque led by Sheikh Nahedh Samarray. We prayed there and went back to Sheikh Nahedh's house for lunch with several of Samarra's dignitaries. After lunch, we headed to the tomb of Imam Ali al-Hadi. The caretakers of the shrine greeted us warmly. Inside the shrine, along with the tomb of the tenth infallible Imam, Ali al-Hadi, is the tomb of his son, the Eleventh Imam, al-Hassan al-Askari, and his other son, Jaffar al-Zaki.

Spiritually, what's even more important to the Shiites than the tombs in this shrine is what is believed to be in the basement. According to Shia belief, the series of the twelve infallible Imams was completed by the Eleventh Imam. Al-Muntathar is not a last name; it's a nickname that means "the Awaited." Shia belief dictates that in 941 the Twelfth Imam went into the basement of this shrine and never reappeared. This event is called the Great Disappearance. The Twelfth Imam is supposed to make a second coming in the future to resurrect justice and enforce good governance in an oppressed world. In this second coming, the Twelfth Imam completes the cycle of governance that the entire series of imams is supposed to implement in our human lifetime. All twelve imams are believed to be infallible because they are direct descendants of Prophet Muhammad. These twelve cannot make mistakes and cannot be questioned about the wisdom of their actions and policies. Consequently, no devout Shiite can question or disobey the views and policies of Shia political and military leaders who represent the Twelfth Imam.

This set of beliefs is no minor matter. The belief in the twelve infallible imams is the very crux of the entire Shia faith and the core around which their theocratic political theory is built. The twelve imams are so significant to Shia life that the imams are often described in Shia literature as "the glue that holds the entire universe intact." The Shiites do not necessarily believe that the Twelfth Imam is still in the basement of that shrine, but the basement certainly represents a gateway to the place where he disappeared. Therefore, it also represents his entrance point back into this world. In other words, the Shiites believe the cycle of governance by imams and their dominion over the whole universe (not just planet earth) will start its last stages from the basement of the shrine in Samarra. The Shiites still wait for this upcoming day with passion, and look forward to seeing the world rid of all injustice and oppression. In this regard, this shrine is certainly more than a graveyard to the Shia people.

To expedite the return of the Twelfth Imam, Shia leaders have repeatedly made attempts to pave the way for his return. The whole idea and concept (on a theological level only) behind the Islamic Revolution of 1979 in Iran was to ready the country for the return of the Twelfth Imam. A theocratic system was installed in place of the ousted monarchs, and Khomeini led the new system carrying the title "Deputy to the [Twelfth] Imam." Khomeini's political opponents and enemies were accused of being "enemies of the Twelfth Imam." The revolutionary courts set up by Khomeini tried and executed countless former Iranian officials and politicians (leftover from the overthrown monarchy) for "fighting against the Twelfth Imam." After the US invasion of Iraq, Shia leader Muqtada al-Sadr set up his own militia that he named "Mahdi Army" and appointed military commanders in it who unquestionably believed that their militia group was ran and managed directly by the Twelfth Imam. This was Muqtada al-Sadr's attempt at making Iraq Mahdi-friendly territory. Critics of Hizbullah, the Shia Lebanese militant organization, also accuse it of having an agenda to turn the entire country of Lebanon into a Mahdi-friendly Shia mini-state that's awaiting the return of the Twelfth Imam. This belief is so significant in Shia theology that devout Shiites are willing to fight and die for it. It is the sole most important motivation of just about any political or military Shia movement that has embarked in recent times on a journey for attaining political power in Iran, Iraq, Lebanon, and other places.

To the Sunnis, however, this entire tale of the awaited Imam is reminiscent of the stories found in *A Thousand and One Nights*.[23] They regard this tale as absolutely fascinating, but definitely a work of fiction. In fact, the more puritan schools of thought among Sunnis view the concept with disdain and ridicule more than amusement. And while devout Shia believers await the return of their absent Twelfth Imam with fervor, ultra-orthodox Sunni believers await the new edition of *A Thousand and One Nights* to come off the printing press.

After visiting the shrine, we took a tour of the city's old market and then went on to the Caliph al-Mu'tasim Mosque, and saw the splendor of its spiral staircase. As I ascended the stairs to the top of the minaret, the brisk breeze hit my face. From the top of the minaret, I was able to look down on the city. Only at that moment did I comprehend the bewildering majesty of the city, and begin to understand the respect it commands. This majestic splendor must have been what made Caliph al-Mu'tasim choose this city to be the capital of his empire, back when this conflict with American forces was an inconceivable notion.

PART II

APRIL 2004: THE FIRST BATTLE

"When the sword is drawn, the passions of men observe no bounds of moderation."
—Alexander Hamilton, article 16 of *The Federalist Papers*

6. DAWN BREAKS: A CITY ENCIRCLED

I did not sleep very well that night after Wadah Khanfar called us to tell us that the Americans were rumored to be preparing an attack on Fallujah. This wasn't that unusual—sleep deprivation and insomnia are unfortunate side effects of being a traveling journalist, and I have particular trouble sleeping when an important job is up the following day. On this particular night, there was also the constant noise of explosions and bombings all over Baghdad. Still, my extreme exhaustion allowed me to sleep for short periods of time, so at least I did get a bit of rest.

When I got up in the morning, lamenting my lack of quality sleep, the first thing I did was ask what had happened in Fallujah. As it turned out, my worst fears had been confirmed over the course of the night. American troops had indeed encircled the city after midnight, and confirmed what Wadah Khanfar had predicted. As we would soon see for ourselves, the number of troops marching around the borders of the city was so massive that an outsider might mistakenly assume the Fallujan mob had mutilated the corpse of George Bush, not the corpses of some hired mercenaries. But no one expected that by the time the sun rose on April 5, the city would be completely under siege and that some 11,000 troops would be cutting off all entrances to the city.

We had to find a way inside the city to cover the siege. The Americans had reason to believe that few journalists would be inside Fallujah if they attacked at night. Because Fallujah is only 35 miles from Baghdad, no news agency or station generally felt it necessary to send a correspondent to reside in Fallujah on a permanent basis—reporters could quickly and easily be dispatched to Fallujah when a need arose. The only journalists residing in Fallujah were native Fallujans who worked for international newspapers and press agencies. One of these journalists was my colleague Hussain Deli, who would play a heroic role in our coverage of the battle of Fallujah. Also, Fallujah had no decent hotels where journalists could stay for an extended period of time. Most journalists started their duty in the morning, conducted some interviews, snapped some pictures, gathered some facts and data, and left for Baghdad by nightfall. In other words, it could be assumed that every night the city was emptied of non-native journalists.

My preparation had to be for a long journey, because I had no idea when or how our crew would be able to leave the city, if we found a way in. I took my suitcase, handbag, and only vital things I might need for survival. I headed to our offices in the Swan Lake Hotel to check on my colleagues as they prepared for the journey. I asked them to double (and triple) check everything they were packing because there was no room for error. These double and triple checks caused us some delay.

When our crew finally headed out of Baghdad at 9AM on the morning of April 5, the streets were extremely crowded. It took forever to get out of the city, and then we had to find our way onto the international highway that connects Iraq to Jordan. This highway was the quickest route to Fallujah. I had traveled this route many times in the past, but this time the trip seemed to move very slowly—because of the heavy traffic, but also because of my overwhelming anxiety about what was in store for us in Fallujah.

Our crew of seven—bureau chief Hamed Hadeed (who luckily for us, was a Fallujan who knew his city well), cameramen Layth Mushtaq and Hassan Walid, engineer Sayfuldeen Muhammad, drivers Abdulaziz Abraham (Abo Omar) and Farqad, and me—had spent the early morning nervously preparing for this momentous trip, knowing that it might prove to be immensely historically important if we did good work. If we survived.

As we edged closer to the Fallujah exit on the highway, we could see many semi-trailers, trucks, and civilian cars pulled over to the sides of the road. By the time we reached the exit, we found all cars stopped or idling some 300 yards from massive concrete blocks that obstructed the entrance to the city. Peering into the distance, I could make out American forces standing at the gates, blocking the entryway with unopposed authority.

Our vehicle was obviously different from the rest of the stopped vehicles because of the large broadcast transmission dish fixed to the roof of our mobile broadcast unit. Luckily, other drivers gave us the right of way because they recognized we were a TV crew. Finally, we got to the front of the long row of cars, and suddenly there was nothing separating us from the American forces except an empty 300 yards.

We got out of the vehicles to explore the situation and talk with the other stranded drivers. The truckers told us that the US forces had entirely blockaded Fallujah, and the portion of the highway adjacent to it, and wouldn't allow anyone coming from Baghdad to enter the city. Truckers coming from Syria and Jordan, headed to Baghdad, weren't even allowed to pass through in order to get to the other side of the highway. Most of the truckers had been stuck there since the previous night.

I asked the crew to wait by the vehicles. I went with Layth (and his camera) to try to negotiate with the American troops for entrance into the city.

Before I was even able to take my first step toward entering negotiations, I discovered that my junior high physics teacher had lied to us—distance is not a fixed measurable quantity. It turns out that distance is directly proportional to the fear clouding the distance between you and any given object or destination. For example, having the barrels of M-16s aimed directly at your head, standing directly in the crosshairs of a sniper's gauge, and being surrounded by fierce troopers with fingers on the triggers of their weapons, can make a short 300-yard walk seem like 300 miles.

No one else dared to approach the Americans. Layth and I walked those 300 yards alone, while everyone else looked on anxiously. I made sure that my walk appeared to the soldiers as normal as possible. I made sure to keep my hands to my sides, to illustrate that my arms and hands were clearly empty. There were soldiers everywhere scanning every inch of our bodies with binoculars. Knowing we were under this kind of scrutiny, we tried our best to give them a full and clear view of every part of our bodies. We kept a few feet of cleared distance between our bodies so they did not overlap and obstruct someone's view. I told Layth to make the camera in his hand clearly visible to them so that they couldn't mistake it for a weapon. Before we left the vehicles, Layth had turned on his camera, but switched off the red LED that indicates its status. He wanted to film the entire scene just in case there was a need to prove anything in the future. To the soldiers, he appeared as if he was only lugging an inactive camera around, but in reality, he was prepared to shoot the whole scene.

I presented my press ID card to the soldiers as I approached them. My ID was issued by the Combined Press Information Center, established by Americans in the Green Zone. The ID was supposed to entitle me to freely move about in Iraq and indicated that I provided coverage for al-Jazeera.

The checkpoint commander inspected my ID. It was clear from his behavior that he was an officer of some commanding rank, and not just a private. He was issuing orders and telling other soldiers around him what to do. He was also in contact with other commanders by radio.

I introduced myself to him.

He asked, "What do you want?" His tone wasn't terribly friendly.

"We're a TV crew from al-Jazeera, and we'd like to be granted entry to Fallujah, please." I answered.

He replied, "All roads are closed now, and no one will be allowed in."

I exclaimed, "But that's for private citizens! We're a news channel."

He repeated, "No one is allowed in. No one."

I argued further, "When you keep us from reporting on Fallujah and keep Fallujans from speaking to our cameras, doesn't that violate our freedom of press and the Fallujans' freedom of expression? Doesn't that seem unconstitutional to you?"

When he saw that I wouldn't give up, and that I appealed to principles and concepts he could relate to, his tone turned friendlier and he was more willing to help.

He reconsidered. "It's really not my call or yours, sir," he said. "I'll have to speak to my commander about this."

I smiled and replied, "That's fine. I've got all day. Take your time and talk to your commander."

"Stay right here for your own security, please," he said, "I'll get back to you with his response."

It was apparent to me after this interaction that our crew was the first (and most likely the only) one to ask for entry permission. Sure, this officer wasn't very welcoming, but after all, he was on a combat mission and must have been very tense. At least he was willing to help. Had there been a TV crew that asked permission to enter before us, he would've already been through the dilemma and known what to do. We were lucky to be the first ones to question the no-admittance policy into the city and to receive some consideration.

We stood and waited, all of us as tense as the situation around us. We could hear the commander yelling out orders on the radio. He didn't say anything in a normal tone or volume. Everything was screamed so loudly that you could barely make out the words.

While we waited, two SUVs drove up, which surprised me because it was so dangerously close to the troops and their weapons. Then I looked closer at the attire of the men and the make of their vehicles, and I realized they were mercenaries. Closed gates almost always opened wide for mercenaries—there was nearly no road to which they were denied access.

There were four plainclothes mercenaries in each SUV. All mercenaries in Iraq seemed to look exactly like the four who emerged from these vehicles. Their heads were shaven, their facial features rough, and their posture intimidating. They wore bulletproof vests and held M-16 automatic rifles. One of the men approached the checkpoint commander, gave him a paper slip, and talked to him for a bit. Although I couldn't make out what they were saying, it was clear from the accent I overheard that the mercenaries were Americans. The man then returned to the driver's seat of his vehicle. Two mercenaries got out of each car and stood guarding their vehicles. They circled their vehicles, holding the weapons at the ready but with the barrels pointed to the ground.

I tried to peek at the mercenaries as much as was possible without arousing any attention. One of them, who seemed to be the boss, was thin and agile. The other seven were massive and muscular. The vehicles were brand new, and each had a blue license plate issued by one of the Gulf States indicating that the vehicles had recently been shipped to Iraq from the Gulf.

Looking back at the highway, I saw dust clouds drift above the road far out to the horizon. I figured that the dust clouds must be related to truckers turning their vehicles around and looking for alternate routes to lead them to Fallujah, or searching for ways to bypass Fallujah altogether in order to get back on the highway and head in the direction of Jordan or Syria.

After twenty minutes of waiting, the friendly checkpoint commander came back with a *no* from his superior. I wasn't shocked, of course; it was only natural they'd deny us entry. Still, I tried to further negotiate with him.

After several intense minutes, he finally said, "Sir, this is really beyond my authority. I can't do anything about this. I repeated your request to my commander exactly as you gave it to me. My commander then moved the request to his commander exactly as I gave it to him with all the details and personal identification information and your news channel information. Everything you said was delivered to the highest commander available, and the answer still came back as a *no*. We're in a state of emergency. We're facing a very tough situation here."

Then, as he moved toward the entrance, he called over his shoulder, "Just so you don't feel bad, look over there." He pointed to the mercenaries and continued, "These men are private contractors working for the US government. They have clearance to pass through any military checkpoint, and you know what they got this time? They got a rejection for their request just like you did."

Because one has to give credit where it's due, I must say that the checkpoint commander was sincere, decent, polite, and professional. There was nothing brutish about him, and nothing that would make me feel the way I did when I looked at the thuggish mercenaries. He looked and behaved like someone I would enjoy talking to over a cup of espresso, had I met him in a café instead of at the entrance to a combat operation.

I figured that it wasn't going to get any better than this in terms of trying to get help from the US forces at this particular checkpoint. My request had already been denied by a very friendly and helpful man. So, I tried to get some information from him that could help me and my crew.

I approached him again and asked, "Are all roads to Fallujah closed off or just this road?"

He replied, "All I know is what I was told to do—I was told to close this particular road. You can look for other roads into the city if you want, although I'm not sure you'll find any that are open. I believe we've encircled the entire city."

I asked for one final request, "Do you see that broadcast dish on our vehicle's roof? Can we open it and broadcast images of this scene to our headquarters?"

He replied, "No, sir. This is a military operation area and all filming is strictly forbidden."

I thanked him for his cooperation and left. I figured there was no sense in making any further requests since we had already been denied everything. Also, this officer was constantly getting yelled at by his commanders over the radio, and I didn't want to add to his burden. So, we started walking back to join the rest of the crew. We overheard the mercenaries trying to contact some people to let them in. They had their own communication devices, and their cars seemed to be equipped with state-of-the-art technology.

Layth told me on our way back to the crew that he managed to film my interaction with the checkpoint commander without anyone taking notice. He had also filmed highway exit signs clearly reading "To Fallujah," and recorded shots of the surrounding scenes. This was like Layth. He always knew what was worth filming and what wasn't. Although he wasn't a journalist, he knew what was newsworthy. He always found a way to film the important events, even in the most treacherous of situations.

As we walked toward the crew, I couldn't escape the contrasting images of the checkpoint commander and the man who appeared to be the boss of the mercenaries. Both were leaders in their own right and undeniably in charge of a team of men, but the two men were a world apart. I thought to myself: why can't the mercenaries behave like normal people, like the checkpoint commander? Why couldn't they appear like normal people either? Sure, the US soldiers weren't all like the checkpoint commander. They weren't all that friendly, but they were like any other group of people you come across: some decent, some mean, some well-mannered, some nasty, some inviting, and some repulsive. The mercenaries weren't like that at all. The mercenaries were a universally angry group of men with no patience for humanity, for compassion, or for civility.

As we walked back to the crew, I was desperately trying to think of an alternative route to Fallujah. I told Hamed Hadeed what happened with the checkpoint commander. Then a thought occurred to me.

"You're a Fallujan, Hamed," I said to him. "You should know all the roads that lead into the city. We're talking about dirt roads, farm roads, country roads, any roads that will take us inside. One of those roads must've escaped the Americans. We're not giving up unless we try every single road into the city and find them all closed."

Hamed started listing off alternative roads. He said, "There is the Old Road... the Abu Ghraib road... the Khand Dhary Road... the Amreya Road... the Fallujah Dam Road by the Euphrates..."

I interrupted him, "No, these are all known roads. They're probably already all closed. We need to take the less traveled roads this time... something the Americans wouldn't have heard about, preferably a farm road of some kind. Our chances are much better there."

Hamed replied, "Then let's try the Naimyah Road. No one knows that road except the people of Fallujah and its surrounding communities. We'll get into the city from its western side, and travel through the Martyrs' Neighborhood. They also call this road the Irrigation Project Road because there is an irrigation canal there that channels the Euphrates water from Fallujah toward Abu Ghraib."

We reversed our vehicle and got on a long winding dirt road peppered by bumps, rocks, holes, and all sorts of other unexpected obstacles. Very few cars were driving along with us, which indicated that Hamed was correct—few people knew of this route. We took several turns on different dirt roads until we got to the Irrigation Project Road, which ran alongside the canal. We could see American choppers swarming the skies above us, indicating that there was indeed a real emergency situation in the city. There were some cars driving along with us for part of the road, but soon we were all alone by the canal. We were not, however, on the Fallujah side of the canal, which posed a problem. I asked Hamed if there was a bridge at some point ahead that would let us cross the canal. He said, "Yes, but not before we get to Naimyah. And that bridge too may very well be closed off by the Americans already."

Everyone was praying that we would eventually find an entrance point into the city. I was worried about the entire situation, but at that point I was most concerned that after all this trouble and risk we might end up finding the Naimyah Road closed. I tried to think of alternative ways to cross the canal should we need to resort to desperate measures. The canal was only ten or eleven yards wide, but its current was swift for its size. I couldn't see any canoes or rafts along the sides of the canal.

I told Hamed about what was on my mind.

He said, "We'll swim if we have to."

I inquired further: "There are no canoes? No small boats? Nothing we could use around here?"

He replied, "I don't know, but I doubt it. It's only a canal, not a river."

After all the anxiety surrounding our slim chances, we were relieved to see the bridge ahead in the distance. We had seen no Americans except for the flocks of choppers hovering above the area. As we approached the bridge Hamed said, "Behind that bridge is Naimyah. You can see Fallujah from there."

I was starting to feel partially relieved until we crossed the tiny bridge and saw cars pulled over to the sides of the road. Then we spotted American troops blocking the road with massive piles of dirt. Behind these piles stood soldiers on tanks and a flood of armored vehicles. We pulled over, and decided we would make another attempt to negotiate, just as we'd done with the guards off the highway. We had come all this way, and it wouldn't make sense to leave without trying to gain entrance.

I walked toward the soldiers blocking the entrance until one of them yelled at me to stop. I obeyed, and raised my press ID card high in the air for him to see.

I said, "I'm a journalist, and I have a TV crew with me from al-Jazeera. I'd like to talk to the checkpoint commander please."

One of the soldiers walked toward me, and the rest of them stood in a fire-ready position, looking not the least bit frightened to shoot and kill. I introduced myself and presented the IDs of all of the people in my crew, just as I had done with the other checkpoint commander. I was expecting equally decent treatment, but luckily I didn't let my hopes get too high. This checkpoint commander was nothing like the other one. He was stern and tense, and did not take the time to do or say anything politely. He allowed no room for negotiation.

In response to my request to speak to the commander, he yelled, "This is a closed military area, and no one is allowed in!"

I said, "But we're journal…"

He interrupted, "I told you nobody is allowed in. Nobody means nobody. You have to leave right the hell now!"

One of the few civilians standing in the area was a local doctor who worked at the Fallujah hospital. After my confrontation with the officer, this doctor told me he'd been trying to get in the city since the morning but found all roads closed. He was desperately trying to get into the city so he could help those who were in need.

I asked the checkpoint commander, "Could you please let this doctor in?"

He replied, "The doctor's problem is not your concern, and I already told you to leave with your crew immediately." After this response, I figured I had nothing to lose if I asked him one last question. He wasn't giving us permission for anything anyway, and I wasn't too concerned about staying on his good side, because he probably didn't have one.

I asked, "One last thing—can we turn on the broadcast dish so I could send a message to our news channel? I won't film anything you don't want me to film."

He didn't take the time to consider my request. We received one final admonishment: "If you don't get the hell out of here with your damn crew, we're going to fire at you full force! Got it?"

I nodded and walked away, smiling, knowing I had pushed the man's patience to the limits. On my way back to the truck, I wondered to myself why mercenaries were gathered around the polite checkpoint commander and not around this one. Maybe they sent out the mercenaries to the nice guy to balance his decency with some indecency. This guy was mean enough on his own—he didn't need any help in that department.

As I continued to walk toward our vehicles, I paused to answer a call on my cell phone. On the other end of the line was the producer for the noon news segment, calling from the headquarters in Doha. He asked if I had input for the noon segment. He then transferred me to the on-air line so that my colleague Abdussamad Nasser (the anchor presenting the live segment) could ask for my input as well. Abdussamad inquired about the situation in Fallujah, and also asked where I was located at the moment. I gave him an overview of the scene unfolding around me.

In the middle of my conversation with Abdussamad, I heard the checkpoint commander start to threaten me again. This time, the yelling was much louder, and he was screaming through a megaphone while standing atop an armored vehicle. He warned me one last time that if I didn't leave the premises he was going to aim his gun in my direction, and shoot to kill. Given this warning, I told Abdussamad that we were in a danger zone, and asked him to call us later.

I followed the commander's orders and headed to the crew waiting for me back at the vehicle. I asked the drivers to move the car immediately but not to venture out too far. I only wanted the vehicle to move out of sight of the troops blockading this entrance. Luckily, the area near the checkpoint was surrounded by tall thick trees, providing enough space for us to hide and plan our next move. Some fifty yards away from our spot, there was a sloping dirt road that led to a warehouse where gas cylinders were sold for home use. We took the vehicle down the slope and parked under the cover of trees.

I asked Hamed, "Is Fallujah still pretty far from here?"

He pointed to some houses about a mile and a quarter away: "That's Fallujah right there."

I was surprised, and replied, "If that is Fallujah, then we can get there walking if we need to. We're on the right side of the irrigation canal this time, so the water is no obstacle."

He replied with mutual surprise, "You want to cross on foot to Fallujah, with the choppers swarming the skies like bees? People around here dress in gowns and robes, not dress pants. No dress shirts, and certainly no ties. The soldiers in the choppers would single us out immediately as foreigners, even without their binoculars, and we would be prime targets. We also have all this heavy broadcast equipment. We can't carry that on foot."

I thought for a minute. "It might be our only way. We'll figure out something for the equipment. In the meantime, try to think of a local who could be our guide if we decide to walk," I said.

Hamed was an honorable and genuine man. I never received a negative response to any question I asked him, and he never denied me anything I requested. He was always positive and responsive, and this journey was no exception. He was also very daring and courageous. Whenever we were faced with a dangerous situation, Hamed would look at me, and without me even asking for anything, he'd say, "Ready at your command."

Hamed belongs to the Jomaylat tribe, one of Fallujah's biggest and most influential tribes. Around areas like Fallujah, one's tribal history plays a large role shaping an individual's personality. Because of the deep respect these people have for tribal lines, one needs to be on his best behavior at all times so that his tribe of origin doesn't get a bad reputation. Hamed has always been modest and friendly, and enjoys a great deal of respect from people around him. He's also quiet, responsible, and an outstanding crisis manager. All these redeemable character qualities played a significant role in helping us to overcome obstacles in our mission in Fallujah. As for Hamed's family, the Hadeed family, they were some of the most generous and giving people I met during my time in Iraq.

After some thinking, Hamed said, "Let me go to find a distant relative of ours. He lives around here. He must know one of the less traveled roads into the city—something the Americans haven't yet discovered or blocked. I'll be back soon."

Hamed disappeared into the forest. I turned to gaze at the city of Fallujah, which sat across the barren section of land known as the Naimyah Desert Patch. I was considering all possible avenues into the city, any of which would accomplish our hope and determination to cover the events that might be transpiring there. I considered the possibility of waiting until darkness took hold of the skies. Once night fell, Hamed and I could walk to Fallujah alone, carrying our satellite phones. Once into the city, we could read our reports live on air using the phones. With any luck, we could paint a clear image of the situation in the city with verbal description alone. But this plan had its flaws. Al-Jazeera is a televised news channel, not a radio station. Because of that, cameras are essential to adequate coverage. I considered the possibility of taking the cameramen and their cameras along with us; they're light enough to be carried on foot. Then again, what would be the point of risking the cameramen's lives and ours if we couldn't broadcast the images they captured? For the broadcast we'd need the broadcast vehicle too. There was no way around these problems.

As I was sitting consumed with this paradox, I noticed a small white car coming toward us from the direction of Fallujah. The car was moving slowly across the desert rocks, and slowed even further as it tried to cross the slopes. I started to hope the car would continue coming in our direction. I assumed the car was coming from Fallujah, and wanted to ask the driver about an alternative route into the city. The tiny white car bobbed across the desert, disappearing and reappearing as it went across the hills.

When the car was close enough, I ran toward it and attempted to flag down the driver. The car was an old Toyota Cressida, and the driver was in his 40s.

I greeted him and asked, "Where did you just come from?" He noticed my Egyptian accent, which is very different from an Iraqi accent. Fallujah is usually a place where foreigners never venture, so my accent aroused immediate anxiety.

He asked suspiciously, "What do you want?"

I replied, "I, personally, don't want anything. I'm part of a television crew. We're from al-Jazeera satellite channel. Do you know al-Jazeera?"

He didn't say whether he knew al-Jazeera or not. Instead, he simply gave me the same quizzical look. He then asked, "Al-Jazeera? What does it want?" I explained our story to him, and told him we'd be grateful if he'd lead us to Fallujah.

After I explained our background and our story, the man seemed to be a little more at ease. He said, "I just came from Fallujah, as a matter of fact. I traveled along a dirt road that winds around the barren hills. Smugglers and outlaws made that road long ago. I don't think the Americans know about it because it was still open when I crossed, but it's still very dangerous because of the terrain and because of the helicopters overhead. If I weren't so desperate for cement to fix the walls of my house, I wouldn't have gone out today. This is the fourth time I traveled this road today to get cement, and it's the last. There are choppers all over. The desert is wide open and empty, and the road is completely exposed. I've got kids at home. I can't take any more risks than I already did."

Despite his warnings, I was ready to start jumping up and down in joy when I heard from the driver that there was indeed a road still open, albeit a dangerous one. I asked him to guide us along the open road into Fallujah. He refused. I asked again, telling him he'd be helping his own family and his own people by guiding us into the city, because the crew was there to report on the plight of the natives in Fallujah. The man seemed not to understand what I was referring to, and he flatly refused to help us.

Just then, Hamed returned from his quest to find us a guide or a safe route into the city. I ran to him in a hurry, asking if he'd found a safer route than the road I had just learned about. He said he had found nothing open. He had asked everyone he knew in the area, and all roads had been blocked, including country roads and farm roads.

I pointed to the man in the white Cressida, "This man over there says he came from Fallujah on a road that was used by smugglers. I asked him to help but he's too scared to go back. Maybe if you offer him some money in exchange for the service of guiding us, he might reconsider." Hamed said he'd talk to the man and see.

I walked Hamed toward the Cressida, thinking I'd introduce him to the driver, but before I could step in, Hamed greeted the driver and spoke to him like they were already friends. The man didn't recognize Hamed immediately, but after Hamed mentioned his family name and talked with him a little more, the driver remembered that Hamed was one of his distant relatives—in fact, Hamed had attended his wedding years ago. The two men belonged to two different clans within the same tribe. The driver was a member of the Msalmy clan, part of the Jomaylat tribe. The Msalmy clan lives on the outskirts of the Naimyah desert.

After finding out this coincidence, Hamed and the driver started catching up on their mutual relatives. Both men gave the latest social changes that had taken place in his clan. I figured this had to be good for our chances to win the man's help, but I was too eager, too impatient, and too scared to wait much longer for Hamed's character to work its magic. I also didn't think that this kind of family reminiscing was an optimal use of time when military choppers were hovering so close above.

I whispered to Hamed, "Enough already. Have you offered him the money yet?"

Hamed said, "Are you insane? You want him to drive away offended from here? I can't do that."

I had a hard time keeping my voice low, but I then asked, "How else are we going to convince him to reconsider?"

Hamed said, "There are ways other than money. You offer money in circumstances like these to non-tribal people, but never to clansmen, and certainly not one who belongs to the same tribe as you. Next time you cover a war, try to learn the culture of the region you're going to be covering. You have to learn the tribal code, man. You have to learn the tribal code." He smiled, tapped me on the cheek, and returned to his relative.

Hamed started talking again to the driver, and I could tell the driver was still refusing his request for help. Hamed kept talking. I could see hesitation begin to show on the driver's face. This hesitation began to take the place of rejection, and finally he agreed to show us into the city.

I could barely contain my happiness when I saw that the driver agreed to ride with us. I offered him the seat next to Abo Omar, the driver, but he refused. He told me to keep my spot up front and that he would sit behind Abo Omar and direct him from there. Before we took off, I paused to address the crew. I wanted them to think one last time about whether they wanted to embark on such a dangerous mission.

As I faced them I said, "I hope you're all aware of the danger involved in this mission. We could get shot by a missile from one of the choppers above us, or we could get hit by an artillery shell as we pass through the open areas between the hills. And if we don't get fired at on our way into the city, you can be certain that we will be under fire during our coverage. In other words, the danger isn't going to be over when we reach Fallujah. If any one of you wants to return to Baghdad, please speak up now, because as soon as we enter the city in this van, we'll be at the point of no return. No one would be angry with you if you didn't want to keep going to Fallujah. I promise."

No one showed even a shade of hesitation at the thought of continuing the journey onward to Fallujah. Most of us piled into the van, while Sayfuldeen Muhammad, our engineer, and Farqad, the other driver, trailed us in the broadcast vehicle. We took the vehicle down a dirt road that detoured around some buildings and headed down toward a small valley. Luckily, the buildings hid us from the American battalions, which lined the main road by the Irrigation Project. I was constantly afraid these troops could still see us through the gaps between the houses. Msalmy assured me that they hadn't spotted him on his previous four trips, and probably wouldn't spot us now.

Most of the time, my eyes were focused upward, monitoring the movement of choppers. Occasionally I would look to the road ahead of us. The surface of the road went from bad to worse as we edged closer to the city. The potholes became more frequent, the slopes got steeper, and there were perilous patches of soft desert sand that offered the severe risk of getting stuck. Occasionally, I also glanced at the side mirrors to see how far behind the broadcast van was. I instructed Abo Omar, "Don't let the satellite van get too far behind us. Their vehicle is very heavy because of all the equipment, so they can't move as fast. They will get stuck in the sand much easier than us."

I asked our guide about the road and its history, and how it could be that the Americans or other locals had no knowledge of it. He explained to me, "This road was used by outlaws during Saddam's rule, usually for smuggling cigarettes and other heavily-taxed goods. After Saddam's regime was toppled, the road became deserted because there was no longer a need for it. The locals know of the road but don't use it, because there are now alternative roads that are paved and safe."

I tried to be calm, but it was very difficult. Time moved very slowly. Every inch we moved down that creepy road felt like a very slow mile, and every split-second felt like time passing in years. Any minute the choppers could spot us and shoot us down, or the tanks encircling the city might see us through the gaps in the buildings, and fire at will.

My heart felt like it was hanging still between the ground and the heavens, just as it had when I went through similar experiences covering the Soviet–Afghan war and the Bosnian war.[24] In the Soviet–Afghan war, I drove on roads that the Soviets repeatedly showered with bombs and rockets. Several of the convoys I accompanied were subjected to nightly shelling by the Soviets. I was once part of a group of journalists with a convoy that was to meet Lt. General Shahnawaz Tanai.[25] Our convoy was targeted and hit in the Kunduz province. Several people were killed and more were injured, and the journalists who weren't harmed were psychologically scarred from the incident. I encountered similarly devastating situations during my coverage of the Jalalabad battle. Also, during the coverage of the same war, I took a trip to the outskirts of Kabul. This journey contained several dangerously close calls from which I barely escaped with my life.

My experience covering the Bosnian war wasn't any safer. One night I found myself traveling down long, winding roads that connected skyscraping mountaintops, and I was the passenger in a car driven by a man speeding more than any sane human being should. The road was blocked by several Serbian checkpoints. The side of the road was littered with the carnage of vehicles that had been destroyed by heavy shelling and bombing. My driver was taking me to the hidden tunnel that led to the Bosnian capital, Sarajevo. We were attempting to bypass a siege that was occurring around the capital city. The tunnel had been dug out starting from underneath the airport, and was the only lifeline the city had during the siege, which lasted for years. That tunnel is now a tourist attraction.

Through all of my experiences covering besieged cities and battles in several different countries, I have learned that every place has its own kind of fear and danger. My time in Bosnia and Afghanistan did not in any way make my time in Fallujah any less difficult or frightening. No amount of training or experience could possibly get a journalist to a point where traveling under the pressure of possible shelling, bombs, or bullet fire is a routine affair.

I looked out the window at the broadcast vehicle behind us. They were falling behind. I asked Abo Omar to stop our van until they could catch up to us. Our guide said that the danger was too great to stop—if we halted our vehicle, we would be much easier for the choppers to spot. I understood this, and asked the driver to slow down as much as possible until the vehicle could catch up. The driver obeyed, and the other vehicle began to inch closer. By the time they caught up, we were much closer to the houses in Fallujah that we had seen from a distance. I was constantly watching the decreasing distance between us and the edges of the city. We all sat silent with fear; our bodies tight with tension. If Abo Omar had turned off the engine, we would've heard the frantic pounding of each others' heartbeats. One could almost swear that the vehicle became a vacuum as we got closer to the city—we all gasped, inhaled, and held our breath in anticipation of the moment we would reach Fallujah and exhale in relief.

As we approached the Fallujan houses on the edge of town, I couldn't believe we had found a way to get into the city. I told myself that these houses must be in a small town close to Fallujah, and that we'd have to go through another frightful road in order to get to Fallujah proper. We couldn't be here already.

When we reached the houses, I asked our guide: "How long is left before we actually get to Fallujah?"

Hamed and the guide turned to me in excitement and said in unison, "This is Fallujah!"

I could finally breathe again. We had made it!

Hamed informed us, "We're in the Martyrs' Neighborhood. This is Fallujah's west side, if you will." I wasn't thinking about the dangers that were somewhere ahead of us, or of the difficulty in covering the actual combat operations inside the city limits. I just couldn't believe we made it to Fallujah safely, despite the choppers and the ground troops and the risk of our vehicles getting damaged on the dilapidated road.

But my happiness didn't last very long. Just inside the city walls, we were ambushed. A group numbering no less than five individuals emerged suddenly from one of the city buildings, and each person carried an automatic weapon. I couldn't tell if these men were insurgents or robbers—the latter was a distinct possibility since the road generally wasn't used by anyone other than robbers. The group yelled at us to stop. Abo Omar slammed on the brakes to bring the car to a screeching halt. Since Abo Omar and I were in the front seats, all the weapons were aimed at us. I thought to myself: What luck… we just took a huge risk and succeeded in evading the military of a superpower only to fall in the hands of these jerks?

Our guide looked out the side window, full of rage at the armed men threatening our vehicle. He told the men to leave us alone. Surprisingly, the men seemed to recognize him, and knew him as much as he knew them. When he told them to leave, they obeyed. They lowered their weapons and opened the road for us. It was clear that they were locals ready for American troops to arrive, and had mistakenly assumed we were part of the enemy operation.

Our guide refused to leave us until the dirt road became a paved street. Once there, he hopped out of the van and pointed to one branch of the paved road. He told us to follow the road all the way to downtown Fallujah. I got out of the vehicle to hug our guide and thank him for everything he had done—I didn't know how to express enough gratitude for the risk he had taken in assisting us in our mission. When I asked him how he was going to get back to Naimyah to retrieve his car, he said not to worry—he'd figure out something.

To this day, I still recall vividly this man's smile and his warm demeanor—all of the physical attributes that make up the modest man who risked his own life to help us. His simple, rough hands gave him away as a hardworking man who struggled each day to provide food and money for his family. Yet, he refused to take even a single penny in exchange for his assistance, and the mere offer of any monetary compensation was an insult to him.

He couldn't have known it back then, and he may not know it now, but without that man, no televised media would've been able to cover the battle that raged that day between his people and the American troops in the first battle of Fallujah. Without him, one of the most horrendous military operations that took place in the battle for Iraq would have remained undisclosed to the global community, and its images hidden forever from the history books.

7. DAY ONE: OPERATION VIGILANT RESOLVE BEGINS

Once we had parted ways with the man who had guided us into Fallujah, it was up to us alone to defend ourselves from this city, its insurgents, and the American occupation forces. This was a massive responsibility. I was still too astonished to comprehend the situation we were in—I could not believe we were riding through the streets of Fallujah, and that we had found a way to foil the Americans. I looked at the houses and buildings as we sped by them in the van, and could not conceal how dumbfounded I was.

I asked Hamed, "Is this really Fallujah? I mean, did we really make it here? I can't believe we're here."

Hamed responded with a confident smile: "Indeed it is. Indeed it is! This is my town, my man! Welcome to my home!"

I gestured to the houses as we passed them, "And these are really Fallujan streets and houses? Not some streets or houses in some generic suburb on the outskirts?"

He nodded, still grinning at my disbelief, "Yes, we are in Fallujah, the very city itself. The Martyrs' Neighborhood, then this road will take us through the Nazzal Neighborhood as well. From there we can go downtown."

He saw the expression on my face change from excitement to anxiety upon the mention of the longer route to downtown Fallujah.

"I know what you're thinking," he said, "but don't worry. There can't be any more military checkpoints between here and downtown. Nothing and no one is blocking our way now."

He slapped me on the back and gave me a reassuring smile. I could barely contain my happiness. He shook his head and laughed at me.

"You've got to be the first person I've ever seen who is ecstatic to have bypassed a military siege only to be put in even more danger of being attacked by military forces," he said.

We continued the drive through the city. After a few moments, Hamed asked, "Do you want to go to my folks' place so we can unload, or do you want to go straight downtown and get some work done?" While in Fallujah, we planned to stay at Hamed's parents' house in the city.

I thought for a moment, and answered, "Let's go to the heart of the city first—to the old market, where people might be gathering. We have to see how ordinary people are feeling in the midst of the siege. We need to get to the emotional scene behind this siege as soon as we can." Hamed nodded his head in agreement and the van headed for the old market.

I turned to the rest of the crew to give them a preparatory speech. They looked at me in expectation, and I tried to muster the most encouraging words I could, "I think it's rather clear to everyone that we've got a colossal task and a very critical mission before us. Our mission is to convey to the world the real situation of this besieged city and the condition of its people. We have to be patient and diligent in this task. We can't possibly achieve anything meaningful here unless we work together." I paused and looked around at the faces of my crew members; each one of them was in total agreement of the rules I was setting down. I was confident that these crew members would support our mission to the end.

I continued, "Each and every one of us has got to give everything he has to this project, and push as hard as humanly possible in these next few days. And, we've got to go into this without any misgivings toward one another. Any one of us could be killed at any moment out there." I paused again, while the crew members digested the sobering words I was offering them. These were harsh realities for anyone to accept, but harsher still for a crew possibly marching to its death.

I paused to catch my breath and let the men digest what I was saying. Then I continued with my speech, which I hoped was inspiring and encouraging them, "This is not the time for an unclear conscience," I said. "This is not the time to worry about petty anger or small arguments. We need to be forgiving and understanding of one another and work as a team. It is our responsibility to watch out for each other. We need to look out for the security of the entire crew at all times. If we go into this city united, then we will come out united."

I glanced at the city whizzing by us, and thought about the scene that lay ahead in downtown Fallujah. I continued, "I'm not entirely sure just yet, but it seems to me that no one else from televised media is here. This means we're the only hope this town has for broadcasting what's happening on Fallujan soil to the rest of the world. Our primary responsibility is to conduct our work in a completely professional manner, and to deliver the truth of what we see to the whole world." The crew nodded in agreement with my words, and I saw no dissent among them.

I had one more final order of business to cover before we arrived in downtown and began what we hoped would become historic coverage of this war.

"Since you're all Iraqis, and I'm the only foreigner among you, I'd like you to do one final thing for me, please. In the course of this coverage, if I happen to get killed, please do not waste any effort shipping my body to Egypt or Doha. I would instead like to be buried here, alongside people who are brave and proud, than in some regular old cemetery with people who may or may not have lived lives of valor." There was a round of sober nods, and I could see that the crew members would assuredly take care of my needs if I ran into deathly circumstances.

I gave the crew one last half-smile of encouragement. I was proud of them. I expected that because this crew was handpicked from the finest professional journalists and media staff in the region, I was blessed with crew members that would listen and accept any direction given to them. Each of these men was well-known for their patience, perseverance, and altruism. I was lucky to have these men to work with on such a dangerous mission.

The van continued to cruise along the streets of the city. As we neared the city center, we chose to head toward the area where restaurants were located instead of heading directly for the old market. Since it was one o'clock, we imagined crowds would be gathering for lunch. We hoped to interview the crowds to get a feel for how the locals were reacting to the siege.

We arrived downtown and cruised past a few of the restaurants. We stopped and checked out a few popular lunch places—the Nomad, the Zar Zoor Fallujah, and Haj Hussain's Kabob Place—but we found most places closed. The streets were nearly deserted. I began to feel a gnawing sense of anxious disappointment. However, there were a few people on the road who soon recognized us as the al-Jazeera crew, and came to speak with us. Soon thereafter, people came toward us from every direction, begging for our attention. Each person wanted to tell us about their situation immediately, and the interview scene quickly turned chaotic. I asked the crowd to please be patient and let us interview one person at a time. I asked Layth and Hassan to assist by recording the statements given by the people.

While Layth and Hassan were busy recording statements, I got a call from Doha asking for our whereabouts. It was clear that the people in Doha were expecting me to say that we had been denied all entrances to the city, and that we were heading back to Baghdad. I gleefully informed them of the opposite: we had bypassed the siege, and were at that very moment standing right in the very heart of Fallujah.

The producer was ecstatic, and transferred me over to our colleague and anchorman Abdussamad Nasser for a feed to the live news segment. I confirmed to Abdussamad, and to the viewers, that we had infiltrated the siege and placed ourselves under the threat of American occupation brutality just like the city residents, a confirmation that I later learned was a big blow to the morale of the troops encircling the city. Among the things I included in my brief report was a sentence that went like this: "The people are in fear. The city is in fear. Most shops and stores are closed, and the city is largely deserted." I did not inform Abdussamad, the viewers, or anyone else of the exact details of our infiltration of the siege, and have not shared them with anyone until the writing of this book.

A short while after I completed my report to Abdussamad, I was told by the townspeople people that some "angry people" were looking for me. I wasn't surprised that people were looking for my crew and me, because it's not uncommon for people to flock to our crew when they have news about the controversial situation we are covering. I continued to work with Layth and Hassan to collect statements, and waited to see how these "angry people" would materialize.

I spotted one of these discontented bands coming toward me and my crew a few moments later, with an obvious bone to pick. I was curious what their frustration might be, and approached them, intrigued.

One of the men confronted me as the spokesperson for the rest of the angry mob.

"How dare you say that we're scared, Mansour!" he exclaimed. "We're not in fear of these Americans, and we're not scared. Speak for yourself when you broadcast on television, or speak for the American troops, if you want. But don't lie about us to the world, especially when you haven't even asked our permission. We do not accept you describing us as 'in fear.' Apologize for this description of us in your next report!" he demanded.

I was taken aback by this reaction. But I also spotted an ideal opportunity for news.

I asked, "How about I let you record your statement and testimony to the condition of your people so I can air it in our next report? Would you be willing to stand before the camera and say your piece? Would that make up for the errors I've made in my broadcast?" One of the men was more than willing to explain this situation to my viewers on camera.

I met several city residents within the next few hours that confirmed what I had been told by this band of angry citizens: the Fallujans were not responding to this siege with fear. I noticed that there was a range of reactions among Fallujans—emotions varied from defiance to shock to confusion—but never once did I hear a Fallujan indicate fear of the Americans. In fact, the majority of locals I met brazenly dared the American troops to invade Fallujah. These dares came from all types of citizens—including teenagers, children, elderly persons, and physically handicapped people. Some Fallujans were in shock that American troops were willing to punish an entire city simply because the troops had a problem with a few small bands of insurgents. But of all the different views I heard, no one accepted my televised "characterization," as they put it, of the city and its people as being in fear. These citizens were anything but afraid of the troops surrounding their home.

The Early Stages of Mayhem

After we had spent some time taking statements and assessing the mood in the streets of Fallujah, some residents informed us that warplanes had already bombed a few houses on the northwestern edge of the town, in the Golan Neighborhood. We decided to check it out. When we arrived, we indeed found the locals gathered around a partially destroyed house. The roof had obviously been heavily bombed. Surrounding houses were destroyed by bombs. The townspeople said the bombs that were dropped had to have been cluster bombs,[26] because witnesses reported that once a large bomb hit, other small bombs scattered to destroy the surrounding houses. Some of the residents were holding up shrapnel, shells, and other remains of the dropped bombs for us to record on film. We filmed all of this, and interviewed the owner of the house destroyed by the largest bomb. I recorded the closing segment of this report—what we call the report signature—in the midst of the rubble.

Just before leaving the scene, we heard distorted voices coming through megaphones, and quickly realized these voices were coming from military vehicles. These vehicles were circling the Golan Neighborhood on the other side of the Euphrates. The voices demanded the residents hand over the "evildoers" who were responsible for the killings and mutilations of the four mercenaries. The words were coming out in fluent Arabic. It was no surprise to anyone, because there were definitely Iraqi mercenaries and mercenaries of other Arab nationalities working on behalf of the American troops. Some Arabic-speaking mercenaries served as speakers, others as translators, and others as security guards. Because the voices were so close, I asked the cameramen to accompany me to the closest point where we could get a clear shot of the military vehicles. The residents warned us not to film these vehicles because the troops were shooting at anyone and everyone they could see. But we knew that we had to get our film, no matter how dangerous it was. We walked along the edges of the neighborhood, and eventually the vehicles got so close that we could see them through gaps between the houses. We took some footage of the vehicles rolling through the streets, and also captured the audio of the soldiers shouting demands into their megaphones.

After our investigation of the explosions in the Golan Neighborhood had concluded, we headed out to Hamed's parents' place. We wanted to set up the satellite broadcast equipment at their house so we could transfer the images and data we had already filmed to the Doha headquarters. Hamed's folks' place is on Dam Street in Fallujah, in the Nazzal Neighborhood, close to the heart of the city. Dam Street separates the Nazzal Neighborhood from the industrial area of Fallujah. This industrial area covers mostly the eastern entrance of the city. This eastern side of Fallujah is connected to Baghdad by a main street that goes directly through downtown and eventually through Ramadi, the capital of the Anbar province.

Hamed's family was waiting for us when we arrived. All of Hamed's relatives were extremely generous and welcoming. In particular, Hamed's oldest brother Sami and his two sons Imad and Ziyad were a great help to us. These men emptied the main living room for our use. We unloaded everything from the van into the living room and parked the broadcast vehicle inside of the fenced yard. The engineer, Sayfuldeen, finished the set-up of his satellite telecommunication equipment, and I prepared to record my report for the midday news segment. We used the roof of the house as our filming location because we needed to broadcast from a place that was higher than the surrounding area in order to expose as much of the horizon as possible. Unfortunately, most Fallujan houses are similar in height. The buildings expand horizontally, never vertically, and are one or two stories high at most. This meant that even when filming on the roof we really couldn't expose much of the city. The only thing tall enough to appear in the background of our film was the Guided Caliphs' Mosque; its tall minarets stood majestically in the distance.

My midday news segment included a brief report on the condition of the city and our attempts to bypass American security. We revealed no direct details, but we showed some of the footage Layth had secretly filmed of our negotiations with the first checkpoint commander at the Fallujah exit off the international highway. This footage showed shots of "To Fallujah" exit signs and the endless streams of backed-up traffic. We included our recording of the troops in the Golan Neighborhood demanding that Fallujans hand over the "evildoers." Initially, I hesitated to include that scene because the word "evildoers" seemed like such an archaic and silly term, but I decided that I should report the situation as I heard it. It was the troops' decision to use such an infantile word—a word that I'd thought to be extinct until that point.

My midday news report included a summary of what the locals had said about bombs being dropped on different parts of the city. Bombing appeared to be focused on the Golan Neighborhood, where eight civilians had already died. We broadcast recorded testimony from a civilian about the cluster bombs, and also showed footage of civilians holding shrapnel and other remnants from those cluster bombs. The report also covered the first statement issued by the American forces since the siege began, which dictated a city lockdown from seven at night until six in the morning.

After we were done filming, this recorded report was aired repeatedly on al-Jazeera—in every daytime news segment and some of the nighttime segments. My colleagues in Doha then asked me to prepare a second report to be aired during the nighttime news. Because a two-minute televised news report could very possibly mean a whole day's worth of work for a correspondent, it wasn't easy to concoct a report from the information I had on hand. I had to make another tour of the city to find out the latest developments for this next report. In it, I discussed the current operation in Fallujah, which had been code-named Operation Vigilant Resolve by the American forces. I also covered how warplanes had dropped leaflets warning residents of the consequences of hesitating to hand over the "evildoers."

I also covered the American forces' decision to enforce a curfew. All medical care centers, clinics, and hospitals were closed in adherence with this curfew. Since the field hospital established by doctors from the Fallujah General Hospital was not in operation just yet, this meant there was nowhere for Fallujans to go for medical care. This nighttime report included images we filmed after curfew hours: images, for example, of an elderly man desperately looking for medical attention for a very young girl. The report also talked about the decision that had been made to close all city schools until further notice.

The report also included footage of other disturbing images from around the city. This footage, shot by Layth, showed American troops occupying the steel bridge where the corpses were hung after the mutilation. The bridge connects the two sides of the city, which sit on opposite banks of the Euphrates. The bridge also connects much of the city to the Fallujah General Hospital, so the occupation of the bridge by American troops meant there were even more reasons that people would have difficulty getting medical care. To get this footage, we relied on the help of locals, who discreetly helped us get just a few yards from the bridge so that Layth could get a clear shot of the troops. We were able to capture some very high-quality images. These images were so wonderful that they were aired in that evening's report as an al-Jazeera exclusive.

I also appeared in a live broadcast from Fallujah that evening. My colleague Jameel Azar was the host in Doha, and the news segment presenter. Because battles between American troops and Muqtada al-Sadr's militia were raging in other areas of Iraq, my former colleague Atwar Bahjat (the one who would later be murdered) was participating in the same news segment, broadcasting live from the southern city of Kufa.[27] I spoke about the explosive fighting that was erupting just about everywhere in the country. I also narrated eyewitness accounts of American warplanes hovering above Fallujah, and reported on the blockade of all roads leading into and out of Fallujah.

In his memoirs, Paul Bremer briefly describes this first day of the siege, including his conversation with General Rick Sanchez about the situation. Bremer writes,

> He told me that before sunrise a combined force of 1,300 Marines, Iraqi Civil Defense Corps, and New Iraqi Army troops had set up roadblocks around the city, establishing an armed cordon. Loudspeaker Humvees supported by armored vehicles entered Fallujah, announcing a dusk-to-dawn curfew and threatening to overwhelm insurgents who refused to turn in their arms and surrender. The situation there was just as complex and dangerous as the crisis we faced in Sadr City and the south.

Although Bremer only mentions 1,300 Marines, the overall count of the forces that attacked Fallujah was a much higher number. Fallujah's industrial area alone was attacked by a force that was 2,000 soldiers strong, as reported in a statement issued by another US commander. Some experts estimate the forces that engaged in this operation to be over 11,000, not counting the Iraqis who acted on behalf of the United States.

The Challenge of Collecting News

On the first day of the siege, city utilities and services in Fallujah remained operational—electricity, water, and phone lines. Telephone access, of course, made the job of gathering and broadcasting news significantly easier. Hamed had relatives living all over the city. He would frequently call his relatives to find out where in the city problems were developing. He also used the phone to check the validity of information received from unauthenticated third parties. When he got information regarding a particular area, he would call people he knew who lived there. Then, he would ask his acquaintances to check and double-check the stories.

Covering this siege was going to be difficult no matter what, but I would be lying if I said that covering the news angle wasn't made slightly easier to some extent by my experience covering other conflicts as a journalist. My previous experience in journalism includes positions ranging from entry-level to managerial. In addition to the wars in Afghanistan and Bosnia & Herzegovina, I was also in Kuwait for two months during Saddam's invasion in 1990. I have also been editor-in-chief for seven years for one of the most widely circulated political periodicals in the Gulf region. This experience enabled me to develop a decent and solid set of methods to use in order to evaluate the level of authenticity of the news claims we received—and it was of utmost importance that the news we reported be accurate and legitimate. We were working for a satellite news channel that provided its coverage to the entire world. We had to be absolutely certain that we didn't provide any information that might turn out to be false or exaggerated, which would damage the channel's credibility worldwide. At the very least, we verified every news claim from at least two different unaffiliated and credible sources for all news that we didn't witness firsthand, along with everything that wasn't verified on film.

We were also responsible for covering more than the city of Fallujah—really, the entire Anbar province. Our correspondent in Ramadi was in touch with us the entire time, as were our other correspondents in Qa'em and Hadeetha. On top of all this, we had continually had unauthenticated third parties calling with news and developments from all over Iraq. It was absolutely critical that we manage the news-gathering process accurately. Our checking and double-checking meant that we ended up excluding from our coverage many of the "news" items we received.

Our strict adherence to verifying all the news we received, however, led to some amusing moments. One was when Hamed received a phone call from a person claiming that an American military chopper had been shot down in Amreyat al-Fallujah, a small village close to Fallujah. Hamed took down the caller's personal information and began asking questions. Overhearing the potential in this conversation, I jumped in. I showered Hamed with questions to ask the caller: "What time did it happen? Is the chopper in flames or not? Were there any eyewitness accounts of injured or dead soldiers? Did American reinforcements arrive for rescue?" Through Hamed, I battered the caller with so many questions that the conversation became more like a full-fledged interrogation rather than a routine news interview.

The man gave Hamed answers to my questions, and Hamed repeated the caller's answer out loud to us. I recorded everything Hamed said.

As the call was wrapping up, I told Hamed to ask one final question: "Ask him what color the chopper was." Hamed paused in his conversation with the caller and looked at me, puzzled that I was posing a question about such a small, mundane detail.

Despite the chaotic situation we were in, and despite the pressure of being in a war zone, everyone in the room suddenly burst out laughing at my ridiculous question. Hamed laughed as he relayed my question to the man. The caller replied sarcastically, "Well, it certainly wasn't a bright rainbow-colored delight, and there weren't any Care Bears or anything painted on the rudder. It was some awful, dull military color, if you really want to know."

After Hamed relayed this response to me, I asked again, "So he doesn't know what color the chopper was?" Hamed repeated my question for the caller.

The caller paused for a bit and then burst out, "Seriously? You're asking me this question seriously? I'm telling you there are dead people on a battlefield and you're concerned about the color of the chopper they were in? I don't think they really care what color their chopper was because now they're dead. Next, you're going to ask me what my favorite color is."

I interrupted Hamed's relay of the frustrated man's ranting, and explained to him that my question wasn't actually all that ridiculous, although I understood why everyone reacted as though it was. The caller claimed what he saw was a military chopper, and I needed to know what color it was to make sure it was indeed a military chopper. If it was any color other than the standard desert-sand or green camouflage, then the chopper may very well not have been a military chopper. It was a matter of authenticity, not silliness.

Although this man didn't know it, his interrogation was actually rather lax compared to many of our others. Many of the people who called us with claims of destroyed military vehicles or choppers were asked to take pictures of the wreckage and bring it to us in order to substantiate their claims. In spite of the great difficulty one faced moving about the city, many of these people were glad to risk their lives in order to deliver pictures they took with their personal cameras.

After we finished with the caller reporting the downed helicopter, I told the colleagues around me, "If the factors and circumstances surrounding a news claim are not all absolutely and verifiably right, refusing to release that piece of news is a much smaller risk than releasing the news and finding it to be false. The whole world is watching us, and every single televised news outfit is quoting us and borrowing our images. We can't afford to be anything less than one hundred percent accurate and absolutely right in every single piece of news we report."

Because of these strict rules, we disqualified many news items that we instinctively felt were accurate, but didn't meet the criteria for accuracy that we had devised. Later on we discovered that the many of these news items were indeed valid, but at the time of discovery we could not take the risk without the immediate proof.

On this first day of the siege, another report I had prepared for the night news segments was aired on the *Day's Harvest*. The report summarized the developments that took place in the second part of the day. The Americans had bombed a civilian house in the Educators' Neighborhood at 4:30PM. A missile carved out a massive hole in the home's entrance, and destroyed other parts of the house. The homeowner was interviewed and spoke about the damage.

Later that night, as we were doing the segment for the *Day's Harvest* at 11PM, Fallujah was being heavily shelled by American forces. Thick clouds of choppers swarmed the skies over Fallujah, with surveillance aircrafts scattered among them. During this broadcast, an artillery battle also broke out between the insurgents and the American forces, and this battle lasted for half an hour. Because all of this was happening under the cover of darkness, we could see nothing except the pulse of light from the bombs as they fell. The sounds of the battle, however, made the situation gloomily clear. I covered some aspects of this battle during my live report. Confrontations in all areas of the city were escalating gradually, and were now much worse than when we first entered the city, I told viewers. And we'd received reports about Americans bombing civilian cars that traveled on the road after curfew.

Nearly the entire population of Fallujah knew that we were broadcasting from the rooftop of the Hadeed family house. The Hadeeds' phone rang with constant news from the townspeople. Some people even called to ask for our help in fleeing the city and the siege, and asked desperately for clues to an exit not blocked by the Americans.

In light of all this violence, many people who lived on the outskirts of the city moved to more centrally located neighborhoods, staying with relatives who lived closer to downtown. Indeed, much of the bombing concentrated on the outer neighborhoods. From atop Hamed's parents' roof, I could see clouds of smoke rising from houses in the Golan Neighborhood, which had been repeatedly bombed. The Golan Neighborhood suffered the heaviest losses due to its location on a major confrontation line between the Fallujans and the American forces—each fighting from one side of the Euphrates.

Our correspondents in other cities confirmed that during the first day of the siege, fierce battles broke out across the entire Anbar province—in cities like Ramadi, Qa'em, Hadeetha, Khaldiya, and Barwana. The occupation authorities had previously issued gun permits all across Iraq, after looting and armed robbery became ridiculously common because the occupation couldn't keep the citizens safe from criminals. One of the decisions American forces made on the first day of the siege was to repeal all gun permits granted to Fallujans, and essentially render Fallujans unable to defend themselves with any sort of weaponry.

The Day's Harvest ended at midnight and our live coverage ended with it, but the battles in the city continued. The night news bulletin producer, Amro al-Kahky, asked me to shoot a third report to be aired on the morning news segments. He wanted a summary of all the developments that had taken place after midnight so that viewers in the US, Japan, and all other countries in other time zones could stay up-to-date. He wanted to make sure that viewers from the furthest point in the East to the furthest point in the West were getting a clear image of developments in Fallujah as they unfolded.

Despite my exhaustion, I accepted his assignment. Normally, compiling three reports in one day is a task too heavy for someone who is reporting under the constant threat of missiles and gunfire. Amro was working the graveyard shift after a nap—a nap he was allowed because two other producers had manned the first two shifts. Working in shifts was not a luxury we could afford on the battlefield with such a small crew. I figured, however, that I might as well make my exhaustion worth it and produce a third report for the rest of the world. I wrote my report, selected the images and the footage I wanted, recorded the narration, and finished the entire montage sometime close to 2:00AM.

When I finished my report, Sayfuldeen, the telecommunication and broadcast engineer, was still awake. I asked him to send the report to Amro in Doha. It was then that we discovered that the satellite transmitter was broken. We were unable to send any information to our main head-quarters in Doha. This presented a major problem.

We tinkered with the transmitter for over an hour, and tried desper-ately to jump-start the machine, but had no luck. By 3:00AM, we decided we couldn't spend any more time on it that night. I informed Doha of the situation and told them that we'd work on a remedy in the morning. I also told Sayfuldeen that it was better for us to get some rest so we could get moving into the city when the curfew lifted at 6:00AM. We still had to make a morning tour around the city to find out what had taken place during the night, even with this technical problem. We had more than our share of work ahead of us, and it was best to tackle that work with as little exhaustion as possible.

8. DAY TWO: US FORCES FEEL THE FIRST STING OF DEFEAT

"Civilian hospitals organized to give care to the wounded and sick, the infirm and maternity cases, may in no circumstances be the object of attack but shall at all times be respected and protected by the Parties to the conflict."
—Part II, Article 18, Fourth Geneva Convention

I tried my best not to think about the transmitter when I went to bed, but it seemed the more I tried not to think about it, the more anxiety I suffered. With the transmitter failing and my mind spinning, there was no hope of any real rest that night. I happen to be a very light sleeper who can easily be awoken by the smallest noise, so the sounds of raging battles and exploding bombs didn't help matters. Some of the explosions were distant, but others shook the very foundation of the house I was sleeping in. I did manage to sleep for a very brief period late in the night, only to be awakened by the dawn call for prayer from nearby mosques. As I mentioned earlier, Fallujah is known as the city of mosques and minarets, so finding a mosque in Fallujah is about as easy as finding a bar in, say, the American city of Milwaukee. When the call for prayer goes off in Fallujah, no one is exempt from hearing it.

The rest of the house was awakened as well. When everyone was up and refreshed (as much as possible under such conditions), we sat down to plan our mission for the day. We needed to move efficiently, the minute the curfew was lifted.

Hamed called his relatives in other parts of the city to learn of the latest developments. We found out that most of the bombing was still focused on the edges of the city. The Military Neighborhood, the Golan Neighborhood, and a few other smaller neighborhoods had taken most of the American wrath during the night. There was still little opportunity for those injured to get medical help. Because the Fallujah General Hospital was under the control of the American forces and the field hospital in Fallujah wasn't open yet, there was only one possible place for Fallujans to receive medical attention: the private hospital of Dr. Taleb al-Janabi, in the Military Neighborhood, on the east side of the city.

To find out how many people had been killed or wounded overnight, we figured we needed to visit Dr. al-Janabi's hospital. We also wanted to make a tour of Fallujah's schools to see if there was any school life left on the second day of the siege. Our most pressing task, however, was to fix the satellite transmitter so that any news we gathered could actually be sent back to headquarters.

We chalked out a plan for the day. I was to head east toward the Military Neighborhood and try to film the area where American troops stood at the entrance of the city. I also intended to film the areas that were bombed during the night. Then, I was to head to Dr. al-Janabi's hospital in the same neighborhood in order to get some numbers on casualty counts and some information about how many people were wounded or trying to get medical attention. The cameramen, Layth and Hassan, were to accompany me. We'd travel in the van, and Abo Omar would be our driver.

Hamed was to make some calls and work with Sayfuldeen, who was still trying to fix the transmitter. He was also supposed to get in touch with our colleague Hussain Deli, the Fallujan correspondent who lived in the Republic Neighborhood, in midtown. Hamed had a small camera with him to capture images of any bombings that may have targeted the midtown area and it surroundings.

We agreed to meet back at the Hadeed family house at 8AM. Our colleagues in Doha had requested that I make an appearance on *Al-Jazeera This Morning*, which normally starts airing at 8, in any case. I was expected to provide the usual summary of the developments that had taken place since the last news bulletin.

Before we set off, I took Hamed aside and told him that there had to be a better division of labor, or we would never accomplish all the things expected of us. The responsibilities given to me alone were too many for any single person in any circumstance in a war zone. On top of all that, we were certain by that time that we were the only televised media present in the city. This made the responsibility on the shoulders of the entire crew much greater, and the load on me even more suffocating. I asked Hamed to try to help to prepare news reports, in order to take some of the pressure off of me.

Hamed was concerned that his limited experience in preparing news reports wouldn't allow him do a good job. He had made a televised news report only once in his life.

I told him, "War doesn't just create military commanders and political leaders. It also creates fine and brave journalists. You will be made a fine journalist by this Fallujan war." He listened to my words and agreed, as I knew Hamed would—he is a courageous and brave man. I informed the newsroom's editor-in-chief at the Doha headquarters, Ahmad Alshaikh, and he welcomed the idea.

Hamed's home was only 200 yards away from Main Street, the start of our route. Main Street connects Fallujah's east side to its west side. My group and I headed east on Dam Street, and we then crossed the short distance to Main Street. Layth sat in the front passenger seat. As we turned onto Main Street, he whispered to me over his shoulder, "Ahmed, very carefully look to your right. Look at the rooftops of the industrial work-shops. Don't be obvious."

I followed his directions. When I looked at the industrial rooftops, I saw US soldiers standing, literally, less than a few yards above our heads. If they chose to fire at us, their shots would come at very close range and would be very harmful. To avoid any chaos or panic in the van, I told Abo Omar, "There are armed American soldiers on the rooftops. Keep driving at a steady speed, and don't give any indication that we know there are soldiers present. Do not hesitate or touch your brakes for even a second."

We had written "PRESS" on the hood of our vehicle in both English and Arabic. The font was so large that the soldiers didn't need any magni-fying devices to read the word from a distance, let alone from a few yards. They were also close enough that if they wanted, they could examine us intimately with the aid of their binoculars, and make out the details of every piece of equipment we had with us in the van. The camera held by Layth in the front seat looked especially suspicious. A camera like his held on the shoulder could easily be mistaken for a shoulder-missile launching mechanism if seen from a distance and from the wrong angle.

Layth realized this danger without any word from me, so he kept the camera on his lap and left its lens sticking out the window so it was obvious that it was a camera and not a weapon. While the van rolled down the city streets, he filmed the soldiers standing ready in their hideout spots. These images became al-Jazeera's first exclusive images of American soldiers in the siege of Fallujah.

Dr. al-Janabi's hospital was located at the end of Main Street near an entrance to the city, in the Military Neighborhood. When we spotted the hiding soldiers, we were at the opposite end of Main Street, so we still had to go all the way through the industrial area to get to our destination. We drove very carefully, and exercised the utmost caution. We could see that all the shops were closed and everyone who lived in the area was apparently hiding out inside their homes. The city was shrouded with an eerie, tense fog. As soon as we could see the entrance of the city near the hospital, we could also see the two tanks that stood guarding the city, with their barrels pointed inside the city limits and straight at us. It was as if all that existed in the city were our crew, the troops hiding on the roofs of the workshops, and the two tanks.

Once we cleared the industrial area and approached the two tanks, we discovered far more troops were hiding in the area than we'd first noticed. Some soldiers were on foot; others were in armored vehicles. We couldn't run from these soldiers, much less hide from them, so we had no choice but to keep calm and pretend we were not afraid of the danger that had suddenly presented itself. We couldn't afford to agitate a single soldier in the sea of troops that had suddenly flooded the area. There were as many weapons in sight as there were hairs on my arms, so we just kept driving at a steady pace. Finally, at the entrance of the city, we turned left to get to the hospital.

The hospital was only a hundred yards or so from Main Street. It was clearly recognizable, but the entrance was blocked by a bombed pickup truck. The truck was still smoldering, and through our open windows we noticed a strange odor coming from its direction. I nodded at Hassan and Layth, indicating that one of them should film the wreckage of the truck.

Hassan looked concerned. "I don't have a good feeling about that strange smell. I'm not so sure anyone should approach the truck."

Before another word was said, Layth stepped forward. He took a few steps toward the bombed truck and suddenly turned back. He ran toward the van with one hand over his mouth and the other clamped on his nose. As he ran, he yelled: "The smell is burning human flesh! There is blood spattered all over the front cabin, and there is a smoldering human corpse in the trunk of the truck."

Layth told me to go check out the horrific scene for myself if I wanted, so I could report on it later. I tried to muster up enough courage to check out the scene, but it wasn't in me. I had never completely recovered from the mutilated civilian corpses I had encountered during the Afghan and Bosnian wars; they were images that had permanently planted themselves in my memory. I didn't wish to revisit this experience, especially considering how much potential for similar, unavoidable images we had in our immediate future.

This truck was clearly a civilian vehicle, and the victim in the trunk was probably an injured person being rushed to the hospital. The American troops obviously hadn't paused to consider the nature of the vehicle's trip through city streets, and instead decided to bomb the truck and obliterate any possibility of danger. I wanted to make sure this assumption that the Americans unfairly bombed the vehicle wasn't far-fetched, so I noted the question for the hospital's management.

Concrete blocks were scattered about the front of the hospital, and a janitor was mopping up one of the many blood puddles that decorated the hospital's entrance. It was evident that the hospital had been bombed too, not just the vehicles out front. We went inside the hospital, and I told the receptionist that we were a crew from al-Jazeera. Dr. al-Janabi and his hospital manager came out to receive us. Al-Janabi told us that he, along with the rest of his staff of doctors, was now residing in the hospital. They had turned the hospital into an emergency hospital, open to the public free of charge. This decision had been made after the American troops occupied Fallujah's public hospital, banned entrance to its staff of doctors, and prevented the wounded any access to health care inside its doors.

Al-Janabi told us about the conditions in and around the hospital. "It hasn't stopped raining bombs and missiles since last night. I informed the troops of the hospital's location so they could stay clear of us, and they still bombed here several times. We have a huge lighted sign on the roof that says 'hospital'—as if our verbal instructions weren't enough. They know very well what we are and what we do. And that still doesn't stop them from bombing us."

Layth and Hassan went outside to capture images of the bombed entrance, and I stayed to talk more with Dr. al-Janabi. I asked him about the bombed-out pickup truck outside his gate.

He explained, "The vehicle arrived here around 4AM. There was a severely wounded man in the trunk who was brought here by his father and brother. Their house had been bombed during the night. As soon as they arrived at our gate, the vehicle was bombed, even though it was clear those inside were seeking medical help. We tried to save the brother and the father, but their injuries were too severe. They expired, just like their charred family member outside."

"Were they speeding?" I asked, "Could that have been what made the troops get concerned enough to bomb them?"

He replied, "No, they weren't speeding, but they were out on the streets before that curfew was lifted. You know how it goes. Injured or not, half-dead or not, anything that moves before the curfew expires is fair game as far as the Americans are concerned."

Dr. al-Janabi then took me on a tour of the hospital, introducing me to some of the injured civilians receiving health care in the hospital. We caught much of this on tape. Then, we recorded a plea from Dr. al-Janabi, asking the American troops to leave the hospital alone and allow the doctors to provide care for the wounded. He pleaded that they not bomb the hospital or any vehicles coming in its direction, because there were inevitably wounded people inside.

I stood there watching the cameraman record the doctor's plea and thought to myself, Look at what's become of me. I've gotten so used to this gore and blood and so used to the fact that I can't do anything to alleviate the pain of these people that as this doctor records his plea I'm not even reacting. He's telling me about bombs being dropped on people already wounded by other bombs, and all I'm doing is putting a camera in front of him and nodding, like he's telling me about his recent trip abroad.

I was extremely bothered by how desensitized I'd become. I forced myself to stop thinking in that direction because I didn't want to get too upset to carry on with my duties for the day, but my discontent remained in the back of my mind.

After getting a proper look at what was going on in the hospital, we headed out to look at the rest of the Military Neighborhood, the cluster of houses behind the hospital. We filmed some of the houses that were bombed during the night, and viewed some of the other destruction. Then we moved on to visit the Wefaq Junior High School, to see if there was any lively school activity despite the siege. Out of the 500 students who normally attended the school, we found only twenty present in school that day.

The school principal, Muhammad Howaydi, said, "I couldn't cancel classes like the rest of the schools in the city because my students were supposed to take their tests today. But as you can see, very few people showed up because of the repeated bombing. This is an entirely civilian neighborhood, despite its name. It is called the Military Neighborhood only because at some point during Saddam's rule, large numbers of people who worked for the Iraqi military lived here. This isn't the first time this neighborhood was targeted with intense bombing. [The Americans] do this every time they have a quarrel with this city. What are they doing? Taking revenge on schools and hospitals in a civilian neighborhood just because it bears a name from the Saddam era? Saddam's military is no more, and the people who live here are not part of any military, so who are they targeting with their bombs?"

Howaydi repeated that the bombing was random, intense, and never-ending. He said that most of the neighborhood's residents had left their homes because they were in constant danger. They were staying with relatives closer to downtown and away from this doomed neighborhood, even though it was home.

We finished up our tours and interviews in the Military Neighborhood, because it was nearly 8AM, our meeting time, and I was expected to provide live coverage for the morning news segment.

When we returned to Hamed's parents' place, we found Sayfuldeen still laboring to fix the faulty satellite transmitter. In light of this problem, I provided my live coverage to the headquarters using my cell phone only. After I provided my coverage, Sayfuldeen stayed on the phone with the satellite telecommunications engineer in the Baghdad office. For the next two hours, they tried together to troubleshoot the transmitter, to no avail.

At this point, I was getting fed up with the transmitter. I placed a call to Ali Salem, the head of engineering at al-Jazeera headquarters, to see if he could be of any help. I found out that he was in Paris, but I was still able to reach him on his cell phone. I asked him to help our engineers over the phone. Salem agreed, and stayed on the phone to troubleshoot with Sayfuldeen for half an hour, still with no luck. His conclusion at the end of this trial was that there was no other option for fixing the problem beyond replacing one particular broken part in the transmitter. In other words, we were not going to be able to repair the satellite using the resources we had in Fallujah.

I consulted with Hamed about our problem. Did al-Jazeera have another transmitter somewhere?

He replied, "Even if there were an extra transmitter, what use is it if it's outside Fallujah? We can't get out of here to get a new transmitter. We barely got inside as it is."

I thought for a minute, but came up with no better solution. I proposed we do more investigating. "Let's find out if an extra satellite exists in the first place, and then we'll worry about how to get it," I said.

Hamed agreed, as always, and contacted the Baghdad office to ask about a transmitter. He learned from the headquarters that there was indeed an extra transmitter, but it was an older model. This older model worked on satellites via the internet, whereas the newer version we had with us worked on direct frequencies. This meant that engineer Sayfuldeen couldn't operate this older transmitter, even if we had access to it, because he wasn't trained on it. But there was another telecommunications engineer in Baghdad—coincidentally, also named Sayf—who did know how to operate it, and if he came with the transmitter he could assist in working with it.

I told Hamed, "This is good news. We do have access to a transmitter. But you're right that it's going to be dangerous and risky to try and bring Sayf and the satellite into Fallujah. We'll have to direct Sayf to the smugglers' road from the Naimyah side of the desert, and have him come with the transmitter in the same entrance we did. Hopefully the American forces haven't found out about the road yet... we'll just have to put all our hope into the road still being open."

After the decision was made that we would use the smuggler's road to bring a new transmitter into the city, Hamed volunteered to travel back to the outskirts of the city to retrieve the satellite. Hamed was the bravest of all of us, and didn't give me or anyone else the chance to volunteer before agreeing to put his life on the line again. He made his calls back to headquarters and worked out the details.

"I'm ready," he said, after all the arrangements were made. "I arranged it all with the Baghdad guys. They're going to bring the equipment to the Abu Ghraib area, and I'll exit the city through the smugglers' road, then follow the road up to meet them. I'll meet them at the closest safe point, and then return here with Sayf and the new transmitter," he said.

"Are you sure you want to do this?" I asked Hamed. "Maybe you should think a little more about it before you leave. Maybe you should take someone with you."

He replied without hesitation: "Thinking twice is a luxury we can't afford under these circumstances. I've already done this trip once, so why shouldn't I do it a second time? It is the same risk and offers the same possible consequences. And why should I take anyone with me? Just to risk someone else's life unnecessarily? This is a one-man job, and I won't put anyone else's life on the line."

I nodded in agreement, and said my goodbyes to him. I wished him a safe journey and a safe return. After he left on his dangerous attempt to infiltrate the American siege, Layth and I headed again toward downtown. I was still thinking very much about Hamed, and the possible danger he was heading into. I hadn't told him one thing—I had kept it from him because I didn't want to damage his confidence—but the reality was that the risk he was taking by traveling this road now was definitely not "the same risk" we had taken earlier. It was a much bigger risk this time because the circumstances in the city were so much worse. By this second day of the siege, we could smell blood in the air and the smoke of bombs and gunfire hung loosely on every building and person in the city. When we had first entered the city, we could only sense danger and threat—it wasn't immediately obvious as it was now. Also, this time he had to go over the smuggler's road twice, not just once like the first time. That amounted to twice the dangerous distance, and seriously multiplied the possibilities of being bombed, shot, or ambushed.

Because I was very concerned about Hamed, I decided to stay in contact with him via phone during his entire trip. When he informed me that he had cleared the city of Fallujah completely, I nearly exploded with enthusiasm and relief. I couldn't believe the American forces were still unaware of that road, when they had been so aware of the rest of the entrances and exits in the city. But I was still nervous despite my initial relief—Hamed wasn't out of the danger zone yet, not by a long shot, because he still had a return trip to make once he retrieved the replacement satellite.

As for Layth and me, our trip into downtown turned out to be dangerous as well. After we left Hamed's parents' home, we voyaged to the Golan Neighborhood where battle skirmishes were exploding everywhere. Our van got trapped several times by heavy fire. In one instance, we were stuck for two hours on one of the side roads, waiting in our vehicle for the fighting to subside. The fighting on the main road was happening between buildings and in open spaces. The gunfire was so intense that our vehicle would've been reduced to a sieve had we tried to escape. While we were waiting here, we heard a massive explosion that sounded like it occurred on the edge of the Golan Neighborhood. Soon thereafter, we were told that an American chopper had been shot down. Hearing such astounding news, we wanted to get to the scene and film the downed chopper, but the residents warned us not to leave our hiding spot because American snipers were all over the Golan Neighborhood and the gunfire was even heavier and more dangerous there than where we were hiding at that moment.

Over the next few hours, downtown streets began to fill up with fortification points, concrete blocks, and massive rocks. Marks of civilization began to disappear—the old market was closed, and the vegetable market had nothing left besides a few clumps of onions and garlic. Most of the downtown shops were closed. Gunmen and armed insurgents roamed the streets openly, without fear of American retaliation—a sure sign that the confrontation had taken a much more drastic and dangerous turn. We hadn't seen any insurgents in broad daylight on our first day in the city.

It was very clear that Fallujah had become a much more frightening place over the course of the two days, but despite this fear, one Iraqi made a statement that reflected the fearless attitude of most of the city's residents. He said, "We Fallujans either live with dignity or perish in martyrdom." The statement was recorded and included in the afternoon news report, and demonstrated the exact attitude of Fallujans and insurgents alike on this second day of battle.

We headed back to the Hadeed family house to regroup. On the way back, the streets were in complete disarray. There were sudden eruptions of fighting on the streets, and no one could speculate when or where the next outburst could take place. We often found ourselves stuck in the middle of fire exchange with little to no warning. It didn't really make much difference whether we moved or stayed put, because the line of fire was constantly shifting. It was slightly safer to take the alleys and side roads— the locals told us that the American troops were trying to advance along the center of Main Street and using other main roads in town in an attempt to infiltrate the insurgents' defense lines and take over blocks of the city.

The troops were trying to advance along that east–west axis of the city from both ends simultaneously. Fierce battles raged on the east side of the city, in the industrial area, and also in the west side, in the Golan Neighborhood. The troops were apparently trying to gauge where the insurgency was weakest so that they could advance from that side.

The troops did indeed advance further on the east side than they did on the west side. On the east side, the troops advanced along Main Street until they reached the Guided Caliphs' Mosque, which overlooked Dam Street. After this advance, the troops were a few yards from the Hadeed family house. It wasn't long before insurgents appeared, rather suddenly, and began shelling the troops heavily enough to force a retreat to their fortifications outside city limits. All this activity unfolded just steps outside Hamed's home.

In light of the fighting in the vicinity of the Hadeeds' house, we parked our vehicle a good distance away from the house and moved on foot through back alleys and narrow side roads. We couldn't drive on Main Street anyway, because the skirmishes along the eastern entrance of the city and on Main Street were still quite fierce, despite the fact that they were decreasing in number. When we reached the Guided Caliphs' Mosque, we encountered some insurgents who appeared to be in control of the area. These men granted us permission to film their activity, but denied our requests for interviews. They even refused to talk with us "off the record." We tried to negotiate further and convince them to talk with us, but we got nowhere. After our attempted negotiations, things suddenly got very tense and the men ordered us to leave the area without filming anything. As we left, we heard the commander of the insurgents holler instructions for the squad to move to the industrial area in an attempt to expel the American troops who seemed to be gaining control of that part of the city. When the insurgents reached this part of the city, we heard the sound of thunder-like collisions as battles broke out between the two sides.

We kept moving on foot through the city until we reached the Hadeed family house, where the fighting had subsided, if only for the moment. We arrived to find the best release for our tension we could imagine under such circumstances—Hamed. He had completed his insanely dangerous mission and had come back with the replacement transmitter. I couldn't believe our luck. The last call I'd had with Hamed, he had told me that he had the transmitter, but because of the dangerous roads we were on, I hadn't been able to stay with him on the phone on his return trip. While Layth and I were walking back to his home through the fighting downtown, I had no idea what he was going through. I couldn't believe he had been able to infiltrate the siege twice, survived the high odds of being bombed or killed, and replaced the transmitter all in a mere three hours.

"Where is the transmitter?" I asked excitedly.

Hamed replied, "It was raining bullets from the side where we entered Fallujah. We had to leave the vehicle at the city entrance, with the transmitter inside, and walk on foot to safety. As soon as the battles stop and the troops leave that area, we'll run and get the vehicle. It's not very far from here."

Although the transmitter wasn't technically in our possession yet, the means to continue broadcasting was within our grasp. Despite the difficult day we had experienced, we were all grateful for this stroke of luck.

Rasheed Wally

As we were talking about the transmitter and Hamed's journey, I heard Rasheed Wally's distinctive laugh coming from the living room. I knew then that the van and transmitter had definitely made it to us, and we didn't even have to brave the streets to retrieve them. Wally was one of finest and most outstanding employees at al-Jazeera's Baghdad bureau, and had proven his incomparable character once again by bringing our most desperately needed piece of equipment to Fallujah.

Wally was a man who never lost his humor even at the most dangerous and critical of times. His philosophy was that life was too short to wait
for good times to come along. He believed that one could make the good
times happen by having a positive outlook. Because of this philosophy, he
often did not have to suffer the effects of blinding fear because he quite
literally laughed in the face of fear. Whenever there was a dangerous
mission, Wally was always one of the first to embrace the mission as if it
were a routine and mundane task. He had taken on so many dangerous
missions and saved so many lives that he was nicknamed the "Savior"
around al-Jazeera's Baghdad Bureau. His efforts in bringing us the
replacement transmitter only strengthened this glowing reputation.

Wally was no ordinary driver. He was an incredibly skilled man, and
he was willing to assist anyone and everyone who needed help. He had
traveled throughout Iraq and in many other countries in his work accompanying al-Jazeera crews on missions. My first time traveling with Wally
was in July 2003, when he took me from Amman, Jordan to Baghdad. I
normally like to stay quiet when traveling, especially when in a car, so I
can ponder the landscape and speculate on the makeup of the towns I
travel through. On this particular trip, however, Wally didn't let me have
this introspection. Although we had just met, he immediately opened his
faucet of jokes and let it flow all the way from Amman to Baghdad. I
never laughed so wholeheartedly in my life, and I didn't even miss the
opportunity to meditate on the landscape I was traveling through. Every
single crew Wally worked with loved him, and thereafter requested him
by name. We were very happy to see him.

When the fighting subsided, Wally had been able to bring the vehicle
and the transmitter from the edge of Fallujah to Hamed's house. For
obvious reasons, now that he was here he didn't want to leave. He
suggested one of the two other chauffeurs drive the faulty transmitter to
Baghdad and stay there.

I understood his objections, but I told him, "No, buddy, that's just not
going to work. You have to be the one to complete this mission. This is
going to be the fourth infiltration of the American siege that we've risked
since the fighting began, and that means the highest odds of danger yet.
No one would dare take on such a mission besides you, and you know
that you would perform at a level far beyond anything the other chauffeurs could offer. We need you." After some encouragement, he eventually
agreed. He then left to head to Baghdad with the faulty transmitter. He
took with him Farqad, one of our two chauffeurs, and Sayfuldeen, the old

telecommunications engineer. Sayf, the new engineer for the replacement transmitter, stayed with us in Fallujah.

A few weeks after this incident, I received bad news about Wally. After things had died down in Fallujah, Wally was with Layth and Abdulazeem in Karbala, covering the American invasion there. Wally was helping Layth with his camera work, and setting up headquarters on top of the roof of the Khuddam al-Hussain Hotel. He was helping Layth find the locations of American troops so that Layth could film them. At this precise moment, an American sniper spotted the activity, and shot Wally in the head. He was killed instantly. That incident took place on the evening of Friday, May 21, about a month and a half after the first battle of Fallujah. Wally was survived by six children, and was al-Jazeera's second casualty in the war on Iraq, after Tariq Ayoub.[28]

Unfortunately, viewers watching these battles on their television sets across the world have no way of seeing or knowing about unsung heroes like Wally. They see journalists, correspondents, and television show hosts like me, and think our work in the battlefield is the most courageous thing on television. In reality, there is an entire army of sincere, hard-working people who risk their lives far more than we on-air journalists ever do, just to make our appearances on camera possible. These heroes remain entirely nameless to the public, even in their death. Wally was one of these heroes. If we public figures, who write and publish, do not dedicate a few pages in our publications to these heroes, the public will never know about the people who made us public figures to begin with. For this reason, I take this small moment to pay tribute to Rasheed Wally. There are many others like him, and the viewing public should try diligently to remember that fact when watching coverage of battle zones like Fallujah.

New Life & Narrow Escapes

Having a replacement transmitter breathed some much-needed life into our crew and its mission. We immediately turned on the device, and sent all the images and reports we had recorded to Doha.

Just as order was being restored in our makeshift newsroom, violence exploded over our heads. An American assault was being launched from the choppers above us, aimed at the insurgents infiltrating our area. Despite the immense danger, we got on the roof in an attempt to film the choppers as they littered bombs across the neighborhood. The choppers hovered so close above our heads that it felt as if the pilots were not planning on stopping at annihilating the insurgents but would finish us off as well. The insurgents were retaliating in fine fashion—they were showering the chop-pers with a constant stream of gunfire. It was difficult to tell if we had a better chance of getting bombed from above or shot from below.

"Enough filming," I eventually shouted to Layth. "We got the images we need. Let's go back inside." We couldn't escape the Americans' bombing inside, but at least we could escape the insurgents' bullets. We got off the roof and went inside to hide, fearing the collision of a bomb at any second.

After the fire exchange subsided a little, Layth risked a walk outside to search for cigarettes. Layth was as dedicated to his smoking as he was to his work. War or no war, bombs or no bombs, he had to have his ciga-rettes. He found a small tobacco kiosk close to the Guided Caliphs' Mosque, about 200 yards from us. He got his cigarettes and ran back. Just after Layth returned, American forces began another attempt to advance ground troops into the city. Protection for their forces was offered by the choppers hovering above the area. The insurgents intensified their fire in response to this method, and suddenly the whole area turned into a death zone. Luckily, Layth was already out of the street.

While this insanity was going on outside, it was time for us to record the noon news bulletin for al-Jazeera. The viewers could hear the fierce-ness of the battle in the background as I gave a detailed update and ran the latest images in the news segment. The report included the following information: the troops were advancing in military vehicles on Dam Street, and chasing after the insurgents who were firing at them. The closer the troops got to the rebels, the heavier they fired back. The troops continued to advance on Dam Street until they reached the front yard of the Hadeeds' house and continued to the steps of the Guided Caliphs' Mosque. This was the farthest they had been able to advance into the city. They held their position very briefly, until they were assailed with gunfire from the insurgents. The insurgents took no care to give them breathing room, and offered no chances for recovery. Eventually, the troops gave up and retreated to their original positions on Main Street, around the eastern entrance of Fallujah.

As the Americans retreated, we advanced with our film equipment. We ran out with our cameras and microphones, and made our best attempt at capturing the aftermath of the battle. The cashier who had sold Layth his cigarettes was now reduced to vapor and fluids, and his kiosk was simply a pile of dust and rubble. The American troops had fired at him with artillery big enough to bring down a house, which was more than enough to raze his weak plywood shack. Layth took the discovery of this casualty the hardest, because he was the last person who spoke to the victim, a few seconds before his demise.

Before they retreated from the Guided Caliphs' Mosque, the American troops performed random, unexpected searches throughout the Nazzal Neighborhood and the Officers' Neighborhood. We interviewed some of the victims of these searches afterwards. A man who lived in a house adjacent to the Guided Caliphs' Mosque told me he didn't know where the troops dropped on the house from, and suddenly they were inside. He had been sitting with his children in the family room, and no one saw the troops coming up the sidewalk, climbing the sides of the house, or even knocking on doors. They entered the house without warning and without permission. According to this man, the troops ransacked the house in an effort to find weapons or hidden insurgents, frightened the children, and then exited the house as quickly as they came. I recorded the man's statement and included it in following news reports.

After the American forces retreated from the area around Hamed's house, we went downtown again to record the developments there. Hamed was shooting his first report, as we agreed upon earlier. I walked him through most of the steps of preparing a report and gave him some of the images that Layth and Sayf captured during our morning tour. I showed him how to organize the footage and the images, and reviewed the report with him. From there on, Hamed would record all the news reports for the Fallujah coverage by himself without any help from me. Although he was a little nervous, I had the utmost confidence in his abilities.

Our goal downtown was to film Hamed's report signature in front of the old market. There were no stores open, and some parts of the market had been bombed during the night. We found a flyer on the ground near the market. The flyer included pictures of some minors and teenagers who had supposedly participated in the mutilation of the mercenaries. The Americans were offering a bounty of money and rewards in exchange for handing over those who participated in the mutilation of the mercenaries. We found another flyer on the ground, this one created by the people of Fallujah. This flyer included a plea to the United Nations to intervene and demand the US end its siege of Fallujah. We filmed the report signature in this place, and made reference to these flyers and the information contained on them.

When we returned to the Hadeeds' place, we heard painful news. The Hadeeds' neighbors' eighteen-year-old daughter, who had earlier that day stood by the window watching the troops advance on Dam Street, had been killed. As the troops buckled from the heavy fire from the insurgents, their snipers had fired directly at the girl. When her father ran to her rescue, he too was shot. Her wounds were fatal, and she died on the spot. Her father's wounds hadn't been severe enough for immediate death. He was transported to Dr. al-Janabi's hospital.

The feeling I had gotten earlier revisited me—the dead, desensitized feeling I had when talking to Dr. al-Janabi. I felt like a machine. A tape recorder, to be exact. I recorded the aftermath of the murder and wrote my piece of news on the end of this young girl's life, and my emotional reactions remained at bay. It is strange how damaged one's psyche becomes after working for so many years against the backdrop of so much bloodshed. That girl had her whole life ahead of her; she was only eighteen. Normally, a scene like this would make me cry involuntarily. Not this time. I wasn't crying outwardly, but deep down, I knew my emotional well-being would not be intact for a long time. Below the surface, I was devastated, destroyed by the things that were going on around me.

The Faulty Logic of Kimmitt and Bremer

I presented the story of the Hadeeds' neighbor and all the other details of the battle on Dam Street in a live report during the news bulletin presented by my colleagues Jameel Azar and Layla Shayeb. These developments led to the scene in Fallujah receiving headline news status in all of al-Jazeera's news segments. The horrific images that the al-Jazeera cameramen had captured were then circulated across the globe by world news agencies, and this circulation made the situation appear exactly as it was: a human catastrophe.

In the news segment following our coverage, Jameel Azar hosted General Mark Kimmitt and asked him about this situation.

Jameel asked, "Are you surprised to face such fierce resistance in Fallujah?"

General Kimmitt responded, "We're getting closer to handing over sovereignty to the Iraqi people. We were expecting an escalation of that kind."

Jameel pushed for a more honest answer. "But the casualty counts among civilians indicate that what's commencing is an operation for revenge, not for providing security to the Iraqi people."

General Kimmitt replied, "There certainly isn't any vengeance on the side of our troops, but the combat operations we're engaging in are happening in tough places, and everything we're doing falls within the context of self-defense."

It was more than difficult for me to listen to General Kimmitt's justification for American destruction after all we had been through in the last few days. I thought to myself, Self-defense? What kind of self-defense entails an oppressive siege on 300,000 people whose only crime is being a resident of a city? What about the battles raging across other cities in Iraq? Are they all cases of "self-defense" as well? My understanding of self-defense is that when you, your loved ones, or your home are attacked, you fight back to defend yourself. Barging into other people's homes with weapons is never self-defense.

Of course, every person sees the world through the lens of his or her own experience. Mark Kimmitt works for an institution that understands only two things: defense and offense. It was unsurprising that he'd use the term "self-defense" to describe what his troops were doing to Fallujans. For politicians and military men, justifications for crimes are often instilled during training. Although understandable in that regard, this explanation still did not make it any easier for me to accept Kimmitt's words.

Paul Bremer gave another perspective on the events unfolding during this first battle of Fallujah. Bremer saw the human catastrophe created by the clash between American government and Fallujans as a chance to promote democracy. On Sunday, April 11, a few days after the siege began, Bremer justified American military action on NBC's *Meet the Press*:

> I believe we are seeing the few thousands of Iraqis who do not share the democratic vision of the future of Iraq that the vast majority of Iraqis do show. Poll after poll, 90 percent or more want democracy here. What we see in these insurgents in Fallujah and in the mobs that support Sadr, we are seeing anti-democratic forces, enemies of freedom, and they simply have to be gotten out of the body politic here for Iraq to move forward. And that's the process we're in now. There will be some people, like the driver, who have that view, but that's not the majority view.

After hearing statements like this one, I couldn't help thinking to myself, So, the bombing of an injured person in front of a hospital, the bombing of a person selling cigarettes, and the targeted sniper's shot to the forehead of a teenage girl are all part of the process of getting the insurgents "out of the body politic"? The killing of civilians like these is necessary for Iraq "to move forward"? Don't these incidents seem even remotely like acts of revenge? And do you *really* think that 90 percent of

Iraqis support you in committing these deeds? If Iraqis support these deeds, then why did outbreaks of rebellion and an upsurge in resistance operations against American troops take place all over Iraq when Americans attacked Fallujah?

It occurred to me after hearing statements like Bremer's that a skewed view of the world often results in a terribly skewed logic.

The American Occupation Spawns Unlikely Alliances

As evening turned to nightfall on the second day of the siege, violence began to spike even more sharply. Skirmishes broke out on all sides of the city. The sound of artillery bombs and explosions came from all directions, and bled beyond the official borders of Fallujah. We heard reports from several other cities in the Anbar province indicating that insurgents had upped their operations against American forces in order to show solidarity with Fallujans. On the second day of the siege, the insurgents in Ramadi waged an attack that killed more than twelve American soldiers. Coverage of this conflict was an al-Jazeera exclusive, provided by Hussam Ali, al-Jazeera's Ramadi correspondent. Ali also reported that there were explosive battles going on in downtown Ramadi, and that several American soldiers were either killed or wounded there when insurgents surprised them with mortar attacks.

Later on in this second day of the battle, the Association of Muslim Scholars in Iraq (AMSI) issued the following statement: "The targeting of our fellow Iraqi civilians, the repeated aerial bombing they are forced to endure, and the subsequent siege they are being subjected to now in Baghdad, Azamiyah, Kazimeyah, Revolution City, Shola, Najaf, and Fallujah is a shameful disgrace on the head of the coalition forces."

The report we aired at noon that day included stories of activity in Ramadi and the statements issued by AMSI. On the following day, a statement issued by American forces confirmed our claims about the scene in Ramadi. Twelve American soldiers were killed and 24 wounded in a battle that lasted for several hours.

Ramadi wasn't the only city that rebelled on Tuesday in solidarity with Fallujah. In the town of Saqlawiyah, a large operation was also waged against the Marines.[29] Battles also broke out in Sadr City, Baghdad, Najaf, and throughout southern Iraq. In particular, insurgency action and resistance intensified in the cities of Diyala, Baqubah, Samarra, and Tikrit. This activity couldn't be explained simply as insurgents trying to ease the pressure on their comrades in Fallujah; these were joint operations in which insurgents and townsmen were cooperating as a sign of solidarity with Fallujah as a town, regardless of factional affiliation.

Although throughout this conflict the insurgents enjoyed boasting about being the main catalyst behind this massive and synchronized rebellion all across Iraq, the reality was slightly different. Certainly, insurgents produced the right type of propaganda to further inflame the locals in each respective town, but the main catalyst behind all of this activity following the siege on Fallujah were the actions of the American forces. The viciousness with which American forces attacked Fallujah was abhorrent to the average Iraqi, and the indiscriminate bombing was appalling enough to enrage even the most peaceful or indifferent of Iraqis. Suddenly, there was no room for pacifists who sought non-violent solutions to the problems with the occupation. This attitude was no longer acceptable to Iraqis. Every town had to stand in solidarity, and every town had to refuse to tolerate occupation on its soil as long as the Americans continued to commit war crimes. The more desperate American forces became and the more horrendous actions they committed, the more Iraqis united with Fallujans and the insurgents.

The viciousness displayed by the Americans was enough to drive any people to make unusual alliances. This was precisely the case with Iraqis, who, when exposed to the behavior of American forces, allied with insurgents and accepted violence as the only way out of the conflict. After the Americans occupied Iraq, they lost the support of civilized, moderate Iraqis, and these lost citizens turned to the insurgents. The insurgents took these groups into their arms and said, Welcome back, fellow countrymen! God is on our side. The insurgents may have played their cards right in this campaign to win over the general population of Iraqis, but it was the Americans who dealt them.

In his memoir, Paul Bremer acknowledges the mess that American forces were experiencing in Iraq during the battle of Fallujah. He writes,

> As we await the next word on the attacks, the Station Chief has presented me with an overall assessment of the situation in Iraq, which was apparently requested a week ago by the DCI in Langley. It is over-the-top pessimistic. "Catastrophic" failure awaits us as a "progressive collapse of Iraq" is under way. Four pages of this, which begins to smell of a classic "cover your ass." The Agency has become so totally shell-shocked by the beating they've taken in recent years, that virtually everything they write only emphasizes the negative.

Chapter 12 of Bremer's memoir, from which this excerpt is taken, is appropriately named "Hitting the Wall."

The Battle at Naimyah Road

The bombing only intensified around the edges of the city as the second day marched into night. Sounds of massive explosions came from every single direction, above our heads, and beneath our feet. Near sunset, some townsmen Hamed knew arrived at the Hadeeds' house. These men came specifically to inform us that insurgents had just waged a massive attack against the troops blockading the Naimyah dirt road. They said it was a fierce and horrifying battle, but it had been an obvious victory for the insurgents. The insurgents had killed and injured a large number of soldiers, and destroyed the whole site. The choppers hurried in after the confrontation, airlifted the casualties, and left the site in flames. The townsmen didn't come just to deliver the news, however. They wanted us to go with them to see for ourselves and film the scene.

I knew this was very serious and groundbreaking news, but I couldn't broadcast this enormous insurgent victory on air unless I had indisputable proof—the word of the townsmen wasn't enough for us to go live just yet. We weren't talking about a minor retreat by US forces as had happened with the attempts to advance into the city, and we weren't talking about a stroke of luck for the insurgents that brought down a chopper. We were talking about the total obliteration of an American military site and an undeniable defeat of US forces orchestrated by a handful of insurgents. I needed verification, and the townsmen were more than happy to take us to the scene where we could get verification for ourselves.

I was concerned for the safety of my crew, though, at such a fresh battle scene. I knew the dirt road in question was the same dirt road where the checkpoint commander threatened to kill us if we didn't move, and also wasn't far from the smugglers' road, where Hamed had encountered so much gunfire on his trip to recover the transmitter.

One of the townsmen reassured me, "The dirt road is only a fifteen minute drive from the paved Fallujah streets. We have just come from there, and there is no one around. The Americans ran away after the chopper carried off their dead. The road will be totally safe to drive on, if we move quickly."

His words didn't help much, however, because I didn't know him or his companions, so I didn't know whether I could trust his word. I took Hamed aside and asked him how he felt about their credibility and the possibility of ill intentions on their end. Maybe it was a trap. Maybe going to see the battle scene would lead to an ambush by insurgents who were unhappy about something we had broadcast.

Hamed smiled and said, "If this is your concern, then you've got none. First of all, I know some of these townsmen very well. These are good people. You have my solemn word that they are definitely trustworthy. Secondly, if the insurgents really wanted your head or mine, they wouldn't have to go to these lengths. The insurgents are mostly local Fallujah people. They know who I am, even if I didn't know them personally, because they recognize my family name. And because they know my family name, they know exactly where we're staying. It's easier for them to hunt us down than it is for the US forces to find us."

He could see I was still concerned. He patted my shoulder and offered a solution: "I tell you what. I know how to deal with fellow Fallujans more than you do. I'll go with them. You stay put."

I grabbed his arm before he tried to leave with the townsmen. I was still concerned: "No, no. Wait. Let's think this through. This isn't safe at all, because—"

He interrupted, "Think what through? These men just told you the troops ran away after the battle. The roads are wide open and clear of all danger, if we stop sitting around and talking about all this and just get going. We don't have time to think. We have to take action right now."

Without giving me a chance to reply, Hamed turned to the gathering of people in his home, looked at the cameramen, and said, "I'm in to see the wreckage of the fight. Who's going with?" Layth leapt at the opportunity, because he's nearly as fearless as Hamed. Leaving me no further room for protest, they left the house to film the aftermath of the possibly groundbreaking news.

What Hamed hadn't let me finish saying is this: if you're a hunter who's injured a wolf on the hunt, and you ran out of ammunition before the wolf died, then you'd better hide because the wolf will come back at you with a vengeance as long as he is still breathing. Sure, the insurgents could revel in the fact that they'd won a clear victory over the troops at Naimyah—but that was their only victory so far. The larger battle was far from over. The insurgents had clearly defeated the troops at one limited, albeit significant, site. The troops, on the other hand, were encircling the entire city and still held the upper hand in battle. The "wolf" in this case wasn't that company of soldiers at the Naimyah Road; the wolf was the US forces throughout Fallujah—and they were more than willing to retaliate. The Americans definitely wouldn't want insurgents to benefit from the abandoned armaments and weapons left by the soldiers, and they most certainly wouldn't want to leave behind papers or other clues that could help insurgents in future attacks or help the media in documenting the defeat the troops suffered there.

After a period of waiting anxiously to hear back from them, it started to seem as though it would've been easier to go with them than to sit at Hamed's parents' house worrying. I called Hamed and stayed with him on the phone his entire trip, just to relieve my fears.

When the crew arrived on the scene, they saw the remnants of what must have undeniably been a gruesome confrontation. The stretch of land where the conflict took place was still smoldering, and the smoke from gunfire hung heavily in the air. Not a single soldier was in sight. Layth filmed everything, even the half-empty food packages left behind by the American troops. The crew surmised that the Americans must have been eating when the insurgents ambushed them.

We never did get an actual casualty count for the attack, but it was evident from the images alone that a very high number of casualties must have resulted. US sources never declared the exact count for this particular attack, and this was true for many other attacks as well. US statements after this attack explained only that "a number of soldiers were killed in Anbar," leaving the count and location quite vague. Fallujah is only one of many cities in the Anbar province, and the Naimyah dirt road was only one of many attack sites in Fallujah. In fact, one of the statements the Americans made tried to justify this vagueness by saying that "disclosing any further information about these incidents [attacks] could subject soldiers to more danger in the future." So, the vagueness was clearly intentional.

Hamed and Layth returned to our headquarters after an hour or so. It felt to me as though they'd been resurrected from the dead because of the fears that had plagued me in their absence—I had been so sure they would be harmed on this particular mission. We congratulated them on their safe return and on the unbelievable footage they captured. Layth was sweating as though he'd run a marathon. He handed us the tape to send to Doha while he sat and chain-smoked, still having difficulty himself believing they'd made it back unharmed.

We sat watching the tapes as they went to Doha, and everyone was talking about the magnitude of the defeat, the anticipated reaction by the US, or the exclusiveness of this footage for al-Jazeera. The conversation included everything except the fact that people, probably quite a few people, had just been killed where our crew had moments ago been filming. Perhaps the main reason for this insensitivity was that no corpses were left on the scene, which might have made the reality more concrete and emotionally devastating.

Still, the image of the scattered food packages got to me. I couldn't stop thinking that this horrible confrontation was the last thing some young American soldiers experienced, and that the food we saw was the remains of their last meal. The American soldiers were mostly very young people in their late teens and early twenties. Their bodies were definitely growing faster than their minds, like teenagers all over the world. Many of them didn't have enough self-awareness to decide for themselves if they really wanted to support this war or not, or if entering the army was the best decision or not. When those kids died, they were eating military food, which looks and smells remarkably like dog food, and waiting on orders to fight a messy and gruesome battle for ownership of a city they'd probably had never heard of before they enlisted. These were the last moments of their lives.

I'm sure some of these kid-soldiers were eating the tasteless military food, looking at the desolate Naimyah Road, and thinking of their own homes. Perhaps they were lifting their spirits by thinking of the next Thanksgiving. Perhaps they were going home as soon as their service was over, and on next Thanksgiving, they were going to have their mom's home-cooked turkey and stuffing, fill up on all the fixings, and enjoy being with family and loved ones in a familiar house brimming with warmth and love. Or maybe they thought about Christmas—about eggnog and peanut brittle and exchanging presents—and about all the weight they were going to involuntarily gain during the next holiday season they could spend with their families in America. It seems that very suddenly the promise for a happy future for these soldiers was cut unfairly short. These young men weren't even allowed to finish an awful last meal that came from a cardboard container while sitting on a desert road under threat of insurgent ambush. In sum, the lives of innocent, perhaps naïve, young people were cut drastically short because Bush sent them to face the insurgents—fighters who weren't so naïve and innocent, and knew exactly what they were doing and knew exactly what they wanted. What they wanted was to see no invader desecrating their soil and subjecting their people to cruelty and injustice, and they were determined to get what they wanted even if it cost them their lives. Pitting insurgents against these young American soldiers was an unfair battle.

My thoughts about the lost lives of these young American soldiers were interrupted by reports of US reactions to the attack, which came to us on the phone from Hussain Deli. The images, borrowed from al-Jazeera by international media, had been circulated across the world in a matter of minutes. These images sent the US forces into panic mode. The images obviously dealt a big blow to the ego of the US military, because they proved that the position of American forces was only getting worse despite their near-airtight encirclement of the city. The American forces were losing what was supposed to be an easy victory to bands of insurgents. Following release of our filmed images from Naimyah Road, the already indiscriminate and genocidal bombing in Fallujah became even less discriminate and more genocidal. Essentially, the Americans started bombing without aim, trying to claim victory with a sheer show of strength.

One hour after we broadcast the images, our colleague Hussain Deli delivered some painful news. An American warplane had bombed a house in the Golan Neighborhood, and had killed more than 20 people in a single strike. This attack was particularly disturbing because Hussain reported that the victims were mostly young children and women. Hussain told us that he was at the site filming the aftermath and the recovery operation as the neighbors started to retrieve the corpses. Hussain spoke of the bodies of dead, small children and their severed limbs. He spoke of a woman whose skull was smashed by a falling concrete beam. He spoke of men whose faces had been scraped off their skulls by the falling steel rods. He painted images that were disturbing and devastating enough that one didn't need to see them in order to feel complete anxiety about the future of the situation at hand.

More Destruction in the Golan Neighborhood

During the second day of the siege, Dr. Rafie al-Issawi, director of the Fallujah General Hospital, attempted to turn the public clinic in the Republic Neighborhood into a central field hospital for Fallujah, along with the help of many other doctors from the area. This medical staff was attempting to give people access to medical care they normally would have received at the Fallujah General Hospital. The number of injured people was growing exponentially, and there were no medical care centers to accommodate these casualties besides Dr. al-Janabi's private-turned-public hospital. Al-Janabi's hospital was on the eastern edge of town, which meant it was quite a distance for some Fallujans, and the area was also constantly under heavy fire. The US forces had been making repeated attempts to invade the city in the east. Also, al-Janabi's hospital was certainly not big enough to accommodate the needs of a city the size of

Fallujah in the wake of a genocidal episode of such proportions. The doctors also tried to turn clinics on different edges of the city into field hospitals to accommodate other areas of the city. The central field hospital was small anyway, but the other field hospitals were even smaller, and the central hospital still had to take the biggest load of work due to its location.

We kept good communication with al-Issawi because he was our primary source for casualty counts on the civilian side of the battle. We interviewed him several times during our live news broadcast to provide viewers with official casualty counts so that no one could accuse us of spreading rumors about massacres without official proof.

One of the massacres that Dr. al-Issawi spoke about was the same massacre in the Golan Neighborhood that Hussain Deli had covered. A man named Khamis Nimrawi lived on the edges of town close to a large concentration of US forces. He thought he'd be safer if he moved somewhere a little deeper into town. So, he took his wife and children, his four brothers, their wives, and all of their children and moved temporarily to the Golan Neighborhood. They all stayed in one house—Khamis's friend's place. Unfortunately, they found little safety at Khamis's friend's place. The US warplanes bombed the house, completely destroying the structure and killing 24 people inside. The only survivors of this bombing were Khamis Nimrawi and one infant child.

We aired the story of this bombing as breaking news at 11:00PM on the second day of the siege, on the *Day's Harvest*. There were other news items covered in our report such as the fuel crisis in the city, the dire need for restocking diminishing medical supplies while the number of the injured was on the rise, and the horrendous corpse disposal problem that had emerged because people were unable to bury their dead amidst continuing violence. We also aired Dr. Rafie's call for Fallujans to donate blood, and we informed viewers about the Golan bombing that had killed 24 people; we promised that footage was on its way.

On the second night of the siege, Hussain Deli had to deal with the possibilities of extreme danger to deliver his film of the massacre in the Golan Neighborhood to us at the Hadeeds' place. On top of the curfew, there would be random bombing by outraged American forces, and we were at risk for becoming targets anywhere in the city. Hussain Deli refused to miss the chance to air the horrendous footage. He arrived at our location just before midnight, when *Day's Harvest* ends, and just in time to air his images. We warned the viewers of the graphic nature of the footage, and then we aired the images. The wreckage from the bombing consisted mostly of plywood and a scattering of internal organs and other dismembered body parts, many that had once belonged to children. The ghastly scene was covered over with blood and black dirt.

There was no question that this was the worst and most devastating footage we had shot and aired so far in this battle. Many of us, viewers and journalists alike, never recovered from the sight of small, child-like hands sticking out of the dirty mess. These images still haunt me to this day. After we aired these images, the entire crew became submerged in a heavy fog of depression. This footage wasn't film of empty burning vehicles, like the footage we had shot of Naimyah Road. There were pieces of bodies here. This was footage of civilians, not combatants. And these weren't just any civilians. These were children—civilians so tiny that they couldn't have been more than five or six years of age.

The hideousness of this violence was a forewarning of the greater violence that was to come. It occurred to me that the scene unfolding in Fallujah was perhaps like what must have happened in North America when the Europeans first battled the Native Americans. Like the Fallujans, the Native Americans were a group of people whose homeland was invaded, who were grossly mistreated and abused. Native Americans, like the Iraqis as of yet, have never truly heard an apology for the actions of invading parties, and it's clear that today's American forces attack with similar philosophies to those who "conquered" the Native American people. This recent massacre was demonstration of a continuing American attitude of disrespect toward the people residing in the places whose resources or land they want. This massacre also demonstrated that the soldiers were indeed like the wolves I'd wanted to warn about: they were severely injured and suffering quite a bit. They were definitely going to inflict further punishment on the ones who caused those injuries.

Later that night, as I tried to get some sleep, I had immense difficulty turning off my brain and allowing my body to rest. Despite severe exhaustion and two days' lack of sleep, I still wasn't able to get any rest. Images of the buried children and the smoldering battlefield by Naimyah Road played on a continuous loop in my mind. On top of those disturbing images, I was plagued by the sound of constant bombing. Normally, the insurgents moved around the city only under the dark cover of night, so when they attacked, you expected that the Americans would attack too. On this night, however, the Americans were suffering from damaged morale, and were looking to exact revenge. The insurgents, on the other hand, were feeling victorious and wanted to seize an opportunity to exploit a weakness in their enemy. The combination of these two elements was a night of battle ruled by previously unforeseen brutality and force. Everyone in the city of Fallujah who wasn't fighting for the insurgents or defending the Americans faced the same fear. As the bombs fell constantly overhead, those not engaged in battle sat emerged in the all-consuming anxiety that the next bomb would drop on them.

9. DAY THREE: FUNERAL PROCESSIONS AND SNIPERS

Just after dawn on the third day of the siege, everyone in the crew sat waiting for the clock to turn to 6AM, for the curfew to be lifted. In the meantime, we had split the crew into three teams to gather the morning news from as large an area as possible. The first team, made up of Hamed and Layth, was to go downtown to report on conditions at the central field hospital, and then they were to proceed to the Golan Neighborhood. Once there, they would see if there were any new develop- ments at the site of the previous day's massacre. The second team was comprised solely of Hussain Deli, who always ran a one-man show, with excellent results. Hussain had the task of hanging around the city center to look for skirmishes, gunfights, or any other outbreaks of street violence. He was going to carry a small camera with him, and his job was to catch the news happening on the streets. The third team was comprised of cameraman Hassan, driver Abo Omar, and me. We were to tour the worst part of town, the east side, where US forces were stationed. Our responsibility was to cover the entire east side of the city, including the Military Neighborhood, the industrial area, and Dr. al-Janabi's hospital.

After the curfew was lifted, our crew headed down Dam Street and turned east on Main Street. The industrial area sat to the right, the Officers' Neighborhood to the left, and two big tanks blocked the street ahead. The guns of the tanks were pointed directly at our heads. Some soldiers combed the industrial area to our right, while other groups of soldiers were stationed on the roofs of the workshops. With so many soldiers in various states of alert, it was clear that the Americans were preparing for yet another operation.

Just about every soldier who spotted us pointed a threatening weapon at us. In the face of this harsh welcome by the Americans, we nearly panicked.

I whispered to Abo Omar, "Don't hesitate. Keep driving. Act as if you don't see them, and act as if no one in this van is frightened. We don't want them to think we're doing anything out of the ordinary."

"But this isn't like the last time we came over to this side of town. The road isn't open. The tanks are blocking the road and the barrels of their guns are facing right at us, ready to shoot at any second. Where am I supposed to drive to? There's nowhere to go. Am I supposed to drive right into the barrels so that they can take better aim at us?"

I tried to reassure him. "If we turn back now, they will definitely fire at us. They'll get suspicious. But if we keep driving forward, they might not. There are soldiers all over the roofs of these workshops on the right, and they're inspecting every detail of this van. We have "PRESS" spelled out on the hood of the vehicle. They know we're journalists. When we get to the tanks, either they let us through, or they turn us back without firing. We can't escape from these tanks except by going right to them. At least they know we're not insurgents."

Despite my reassurances, we were all very nervous. In a matter of minutes we could easily become just another three names added to the long list of journalists killed in the Iraq war. The casualty count of journalists and crew members had already reached 33 one year into the war. Burhan Muhammad, a cameraman for ABC News, was the most recent. He had been killed in Fallujah on March 26, while filming a particularly fierce confrontation in which the US forces suffered a high casualty count. Not many people outside Fallujah knew about his death, since Burhan's camera and film were destroyed along with him. It's never an easy thing to find yourself under fire and your best bet to choose between two undesirable options—none of us wanted to end up another statistic, but as I said to Abo Omar, we really had no choice but to keep driving.

The further Abo Omar drove down the road, the more nervous we all got. I figured maybe if I got every person to focus on his duty, I could get our minds off our fears. So, just as I told Abo Omar the chauffeur to keep driving, I asked Hassan the cameraman to start filming. I asked him to focus his lens on the two tanks and the troops on the roofs above us, but he wasn't as daring as Layth. His fear made him clumsy, and he wasn't able to film anything. I couldn't blame him. I was at least as scared as he was.

Abo Omar continued driving toward the tanks, trying desperately to maintain an even speed. We wanted to change routes, but there were no visible places to turn off the road. The only turnoffs we knew were located at the end of Main Street, close to Dr. al-Janabi's hospital, which is where the tanks were anyway—defeating the purpose. We drove up to the tanks in complete silence, our hearts up in our throats. We didn't stop or slow down, and the soldiers didn't ask us to stop either. They simply kept staring us down, holding their weapons ready and their fingers on the triggers. We were no more than a few feet away from the tanks when we turned on the side street that led to the hospital. The soldiers kept us in their aim until we reached the front gate of the hospital. We breathed a collective sigh of relief, and then focused on the task at hand: investigating developments at the hospital.

Several pools of blood now marked the entrance to the hospital. It was obvious the night had been another bloody one on the east side of town. Al-Janabi came out to greet us. He told us that the hospital had been bombed, again, during the night. The effects of the bombing were clear on the front of the building. He also told us that the hospital received large numbers of wounded people, including Khamis Nimrawi and the baby—the only survivors from the Golan massacre.

Al-Janabi led us to a room where there were two babies staying, one of whom was the Nimrawi toddler. He couldn't have been more than a year old. The other baby was about eighteen months old. Both of them were crying, and what was left of their limbs twitched in pain. Their bodies were wrapped in gauze as though they were being mummified. We filmed the scene in the nursery, and I left the room as soon as we finished. It was too difficult a sight to linger. We aired the footage on al-Jazeera the same day, and the images found a place in my memory alongside those of the children buried in the wreckage of the Golan massacre, and the multitude of other horrors I had seen since we began our coverage just a few days earlier.

We traveled next to Khamis Nimrawi's room, where we found the stricken man distraught, screaming, and demanding things from the staff. Khamis had suffered injuries to his head, hand, and leg. He was angrily calling for the baby who'd survived, even though he hadn't been told yet that anyone had survived the bombing besides him.

He said, "Bring him to me, please! I recognize his cries. He's crying in the other room. I just want to smell him. Please, doctor. I beg you. Tell me I'm not going crazy. I can tell his cries from among a million other babies. It's him, right? The baby survived, right?" He was throwing angry, violent words at the hospital staff and the three of us. He didn't want to really believe that what happened to his family actually did happen, and his pain was obvious. We filmed that painful scene and aired part of the footage the same day.

I knew Nimrawi was in complete shock, but I tried to get him to speak logically, so he could tell the world his story.

I prompted, "Could you please tell me briefly what happened to you? How did only you and the baby survive your ordeal?"

He calmed down just a little bit when I spoke with him, and was able to focus on what I was asking. He began to explain: "We were joined at my house by my three brothers, their wives, and their kids. Their families were all seeking refuge from the indiscriminate bombing of the Americans. So, we were four families in one house—26 people total."

He paused to take a deep breath. It was clearly difficult for him to recall the circumstances of such a tragedy.

"The Americans started bombing in our neighborhood. Everyone ran to one of the interior rooms, thinking they would be safer there. In the midst of the chaos, no one remembered the baby sleeping in another room. I was on the other side of the house while the rest of the family was hidden in a couple of other rooms. Those rooms were all bombed. The only survivors are me and the baby, because we were in other parts of the house.

He paused yet again, and took a shaking breath: "Eight adults are dead, and sixteen young children."

The sad story of this man was unfortunately not unique, and it was certainly not the last evidence of violence we would see in the residential neighborhoods of Iraq. On the following Friday, another resident, Salih al-Issawi would also lose his entire family when his house was hit by an American bomb. When I went to see Salih, I found him in denial and shock just like this man, and unable to dissect the truth from the nonsense.

After we aired the story of the Nimrawi family, it became headline news around the world. General Mark Kimmitt's response to the journalists who were grilling him about the horrifying images couldn't possibly be more cold: "My solution is quite simple: change the channel."

My response to statements like these is to wonder how General Kimmitt would've felt if someone told him to change the channel on September 11, 2001, when every station across the world was broadcasting images of Americans dying at the hands of a foreign monster.

A Collision of Chaos and Grief

Once we finished filming the wounded at the hospital, we went back to the Hadeeds' place. We took the advice of the locals and used a side road in order to avoid heavy shelling as much as possible. We sent the images we had filmed at the hospital to the Doha headquarters for my colleague Lina Zahr Eldin's morning news segment. I also updated the Doha newsroom on the latest developments, and asked them to prepare an in-house report using the images we provided. We didn't have time to prepare the report ourselves because we had to run back downtown to film the funeral procession for Hamed's neighbors' teenage daughter. The funeral procession was planned to take place at 10AM in Fallujah's old cemetery, close to downtown.

We were expecting that this girl's funeral procession would be the only one going on at that time, so I thought I could cover the event alone with the assistance of one cameraman. When Hassan and I arrived at the old cemetery, however, we found a scene quite unlike anything we'd expected. We found countless funeral processions going on at the same time—the cemetery was flooded with fresh coffins and mobs of people paying their respects. These funeral processions were anything but typical. Many of the people attending these funeral processions were intensely angry along with their sadness, and an atmosphere of unrest permeated the entire area.

We began to film the scene in front of us. While we were filming, one of the outraged funeral attendees noticed what we were doing and accused us of being "agents of the murderous occupation." He continued to assault us with related accusations, and with each one, he grew angrier and more obnoxious. His main point seemed to be that we were filming the crowds in order to submit the images to the Americans. Despite the fact that these were supposed to be mournful, solemn, and respectful services honoring the dead, this man's hatred for the Americans would not allow him to honor the grieving process; instead he was literally mad enough to do nothing but assail us with fraudulent accusations.

I can't possibly put in words how much his words hurt me. Before coming to Fallujah to cover this battle, my crew and I had been living in the safety of our homes, away from all this danger, and reporting the news from the comfort of our fancy offices. We had all left that comfort and security and placed ourselves directly in danger—and all to expose the suffering in Fallujah. We were risking our lives, every single minute, so that the rest of the world might know of the misery suffered by this man and by many others like him. I had left behind a pregnant wife who was due any minute, knowing full well that she was going to give birth to my only son in my absence. I came to Fallujah with the full knowledge that I could die before I got the chance to see him and hold him, much less watch him grow up. I didn't leave my wife and my daughters just to come to Fallujah and get pummeled by hurtful comments from those I was trying to help. We weren't expecting this man or any other Fallujan to thank us for doing our job, but we were also not expecting them to accuse us of being agents of the very occupation forces we were working tirelessly to expose to the rest of the world.

I searched the crowd for a face that would lessen the pain brought on by the words of this man—a softer face, a face that showed support and empathy for our work. My search was in vain. While no one rose up to support this man's words, the rest of the crowd simply stared at us in confusion, and did not bother to tell the man to keep quiet, or to deny the truth of his words. I could sense that the deep pain people were feeling for those they were burying that day was overwhelming. This crowd was overrun by sadness, by worry, by confusion.

At that moment I realized that I had more to worry about than the sting of the angry man's accusations. When a crowd teeming with anger and helplessness meets two unarmed outsiders, the outsiders—us, in this case—might find themselves in dire circumstances. One single outspoken man could be a catalyst for an uprising of anger and violence. In no time a mob could develop and turn its sights on the two of us. I was also acutely aware that I was the only non-Iraqi in the crowd, and I was surrounded by angry men accusing me of working with foreign authorities. I knew I would be in a lot of trouble if this escalation didn't end. If just the right combination of pressure and anger took hold of this crowd, the two of us could end up facing the same fate as the mercenaries. There weren't any insurgents at the cemetery, but there were many armed men. They were mostly tribesmen, and it's a normal thing for a tribesman to carry a weapon of some sort, usually a light pistol, at all times. Even though these men weren't insurgents, I knew that the presence of weapons made our situation even worse.

I thought to myself: What next? At first we were worried about being bombed by the Americans, then being murdered by the insurgents, and now we feared the wrath of an armed, angry civilian mob?! Was there anyone in this city not out for blood?

I tried not to let the angry man distract me from my purpose at the cemetery, but the place was tightly packed, and barely left any room for escape from his fiery accusations. The man followed us as we moved through the crowd. All attempts we made to evade him were in vain. He followed right behind us, constantly yelling his accusations. Not a single person stepped forward to say a word in our defense. The situation got worse when people noticed that neither me nor Hassan were Fallujans; they began to consider the validity of this man's accusations. My accent is distinctively Egyptian, and it was clear when I begged off his accusations that I was not a native. Hassan is an Iraqi, but not from Fallujah. Fallujans could easily identify Hassan's Baghdad accent, so he was considered just as much of a foreigner as I was. Our foreign origin made us even greater targets of the mob hatred.

I looked around, and I decided the best solution was to ignore the crazy man. This is what I do most of the time when I encounter this kind of opposition while filming, since most unpleasant situations I face seem better ignored and rarely amount to a clear and present danger.

A man came up to us and whispered something that reinforced my decision. "Don't bother replying to his nonsense. If you are patient, you'll be a better person for it. He's just an emotionally wounded man, like the rest of the living victims you see at these funeral processions."

After this consolation, I continued to bite my tongue. I asked Hassan to try to lead me further away from him. We picked up our pace and made it to the entrance of the cemetery, but he still followed close behind us. At the entrance stood a mosque where people performed the prayer for the dead before burial. There was a new wave of funeral processions coming through the entrance. The sight of more coffins and more funeral processions further agitated the people who were already in the cemetery. Very suddenly, everyone in the crowd was overcome with anger, and it was clear that an explosion of violence wasn't far behind. The man's accusations continued. Enough people eventually noticed Hassan holding the camera and me holding the al-Jazeera microphone, and they suddenly surrounded us. They began to unleash incoherent, angry shouts in our direction. I couldn't make out most of what they were saying, but I could tell that they were accusing us of doing nothing for them, even though we had been broadcasting images and updates from Fallujah since the start of the siege, and had done nothing but work to tell their story to the rest of the world. Somehow, these people felt that we were the party responsible for and capable of lifting the siege and ending the bombardment! I couldn't believe what had come over this crowd.

Obviously, ignoring the man's accusations had not been enough to save Hassan and me from the violence of this crowd. But what other options did I have? I could have lashed out at the man when he was the only one verbally attacking us and it might have scared him off, but that would be unlikely in the face of an entire crowd. Regardless of how effectively I lashed out, I couldn't possibly scare a mob of people into believing my innocence. I figured that my only option was to appeal to their logic, and I hoped that maybe that way I could contain their anger.

I ascended the first few steps of the minaret's staircase. I yelled at the top of my lungs, begging people to quiet down and give me their attention. I shouted for a good amount of time, pleading with them to quiet down, until eventually a hush descended over the crowd. In this silence, I saw their faces searching, asking what I could possibly say to make this situation any less repulsive.

I said, "Listen folks, I have heard some very hurtful and threatening remarks from some of you today. I'm not blaming any of you for your angry comments. Why is this? It's because I'm living with you and going through the same suffering you're enduring." I could see that I had their attention. The anger was fading from their faces, and their attention to logic was returning.

I continued, "I know you're all devastated by what the American forces have done to you, your neighbors, and your families. My cameraman and my crew are here in Fallujah to convey your hurt and suffering to the rest of the world—not to help the American forces. We're living with you every day here, facing the same miserably high odds of getting killed that you're facing. Until this siege is over, we all face the same risks. But this uncontrolled anger isn't helping us broadcast the news of this miserable war. Either you help us, and cooperate with me and the crew, or we'll leave you here and find other developments to film and other stories in this city to share with the world."

I continued, soberly, "Believe it or not, you're even safer than we are, because we are high-profile journalists. At least you get to stay put in your houses most of the time. If the Americans don't bomb the house where you're hiding, you won't be killed. We can't afford the luxury of staying inside. Wherever the Americans bomb, we run to the scene to film and interview. We risk our lives to save your city and your people, and in return we're being accused of being American agents or of failing to lift the siege off the city. Where's the logic in believing that a crew made up of a few men can be responsible for the world's dead silence toward the atrocities being committed against your people? How are we responsible for this? If you don't help us film this war, I'll simply clear myself of any responsibility for conveying your voice to the rest of the world. Is this what you want? I can tell you for sure that I came to Fallujah to film your stories, not to be accused of espionage. What I want is for you to step forward and let go of all your feelings, all your pain, all of your hurt and suffering. Let it all out on my microphone and in front of Hassan's camera. I promise you we will deliver your messages exactly as you want them to be delivered. We won't edit out anything. We'll air it just as we filmed it. This way next time someone accuses us of editing out images or playing with the tapes to deliver intelligence messages to the American forces, you can respond in our defense."

I felt much better after I had spoken out against the man's accusations and those of the angry crowd, and I had managed to dull the crowd's anger in the process. After hearing me speak, people in the crowd became much more cooperative.

While still standing on the high steps, I said, "I'll step down now with my microphone in hand. Hassan will run his camera. Please nominate one or two people to represent you. These people will speak on your behalf because we don't want chaos to break out again. One or two people are enough to deliver your message."

People calmed down, and eventually two people came forward to speak on behalf of the crowd. The first speaker was one of Fallujah's public figures, a man named Shaikh Abdulwahab al-Qaisy. He made a plea on behalf of all Fallujans for the people of the world to stop being silent about the brutality in Iraq. He spoke about the horrific body disposal situation in the city that forced the residents to reopen this abandoned graveyard because there were no other places to bury the dead. He mentioned that old graves were dug open again to accommodate the 50-some victims who were killed within the last two days alone.

The other speaker said, "Americans keep crying 'foul' to the rest of the world when they're faced with violent resistance in Fallujah. Who is the aggressor here? Are we attacking them in their cities? Are we placing their families and children under siege? No. They're the ones who've traveled thousands of miles and crossed continents and oceans to come here to wage war against us. We're obviously in a self-defense situation. They have no right to cry 'foul' regardless of what the resistance does to them. If they don't like the way our resistance works, then they need to leave this country. They can't tell us what's moral or immoral in terms of resistance when they are illegally occupying our land."

He then said a few words in broken English, followed by some Arabic words, in an attempt to deliver a message to Americans. The gist of this message was, "Is this the democracy and freedom America promised us? America must leave Iraq for Iraqis. They must leave us alone to elect our own government instead of bringing with them this so-called Governing Council."

The small crisis of being in the middle of an angry armed crowd was averted, and the anger of the people in the cemetery was expressed on camera. But the bigger crisis of rising fatalities among civilians wasn't averted or contained in any way—that crisis remained the difficult burden of all Fallujans.

A City Held Captive

We stayed at the cemetery and filmed for another hour or so, then walked back to the Hadeeds' place. We wanted to send the images to headquarters in Doha. We had been able to capture a good group of images from the east side of the city along with what we got from the cemetery, and Hamed was able to get images from midtown, the west side, and the Golan Neighborhood, where battles were raging.

By the time we arrived at the Hadeeds', the situation in the Nazzal Neighborhood had become very dire. American forces were making another attempt to penetrate the center of the city. The troops had reached the Guided Caliphs' Mosque and were advancing along Dam Street, where the Hadeeds lived. To avoid the clashes between the insurgents and the rapidly advancing forces, we used back roads and alleys to get to the house. We arrived at the house just in time for al-Jazeera's noon news segment.

I gave a live update on the latest developments in the city amid the constant sound of escalating violence all around the Hadeed home. The 1st Marine Regimental Combat Team, under the command of Colonel John Toolan, was making another attempt at further invading Fallujah by land. These Marine forces were amassing at the Hadeeds' front gate. Quite literally, bullets were coming from every single direction—I had to take cover several times during my report to avoid stray bullets that found their way through the window panes. On top of the constant gunfire, choppers were hovering directly above our heads, and dropping bombs at their leisure. Marines ran up and down the street, yelling commands to one another as they chased the insurgents.

As I was attempting to dodge bullets, one of the missiles entered the room, passed immediately above my head, and exploded in a violent spray of fire. I leapt from the wooden platform I was standing on and jumped for cover, the adrenaline of fear pumping through my body. The rest of the crew ran for cover as well. When the house began to shake from the force of the bomb, the camera became tipsy on the tripod as well. Thinking quickly, Layth snatched the camera and filmed the scene by hand while taking cover. He was able to film me while I continued to provide my live coverage in a very unflattering squatting position, seeking shelter from the assault. Choppers continued to maneuver around the neighborhood, occasionally switching positions and taking turns firing missiles at some of the houses around us. In return, the insurgents fired shoulder-held rockets and showered the Marines with bullets and other projectiles I couldn't recognize. It was a horrifically fierce battle by anyone's standards, and it was raging on all sides of where we were hiding.

Until this violence, we had been filming three stories higher—in the tiny attic on top of the roof. From this spot, we were able to broaden the camera view and catch a small panoramic look at the city. When battles started breaking out directly above our heads, we had been forced to change our filming location to the second floor of the house, the actual roof, so that the attic could provide us with some cover from the battle. Naturally, we couldn't film as much of the city as we were able to before. The cameramen didn't mind standing on top of the attic, but I couldn't allow them to. Although the images were significantly important for our coverage of the battle, the safety of the crew was more important.

My colleague Bassam Elkadiry asked me to have the cameramen point their lenses at the choppers to show the viewers how the choppers were involved in the battle. A battlefield is always far more complicated than what the newsroom people can see, and it's understandable that my colleague didn't see the immense danger that would come from getting such a shot. My colleague and everyone else in the newsroom could only see what the lenses were pointing to, and the cameras were very limited in their movement in such circumstances.

Because of these things, I had to deny his request. "I can't do that. My concern right now is the safety of the crew. I told everyone to leave the roof except for me and the cameramen Layth and Hassan. It's a much more complicated scene than what you can see."

The battle continued raging for about twenty minutes, but it felt like twenty years. When the horrific battle was finally over, so was the uneasy live news segment. We congratulated each other, confident that the risk we had taken in filming the scene outside the Hadeeds' doorstep had paid off. We were able (at least in part) to illustrate for viewers the seriousness of the combat going on in Fallujah. Our crew and the entire al-Jazeera channel wanted to reach millions of viewers with the truth of what was going on in Fallujah, and we were confident we had done so.

I, on the other hand, was hoping to reach millions of viewers except one. That one person was the only thing on my mind after we completed filming this particular battle.

Personal Sacrifices

During my coverage of the siege, my wife was glued to the television set, just like everyone else in the Middle East. I was hoping she'd never see the news segment we'd just filmed. I didn't want her health, or that of the baby boy she was carrying, to be put at risk because of the insanity I was involved in. I desperately hoped she had missed the news segment covering the battle at the doorstep of the Hadeeds' home.

Fortunately, she hadn't been watching television when the battle broke out, but we do have relatives, and the footage was shown all across the world. Immediately after the battle, our family members, friends, and co-workers all placed calls to our home, asking about my safety. When they told her what they saw, she was worried sick and remained that way until I called her that evening. She didn't get to watch that battle footage until much later, when I was preparing the material for this book and watching the taped footage at home. Then she was worried all over again; this time for my safety after spilling the secrets of such amazing horror.

My wife has put up with a lot since our marriage in 1987. She has constantly tolerated hectic work schedules that force me to travel without advance warning, and leave her and my family alone for uncertain periods of time. The uncertainty I cause her to live with whenever a war breaks out is something that most women, and most people, would never be able to sustain. On top of all that, the ever-present danger of my work as a wartime correspondent has to be a continual source of anxiety. She has definitely put up with a lot more than I could personally manage to put up with for anyone, and she has sacrificed more for me than anyone I know.

My wife and I got married during the Afghan war, the coverage of which provided me with enough material to write four books. Despite this dangerous and hectic time, my wife stood by me. She was also a constant source of support in the years that followed, when I spent countless sleepless nights at the office with my manuscripts, trying to get all the information exactly the way I wanted it. My wife was careful to never let me know how scared she was, and tried her best to contain her worries so they didn't add to my anxiety. She has always kept an emergency suitcase packed and stowed under our bed, just in case I get a sudden assignment. That suitcase contains basic survival items, warm clothing, and dried foodstuffs. She keeps another suitcase packed as well—one that doesn't include items of survival—ready at all times for my constant journalistic travels. These two suitcases have been always ready for me—from the day we got married and until this very moment, as I sit and write my chronicles of this war.

In 1990, four years after our marriage and my work in the Afghan war, Iraq invaded Kuwait. Suddenly I was again plunged into a world of chaos and danger. With barely a moment's notice, I was onboard the last commercial airliner to enter Kuwaiti airspace on the eve of the invasion—August 2, 1990. This plane happened to be the British Airways airplane whose passengers were taken to Iraq as hostages, me included. During that entire time, my wife was in Egypt while I was held in Kuwait with no means of communication. She had no idea if I was dead or alive. Nada, my eldest daughter, was born during that unpleasant episode. Saddam Hussein released the last hostages months after the flight. I didn't get to see my first daughter until she was five months old.

My wife also suffered through my experiences covering the Bosnian war in 1994. During this conflict, I was under siege for over a month, and communication was spotty at best. In this American–Iraqi war, Fallujah was the danger interrupting our lives and our security. But she never complained when she called me in Fallujah, and she never took issue with my absence from our home and our family. The only thing I heard from her were wishes for a safe return home. She never asked me to leave Fallujah, or any other war-plagued city for that matter, even though deep down she was trembling in fear. From the first day of our marriage, she realized that my stubborn personality and indelible eagerness to cover any conflict could not be sustained. She knew that no paycheck, no matter how big, could possibly allow me to accept these horrific assignments if I didn't believe that what I was doing was being done for the sake of humanity first and foremost.

This is definitely more than any other woman I know is willing to put up with for the sake of a spouse, and I am in this incredible woman's debt.

US Forces Retaliate: The Emergence of Sniper Power

After the worst of the battle on Dam Street was over, we noticed Marines moving up and down the street performing searches of civilian households. Layth discretely filmed this activity from holes in the edge of the roof. He also filmed tanks and armored vehicles entering Fallujah from the west side aided by a cover of choppers and AC-130 gunships.[30] He wasn't able, though, to film the insurgents firing shoulder-held rockets and unleashing showers of bullets from rooftops and alleys, something they did for the entire length of the six-hour battle.

Some sources estimate that the number of US soldiers who participated in this single west side battle was close to 2,000. This gives us an idea of the real size of forces surrounding Fallujah, a number estimated by some observers to have reached over 10,000 soldiers. This number does not include the other forces that participated in the operation such as the National Guard forces or the New Iraqi Army forces. Captain Christopher Sullivan[31] of the First Battalion, a unit that was participating in the attacks that day, told the media that the purpose of this operation was to arrest small groups of insurgents and terrorists. Obviously, the numbers do not match this supposed purpose.

From Hamed's parents' house, we watched the Marines moving along Dam Street in the direction of the Nazzal Neighborhood. In the midst of the house searches, bombs suddenly fell from the sky—bombs aimed directly at a tire warehouse across the street from the Hadeeds' home. The warehouse went up in flames, and we were lucky enough to film to whole incident from the rooftop of the Hadeeds' house. These sudden bombings were not becoming any less frightening as they became more commonplace. We sent those pictures to al-Jazeera headquarters right away.

After they left Dam Street, the armored vehicles continued along Main Street until they reached downtown. The Marines had advanced on the industrial area and the Nazzal Neighborhood simultaneously, which indicated an even more intense drive to move into the city than there had been in previous days. But soon the insurgents retaliated and went after the Marines, and Dam Street became inaccessible. In fact, we couldn't even peek out the front door.

Hamed was making phone calls and collecting information from all over Fallujah, mostly concerning the movements and advances of the Marines. We continued to compile updates. He had to talk fairly loudly to be heard over the noise of the activity outside. I was speaking just as loudly on the phone to headquarters. In the midst of this, Layth came running down from the attic to hush us.

He spoke with genuine alarm. "Folks, keep it down please! The American forces are surrounding us."

We could tell that he was genuinely frightened. I said, "What's new about that? They have been surrounding us from day one! That's why we're here."

He shook his head urgently, "No, I don't mean us as in the residents of Fallujah. I mean us in this house. You can't look out the window because they might shoot you—they've smashed out all the windows in the building across the street and put in sandbags for their snipers. I'm afraid they're targeting us... or at least are keeping us in their scopes in case they decide to target us."

I understood Layth's fear, but I had started to expect more of the same: the Marines would advance; the insurgents would unleash fire on the Marines; the Marines would retreat.

This time, however, the Marines had made bold advances, and they weren't buckling under the blows of the insurgents. They had taken over a very strategic building in the city—a factory in the industrial area across the street from the Hadeeds' house. Next to the factory, there was a motel that normally provided inexpensive accommodation for factory workers who weren't from Fallujah. The four-story motel was a relatively tall building in Fallujah—most other buildings don't exceed two or three stories. That motel was a constant obstacle when we tried to film swarming warplanes and choppers as they whizzed around the area. It was higher than the Hadeeds' place and obstructed the view of the camera. That building was crucial to anyone hoping to get a good shot at the surrounding buildings—snipers, for instance—so it was no wonder the Marines had sought to take it. It was an important victory.

After they had stormed and occupied the building, the Marines placed an unusual number of snipers on the rooftop of the motel and surrounded them with small fortifications. The snipers were clearly visible at times, and we counted how many there were when we looked at Layth's film. This number of snipers was a clear indication that the Marines were changing their approach. From that point on, everyone and everything in the city was in target range of the snipers. Months later, I would learn that some time during or after the second battle of Fallujah, insurgents leveled that motel with massive explosives, in order to make sure the Marines could no longer enjoy the obvious advantage of its commanding heights.

The intensive use of snipers wasn't the only change in American military strategy around this time. The Americans also started relying heavily on F-16 Fighting Falcon jets,[32] which were pretty much out of reach of the shoulder-held rockets used by the insurgents to gun down several choppers. On this third day alone, the insurgents claimed responsibility for shooting down three choppers and destroying twelve armored vehicles and several military jeeps with small rockets. These heavy losses were good reason for the American forces switch to war machines that were harder to bring down with a small rocket.

As reported by USA Today, the heightened state of emergency and heavy casualty count in these middle days of the battle caused the Pentagon to cancel time-off and leave days for all US occupation forces in Iraq, including pre-approved leave for as many as 24,000 soldiers. The Pentagon needed every soldier on the ground to try to staunch the hemorrhaging of its force. After the difficult third day of the siege, American commanders made plans to bring more troops and reinforcements to Iraq.

It's important to note, though, that the casualty counts among the Marines and the US Army on that third day included only the direct losses the Americans suffered in battle. The losses from the American-trained New Iraqi Army and Iraqi Civil Defense Corps, who were meant to aid American forces, were not part of that count. And in reality, many of these American-trained Iraqi forces bailed on the Americans when the situation spiraled out of control. These "allies" simply ran away in the face of danger.

The bitter disappointment of the unexpected US losses in these first few days of battle are vividly described in Paul Bremer's memoir:

> As the Marines pushed deeper into the city, the Iraqi police and Civil Defense Corps forces backstopping them either abandoned their posts or went over to the other side. The local police commissioner was caught working with the insurgents. Iraqi Civil Defense soldiers had proven to be "useless" according to a senior Marine officer. Almost half of the first battalion of the New Iraqi Army deserted on the way to Fallujah. Of the five battalions of the Civil Defense force in Baghdad, almost a third did not report for duty on Tuesday, April 6—the second day of the siege. The battalions recruited from Sadr City had eighty percent absenteeism. All over the south, Iraqi policemen were absent or passive. "So much for the Iraqis taking over their own security," I told Dick.

In Bremer's account, it is clear how miserable the state of affairs was for American forces trying to execute the offensive on Fallujah in the face of such powerful insurgent forces and the sudden disappearance of those they had trained.

US Forces Target Fallujan Mosques

"… [I]t is prohibited to commit any acts of hostility directed against historic monuments, works of art or places of worship which constitute the cultural or spiritual heritage of peoples, and to use them in support of the military effort."
—Protocol II, Article 16, Fourth Geneva Convention

By this point in the siege, prayer calls were exploding from the speakers of Fallujan mosques almost non-stop. Clerics were using the prayer calls as a forum for begging Fallujans to have patience and not resort to violence. Usually, giving the prayer calls was a job allotted to one man—a cleric or an ordinary worshipper. These calls would come at varying times throughout the day from different mosques throughout the city. When these prayer calls were given from a multitude of mosques simultaneously, the collective noise was quite deafening, even frightening, especially to a person who could not understand the language. For this reason, the effort the clerics took to secure peace in the city seemed to frighten the Marines rather than console them. This would not have been the case if the Marines had been able to understand and decipher each prayer call.

Because of the disturbing noises coming from each mosque, the Marines thought these mosques were housing bands of armed insurgents making battle cries, when in reality most of the time the only person in these mosques when prayer calls were made was an unarmed old man, straining his voice in prayer in front of a microphone. In a desperate effort to quiet these prayer calls, Marines began attacking mosques, claiming that insurgents were taking up fortifications there. After their big advance on the third day, the Marines sent snipers to the tops of the minarets of the Guided Caliphs' mosque. Once there, they used the minarets as outposts from which to aim at people in the Officers' Neighborhood, the Nazzal Neighborhood, and the Military Neighborhood. A resident of the Officers' Neighborhood called to inform us that one of the snipers at the Guided Caliphs' Mosque used this vantage point to kill his eighteen-year-old son.

After the snipers took up residence on the minarets, we started getting reports from the field hospital of a huge increase in the number of dead and wounded shot by snipers. The casualty counts included women, children, and elderly people—not just young, agile men whom one might imagine being involved in the insurgency. I was able to talk with one of these victims, a 75-year-old man, during a visit to the field hospital. Another person we interviewed during that same visit was a man who'd lost two young brothers to sniper fire, and his parents were critically injured. During this visit, we also filmed several minors, including very young children, who were killed or injured by snipers. These were not accidental casualties. These deaths and injuries were inflicted by trained snipers, who had the unfortunate victims in the bull's-eye view of their scopes.

With snipers in place on the minarets of the Guided Caliphs' Mosque, the Marines began an attack on the Abdulaziz Samarray Mosque, in the Nazzal Neighborhood. This was also the headquarters of AMSI. We were a couple hundred yards away from the mosque when the attack began.

Before ordering Marine troops to storm the mosque, Lt. Colonel Brennan Byrne, commander of the First Battalion, Fifth Marine Regiment, called in a heavy air strike.

Later, when pressed for an explanation for the bombing, Byrne was quoted in the *Sydney Morning Herald* saying that the Abdulaziz Samarray Mosque was bombed because "we wanted to kill the people inside," which he and his men took to be about 40 armed insurgents. Another spokesperson for US forces was quoted in the *Washington Post* on April 8 confirming that F-16 fighter jets fired a missile at the mosque and dropped a 500-pound bomb in order to destroy part of the outer wall and expose the insurgents hiding within. From the Central Command headquarters in Tampa, Florida, Captain Bruce Frame said that the initial information he received stated that the bombing of the mosque happened after five Marines were fired at from within the mosque, an act that forced the Marines to release the bombs from above.

The US forces maintained that because of the attacks from the estimated 40 insurgents hiding within it, the mosque lost its religious protection under the Geneva Conventions and became fair game as a military target. Despite the great lengths these US military officials went to in order to justify the attack on this mosque, however, when the Marines finally broke into the mosque from the ground they found no evidence whatsoever of insurgents. In fact, there were no bodies at all in the mosque—living or dead—to suggest that this mosque had recently been an insurgent outpost. It was clear from this discovery that the Americans had either taken the opportunity to bomb a sacred Iraqi relic for the satisfaction of revenge or had not truly had sufficient evidence to assume this mosque to be a dangerous hiding place for the enemy.

Paul Bremer spoke of this event in his memoir as well. He writes,

> The 1 MEF pressed ahead in Fallujah, with the Marines encountering in-depth defensive positions, with machine guns and mortar pits protected by riflemen and snipers. The enemy was fighting out of schools, hospitals, apartment buildings, and mosques, just as Saddam's forces had done. As the fighting increased, casualties mounted and Al-Jazeera documented each one. A Marine Cobra gunship fired a missile at a sniper in the minaret of a mosque killing more than ten Iraqis, most likely all insurgents. But the edited television images provoked a sharp emotional response from Iraqis across the country.

Although I never did like Bremer's memoir, I liked this paragraph, for selfish reasons. Bremer admitted that our crew "documented each one" of the casualties that were mounting due to the American forces' indiscriminate bombing, and I appreciate when a man gives credit where it's due.

We received footage of the mosque bombing from an Iraqi engineer who lived in the Nazzal Neighborhood. He had filmed the bombing with his handheld camcorder, and then risked his life to run through the streets and get the footage to our crew at the Hadeeds' place. The footage showed the Americans clearly targeting the minaret, and therefore proved that this bombing was undoubtedly intentional. After we reviewed the footage, we broadcast the images to Doha, and they in turn played the footage repeatedly during breaking news bulletins.

The bombing of this mosque along with other controversial bombings around the country put Paul Bremer in a difficult situation. He had an understandably hard time justifying the actions of his country's forces to members of the Iraqi Governing Council. During their April 7 meeting, which was attended by Bremer and Rick Sanchez, Bremer had to listen to several Iraqi representatives speak very emotionally about their opposition to the "ruthless attacks" the Marines were waging on Fallujah. One representative after another took turns to speak about the miserable state of affairs in the city. In his memoir, Bremer mentions the weak argument he used in response to the Governing Council members: "When they had finished, I asked for the floor. 'We all regret the loss of innocent life,' I said. Without giving credence to Al-Jazeera, I noted that in every war civilian casualties occurred. Our military took extraordinary care to avoid them."

When Bremer was confronted by Governing Council members instead of Iraqi citizens or non-American media, his primary concern was still not to "give credence" to al-Jazeera. Even though we had nothing to do with his miserably weak situation, he was concerned with how we'd "spin the story" as he puts it in another part of his memoir. What he really should've worried about was how to end the senseless, indiscriminate bombing that his army was carrying out. At the very least, he should have been concerned with whitewashing the image of his forces, and not with what al-Jazeera had to say.

Following the attack on the mosque and the statements made by American forces, the imams and clergymen of Fallujah issued a public statement, and sent a copy to us. We read some of this statement during our live broadcast. The statement warned occupation forces not to violate the sanctity of places of worship. It said, "Occupation forces desecrated our mosques, and we want to declare to them that our mosques represent a red line that cannot be crossed, because they are symbols of our dignity."

The bombing of the Abdulaziz Samarray Mosque did not only enrage Iraqis and Muslims. Non-Muslims around the globe were upset by this development. In an April 8 article in the *Independent*, Robin Cook, former secretary of state for foreign and commonwealth affairs of the United Kingdom, wrote an article entitled, "Iraq will never be sorted out until Mr. Blair and President Bush admit their mistakes." In the article, Cook commented, "The first step is for the US to stop making things worse by trying to crush any resistance with overwhelming force." He continued later, "The second step should be to medi-vac Paul Bremer for a period of compulsory rest and recuperation in case he really is daft enough to storm a mosque." Cook echoed the common international call for Bremer to step down following this particular bombing.

The Abdulaziz Samarray Mosque wasn't far from the Hadeeds', but we were surrounded by Marines and unable to get out to the site to film anything in person. Any movement would have put us right in the line of sniper fire. Hamed called the people who were living right next to the mosque, and asked if any insurgents had been seen going in or out of the mosque before the bombing occurred. The answer was a definite no. One of the people Hamed called added, "There were definitely no insurgents during the day, but there were calls for prayers and patience blaring out the speakers of the minaret all day long. The Marines may have been scared of these calls, so they bombed and then claimed there were 40 insurgents inside. We didn't see a single insurgent. The only person that we know of inside the mosque was the man praying."

Hamed asked if it was possible to get Shaikh Makky Kubaisy, the head cleric at the Abdulaziz Samarray Mosque, to speak about the incident, which was attracting attention as far away as Washington, DC. Hamed's thought was that instead of leaving the story open for the military to spin all sorts of fairy tales about the mythical 40 insurgents, it would be better to bring the man in charge of the mosque to speak candidly about what happened. It wasn't easy, though, to get a hold of the shaikh, considering the siege around our immediate area. And night was starting to fall.

Once again, Hamed's bravery helped us out of a tough situation. Despite the danger, Hamed snuck out of the Hadeeds' home under the cover of night. He then made his way downtown by leaping from one house to the next until he was out of range of the snipers, and eventually he was able to find the shaikh and bring him back to the Hadeeds' place. I called my colleague Saeed Alshoely and told him that we had with us the man in charge of the bombed mosque, who also happened to be the Fallujan representative of AMSI. Saeed, who has always been cooperative and professional, said he was ready to put the shaikh on the air immediately. I told him that I preferred to have the shaikh appear on the *Day's Harvest*, since that's the longest news segment of the day and would allow the shaikh more time to talk. And we weren't in any hurry because he had to stay with us overnight anyway; it was too late and too risky to send him home that night, and we didn't want the Marines to shoot him dead for violating the curfew.

When the shaikh appeared on the *Day's Harvest*, his words about the bombed mosque were extremely damaging to the image of the American forces in the international media. He spoke about the details surrounding the mosque bombing, and noted that no one living in the surrounding houses saw any insurgents enter or exit the building. This testimony forced the US forces to retract their earlier statements and admit that there had been no insurgents inside the mosque. When asked about this inconsistency, Lt. Colonel Byrne offered that the insurgents had been hiding in the mosque, and had run out after the first missile was fired from the air. He also said that it was possible that the insurgents vacated their dead from the scene after the bombs were dropped and before the Marines stormed the area, which would explain the absence of corpses. Byrne summarized this situation in this simplistic way, "When we hit that building, I thought we had killed all the bad guys, but when we went in they didn't find any bad guys in the building." Because reporters continued to press him, he eventually caved in and admitted that he had no idea why the insurgents weren't in the mosque and therefore could not logically justify the bombing.

General Kimmitt, however, refused to admit that his forces were unjustified in bombing the mosque. In an interview on al-Jazeera, Kimmitt admitted that a mosque "has a special status under the Geneva Convention that it can't be attacked." But then he qualified this, saying that "it can be attacked when there is a military necessity." His addendum to the Geneva Convention was so enraging that my colleague Katia Nasser offered open ridicule in a news report later that day. In a report that quoted Kimmitt, she commented, "This was General Kimmitt's fatwa [religious ruling or decree], legalizing the targeting of places of worship."

This new strategy of the American forces—destroying mosques as a form of subduing violence—lasted through the second battle of Fallujah, which happened seven months after the bombing of the Abdulaziz Samarray Mosque. By November 2004, most mosques in Fallujah had suffered damage of some kind. These damaged mosques remain as evidence of the severe campaign the Americans took against the cultural and religious identity of the city.

New American Strategy; New American Weapons

On the day of the mosque bombing, F-16 Fighting Falcons began to take the place of the helicopters. Hussain Deli was able to capture good images of these planes as they bombed the already assaulted areas in the Golan Neighborhood. A spokesman for the US forces later acknowledged the use of this type of aircraft—these killing machines have incredible maneuverability, awesome firepower, and can fly at altitudes and speeds that are far beyond the capability of the simple mortar fire the insurgents were using. The use of these fighter jets meant the potential for serious devastation to residential buildings, massive damage to residential neighborhoods, and much higher civilian casualty counts. Naturally, by the end of their first day in use, there were over 150 Fallujans either killed or injured—including women and children—and these victims could all be attributed to the US forces' use of the F-16. This casualty count doesn't even include unrecoverable bodies from the huge number of homes that were completely obliterated in the Golan, Officers', Military, Educators', and Nazzal neighborhoods, along with the industrial area.

When Hussain called to tell me that he captured images of widespread bombing by F-16s, I told him to come back to the Hadeeds' immediately. We needed to air those images as soon as possible in order to prove the reality of our charges of indiscriminate bombing. Until that point, US forces were denying the use of F-16s. They claimed their bombing was only done by helicopters in order to minimize damage to civilians. Hussain said he was only a hundred yards or so from us, but he couldn't quite get to us because he had to cross the street that separated him from the Hadeeds' place, and there were snipers everywhere. I asked him to wait it out until night fell so he could cross a little more safely.

Hussain, however, did not heed my advice. He waited until what he considered to be an open chance to cross, and made the risky passage before evening fell. I was ecstatic when I saw him arrive in one piece. I wanted him to wait until it was time to air the next news segment so he could talk live about the footage he had shot. He hesitated because he had never appeared on camera before, but with a little bit of encouragement, he agreed. The news segment, however, was slightly delayed because of a live broadcast of the program *From Washington*. Hussain refused to wait any longer because he wanted to go downtown to film the casualties and the aftermath of the bombing. We ended up airing Hussain's footage of the F-16 raids on residential neighborhoods without him being present. We also aired footage he captured of insurgent activity around the Golan Neighborhood—images of insurgents firing mortar rockets at the Marines situated on the other side of the Euphrates, and insurgents retaliating against fire from F-16s.

When we aired this telling footage, it was rebroadcast around the world. Americans could no longer continue their denial about their fighting tactics—they acknowledged the use of fighting and killing machines like the F-16, at once admitting to the new strategy they'd adopted in this war.

Without Limits, *Without Script*

Without Limits was regularly scheduled to air on Wednesdays. I had planned to do the show that week from Baghdad—I didn't know that I'd be under siege in Fallujah. This week's episode was the first of a two-part show that I had prerecorded, wherein some former commanders of the Iraqi Army talk about the fall of Saddam's regime a year before. I had already finished doing the montage for the first part of the video and had left the tape at the Baghdad office, but I hadn't recorded the introduction. I arranged for my colleague Imad Bahjat, the show's director in Doha, to air a live introduction from Fallujah, and they could then air the prerecorded segment of the show from the Baghdad bureau.

But I couldn't sit down to write a proper introduction for the show because of the constant chaos in the makeshift headquarters we'd set up at the Hadeeds'. It was difficult to improvise an intro on air, but I had no choice. I stood before the camera, and in no time I heard the director giving his order to play the theme music for the show. He then prompted me to begin.

I tried to improvise as best I could. "Good evening. Welcome to this week's episode of *Without Limits* airing from Fallujah, the city that's currently under siege by American occupation forces in Iraq. I had no plans or expectations to open this show from Fallujah, but I, along with the crew, find myself under siege. But there is a bright side to everything—even this siege has its lucky moments. The same fate that kept us under siege has also made tonight's show possible, because it was prerecorded. The former Iraqi military officers featured in tonight's show couldn't speak on air due to security reasons, so the show had to be prerecorded. Tonight's segment is the first of a two-part show, which means that my crew and I are prepared to stay under siege until next week, when the second part is set to air.

"For the past three weeks, I have been traveling across the villages and towns of Iraq in search of senior military officers who participated in the battle for Baghdad, which ultimately resulted in the fall of the Iraqi regime on April 9, 2003. In my interviews with these men, I was trying to answer the questions that many of my viewers are asking: What's the secret behind the fall of Baghdad—why was it that easy for American forces to take over? Why didn't the Iraqi Army and the Republican Guard stand their ground? Most officers I approached refused to speak on camera, and some of them refused to even meet with me. However, I found other former officers who did agree to share their experiences. In this episode of *Without Limits* I present you with testimony from two former senior officers. One of them agreed to go on record, audio and video, with his real name and identity being known. He is Brigadier General Muzher al-Obaidy. The other guest is a former officer in the Republican Guard, and he agreed to speak under the condition that his identity is kept hidden from the public. Please stay tuned to hear their accounts after the break."

Although the introduction was improvised, I was confident that I had given the viewers a glimpse of the situation in Fallujah, and confident that I had explained how everything we were experiencing was tied to the recent history of this war—including the fall of Saddam's regime.

George Bush Reacts

The political fallout from the events in Fallujah obviously caught the attention of the White House staff. Press agencies reported the day of the mosque bombing that George Bush spoke to his best ally, Tony Blair, and scheduled an urgent meeting to be held on April 16 to discuss this new development. This meeting was of great significance, because in this meeting the two also intended to discuss Bush's intention to target al-Jazeera with bombs and other weapons because of our coverage of Fallujah. The story of this meeting was exposed by the British *Daily Mirror*, and I'll discuss this scandal further later in the book. On the day after the bombing, Bush also held a meeting with the National Security Council to discuss the situation in Iraq.

Paul Bremer also speaks in his memoir about two video-conference National Security Council (NSC) meetings attended by George Bush, Dick Cheney, Colin Powell, Condoleezza Rice, Dick Myers, Bob Blackwill, General John Abizaid, and himself. In these meetings, the group discussed how the military situation in Iraq was spinning out of the control of American forces. As we know, the situation was particularly bad in Fallujah and Muqtada al-Sadr's territories. Bremer writes,

> I was staring at the video image of the White House SitRoom as General Abizaid ran through a series of slides. He listed various cities:
> "Baghdad. Situation calm."
> "Nasariya. Situation calm."
> "Najaf. Situation calm."
> Making sure our microphone was off, I turned to Bob Blackwill:
> "It's as if a British general were to brief London in July 1940. Paris. Situation calm. Right. The city happens to be in enemy hands."

Bremer lists other details of the meeting in this part of his book, and then writes, "At the end of the meeting, the President said, 'we need to be tougher than hell now. The American people want to know we're going after the bad guys. We need to get on the offensive and stay on the offensive.' So we all had our marching orders."

In the next few days, news came of the further deteriorating situation in Fallujah and the "stiff opposition" the Marines were facing there, and Condoleezza Rice called for yet another NSC meeting. Now they needed to work out the specifics of being "tougher than hell." A series of NSC meetings, one briefing after another, and a constant stream of papers moved through the White House to update Bush on the latest developments in Fallujah.

Back in Iraq, AMSI issued a statement declaring a boycott of the United Nations until the Security Council issued a condemnation of American military actions in Iraq. Lakhdar Brahimi, the UN secretary-general's envoy to Iraq, failed to condemn American military actions despite his disagreement with American policies. In his memoir, Bremer writes,

> The next morning, Bob Blackwill, who was meeting daily with Brahimi, told me that he sensed Brahimi was close to abandoning his mission. The level of violence was frustrating his efforts to meet with Iraqis, and he disagreed strongly with our approach to Fallujah. I immediately called him to urge him to stay on. Later, I called Secretary Powell to suggest he pass Kofi Annan the same message.

Bremer concludes, "In the end Brahimi agreed to remain, 'for now.'"

It wasn't a surprise that Bremer was pleading with Brahimi to stay in Iraq. The US was desperate for support. All military and political ambitions were seriously suffering, and the image of American forces in Iraq was being tarnished by the media coverage of their behavior in Fallujah. The Marines turned out to be far weaker in this battle than they claimed they would be, as illustrated by the losses they were enduring at the hands of the insurgents. They also turned out to be much, much less diligent than any army should be in terms of guarding against the needless slaughter of civilians. Any global support, even if it was indirect support from members of the United Nations, was greatly appreciated by Bremer and other parties supporting the American mission in Iraq.

AMSI called for a peaceful protest in light of the mosque bombing and other actions of the American forces. The protest was to start in Baghdad on the morning of Thursday, April 8, and move toward Fallujah in an effort to break the siege around the city. This call for a peaceful protest found Iraqis all over the country listening with intense interest. By then, Iraqis were fed up with news of massacres, and welcomed a message of peace.

Destruction Wrought by American Snipers

Just before night fell on the third day of the siege, I made a foolish mistake. I tried to discreetly capture some still images of the Marines—the snipers in particular—using a small camera facing out the window of the Hadeeds' home. The flash on the camera was set to be auto-triggered by the percentage of light available in room. It was not quite dark yet, and I thought there was enough light out for the flash not to go off. I zoomed in on one of the snipers until I had them in perfectly clear view. Then, I slowly moved the curtains aside and snapped a picture. The light from the flash blinked very visibly, despite the amount of light in the room. I knew the sniper must have seen my attempt to catch him on film.

I was horrified. I moved slowly away from the window, and told everyone to stay out of the living room. One of the guys scoffed at my anxiety, and said that clearing the living room was unnecessary. I told him we couldn't be too careful. Just the night before, the snipers had shot the neighbors' unarmed eighteen-year-old daughter for simply looking out the window. These people were capable of a multitude of unimaginable things. We were taking pictures of this army and their inhumanity in order to show the whole world. We would definitely be a target if we showed our presence to these soldiers in any visible way. Because of my mistake,

I expected the room to be flooded with fire at any moment. We stayed out of the living room until night fell. At that time we felt confident that the snipers wouldn't see us and went back into the room.

The night after the mosque bombing was our first night going to bed under the direct threat of snipers. At this point, the electricity was cut off in the entire city. The only thing that defied the pitch-black darkness in our temporary shelter of the Hadeeds' home was the light from a few candles and one kerosene lantern. We had a small power generator, but we didn't want to use it. Fuel supplies were very low, and we needed to save those for running the broadcast equipment and charging batteries for the cameras.

Because we had no idea how bad the situation would get, we thought we'd check the fuel supplies just to be sure there was indeed enough left for recharging our equipment. What we found out was very disappointing—we had barely enough for a few hours of power. If we ran out of fuel, we'd be totally cut off from Doha because we wouldn't be able to broadcast anything. Our whole mission would come to a halt.

Abo Omar, the chauffeur, mentioned that his car had gas in its tank, and since we were no longer using his car, he suggested we suck the gas out of the tank and use it in the generator. His car was parked in the Hadeeds' front yard, facing Dam Street, the side of the house no longer usable due to the constant presence of snipers. Because of this, we refused to let him go to get the gas. It was too risky. Abo Omar was angered by our objections, and yelled that he was up for the challenge; he was not any less brave than Hamed, and could cross into the front yard to get the gasoline just like Hamed had crossed the smugglers' road to get the replacement satellite transmitter. We knew he was stubborn, but we also knew he was a little bit on the clumsy side. If he went outside, he would probably end up making a lot of noise. So, we told him that if he believed he must go, then he should at least keep quiet so that the snipers couldn't hear him.

Abo Omar moved carefully through the front room, listening to the sounds coming from the building facing the Hadeeds' home. The Marines were talking loudly to one another. We, on the other hand, whispered, in fear of being heard or noticed. Abo Omar stepped outside the door. He was only gone a matter of moments before he came right back inside, trembling in fear. He shut the door and stood with his back against it. He was gasping for air and clearly shaken.

I held him by the shoulders and whispered in fear, "What happened?"

He was unable to talk for a few seconds, and then he explained, "Just as I headed toward the car, I saw a red laser dot on my chest. A sniper spotted me within less than a second of walking out the door! I dropped to the ground expecting to be shot any second. I crawled back to the house and rushed back inside."

He wiped a hand over his face in disbelief: "How in the world did he spot me so fast? I didn't make any noise, and his people were making all sorts of obnoxious noises. There are no lights in the house or the entire city—the Marines have all the lights."

Hamed came into the living room at that moment and heard Abo Omar. "Snipers don't need to see you or hear you to spot you," Hamed explained. "They use thermal detection. That's how night-vision goggles work. They don't need lights to see you. It could be pitch black, and you could be dead silent, and they'll still spot you. If I knew you were going out I would've stopped you! You could have been shot in a matter of seconds!"

I felt then that Abo Omar and I had a new lease on life—we had both had close encounters with snipers' barrels, but somehow we had both gotten away with it. I couldn't help but think that we might run out of luck, because we had certainly had our share of near-misses.

After this close encounter, we left the broadcast dish on the rooftop but moved the rest of the broadcast equipment downstairs. When we first started covering the Fallujah battle, we'd been on top of the roof. As the violence escalated, we gradually descended. That night, when I appeared on air, I was in the backyard, away from the view of the snipers and speaking as softly as I could. By then, we were unable to film anything since we were so low on the ground, and we had to rely on whatever footage Hussain Deli shot downtown, along with the few images Layth was able to capture in his risky manner.

As we sat helpless on the first floor of the Hadeeds' home, we realized how tight a grip the snipers had over the neighborhood we were in. We were barely able to move, and the simplest of tasks became life threatening. We didn't talk about our dangerous situation when we were on air, though. We didn't want the rest of the colleagues in Doha to get concerned, as long as we were still able to manage somehow. The rear entrance to the house was still relatively safe to use, so we were not totally out of commission. But still, we knew that any slight movement would get us right back in line of the snipers' fire. We were at the constant mercy of the snipers, and we were never able to forget that fact.

10. DAY FOUR: IRAQIS UNITE

We weren't sure what to expect after Wednesday's tumult—the funeral processions, the mosque bombings, and the appearance of F-16s and snipers—but every new day in this battle brought new dangers and new surprises. Thursday, April 8, turned out to be a historic day for Iraq, and for me. It was the first time in my life I saw Iraqis from all walks of life—people of varying ethnicities, sects, tribes, and subcultures—unite as one. The irritating sectarian speech that I had grown accustomed to hearing in the Iraqi streets disappeared. Even the insurgents, whom I thought would never have the wisdom or intellect to set aside their differences and work together, united. People across Iraq were throwing aside their cultural differences and uniting in support of the people in Fallujah.

To an outsider, this unification may seem rather unremarkable; it may appear that Iraqis are all the same, and operate under the same set of beliefs and moral codes. That is anything but the truth. The only thing that united Iraqis during the first year of this conflict was the fact that they bore arms against US forces and carried a militant hatred for the American occupation. Otherwise, insurgents and militant groups in Iraq suffered a vast sea of differences, some of which turn them against each other despite their common nationality. Some differences are rooted in opposing religious views; others are driven by different philosophies about Iraqi patriotism. Some Iraqis are Ba'athists; others see Ba'athism as the most hideous ideology in history. Many insurgents preferred working with Americans to working with an opposing group of insurgents.

None of these divisions held fast, however, on the fourth day of this siege. On this day, insurgents united in solidarity with the citizens of Fallujah, and managed to shoot down the sixth helicopter since the start of the siege of Fallujah. The helicopter crashed and burst into flames in a farming field next to the Anbar School in the Golan Neighborhood. And the insurgents adopted the same strategy as the Marines—they began to employ snipers in battle.

As the insurgents were planting snipers around the city of Fallujah, Muqtada al-Sadr's Mahdi Army was escalating its rebellion against American forces in every major city in the southern part of the country: Karbala, Najaf, Kufa, al-Kut, and Thawra City (Revolution City) in Baghdad. This day was by far the biggest victory for the insurgents in this region of Iraq, and the effects were seen far beyond the borders of Fallujah.

The most effective maneuver the insurgents managed against American forces was to cut off their supplies, and effectively turn the military situation on its head by placing American troops in and around Fallujah under siege. The main supply line for the American troops was the Baghdad–Fallujah highway, which passes through Abu Ghraib. In support of the suffering Fallujans, insurgents affiliated with a variety of different groups and beliefs came from all over Iraq in order to intensify attacks on American troops on that highway. American forces were pummeled by mortar fire and shoulder-held rockets. Insurgents set up ambush sites all along the highway, and these ambushes continued all night long. By Thursday morning, insurgents had managed to destroy and incinerate more than ten trailers that were loaded with foodstuffs and other supplies intended for the Marines.

Al-Jazeera and other international media and press agencies filmed the burning trailers, along with scenes of locals looting the contents. It was clear that these attacks on supply convoys were not arbitrary. The insurgents essentially turned the Baghdad–Fallujah highway into a graveyard for charred American military supply trailers. These ambushes were undeniably synchronized, carefully planned, and professionally executed ruthless attacks. These attacks scared the chauffeurs who were working for the Americans, understandably so, and eventually they refused to deliver supplies to the Marines around Fallujah. American forces were forced to airlift supplies and deliver them by helicopters. This caused great delay in the replenishment of supplies, and further weakened the American effort.

Northeast of Fallujah, the insurgents destroyed seven military vehicles on one of the most important supply roads for American forces—the only alternative route to the international highway that connects Iraq to Syria and Jordan—and now had complete control of that route. A few days later, on April 11, I traveled down this particular road and found it still under the control of insurgents. There was not a single American soldier anywhere on the 95 miles of highway.

On the Amreyat al-Fallujah Road, there was even more evidence of insurgent attacks. Insurgent groups managed to destroy a convoy of American military vehicles that consisted of three trailers loaded with supplies and two Humvee vehicles that were supposed to protect the trailers as they delivered their supplies.

Along with these attacks on supply routes, military confrontations with American forces also escalated in Tikrit, Samarra, Mosul, Baqubah, and throughout the Diyala and Anbar provinces. The American grip on the country was slipping, and signs of defeat were surrounding American forces all across Iraq. This was all happening on April 8, on the eve of the first anniversary of the American occupation of Iraq.

The Media and the US Government React

Partly because the historic anniversary of American occupation coincided with such a rash of violence in Iraq, observers and commentators in the Western media wrote extensively about the crisis. The *Guardian* reported that Bush, Blair, and Bremer had started a war that would eventually lead to their demise. The *New York Times* reported that American forces were facing widespread uprisings across Iraq—and these uprisings were not just led by Muqtada's militia, as the Bush administration was claiming.

The setbacks the American forces were experiencing also coincided with the resignation of Richard Perle, one of the kingpins of Bush's core group of supporters, and a leading architect of the war on Iraq. His resignation was seen as the start of defeat for Bush's entire group of hawkish radicals, and perhaps the true start of America's defeat in Iraq. Perl also called for the resignation of George Tenet, the director of the CIA. Tenet eventually resigned in July 2004 amid widespread criticism of the conduct and intelligence reports of the agency.

Three years after his resignation, on April 29, 2007, Tenet made a major accusation on CBS's *60 Minutes*. He attacked the Bush administration, Cheney and Rice in particular, for using him as a scapegoat for their blunders in Iraq. Tenet said he was "thrown overboard" after his seven-year service as director of the CIA. He said the administration made him look "stupid" and that "men of honor [didn't] do this." He described the Bush administration's characterization of him as "the most despicable thing[s] I've ever heard in my life." Tenet then said, "The only thing you have is trust and honor in this world. It's all you have. All you have is your reputation built on trust and your personal honor. And when you don't have that anymore, well, there you go. Trust was broken." When Scott Pelley, the *60 Minutes* reporter, asked him if the trust he was referring to was the trust between him and the White House, Tenet replied, "You bet. You bet."

Tenet's memoir, *At the Center of the Storm*, was published in May 2007, around the fourth anniversary of the American occupation of Iraq. When the book came out, it was one of the most controversial books of the year. Tenet, who was trusted with America's most important secrets from the time of his appointment in 1997 until he resigned (or, arguably, was forced to resign) in 2004, used the book as a forum to wage an attack against the Bush administration and their plans for invading Iraq.

Tenet was only one of the many people Bush would turn his back on during the Iraq war, one of the many people he would sacrifice to save American face. The use of scapegoats became more and more common during the first battle of Fallujah, as American forces suffered greater and greater losses. When defeat in Iraq resulted in a series of nasty games in Washington, there was going to be more than just one victim. One by one, the neoconservatives started eating their own words and Bush turned his back on them.

Later in April, after the disaster in Fallujah, William Kristol acknowledged that these shifts in personnel represented a fundamental change in the thinking of neoconservatives because of mistakes that were made.[33] These remarks appeared in an issue of Kristol's rightwing magazine, the *Weekly Standard*. Robert Kagan, one of Kristol's closest allies, and a co-founder of the Project for the New American Century (PNAC) with Kristol in 1997, agreed in an article published in *Foreign Affairs*. In this article, Kagan contended that the Iraq war was going was making neoconservatives reconsider their priorities.

As for Paul Bremer, he expresses the level of defeat he and the American occupation forces were suffering on the eve of the anniversary of American occupation in his memoir:

> On the morning of April 8, the twin military crises provoked a full-scale political crisis. First, Interior Minister Nouri Badran, who commanded the flagging Iraqi Police Service, submitted his resignation. Even though he cloaked the move in the standard "personal reasons," it was unsettling that he abandoned the government during the ongoing crises. Next, Abu Hatem, the legendary Shiite warrior from the south—the "Lord of the Marches" who held sway over vital tribes along the border with Iran—suspended his membership in the Governing Council. I had visited his tribal homelands in the marshes in September and had seen how popular Abu Hatem was down there.
>
> I reached him on his cell phone in his tribal home in the southern city of Amara and asked him to reconsider. "Let me think," he said. "This is a difficult period." We agreed to meet the next day.
>
> Within minutes, Minister of Human Rights Abdel Basit Turki announced his resignation. He was a moderate Sunni with family and clan ties in the Anbar Province. Next we heard that Pachachi, the senior

GC member, was outraged by the Fallujah operation, which he publicly labeled "collective punishment." He too was on the verge of resigning.

Less than an hour later, Hachem al-Hassani, who represented the Sunni Iraqi Islamic Party, came in to tell me that his party's politburo had voted to "leave the Governing Council" in protest over the Marine offensive in Fallujah. Hachem added that Ghazi al-Yawar, one of the most prominent Sunnis on the Governing Council, also planned to quit the Council that afternoon.

"You must call for an immediate cease-fire in Fallujah," Hachem insisted. He wanted to lead a GC delegation to Fallujah to talk to the city's leaders about resolving the crises.

He begins the following section with an even more anxious line: "We were at the most critical crisis of the occupation. The stakes couldn't be higher."

In this section of his memoir, Bremer also talks about how the messy work of the Marines in Fallujah brought Iraq to the brink of total political collapse:

> It was evident that continuing military operations in Fallujah would result in the collapse of the entire political process and force the postponement of Iraqi sovereignty. I was sure this would cause an upsurge in the insurgency and the deaths of more Americans. At the same time, I felt we needed to continue vigorous military operations against Muqtada.

Bremer thus makes clear in his memoir the defeat the US was facing in the first battle of Fallujah and acknowledges that the Iraqi Governing Council was merely a tool for American occupation to gain legitimacy. Without Iraqis who accepted a role in the political process, the occupation would've collapsed from the beginning. The Governing Council was merely a way of making the occupation more amenable to some of the Iraqi public. But even the Governing Council couldn't politically cover for the United States in the face of what was unfolding in Fallujah.

The March for Peace

AMSI's call for a peaceful protest found many willing participants. Thousands upon thousands of Iraqis from all sects and ethnicities orchestrated a massive protest that traveled from Baghdad to Fallujah—and this activity included the cooperation of infamously opposed Sunni and Shia Muslims. These crowds were chanting as they marched, "Sunnis and Shiites watch each other's back; we will not sell out Iraq."

Along with the peaceful march of protest, the Iraqi Red Crescent sent a huge convoy of trailers to Fallujah loaded with humanitarian aid, medicine, medical supplies and equipment, canned goods, and fresh produce. This entire fleet headed to Fallujah with the intention of breaking the siege, entering the city, and making an entry point for the rest of the convoys of humanitarian aid coming from all over Iraq.

Shaikh Ahmad Abdulghafour Samarray, imam of Umm-ul-Qurra Mosque in Baghdad, issued a statement that Agence France-Presse reported later that day:

> The Red Crescent negotiated with the coalition forces for an entire day to get permission to get these humanitarian aid shipments allowed in Fallujah. We finally got the permission. The shipments contain medical supplies, fruits, vegetables, other foodstuffs, and donated blood to the people of Fallujah. We want to express solidarity with our brethren in Fallujah who are being subjected to bombing and shelling by tanks and airplanes. People are making very generous donations. Some women even donated their entire collection of jewelry for the benefit of Fallujans.

My colleague Abdulazeem Muhammad, who managed to enter Fallujah with the Red Crescent convoy, said that people were donating everything they owned to help relieve the pain and suffering of Fallujans.

The American forces, though, stopped the entire convoy of Red Crescent trucks just outside the road that leads to Fallujah. After hours of grueling negotiations, they allowed only a few small trucks, but not trailers, to get on the road. Most of the small trucks were part of the Red Crescent's convoy. By the time this significantly downsized convoy reached the city of Fallujah, the Marines had put up another obstacle. Despite the negotiations, the Marines at first re-enacted the conditions of the siege, and did not allow the trucks to get inside Fallujah. Finally, as a result of considerable local and international pressure, they eventually conceded and let some trucks inside, the first effective break of the siege.

For our al-Jazeera crew, our colleague Abdulazeem Muhammad successfully entering with the Red Crescent trucks was a big gain. By Thursday, most of us were dangerously exhausted. The amount of work we had to do was much more than any of us could handle. We desperately needed some fresh blood. So when Abdulazeem entered Fallujah Thursday afternoon, he came just in time.

We just weren't sure how to get him to the Hadeeds' place from where he'd entered the city. No one dared to risk the sniper fire except for those with a death wish or those who were simply crazy and brave—people like

Hussain Deli, who wasn't stationed in the Hadeeds' place with us at this particular time. We decided we'd have to figure out a way to get Abdulazeem Muhammad to the Hadeeds' place later, when circumstances changed.

Inside Fallujah, the Marines reinforced their positions in the neighborhoods where they'd recently gained control, in particular, the industrial area and Nazzal Neighborhood. They occupied the Abdulaziz Samarray Mosque, and positioned their snipers on the minarets. The insurgents also reoccupied the Guided Caliphs' Mosque in an effort to control the Officers' Neighborhood and Main Street. All people living in the Military, Nazzal, and Police neighborhoods in the eastern part of Fallujah were practically under house arrest. No one could step outside his or her home because the snipers had orders to shoot on the spot, regardless of whether the person in question was carrying a weapon. City residents didn't even dare look out their windows.

One unfortunate family in the Hadeeds' neighborhood didn't realize that snipers had the authority or orders to shoot anyone on sight. Two of their kids somehow got outside the house, and were shot immediately without warning. The family called us after this tragedy, asking to send an ambulance to take the bodies of their dead kids. We called Dr. Rafie al-Issawi to handle the situation. Al-Issawi told us that the Marines had bombed every ambulance the hospital had sent out to the Nazzal Neighborhood. He said that there had been many wounded people who might have been saved but were instead left to bleed to death because ambulances couldn't get to them. He cited one incident from the night before as an example. Marines bombed one of his ambulances in the Nazzal Neighborhood. The driver miraculously escaped with his life, but had to leave an injured paramedic behind. When the hospital sent out another vehicle to tow the bombed ambulance, the Marines bombed the towing vehicle too. He said that injured people in the heavily besieged area of Fallujah were at risk of dying, and the dead were at risk of rotting without proper burial.

By the fourth day of the siege, it was obvious that people no longer had the luxury of simply worrying about what to do with the gravely injured—there was a new and rapidly growing problem. How to deal with the dead.

11. A CITY UNABLE TO GRIEVE

...[B]urial or cremation of the dead, carried out individually as far as circum-stances permit, is preceded by a careful examination, if possible by a medical examination, of the bodies, with a view to confirming death, establishing iden-tity and enabling a report to be made... Bodies shall not be cremated except for imperative reasons of hygiene or for motives based on the religion of the deceased... the dead [must be] honourably interred, if possible according to the rites of the religion to which they belonged... their graves are respected... prop-erly maintained and marked so that they may always be found...
> —Article 17, First Geneva Convention

When speaking of the horrors of war, most people talk about the tragic impact on the survivors, because at the very least, the dead are no longer in danger. When the tragedy and suffering of a war reaches even those who have died, then you know for a fact that the war is catastrophic beyond human imagination. The tragedy of the dead in Fallujah started on the first day of the siege. Fallujah's main cemetery runs alongside the Euphrates, one of the first areas to be controlled by the Marines. Therefore, no one was allowed to enter this cemetery once the siege began—not even the dead. When citizens wishing to bury dead bodies tried to reach the cemetery that was under the Marines' control, the Marines showered them with bullets. So these citizens returned to the city with even more dead and injured than they'd started out with. Fallujans were forced, instead, to dig up the old cemetery that was within city limits. This makeshift graveyard was enough to accommodate the dead on the first day, when the casualty count was still relatively low. Even the old cemetery wasn't a completely safe place to bury the deceased, however. Some people were killed trying to bury their dead there as well.

By Wednesday, April 7, however, the crisis of what to do with the dead had reached a critical point. Khamis Salih Nimrawi, the man who had lost 24 of his family members, didn't have to endure just the immense catas-trophe of losing his entire family; he had to figure out what to do with their bodies. Locals like Nimrawi had no option but to deposit the bodies at the Abi Ayoub al-Ansari Mosque, where many other citizens were storing bodies of their deceased loved ones until the cemetery opened up.

Some people, particularly those under the siege of Marine snipers in the Nazzal Neighborhood, buried their dead in their own backyards. The family in the Nazzal Neighborhood whose two children had been killed by snipers pleaded with us to film their family as they went through this difficult process. They wanted the whole world to see a family burying their children in their own yard so that maybe somewhere in the world a viewer would be moved enough to do something to stop war, and eventually help to ensure a proper burial for their kids. Unfortunately, when this happened, we were already siege by the snipers at the Hadeeds' place. Even Hussein Deli couldn't go to film the burial because the Nazzal Neighborhood was virtually unreachable for anyone because of the snipers and indiscriminate bombing.

After I told the family that there was no way for us to film their burial, I hung up the phone and collapsed into sobs. I was overwhelmed by the image of what was happening in this family's yard, just beyond our reach. Just a few hours earlier, two of their children were alive and healthy, living among them. Now they were dead and were to be buried right in the yard. I don't want to even think what it was like for that family to handle the job of preparing the bodies for burial without anyone in the world taking notice of their tragedy. And for others it was even worse—at least these children had a grave, even if it was in their own backyard. Some families had no yards at all, or had too many victims in their families to use the yards for burial.

We all felt powerless. Dr. Rafie al-Issawi called us that night to send a plea to the entire world through al-Jazeera; a plea for everyone and anyone who had a shred of humanity, a plea to intervene and help to end the catastrophe going on in the city of Fallujah.

To try to solve this problem with the corpses, Fallujans eventually resorted to turning the only sports field in the city into a cemetery. Graves were dug in this soccer field, and all the citizens who were able to reach the field buried their dead there. Still, this wasn't a complete solution because not everyone in Fallujah could reach the soccer field. Many neighborhoods were under the constant threat of snipers and unable to leave their homes. And even if Fallujans were all able to reach and to accept these temporary burial grounds in light of the severe shortage of proper burial places, what were they to do about the Marines who routinely fired at them as they buried their dead? There was no way past this problem.

Reports of civilians being shot in the simple act of trying to bury the dead continued as the violence in Fallujah escalated. On April 9, Dr.

Wathiq al-Ani, the director of the medical center in the Educators' Neighborhood, informed us that a man named Abdulkarim Ashour Ibrahim was killed as his family and friends took a body for burial after the Friday sermon just past noon. As the funeral procession was going on, the Marines fired intentionally and indiscriminately at the people in it. The first victim was 27-year-old Hamdy Kamel Hassan. The second victim was his 19-year-old brother, Muhammad Kamel Hassan. The third victim was 28-year-old Omar Ali Ahmad. All three victims were residents of the Educators' Neighborhood. These were just the dead. Those wounded by sniper fire were virtually impossible to count.

The same Friday, a sniper aimed and fired at people who were digging new graves in another small, old cemetery inside city limits called al-Ma'adeedy Cemetery, which was located next to a mosque of the same name. Several people were killed during this incident, with the fire coming from more than one sniper.

By that Friday, the number of dead since the start of the siege had reached 500 according to the official count of all medical centers and clinics in Fallujah. This number, of course, accounted for only the dead whose bodies had made it to medical centers and field hospitals. It did not include the dead who were buried under the rubble of their homes. Because of this massive number of casualties, mosques across Fallujah called upon people to donate shrouds for the dead. There was a serious shortage in shrouds, in addition to the shortage of burial places.

These problems only worsened as the violence in the city grew. On the eve of Saturday, April 10, I passed by a field hospital just after midnight. I found dead bodies belonging to one family in a pile in front of the hospital—a family of three generations represented by its dead. There was the grandfather, a man named Muhammad Jassim al-Matloub. Next to him, on one side, lay the body of his son-in-law. Next to Muhammad, on the other side, lay the body of his young grandson. Most of the family of Muhammad al-Matloub had managed to escape their house in the Jubail area of Fallujah that morning. The three dead had stayed in the house for some reason, and a fighter jet had bombed the house, killing them all. The bodies were badly mutilated and their skin was ripped off in some places, exposing muscles and organs. I tried to maintain my composure, but I got weak. It was too painful a sight to keep looking at. I left the cameramen to film the bodies and ran out. We aired these gruesome images on al-Jazeera Saturday morning.

It was bad enough that ill-equipped medical care centers and field hospitals had to handle the job of treating the wounded, but now they had to be morgues, too. Ambulances were almost a guaranteed target for the Marines, so doctors resorted to using unmarked private cars for the retrieval and delivery of dead bodies. Of course, those too were bombed and fired at, but at least not as a guaranteed target.

Along with the critical shortage of cemeteries, shrouds, and morgues came the crisis of unidentified bodies. Some bodies were mutilated beyond recognition, even to their next of kin. Some bodies could have been identified, but the families couldn't reach medical centers to do so. Families were sometimes scattered about, some outside the city limits, some stuck in one neighborhood with the rest of the family in another.

Before long, the corpses started to cause health and sanitation problems. There were no refrigerated places to keep the bodies for identification at a later date. Doctors didn't know what to do with this moral dilemma. How could they bury a body without securing an identity? What would they tell the families who would come later to ask about their loved ones? In the end, many people had to be buried in unmarked graves. This was a hard decision for doctors to make, but they had no choice. It was unsanitary to have dead bodies rotting in the hospitals.

The problem of identification was especially vexing in the case of young victims. Adults don't have to be identified by a next of kin or a family member in order to be buried. They could be identified by a colleague at work, the grocer next door, a friend, or someone they come across as they go about their daily business. Children—any children anywhere in the world—lead lives that are more limited to their parents and neighbors. Children don't work, and they don't interact with adults frequently enough to be recognized. Consequently, a high percentage of the unidentified bodies buried were those of very young children.

One of the graves I passed by had a disturbing tombstone inscription: "Three young children, possibly from the Dhahi family. Not sure."

When I came across this, I imagined being one of those parents, looking for my children lost in the chaos of this horrific war. To keep my hopes up, I count my kids among the missing, not the dead. I look for every shred of evidence that might lead to finding my children safe. I come across this tombstone. What could this possibly mean? Are these my kids? My brother's? My third cousin's? The tombstone says "possibly"—maybe they're not from my family at all.

The magnitude of the possibilities would be enough to drive anyone insane. I sat by that grave for a long time, crying, and thinking all the while of how a Dhahi parent would eventually react upon discovery of this grave.

Such was the situation in Fallujah. This siege was a tragedy for the living, and a bigger tragedy for the dead. Fallujans couldn't even wish to be dead to be relieved of this tragedy; death was not any easier.

Thursday night saw one of the fiercest nights of confrontation between the insurgents and the Marines in the entire siege—the shelling was unending. Just as the Marines had succeeded in gaining control of a couple of neighborhoods in Fallujah, the insurgents had now succeeded in encircling the Marines. The insurgents had cut off all lines of support coming into Fallujah except for what could be airlifted by the few helicopters that had not yet been replaced by F-16s.

I spent the night thinking of a way to break the snipers' siege on our newsroom at the Hadeeds'. We were supposed to do our special coverage of the first anniversary of occupation the next day. Al-Jazeera had dedicated its entire day's program to the occasion; we couldn't let everyone down because the snipers had us in their grip. Commentary from Fallujah, a city that had become so central to the war, was crucial. I had to figure out how to get downtown and do our coverage as planned.

I discussed the situation with Hamed, and he felt it was impossible for us to be able to manage anything realistically and safely. Nevertheless, we agreed to sleep on it, and figure something out in the morning.

The night was so dark and so long that I wondered at times if dawn would ever come. Explosions, sniper fire, and the roar of engine jets marched through whatever light sleep I may have gotten before I was greeted by the sound of morning prayers coming from the surrounding mosques.

II. DAY FIVE: A DEADLY RUMOR

At dawn, I gathered the crew. "Listen, we have to find a way to break the snipers' siege. This is unbearable. We've been practically paralyzed since noon on Wednesday, when the snipers took their positions across the street. Sure, we've been lucky enough to get footage of the F-16s and the humanitarian aid convoy, and sure, the phone lines are still operational, but still, this is not enough. We're not a newspaper or a radio station. We're televised media that relies almost entirely on footage. People have to see moving images as we read our reports."

I felt my voice break with frustration. "For God's sake, I'm appearing live with a bare wall as my backdrop because we're broadcasting from the Hadeeds' backyard. This is definitely not acceptable for a special coverage day. We have to get out of here and move downtown. My backdrop has got to be moving people, and active scenery! We have to be live not just for a few hours. We have to be live literally all day long."

"What do you suggest we do?" one of the guys asked. "You see the snipers outside. You know they're waiting for an excuse to shoot. Just walking outside the door is enough excuse for them. Then, after they've shot us, they will celebrate because they will have silenced the only televised media in the city."

I replied with the plan I had come up with in the night, after much thought. I said, "There is a way. It's not safe, but it is a way. We could sneak out the rear entrance and hide between houses until we clear the snipers' area. This is what Hussain Deli does whenever he delivers footage to us."

Another person in the crew asked, "Even if we were to agree to this, you do realize that this is a much bigger risk than the one Deli takes. He's one guy—it's much easier for one guy to sneak out of the house and hide from the snipers. We're a group. They'll spot us immediately. How will we make it downtown alive? Also, the broadcast equipment is on the rooftop. We can't bring it down now. They will definitely shoot us then."

I had convinced Hamed that my plan would work, and he argued the case alongside me. We tried to convince the others, but we understood that we were asking a lot of everyone.

I said, "Look, we can sit here having this discussion until the end of the siege, when we'll be able to walk downtown without any problems. You're right that I have no guarantees that we'll all make it downtown safely, just as I have no guarantees that we can get the equipment off the rooftop safely. I can't compel you to do something where one of the possible outcomes is your own death. But Hamed and I are going to take the equipment off the roof, and we are going to go downtown. Any of you are welcome to join us, but you cannot stop us."

Maybe because of our fierce determination, the guys reconsidered.

One man commented, "Abo Omar walked outside for only a few seconds, and he was almost killed on sight. The laser beam was pointed right at his chest. But then, he made it back inside safely. At the end of the day, you will face whatever fate you're destined to face. If the snipers are destined to kill us, then they'll find a way to kill us even if we stay in this living room. We came to Fallujah and placed ourselves under the siege for the sake of Fallujans, and it is our job to tell the world about their misery at all costs. Let's finish this job professionally. Let's go downtown."

His words had an encouraging effect on everyone. After this speech, no one wanted to be left behind.

We got our things together, and began preparing to make our way downtown. Hamed called on his two nephews, Sami and Zeyad, who were very fit and agile, to help get the equipment from the roof. These two young men would be able to maneuver the rooftops better than any of us—every other member of the crew was either overweight, out of shape, or too old to perform this kind of task.

The two young men climbed the rear walls of the house to where they couldn't be seen by the snipers. They reached the roof from the rear side and remained there for a while in very dangerous and awkward positions just so they didn't become visible to the snipers. Whenever they had to get a bolt or a nut undone, they crawled slowly toward it on the rooftop, unscrewed it, and returned to their awkward and dangerous positions. Slowly and gradually they were able to pull the equipment toward them, and were able to attach ropes. We then pulled the equipment off the roof little by little, using the ropes. Eventually we had a hold of each piece of equipment. Miraculously, we had managed to get all the equipment safely on the ground with this careful process.

As his nephews were recovering the equipment from the roof under our supervision, Hamed and his elder brother arranged for two pickup trucks to take us downtown. The trucks remained a safe distance from the house, about 500 yards out of the snipers' view. The trucks were hidden between houses where all the other vehicles were parked. This meant, however, that we had to carry our luggage and equipment, most of which was very heavy, to an assembly point at the beginning of a narrow alley, which eventually led to the place where the pickup trucks were parked. We were very concerned about our equipment, because the route we had to take to get to the trucks wasn't level, and would be hard to traverse. We would have to go through winding, narrow alleys and climb several walls to avoid being in the snipers' view.

The entire Hadeed family and some of their neighbors participated in the risky mission of delivering our equipment and belongings to the assembly point. I carried one of my bags in one hand and a bunch of other things in the other. One of Hamed's agile nephews followed me, carrying my other bag. We went individually because it was easier to evade the snipers as individuals, but we still followed one another down the winding road. We were forced to bend our bodies in strange positions as we jumped from one safe spot to the next, but it was a necessary action to evade the shots of the snipers. It wasn't easy, but the entire crew eventually made it to the assembly point, and the Hadeeds and their neighbors made it back to their homes safely. I was beginning to feel as though the opportunity we'd risked our lives for was very close and very reachable, and that the risk had been worth the anxiety. We walked down the alley and headed toward the trucks.

As soon as we reached the trucks, any relief I had been hoping for dissolved immediately. What we saw in front of us was a scene of horror and despair, the likes of which we had not seen even in the darkest hours of the siege.

The Devastation on the One-Year Anniversary of American Occupation

What we saw when we approached our meeting spot was mass hysteria—people fleeing for their lives. Men, women, children, and the elderly ran in all directions, and cars packed to the brim with belongings tried to plow through the thick crowds of people. We found out that the massive crowd was attempting to escape Fallujah because of a rumor that the Marines had left the Naimyah Road open for those who wanted to escape. For those who chose to stay, the people in the mob told us, the Marines were promising imminent death. People believed the rumor, and believed that if they didn't take advantage of the chance the Marines had given them, then they were all definitely going meet their deaths. The insurgents had dealt a massive blow to the Marines at this very place a few days earlier. After that incident, the Marines took control of the Naimyah entrance both by land and air, bombing anything and anyone. It was easy to see why the rumor that the exit was open—for now—would be taken seriously.

There weren't enough vehicles to carry the thousands of people wishing to leave, so most people walked, waving white flags of concession above their heads. We joined the mob to see what developments might occur. The closer our crowd came to the main road that connects Fallujah to Naimyah, the larger the crowd became. By the time we reached the Naimyah Road where the actual exit was, the mentality of the crowd had become almost apocalyptic. We were engulfed in thousands upon thousands of people; a colossal wave of mass migration; an entire hysterical city looking to flee the possibility of extinction. Layth and Sayf filmed this entire scene and the seemingly endless chaos. Hamed suggested that we try to head to the location of the field hospital, which seemed to be the main starting point for most of the fleeing people. When we finally reached the field hospital, things were even worse there: crowds of hysterical people screaming and running for their lives.

We didn't know where to turn or what to do next. We moved without talking and tried to follow our instincts and not lose track of each other. We got out of the pickup truck and unloaded our equipment next to an old wall, and then looked at each other, dumbfounded.

While we stood and tried to get our bearings, I saw a petite woman trying to get her three kids to join the mob and flee toward the Naimyah exit. The kids were too young to understand how scared their mother was. She couldn't get them to run, so she tried to carry all three of them. Her tiny build, however, couldn't bear the weight of all three. She stumbled and fell over onto the sidewalk that separated the pavement from the sand, hitting her teeth on the concrete. When she picked herself up we saw her mouth was smeared with blood. Her youngest had hit his forehead on the hard pavement while the other two had landed face-first in the sand. Despite this setback, the mother did not stop for a second. She picked up the crying kids and tried again. She fell about every hundred yards. One child had hurt his foot and refused to be carried. He ran behind his mother, leaving bloody little footprints in the sand.

I looked at the sandy patch around the hospital, and saw other footprints. There were incredible patterns of little footprints, sometimes *very* little, sometimes very bloody. The woman and her three children weren't the only ones struggling terribly to flee the city. Countless numbers of children were holding white flags and running barefoot on the hot sand.

The white flags were made of twigs and any piece of white cloth the children could find: their fathers' white socks, their mothers' white head-scarves, or even their own little white underwear.

I yelled to Layth and Hassan, "Film this," and pointed to the petite mother, one mother in an immense crowd of mothers and children.

As they got in position to film, I yelled again, "No, wait! This scene is better. Film this."

I pointed to a blind, elderly man who stumbled aimlessly through the crowd. The crowd itself was in total disarray, and parts of the mob were running in all directions. The poor blind elderly man kept going in circles, hitting all sorts of obstacles—lamp posts, walls, cars, other people. He'd fall on the ground, whimper in pain for a bit, and get up again to repeat the whole impossible process. The man never got anywhere outside a circle with a radius of maybe a hundred yards. The crowd was made of one sad case after another.

Pure panic and all-consuming fear had overwhelmed everyone. I was in no position to help, because I couldn't figure out what was going on, and so many people needed help that it was impossible for me to focus on just one. I figured the best way I could help these people would be to film the misery they were going through and broadcast it to the world. So every time I saw a scene I thought captured the devastation we were witnessing, I'd yell "Camera!"

Of course, just after I called for a camera, I'd find faces that bore the signs of an even worse situation, and I'd yell again: "Camera!"

Before long people around me who weren't part of the crew also began yelling Camera! Camera! It occurred to me that even if I had a thousand cameras, I couldn't possibly capture all the destruction and tragedy unfolding around me. This was an indescribable scene of human misery. This was something that we as journalists could never fully explain to the world, no matter how many cameras we had or how much footage we got.

One of the unsettling things about this scene was the palpable antic-ipation of death and annihilation. There was no gore just yet—not a lot of blood, no disfigured bodies, and no corpses. Yet despite the lack of gruesome detail, this remains one of the most disturbing events I have ever witnessed. How to describe the look on people's faces as they try to escape what they believe to be certain death? I had never seen anything like this look before the scene in downtown Fallujah that day, and after the scene it became so surreal it was unimaginable. Is it enough to say that the look on the face of a person trying to escape death is far worse than the sight of a dead body? The eyes look different. The face loses all traces of humanity and becomes something frighteningly strange and horrifically desperate.

I have written, reviewed, edited, and rewritten accounts of my witness to this mob scene more times than I care to remember, and I have never found a version that I believe delivers the scene to someone who had not witnessed it. Perhaps I could try to put the reader in the shoes of one of the unfortunate people caught up in this desperate crowd. But these fleeing people were unified by nothing but fear. Women breastfed their babies, holding them close to their chests despite the constant threat of sniper fire. Young men ran with elderly relatives slung over their backs, as fast as they could. Entire families ran together, all fleeing from a rumor of impending death, even in the face of sniper fire that might at any moment kill any one of them. These people were escaping what they believed was imminent doom—a promise of death that had deliberately traveled halfway around the world.

Harming the Helpless

"Parties to a conflict must respect children, provide them with any care or aid they require."
      —Protocol I, Article 77, Geneva Conventions

I saw a little girl lost in the crowd of people where we stood filming. She was only tall enough to reach the legs of the adults in the thick crowd and she bumped into everyone as they furiously moved toward the exit. She looked searchingly upward, to each passing face, crying for her mother. When I looked at this lost girl as she cried out in dazed shock, I didn't see her face. I saw the face of my little daughter, Riham—and it was with sudden alarm that I ran to try and help her, if any help could be had in this dire situation. I wanted to calm her down and keep her safe.

When she spoke to me, this little girl's voice brought Riham's voice to me. I had only been allowed to hear her young, sweet voice through my cell phone in recent days. I talked to her a little bit every time her mother called me. She had no understanding of what kind of danger I was in—or even what danger is. The only thing she knew is that I wasn't around, and that she missed me. She often asked when I would stop leaving home, and when I would be home for good, like the fathers of her friends. I would have to tell her I was covering a war, and that I needed to stay because danger sometimes unexpectedly creeps in to people's lives, and the world had to know about it.

She would usually respond with something along these lines: "Okay. I guess you can stay there. But why don't you put on the nice ties Mom and I picked for you? Why do you always seem tired when we see you on the news? You always look like you haven't showered in a long time. And your hair is always messed up!"

She would continue, "And you're always in weird places, like in a dirty alley or on the top of a house. You never get on the rooftop when you're at home. But when I turn on the TV, you're always in some dirty or crazy place like that. Mom and I don't like you to look like that or be in these places."

Riham wanted her father around, wanted her father to look neat, and wanted her father to wear the ties she picked out. She had no understanding whatsoever of what war was. The little girl lost in the crowd must've had similar simple thoughts before the siege, and certainly before the occupation—when her life was much more ordinary. She wanted to be with her family. But when the threat of death falls on an entire city, the innocence of a child is ravaged by the fear. Imagine any child who has a special place in your life lost in a crowd of people running for their lives, and maybe you'll be able to visualize how devastating this scene was.

As soon as I offered help, the little girl immediately put her little hand in mine. There wasn't much I could do for her, since I was a stranger. I tried to comfort her, and she assumed I was a friend of her dad's who could lead her to her family. I tried to ask those in the immediate vicinity if anyone knew her, and had no luck. Eventually, a paramedic took her away from me and told me they'd keep her at the field hospital until something could be figured out.

The sight of the elderly was just as painful as that of the children, as they were often just as helpless. I distinctly recall the sight of a very old and very frail woman standing close to the road with her daughter-in-law and her grandchildren. The family was looking for a vehicle to take the old woman to the Naimyah exit because she could barely walk, and she would never make it all the way across the desert. The crowds were too big, and all the vehicles were too full for any additional people. I called on Layth to film this family while I spoke with them, because their despair so aptly symbolized the plight of the people. Layth, however, didn't just film this family; he felt obliged to help them. He began to search frantically for a vehicle. Eventually he found a truck, but there was no place, so he helped the entire family to get on the roof. It was no small feat, because that family had at least six children, the oldest of whom couldn't have been more than seven. I will never forget the helpless look on that old woman's face, nor the tears that came when she saw Layth approaching with a vehicle for her and the rest of the family. Once the family was secured on the roof of the truck, Layth told the old woman goodbye. He cried and waved as the truck headed toward the Naimyah desert exit.

Two hours into our filming of the unfolding disaster of the street mob, I was live on al-Jazeera only via the phone. We hadn't set up the broadcast equipment yet. As I was describing the scene to the viewers over the phone, a black microbus sped toward the field hospital, headed right for where we were standing. I realized there must be some wounded people in that microbus, and ran toward the vehicle. I yelled at Layth to start filming as I opened the middle door of the microbus. Layth ran as fast as he could because he wanted to film whatever victims came out of that microbus before the crowds gathered around the scene.

As soon as I opened that middle door, I realized I had made a mistake. In an urgent, tearful scream, I yelled to Layth over the crowds, "Don't come! Don't film! Stay away. Please stay away! Oh my God. Oh my God. Stay away!" Then I collapsed in uncontrollable tears.

Inside the microbus were the bodies of the old woman and her young grandchildren, who we had just two hours ago helped onto the roof of a truck and pointed toward escape. It was impossible to tell which torn limb belonged to which dead body, and the bodies were piled atop each other in a sickening mass of blood and flesh. Some of the faces were missing flesh, and the bodies were covered with desert sand. There were too many little body parts scattered about in the microbus, little arms, little legs, little torsos all belonging to the children who were on the vehicle. Some children's bodies were still somewhat intact, and their limbs hung onto their bodies by small, veiny threads. Even now, as I sit typing this paragraph, it is impossible to remember these fallen children and their grandmother without crying.

The crowds didn't take long to notice the dead bodies in the microbus. A group began to gather around the microbus, and the small mob began chanting: "There is no God but God! America is the enemy of God!" We were able to capture these chants on my cell phone, and every single listener tuned in to al-Jazeera at that moment was able to hear and feel the desperate anger of these citizens.

My colleague Muhammad Kraishan was on the other end of the line and broadcasting live on al-Jazeera.

"Ahmed? Do you hear me, Ahmed?" He asked, not hearing my responses to his live questions.

Upon hearing the chants of the street people, he announced to the viewers, "It seems that Ahmed has given his cell phone to the protestors to express their grief."

The truth is I didn't intentionally leave anything to anyone. The truth is that when I broke down over the sight of the victims in the microbus, the protestors near me snatched the phone as it fell from my hand. Months later, one of my colleagues would blame me for this mistake as we watched a recorded tape of Kraishan's interview with me. Of course, there was no footage of my collapse because we were only on the phone, but it was obvious that the very instant that the proctors' voices grew louder and my voice disappeared signaled the point of my collapse. My colleague said this was unprofessional behavior on my part. I don't at all agree with this assessment—I challenge anyone who has a shred of humanity to worry about his professional image when he's submerged in violent chaos and directly facing dead, mutilated bodies of children. Even other people who hadn't seen this family when they were alive screamed in horror as medics removed the bodies from the microbus. Sometimes an incident that lasts less than a few seconds can leave a giant imprint on your psyche. I still recall the image of those tangled, bloodied bodies as if they were directly in front of me. I still recall the frightened face of that old woman, a face that had undoubtedly seen a lot in its lifetime. That old woman probably never imagined an ending like that for herself or her grandchildren. She had probably never imagined that her skin might someday be washed over by the blood of her very own grandchildren. It seemed to me the most inhumane and unbelievable way to die.

The little lost girl remains in the back of my mind as well. To this day I wonder what became of her. Was her life cut short along with the rest of the children butchered senselessly that day? Did she find her parents? I won't ever know the true answers to her whereabouts after that day in Fallujah, but I know the image of her suffering won't ever leave me.

Moments later, I recovered as much as I could from my breakdown, and I realized I was still on air. Kraishan was on the other end of the line waiting for my comments. I had to get my head back on straight and proceed with doing my job. I moved on for the moment, but the whole scene was burned into my brain forever.

We headed to the field hospital to film what we could of the scene inside. What we found inside was just as traumatic as what we found in the streets—piles and piles of dead children and severed bodies. Perhaps because my mind was so focused on the lost girl and the dead children in the microbus, it seemed impossible to believe that more adults than children were being killed given the evidence we found—we saw so many small, dead bodies in the field hospital and we heard so many stories about children that had been killed or wounded. Maybe this was because families knew there wasn't room for everyone to escape, so they had to prioritize, and they tried to send their children out of Fallujah. Unfortunately, their children ended up dead. This is my only explanation for the high ratio of dead and wounded children that day.

Cries, very loud cries, bounced off all the walls of the field hospital. Hospital rooms filled up so quickly that doctors were performing surgeries in the hallways. The hospital was just a simple clinic with hardly any medical equipment, so complicated surgeries were very difficult and often unsuccessful. The smell of blood, disease, and death was overwhelming—it was nearly impossible to travel through the hospital and resist the urge to turn away and instead join the mob outside. It was hard to tell which reality was worse.

I looked for a secluded corner anywhere in the hospital—any small, isolated place where I could sit and attempt to process the information I was seeing. I needed somewhere to sob in uncontrollable tears; somewhere to let myself come to terms with all this death and destruction. I knew a mental breakdown like this wouldn't help the victims, but I thought it might ease some of my mental stress. The more I searched for a secluded corner, the more death and blood I came across. So, eventually I stood in a corner, with all the death and screams of pain surrounding me, leaned back against the wall, covered my face with my palms, and sobbed. The sobbing didn't make me feel better. The screams of wounded people in pain just an arm's length from where I was standing didn't let my mind wander from the grisly scene.

This day was one of the hardest trials of my life, one that even now I cannot fully comprehend. The things I witnessed in Fallujah during this siege were worse than anything I had ever encountered as a war correspondent, so much so that I have trouble comprehending them as a human being. This was the only war I have ever covered where most of the dead I encountered were very young children. In this war, Fallujan children were swatted like flies; eradicated in obscenely large numbers and without any regard to their innocence.

After I had let myself react to the emotional overload, I realized I had to get myself together so that I could better manage the crew. We still had a long day ahead of us and, most likely, more gruesome scenes to cover. I tried to forget the image of Riham lost in the crowd, and the devastating images of sick children in the hospital, and headed back out into the streets.

I called Layth and Hassan, "Please try your best to film everything you can of what's going on out here. I'm going to head out with Hamed to look for a place to mount the broadcast equipment. We need to transmit these images to Doha, so we need to set up the equipment as fast as possible."

It was then that I realized I was missing my handbag and my suitcase. My handbag contained everything I needed to do my work: a small camera and my laptop. I panicked. I didn't know how I could possibly find my bags in that mob of frightened and enraged people. I was also overwhelmed with confusion—I didn't know how I lost the suitcase to begin with. I thought maybe I left it by the old wall where we unloaded the broadcasting equipment and our belongings, but I went to the wall and didn't find my bags or the broadcasting equipment.

I told Hamed in an urgent shout, "I don't know where the handbag went. It was in my hand the entire time. I took a few moments in the hospital to get myself together, and I must have lost it then."

As I was talking to Hamed, a paramedic approached. "When I saw you in a difficult situation, I took your bag for safekeeping," he said. "I've been holding onto it for you in this building so that it didn't get stolen or lost." He pointed to the headquarters of the Islamic Party. Relieved, we followed this man through a small patch of barren desert that separated the field hospital from the Islamic Party headquarters. There was nothing in this barren land, except for one of the bombed-out Red Crescent ambulance that had at one time been carrying humanitarian aid for Fallujan residents. This was one of the ambulances the Marines had bombed in the Nazzal Neighborhood.

The headquarters of the Islamic Party, an old theater that had once been converted for political use, was being used as a kind of hospital during this siege. Victims were stretched out on makeshift beds on what was once the main stage. Injured people were scattered in the hallways. The theater was well below the minimal levels of sanitation needed for any kind of medical center, or for that matter, any other use. But these victims and doctors had no other choice. The field hospital was overflowing with the dead and injured. The doctors moved newcomers to this theater and made up for the lack of sanitation by using lots of alcohol and cleaning solutions when treating the injured victims.

The paramedic walked me to the office where he had left my bags. I took out some things and, with his permission, left the bags there. I didn't want to be lugging them around all day.

I talked with the rest of the crew, and we agreed that the best place for us to do our broadcast would be right next to the field hospital. It was close to the city center so we could cover the developments there. It had the electricity we needed to run the broadcast equipment. We didn't have a lot of fuel left to run the generator, so we couldn't be far away from some source of electric power.

We asked Dr. al-Issawi's permission to mount the broadcast equipment on the roof of the field hospital. He didn't mind. Sayf began working on preparing the equipment for transmission as the rest of us sat in the front yard figuring out our division of labor. Our team was expected to create news reports about the events taking place in the city all day long and into the night. We were expected to make more than one report to be broadcast during the live news coverage provided by the crew. To accomplish this all, we divided our work into sections. Hussain Deli and Abdulazeem Muhammad were to follow ambulances wherever they went. Ambulances would, of course, be sent to places that had just been bombed, and this team would follow them to gather the information and film the scene.

Hamed was to coordinate all received information and to gather news from the various areas in the city. He was to provide contact between the crew and the headquarters in Doha, and also gather news from the teams located all over the Anbar province. He had been working with these teams for the past several days. He was also expected to gather news from sources he had contacted over the past few days stationed on the outskirts of Fallujah.

My job was to gather news from the hospital using different sources: doctors, nurses, victims who were able and willing to talk, teams of paramedics, and humanitarian volunteers. I was expected to stay in the hospital the entire time, and my reports would be added to the information supplied to me by Hamed, Hussain Deli, and Abdulazeem Muhammad. Then I would present my reports live to the viewers. The only time I would be outside the hospital was when I had a live segment to present.

Layth and Hassan were to do their standard job as cameramen, filming everything Hamed or I directed them to. Abo Omar the chauffeur was to be backup help for Sayf, the telecommunication engineer, and the cameramen.

I called the newsroom in Doha and informed them that Hamed would be coordinating things, and that they needed to go through him if they wanted to communicate with anyone in the crew. We had to be extremely organized because the situation was itself so chaotic.

Still, we hit a snag very quickly. Within minutes of splitting up to pursue our own assignments, we received word from Sayf that the broadcast equipment wasn't working. Doha headquarters called several times to get my live participation in the special coverage of the anniversary of the occupation, but I couldn't participate with a camera—I had to conduct these interviews via phone only. I provided my coverage from Fallujah as Kraishan and Abdulqader Ayadh provided their coverage from Baghdad. I tried my best to describe the horrors I'd seen that day, but as they say, a picture is worth a thousand words. My coverage fell well below my personal expectations because of the broken equipment.

Sayf kept attempting to jumpstart the equipment, for three hours, to no avail.

"It's pointless to keep trying here," he said, "this place is too low. I need a place with more altitude and no tall buildings." He looked around briefly, and pointed at the building in front of us, "If we move the equipment there, it would work."

We were standing on the rooftop of the field hospital, a one-story building, while the building in front of us was a three-story building. It was the tallest building in the area and looked to be made up of several private clinics.

I said, "Fine, let's go. But we'll have to find the owner so we can ask permission to use the rooftop of the property. How do we find this person?"

Hamed took charge of this task, and went around asking people. Not surprisingly, Hamed got no answer. Everyone was trying to escape with their lives, not answer trivial questions.

Finally, I told Hamed, "Let's just relocate the broadcasting equipment there and run it without permission. If someone objects, we'll leave, but considering your good ties with the people of this area, I bet it could be worked out."

By the time we began moving our equipment, it was almost time for the Friday sermon—a mandatory worship for Sunnis. There was a rumor

circulating that the Muslim scholars in Fallujah had issued a decree reliev-
ing worshippers of this duty under these life-threatening circumstances.
The rumor wasn't confirmed, really, but certainly mosques didn't care if
worshippers missed their services today. Only mosques that were not
occupied by insurgents, bombed by the Marines, or crawling with snipers
held the Friday sermon as usual. Naturally, most sermons that day were
about the war.

Sunnis and Shiites do not pray at the same time or even necessarily in
the same manner. They differ on their views of whether the Friday
worship is mandatory or not. Even when they do agree, they worship
separately. But not on this particular Friday. It was the first, and perhaps
the last, Friday where all Sunni and Shia mosques across Iraq united their
Friday sermons and prayers.

Hamed and I, along with one of the cameramen, decided to attend
one of the services to hear what the preachers had to say. In the meantime,
Sayf and the rest of crew would try to mount the broadcast equipment
on the three-story building and get it to work. We attended the mosque
closest to us, and the sermon seemed tame, considering all the craziness
outside. The Friday sermon at the Umm-ul-Qurra Mosque in Baghdad,
however, was more directed at the chaos in the streets of Fallujah. The
Umm-ul-Qurra Mosque is one of the biggest and most influential
mosques in all of Iraq and is led by Dr. Harith Aldhary, the secretary
general of AMSI. Aldhary called upon all Iraqis "to protest on Saturday,
Sunday, and Monday if possible to show the occupation forces our opposition to what's happening in Fallujah."

Dr. Aldhary grew visibly emotional as he delivered his sermon. He
called upon his congregation to wage jihad against the US. He chanted,
"Off to Jihad! Off to Jihad! The battle of Fallujah is a battle for the history
books, a battle for Iraq, and your loved ones in Fallujah are fighting while
welcoming death and martyrdom."

After we heard the sermons offered in a few of the mosques, we
headed back to the field hospital. On the way, Wadah Khanfar, the director
general of al-Jazeera, called me on my cell.

"Where have you been, man?" He asked.

"We were covering the Friday sermon, and we're now on our way
back to the rest of the crew," I replied.

"Well, quick, get back to the field hospital! They managed to fix the
broadcast equipment, and you're due to appear on air for live coverage
right this second. We're waiting for you."

We hurried toward the field hospital, and just as we were about to run for the stairs, we saw a man wailing over the body of his dead son. As we got closer we were able to decipher his words.

"My son died because of a rumor! A rumor!" he wailed.

It turns out that the story about the Marines opening the exit for civilians to escape was not true. Fallujans were talking about this at the field hospital entrance as we approached, and some of these locals confirmed that they had heard this claim from Marines themselves.

One man said, "I wouldn't have risked the lives of my children if I hadn't been told by a Marine to flee and take advantage of the open exit. He told me this. He told me the Marines were leaving the exit open today intentionally and that I should head in that direction."

This man was not the only one with this story. Several other men with wounded and dead children at the hospital said the same thing. These Fallujans concluded that spreading the rumor had been an intentional attempt by the Marines to misinform Fallujans, perhaps to make the city extremely chaotic, and in the process force civilians to crowd the Naimyah exit and deprive the insurgents of the opportunity to strike the Marines from this area. The Naimyah desert exit was basically an empty battlefield from which the insurgents could stage quick sneak attacks on the Marines. The presence of civilians made this much more difficult.

I don't know that I agreed with this speculation on the part of Fallujans, but I do know that US forces definitely spread false rumors intentionally in Fallujah on several occasions. And although I can't swear that the Marines were the ones who spread this particular rumor, it would not be a surprise.

In any case, most people who believed the rumor and had the means to flee ended up dead or wounded. A small number of lucky travelers managed to actually make it out of the city while the Marines were busy keeping insurgents away from the Naimyah exit. Many Fallujans, however, were caught between the Marines and the insurgents and consequently ended up dead as well.

I got quite caught up in the news about the false rumor that we received on the front steps of the hospital, and I forgot I was due on air until I got another call from Doha telling me I was late. We left the men arguing over why the Marines would spread a rumor of this kind, and ran toward the stairs leading to the roof where our broadcasting equipment was set up.

When we reached the roof, we found the crew airing the tapes that we had filmed in the morning. The tapes contained the footage of people running for their lives, and gave the audience insight into the death and destruction we had waded through since we had begun work in the early hours of the day.

Conditions of a Fragile Cease-Fire

We hadn't been watching television, so we had no idea that al-Jazeera had aired this breaking news in the morning from its office in Baghdad: The Bush administration had offered a preliminary cease-fire agreement. In a statement released by Paul Bremer, the agreement delineated that a

> unilateral suspension of offensive operations in Fallujah [would occur] in order to hold a meeting between members of the Iraqi Governing Council, Fallujah leadership, and leaders of the anti-coalition forces, to allow delivery of additional supplies provided by the Iraqi government; and to allow residents of Fallujah to tend to wounded and dead.

Bremer's statement made clear that coalition forces would "retain the inherent right of self-defense and... remain fully prepared to resume offensive operations unless significant progress in these discussions occurs." A primary condition of the implementation of the agreement was that our crew leave Fallujah. The unilateral cease-fire was to start at noon, but only if we agreed to stop filming and leave Fallujah.

From the start, this tentative cease-fire agreement was marked by conflict and confusion. Press agencies reported that Hachem al-Hassani and Iyad Samarray held talks with Paul Bremer in an attempt to broker an agreement by which American forces would retreat to the outskirts of Fallujah and lift the siege. The Islamic Party also issued a statement that day that read,

> As a result of the painstaking efforts made by the party, and after negotiations that were held—which are still ongoing until this morning—with concerned American parties, an agreement was reached to end the exchange of military operations in Fallujah and its surroundings starting from noon and lasting for twenty-four hours.

General Mark Kimmitt, however, denied that such an agreement took place. He told reporters, "There is no brokered agreement for a cease-fire in Fallujah," and added, "there is no agreement between the rebels and the coalition forces," as Agence France-Presse had reported.

Moments after Kimmitt's statement was released, Lt. Colonel Brennan Byrne, commander of the First Battalion, Fifth Marine Regiment, reinforced Kimmitt's claims. He told Agence France-Presse reporters, "The suspension of offensive operations lasted for ninety minutes but it is over." Byrne also said that planned mediation talks with local tribal sheikhs had never happened. The Canadian Broadcasting Corporation reported that Byrne said his forces had been cleared to resume offensive operations, and that a cease-fire was not in effect.

It should be noted that in addition to these troubling and contradicting reports, it was obvious that this conditional cease-fire was certainly not offered for the sake of helping Iraqis or Fallujans. F-16s were bombing houses, snipers were hunting civilians who were fleeing their homes, and helicopters were finishing off those who hadn't yet been killed by the F-16s or the snipers. The Americans could continue in this manner for many nights to come, if they so chose. No, the safety and security of Fallujan civilians was definitely not the reason for this offer of cease-fire. That was to save the American forces who had been encircled by insurgents. The insurgents had cut off all land supply routes to the troops encircling Fallujah, and without food, they were in danger of becoming too weak to continue fighting.

In the statement about the purposes of the cease-fire agreement, Bremer was quite simply lying through his teeth—in particular, the part about allowing Iraqis to deliver supplies and tend to the victims. The reality on the ground was that Marines were bombing and killing civilians as Bremer issued his statement, and they continued to do so afterward. The Marines were still bombing and killing people involved in funeral processions that started immediately after the Friday sermon, which was well past the noon hour. Bremer's statement had specified the noon hour as the start of the suspension of offensive operations. Minutes after the cease-fire was to be put into action, the agreement was already broken by the US.

Bremer's memoir, though, does admit the truth about this cease-fire agreement, albeit it unintentionally.

> Before another NSC meeting late that Friday, I called Rice to prepare the president for bad news. "The situation in Fallujah isn't good, and we're trying a unilateral move," I said. "But it might not work. The Sunnis are very restive, and we still might have a wave of resignations from the Council. The Shia situation is also bad."

In this passage, there is no mention of tending to the victims or allowing humanitarian supplies to get through. His resorting to "trying a unilateral move" of this kind had nothing to do with humanitarian aid and everything to do with the fact that the American occupation was failing miserably in Fallujah. He was trying to save the Marines from utter defeat. He was trying to save the makeshift government in Iraq from collapsing over his head. The cease-fire was created to avoid the catastrophe of US military defeat, and for no other reason.

After the cease-fire was proposed, there was also talk about forming a delegation from the Iraqi Governing Council to speak with dignitaries and leaders of Fallujah. This never beame more than a rumor, but the Fallujans didn't buy into it in the first place. The general opinion in Fallujah was that any delegation would serve the interests of the Bush administration more than those of Fallujans and other Iraqis. By the time the cease-fire was proposed, most Fallujans had succumbed to one of three fates: they had fled the city, they had remained in the city and lost loved ones, or they were dead. There wasn't much that any delegation would have to offer them. The only ones who stood to benefit from such a delegation was the Bush administration—it might save both political and military face. This was the general consensus I gathered from speaking to Fallujans after these rumors began to circulate.

At this point in the siege, representatives of the Iraqi Islamic Party, which was participating in the Governing Council, began to become more active in this conflict. The party's official representative was Dr. Mohsen Abdul Hameed; but Hachem al-Hassani, an American citizen of Iraqi origin who seemed to have a special relationship with Paul Bremer, handled many of the finer details, along with Iyad Samarray, a British citizen of Iraqi origin. These men were only two of many Westerners of Iraqi origin who came from overseas to represent the Iraqi people, though they had long lived abroad. No one I came across in Iraq had any real respect for these men; people felt they represented the interests of their Western homelands far more often than they represented Iraqi interests. Even Iraqis who didn't disrespect these men still didn't feel positively toward them. These estranged Iraqis simply did not know the least thing about the lives of Iraqis or the country of Iraq; they were naturally weak representatives for the Iraqi people.

The Fallujans' skepticism about the delegation rumor and their disregard for "Imported Iraqi Politicians" (as they termed them) was justified. The Islamic Party designated to work on the behalf of the Fallujans delivered nothing but lies in the end—either the Islamic Party was being dishonest or the Americans were, and if it was the Americans, then the Islamic Party should have refused negotiations to begin with. Either way, when these two groups reported that a cease-fire agreement had been reached, they were reporting false information to the public.

Before word came to us that the Bush administration wanted al-Jazeera out of Fallujah, our broadcast equipment was mounted on the rooftop of the three-story private building and we had been able to film a live battle between the insurgents and several American helicopters in the Golan Neighborhood. The battle lasted for an hour, and our cameras were rolling the entire time. We broadcast the battle live as it unfolded.

Afterward, my colleague Muhammad Kraishan interviewed General Kimmitt and asked, "Aren't these attacks by the helicopters a violation of the cease-fire agreement?" Since the interview was live and Kimmitt had no time to prepare a scripted answer, he answered spontaneously, "Our forces were in a self-defense situation there." His answer obviously did not directly address our objections to violations of the cease-fire agreement.

At this point in the siege, one of the biggest problems was that no one knew who was lying and who wasn't. Kimmitt, moments before this helicopter assault, had denied the existence of a cease-fire. When confronted with direct questions about the cease-fire, however, he justified the violation of the very agreement he had denied was in existence! The self-defense justification for this argument was not what caught the attention of the Iraqi viewer, however; it was the fact that Kimmitt didn't maintain his denial of the existence of such an agreement. It was clear to Fallujans by this point that neither the Americans nor the Islamic Party was concerned about their safety. Each side was simply working to serve its own interests amid the ongoing hostilities, and in the meantime the Fallujan casualty counts were climbing. Fallujans I spoke with about this situation were enraged, to say the very least, about the lack of interest in their well-being.

After the siege was over and I was no longer covering events in Fallujah, I came across an article by journalist Yasser Za'atra, of the London-based *Al-Hayat* newspaper. In this article, Za'atra provides analysis of the so-called suspension of hostilities and summarizes the Fallujan perspective. On May 4, 2004, Za'atra wrote,

> Fallujah was definitely going through a crisis, but the crisis the occupation was going through was definitely bigger. The battle of Fallujah was a new and dangerous turning point for the occupation, very differ-

ent from any other previous turning point. As far as Iraqis were concerned, they didn't lose at the battle of Fallujah. The losers were the Iraqi Governing Council members who went absent [in shame] from world media screens for a few days, except for the ones who were completely shameless and have already completely sold themselves out to the occupation. The battle of Fallujah was a victory for Iraqis especially when it was coupled with what can be described as the rebellion of the Al-Sadr movement. Hence, the Islamic Party's mediation and negotiations were really to save the American occupation, not the defiant city or its heroic people.

This article expressed exactly the views I had reported from Fallujah after the first talk of a cease-fire, and are also what Bremer hinted at, and sometimes confessed to, in his memoir.

Another matter that concerned Fallujans during the cease-fire talks was the role being played by Hachem al-Hassani and Iyad Samarray. Both "Imported Iraqi Politicians," as Fallujans called them, delivered nothing useful to Fallujans. People continued to question al-Hassani's presence when he took two high-ranking positions—minister of industry and minerals in the Ayad Allawi cabinet and speaker of the Transitional National Assembly (parliament), both organizations formed after Bremer's term in Iraq was over.

Al-Jazeera Becomes Bremer's New Enemy

There were plenty of reasons Bremer and the American government could use to justify our eviction from the city. Aside from the footage we had broadcast worldwide of the damage within city limits, al-Jazeera crews outside the city had also managed to film American supply convoys totally destroyed along the Abu Ghraib–Fallujah road. The only alternative to the main highway was the Thra'a Dijla. This road had also been blocked, and was now controlled by the insurgents. In taking control, the insurgents had also destroyed any existing American supply convoys.

In addition to the footage of destroyed American military trailers that was filmed by al-Jazeera and broadcast worldwide, Agence France-Presse reported on Friday, April 9, that "hundreds of Iraqi gunmen armed with automatic rifles and armor-piercing rockets managed to control the road that connects Abu Ghraib with Fallujah west of Baghdad." The report also mentioned that "The firing by the gunmen was at its most dense and deadliest at a distance of fifteen kilometers from Fallujah." The report quoted one of the gunmen as saying, "Let the whole world know that we have no alternatives besides victory or death." The report quoted a second gunman who was holding an automatic rifle and encouraging his fellow assailants. He said to them, "You should know that the people of Fallujah support you and demand you to control as much of this highway as possible." Although these images and events were damaging in and of themselves, Bremer and the American government jumped at the opportunity to accuse al-Jazeera of exaggerating what had actually happened in these places.

Throughout his entire memoir, Bremer does not make a single mention of the American television networks—NBC, ABC, CBS, or Fox. However, he does make three references to the BBC, four to CNN, and nine to al-Jazeera. Most of his references to al-Jazeera have to do with his concerns about our coverage and the image the network portrayed of the Marines. He understood how important it was to control the image of the troops and the spin of a story—and al-Jazeera's work concerned him for this very reason.

Our crew attempted to be no nicer to the Marines than we were to the insurgents—we showed no bias to either. Our job in Fallujah was to show the truth, and we worked not to color the truth with our own personal opinions. We hadn't risked our lives to be spokesmen for someone else. But, not surprisingly, Bremer felt that that we were on the side of the insurgents because we were also from this part of the world. He continually attempted, both directly and indirectly, to question our credibility, honesty, and professionalism because of this fact.

For example, Bremer wrote that al-Jazeera was showing footage of what we "claimed were unarmed civilians dead in Fallujah," hinting that the victims we were showing weren't actually civilians. Does he suggest that we found some dead insurgents, took away their weapons and ammunition, placed their bodies inside a bombed-out house, blew up some children to lie next to the dead insurgents, so that we could "claim" these were all civilian victims? Taking the veiled accusation to its logical extension reveals its weakness. We filmed what we saw, as journalists all over the world do, and what we saw were too many innocent victims. It was not our fault that our footage portrayed American forces in a negative light. We simply filmed the reality of the situation in the city of Fallujah.

So it was to cleanse the image of the American forces in Iraq that Bremer believed he had to get us out of Fallujah. He reports in his memoir that General Abizaid "understood that the political situation would not permit continuation of the Fallujah offensive at this moment. We discussed whether the GC delegation would be able to calm things enough to get the story off al-Jazeera." It's clear in this phrasing that one of his prime purposes in calling the cease-fire was to get us to shut up, not to save the lives of civilians.

The demand for the expulsion of our crew from Fallujah became official that morning, though we didn't know it until later in the day. Bremer stressed this demand in a meeting he had with some Fallujan dignitaries the next day, Saturday April 10th. After this demand was issued that we be removed from the city, the Americans, or someone working with them, began to fire on us as though we were fair military targets, spread rumors that whoever cooperated with us would get bombed, and they sent some of their stooges to accuse us of being "the main reason why the fighting was still going on!" This last accusation was disturbingly hilarious—how could any news network possibly be the main reason for any army failing to maintain control of an occupied region?

When I returned to the roof of the three-story building, I found Layth and Sayf airing the tapes we had prerecorded that morning. We decided that I should be in the Golan Neighborhood for the live coverage. This neighborhood had seen bloody, fierce battles on and off all morning. I stood facing the Naimyah Road, where thousands of people had tried to escape death that very morning.

My live segment started, and I gave a detailed narrative of the bloody events of the day. As I was giving my report, a battle broke out just behind where I was standing. F-16s, aided by helicopters, took aim at the entire neighborhood. The cameras did their work and kept the film rolling, capturing the shocking images. Because this scene was filmed in the background of our broadcast, the entire international viewing audience could see that Bremer's "cease-fire" was nothing but a lie.

We continued to film the F-16s as they showered the city—civilians as well as insurgents—with bombs and missiles. While this was going on, I tried to interview Dr. Rafie al-Issawi, who put the death count at nearly 500, with more than a thousand others wounded. I then interviewed several Fallujah residents who had climbed to the roof as soon as they found out we were broadcasting from there. While we filmed them, the residents angrily insisted that it was their right to remain in their city despite the indiscriminate bombing. Every one of those residents expressed his readiness to defend his city and his hatred for occupation forces that would subject his city to this kind of treatment.

We also broadcast more news about the situation of the dead and the wounded. Victims were now being sent to hospitals by private civilian vehicles. Ambulances didn't dare drive for fear of being bombed, especially in the Golan Neighborhood. The dead who managed to reach the field hospital—only yards away from us—were shrouded, prepared for burial, and sent to be buried either by relatives or volunteers. The wounded victims were medicated at the field hospital while critical cases were sent to Baghdad in ambulances. They were now being allowed to leave the city.

We also broadcast a new story about insurgents dealing serious damage to the Marine forces on the highways outside of Fallujah. These forces were managing to break the siege near the Naimyah Road. Yet, despite these breaches, civilians were still unable to flee the city.

Insurgents, as always, employed the tactics of standard hit-and-run guerrilla warfare. They were able to hit the Marines with enough force to get them to leave the Naimyah Road, but they couldn't secure the convoys of civilians escaping the city. Or maybe they didn't want them to escape. The presence of civilians in Fallujah was critical to the success of the insurgents. The more civilians who died, the further tarnished the image of the Marines became. Domestic and international pressure would be put on Bremer to end the military operation as long as ordinary people continued to die.

In the battle between the Marines and the insurgents, the civilians were the ones to pay the price. Sometimes insurgents would fire, hit, and run. When the Marines came looking for the insurgents and found nothing, they were not above firing in anger at whomever they found. Usually the only person in the way was an unfortunate civilian.

As we were broadcasting, I was preoccupied by the knowledge that we were doing so from private property, and that its use hadn't been authorized by the owner. I feared that the owner of the property would come any minute and ask us to leave. It wasn't unreasonable to fear that his property might be targeted because we were there. In the middle of my broadcast I saw some signs of dissent in the crowds that had gathered. Instinctively, I knew the owner had found his way up to his rooftop—a man I later learned was named Mahmoud Khodair Abo Jamal. When he found me, he told me that we could use his property as long as we wanted.

When I tried to apologize for having used it before seeking his permission, he said, "No, no please. Don't mention it. If you need anything while you're up here, just remember that I'm the host and you're the guest. All you have to do is ask."

Abo Jamal was not the only generous one. Every Fallujan who could offer something to facilitate our broadcast did so. When we needed a land telephone line to get reports from the surrounding areas, Dr. Abdulmalik al-Ani, the owner of nearby pharmacy, hooked up a very long phone line from his shop to the rooftop. That phone line played an important role in our keeping watch on the events taking place in parts of the city we couldn't reach.

As soon as Fallujans saw us on al-Jazeera, they knew what building we were broadcasting from. Several of these citizens risked leaving their homes to warn us that we were in a dangerous position. They said our location was way too exposed to be secure. We could easily be hunted by snipers. But we didn't have an alternative; either we broadcast from a high location, risking our lives but showing the city, or we hid for safety in some obscure location and cut all live events and battles from the broadcast.

The Fallujans understood our dedication to getting the story out, but some pointed out that I wasn't wearing a bulletproof vest or a helmet. I had on no protection whatsoever. But again, we had no options—we had none of that equipment. When we came to Fallujah, we had no idea we'd end up in the middle of a battle. We'd brought only two bulletproof vests and no helmets at all. As events escalated and every one of us became very much at the center of the battle, we had to prioritize. The cameramen were the ones most likely to be hit because they were constantly on the move. So the cameramen wore the vests.

Fallujans risked their own lives to help us. Usually Hamed spoke to them and dealt with their concerns, because I was busy broadcasting.

One of the people who came to help us was a man in his forties. He didn't bother to explain himself to Hamed; when he reached the rooftop he simply demanded that we give him something to do. I felt a little suspicious, so I asked Hamed if he knew anything about him. He told me that he knew the man and that he was trustworthy. The man was called Munther Muhammad Obaid, and he turned out to be very handy. Whenever I turned to the right or the left, Munther was there to hand me something, to help me carry something else, always providing help in one way or another. When there wasn't anything to do, he would run down to the streets to gather news—often without us asking. When it was time to eat, he simply ran out, bought lunch for the entire crew, and brought the food up to the roof. When the sun got hot, Munther gave me a hat. Later in the evening when I tried to return the hat to him, he refused to take it. He asked me to keep it as a souvenir to remember him by. My wife would later keep that hat in a special drawer reserved for the clothes I wore during the coverage of the battle of Fallujah.

Munther made himself my personal bodyguard. In the confusion surrounding our broadcasts, at one point a man approached me without anyone noticing. He was looking at me strangely, and as soon as he got close enough, he jumped on me and began trying to strangle and shake me. He screamed that I was an agent for the Americans. It was clear to me that either he was mistaking me for someone else or his fear had turned into uncontrolled paranoia. I tried to explain who I was, but he wouldn't listen. I tried to push the man off me or to scare him away, but he persisted. Munther had just returned from running errands and quickly came to my side. With the help of some others, Munther quickly dragged the man away. When he returned, he took up a vigilant position next to me.

We stayed on the rooftop to film, and the battles kept raging. They would subside for a few moments and return to their original fierceness in no time. We never did feel the effect of the supposed cease-fire or the unilateral suspension of hostilities. It seemed then that the cease-fire was just another rumor, like the one about the Naimyah exit being open for fleeing citizens. We had heard so many conflicting statements from US officials at all levels of the government that we didn't know what to believe anymore. While some parties on the American side demanded that we leave before a cease-fire would be implemented, other parties said that a cease-fire was already in effect (Paul Bremer was the most notable of these). Meanwhile, the Marines repeatedly violated Bremer's supposed cease-fire live and on air before the eyes of the entire world. These forces would suddenly bomb a funeral procession or a convoy of civilians fleeing Fallujah, and it was obvious that they had no intention of slowing their activity.

The day was nearing to a close, and we had all been pushed beyond our physical and mental limits. I stopped work for a minute and watched the sun set. The horizon was smeared in tones of red, just like so much of what we had encountered that day. Below us, small battles and skirmishes exploded in all corners of the city. I tried to keep track of the fighting while also keeping up with the latest developments reported by the others, who were in contact with other journalists and informants. We were waiting for a call from Doha asking for our updates. There was a delay because an explosion had taken place in Baghdad, and the Doha headquarters got involved with the coverage. After a while, I got impatient, and I decided to call them myself.

I dialed Wadah Khanfar. He answered his cell phone immediately. "Ahmed, you've destroyed us! You're gonna get us shut down!" This was his usual greeting for me when my coverage got too "hot," politically speaking.

"You've destroyed us," he repeated as he let out a big laugh. "You're gonna get us bombed out!"

"Bombed? Your usual complaint is that I'll get us shut down," I said.

He replied, "Well, this time the danger is getting bombed. General Kimmitt is talking about you all over the media. Have you heard what he had to say about you?"

I had no idea. At that point the crew and I weren't aware of anything Kimmitt had said about any of us.

"Go watch al-Jazeera right now. We're airing his statement live, and it mentions all of you."

"I can't. I'm on a rooftop. We have no access to a TV set."

"Well, Muhammad Kraishan just interviewed Mark Kimmitt, and he said: 'Your correspondent, Ahmed Mansour, is feeding al-Jazeera viewers with lies from Fallujah.' Kimmitt is mad at you, man. He's got you on his mind."

Despite my exhaustion, I couldn't help but laugh. I said, "So you weren't kidding! What's gotten into him? Since when do generals target journalists by name? They usually attack us as an institution, but never by name. This is definitely a first! I should be honored."

Wadah said, "I know. It's unusual, but it's happening right now. All kidding aside, I have some more serious news for you related to Kimmitt's threats. I hope it doesn't disturb you. The Americans are demanding that you and your crew leave Fallujah immediately as precondition for a cease-fire. They haven't officially declared this demand yet, but sources very close to the delegates say they're going to ask for your departure tomorrow morning. We aired the news after we confirmed it. It's been on the breaking news ticker all day on our screens. But don't worry. Since nothing has been made official, you can keep on with your duties as normal until the matter becomes clearer."

Despite his reassurances, I got plenty worried. I said, "They can't expel us from the city. They can't do that to us or to Fallujans. If they're not happy with our coverage, that's fine. Let them get ticked off all they want. But what do Fallujans have to do with this? How dare they set our departure as a precondition for a cease-fire? A cease-fire should be put together in the interest of saving Fallujan lives, and should have nothing to do with a TV crew. We're the only outlet these people have to share their misery with the rest of the world…" I trailed off, consumed with disbelief and outrage.

Wadah interrupted my mutterings. "Relax, buddy. Relax. No one said you had to leave yet. I said to keep going until the whole deal becomes official. Who knows if it will. Let's just wait and see what happens."

"Fine," I said, "I'll try to relax. Also, I want you to know that we're sending the cameramen, Layth Mushtaq and Hassan Walid, back to Baghdad. They're too wiped to continue. The rest of the crew also needs rest for the afternoon. Can we rest? Or are you going to come back to us for coverage later on in the day?"

"Unfortunately we will have to return to you later on, but for now, we're busy with the explosion in Baghdad. You guys can rest for an hour or so." I agreed reluctantly, wishing we had more time to recuperate. I told the crew we could rest at least a little, and hoped that could be of some comfort.

Wadah and I worked out arrangements for covering news for the rest of the day. I asked his advice about our bad filming location. Filming on the rooftop of the private clinic completely exposed us to the Marines. We knew that at any second we could get hit by snipers, bombed by F-16s, or shelled by the tanks sitting on the other side of the Euphrates. Our location gave us a good vantage point for filming, but it could mean our deaths.

When I hung up with Wadah, Abdulazeem suggested that we go to the field hospital to watch al-Jazeera's breaking news about Kimmitt's accusations. He wanted to hear more details.

I told him, "No, I want to stay here with the rest of the crew. Wadah already told us what Kimmitt said. We don't need any more information than that."

Abdulazeem continued to prod. "But you need to wash up anyway. You look terrible. Let's go to the Islamic Party headquarters and check things out. Then you can wash, and I'll watch the report."

I reluctantly agreed. We headed over to the Islamic Party headquarters. As we approached the door, Abdulazeem said, "Man, this building used to be a fancy movie theater back in Saddam's days. Did you know—"

"Stop thinking about movie stars and focus on what's important here! Come on!" I interrupted, frustrated with his lack of focus.

He quieted down, and when we reached the door of the Islamic Party building I gave him some work to do. "The Governing Council has put together a delegation team in cooperation with Paul Bremer's administration. I want you to go cover the negotiations between the administration and the dignitaries who represent Fallujans. Wadah is confirming the news that our departure from the city as a TV crew is the first demand the delegation is making for a cease-fire negotiation. I want you to get me either confirmation or denial." He agreed to go, after catching Kimmitt's statements on al-Jazeera. We entered the Islamic Party headquarters and I headed to the bathroom to clean up.

As soon as I entered the bathroom, I heard massive explosions erupt outside, very close by. I rushed back into the hallway. Party officials were shouting for everyone to stay in the building. We tried to leave anyway, telling them we didn't want to be separated from the rest of our crew.

They denied us exit, saying, "The gunfire is right out the door. You can see the glare of the flying bullets. These aren't regular M-16 bullets. These are much higher-caliber projectiles coming from the other side of the Euphrates. The Marines on that side are firing at the rooftop—exactly where you were a few minutes ago."

We looked cautiously out the window. We could see there was an exchange of fire between the insurgents and the Marines. We weren't able to see the insurgents, but it was clear that they were positioned a couple of hundred yards away, and they had lower positions than the Marines. They had to have been positioned in the streets, between buildings, or in alleys because the fire they were returning was at low altitudes. Their strategy was simply to avoid being exposed to enemy fire.

We stayed at the party headquarters until the violence subsided. As soon as we felt it was relatively safe, we crossed the street in the company of one of the doctors who wanted to get to the field hospital. The doctor warned us, "Watch out… bursts of fire are still coming every couple of minutes. Cross the street carefully."

Just as the doctor finished talking, a spray of gunfire headed in our direction, so we bolted toward the other side of the street, covering our heads. We could see the red glare of the massive flying bullets that the party officials had spoken about. We knew that they were not regular M-16 bullets, because those have no red glare.

Over the noise of the gunfire, Abdulazeem yelled, "Look! They're firing at the crew! The rest of the guys are still on the roof!" The doctor screamed out warnings for us to watch out for bullets, but we ran toward the building anyway. We had to get to the rest of the crew to make sure they were okay. We entered the building and started taking the steps two at a time. We reached the top of the stairs gasping for air—I don't know if we were out of breath because we ran so hard or because we were so scared.

"Is everyone okay?" I yelled in panic as I looked at the guys taking shelter on the stairs between the third flood and the rooftop.

One said, "Yes. Luckily we were praying when the shots broke out. It was dusk prayer time and we were kneeling on the floor of the rooftop. Then big bullets zoomed just above our heads. If we'd been standing, we would've been dead."

I paused, thinking. Had the Marines suddenly gone insane enough to attempt to bomb a television crew? We couldn't avoid the conclusion that they had aimed for the al-Jazeera TV crew. This had been a deliberate shot.

First, there had been the demand by Bremer's people that we leave the city as a condition for a cease-fire. Then, Mark Kimmitt directly accused me of spreading rumors and propagating lies. And now here we were, hiding from direct fire, the sole targets. This sequence of events could not possibly be coincidental.

We called the al-Jazeera newsroom and told them what had happened, and their breaking news ticker announced live that our crew had been targeted with fire. We called our families to let them know that we were all safe.

At that time, we had no idea about the NSC meeting at which Bush, Rice, Powell, Bremer, Abizaid, Sanchez, and Blackwill were discussing the problems our coverage was creating. We had no idea that the latter four remained another half-hour after the meeting was over to discuss how to get al-Jazeera to stop spreading news about the American activities in Fallujah. Kimmitt's personal attack on me and the Marine attack on the al-Jazeera crew was being widely portrayed as simple coincidence. In truth, they were the first incidents in Bush's war on al-Jazeera.

Luckily, no one was harmed in this attack. We left the rooftop in a panic, but our broadcast equipment remained there. The owner of the building promised to keep our materials safe, because the equipment was too heavy to move—and his rooftop provided a prime spot for broadcast. With that, the entire crew vacated the building.

It was the end of a long, frightening, bloody day. None of us had the energy or presence of mind to do much. Once off the rooftop of the building, we stayed around the field hospital witnessing more of the suffering we had seen all day long. We asked if there were any new victims. I was hoping the answer would be no because I couldn't handle any more dead children. But there was another family of three generations dead: a grandfather, an uncle, and a grandson. This last straw came precisely at the wrong time. It had been a bloody day, and the last thing we needed was to see more unnecessary death. Our spirits were officially broken.

As we walked out of the hospital, I called Wadah Khanfar and told him that we were now officially targeted by the Marines. He said that Shaikh Hamad bin Thamer al-Thani, chairman of al-Jazeera's board of directors, wanted to talk to us to make sure we were okay. Shaikh Hamad was always in contact with me, but this time it was different. He asked to talk to each member of the crew, most of whom he'd never met and didn't know, and commended them one by one for their bravery and excellent humanitarian service to the people of Iraq. Before I handed the phone to each person, I'd introduce the person to Shaikh Hamad and tell him of the role that person played. He commended them individually for their personal roles, and handed us collective praise for our work as a group. This phone call really lifted our spirits. We were exhausted and very worried about being attacked by the Marines—we needed the emotional support Shaikh Hamad gave us.

This wasn't the first time Shaikh Hamad had lifted out spirits during this coverage, but it was the most remarkable occasion, because it came at a time the entire crew needed so desperately to hear some uplifting words. Shaikh Hamad was in contact with me regularly, as was Wadah Khanfar and the rest of the newsroom staff. They never let us down and always found a way to support us with everything they could offer from Doha. Although we were the only ones in the field doing the reporting, our crew in Doha deserves the highest of praise for its support and dedication.

The Last Generosity of Hussain Sameer

After we hung up with Hamad, I turned to the crew and asked what our plan was. Hussain Deli suggested we eat at his place. We had planned to skip dinner because we were all so depressed, but the call from Hamad had brightened us enough so that our appetites returned.

We had three men carrying our belongings as we walked through the city. I didn't know any of them, but I had seen them helping the crew gather things from the rooftop before we left. Hamed took the time then to introduce these men to me. Two of them were Hamed's brothers-in-law, Hussain Sameer and Nizar Sameer. The third man was called Omar Farouq. Hamed offered to take me, Abdulazeem, and Omar Farouq to have dinner at Hussain Sameer's place; only two or three houses away from our location. Hussain Deli, Layth, Hassan, Abo Omar, and Sayf were going to have dinner at Deli's house and sleep over there.

Before we went our separate ways for dinner, we made a plan for the next day. The plan was for Layth, Hassan, and Abo Omar to return to Baghdad with any of the convoys going there. Hussain Deli and Sayf were to be at our broadcast location by 7:00AM. Abdulazeem and Hamed were to take on the role of cameramen, and also do news reports. The Baghdad office agreed to send us two cameramen to replace Hassan and Layth, who had become too exhausted to continue working. These two courageous men had spent the last few days constantly on their feet. Several times I even saw Layth sleep while standing, leaning against a wall. They were a mess, and they needed to be sent home to rest.

When we arrived at Hussain Sameer's home for dinner, he welcomed us warmly.

As he served us supper, he apologized for the crudeness of the meal. "I'm very sorry. This is all we could prepare on such a short notice. This is well below what I would've served you had I known that I'd be your host. Tomorrow, every single one of your crew has to have supper here— a supper befitting of such good people."

As we were having supper, the newsroom staff in Doha called and asked me to give the latest live update. I gave a brief live update over the phone and then returned to the table.

We talked about the events of the day while having supper. I asked our host if he was planning to leave the city.

He said, "I don't care what the Marines do. This is our home. They're the aggressors and the occupiers. I'm not fleeing my town just to leave it to them."

His six-year-old son walked in as we were sitting. I played with the little boy and then asked him if he was staying or leaving. He replied, "Wherever my dad is, that's where I'll be. I'm staying."

After supper, Hamed stayed to sleep at his brother-in-law's place. Abdulazeem and I went with Omar Farouq to sleep at his house on the other side of the field hospital, not far from where we had supper.

Omar Farouq was the patriarch of a big family. In Fallujah, as in many other conservative parts of the region, the home of a big family hosts more than just the immediate family. It's usually a very large house with sections and suites made of two-bedroom accommodations or semi-separate apartments within the bigger house. Sons and daughters often continue to live with the family after getting married; they just take one of the suites to themselves to have some privacy. Omar Farouq's place was like this. Except that when we stayed there the house was completely empty, because he'd sent his entire family out of Fallujah. Omar was alone in the enormous house.

Omar was a very hospitable person. He tried his best to make us at ease. He offered us each a bedroom of our choosing, or an entire suite if we wanted. We told him that we preferred to stay in the same room. At times like these, huddling together provides a feeling of security, and security was a commodity in very short supply in the middle of the siege. He said in that case, he'd stay with us in the room too.

I had trouble sleeping, as one would imagine. I tossed and turned in my sleeping bag, trying in vain to forget the images of the day. It is unquestionable that it had been a devastating and tragic day for the children of Fallujah. I still have not forgotten the fear on those little faces, or the sight of their small hands holding fiercely onto the twigs with their white flags of surrender. I remember the little footprints I saw on the sands leading to the Naimyah desert, and I remember the severed limbs and broken bodies hauled to the field hospital after the fighter jets senselessly bombed these children for attempting to cross the Naimyah exit.

As I turned to my right side trying to sleep, I felt lumps in my pocket that I had forgotten about— a small packet of cookies one of the doctors had given me in the morning for breakfast, and a piece of chocolate a Fallujan had given me in gratitude for our coverage. I couldn't help but think that even though the siege was enormously overwhelming and indescribably dangerous, small acts of kindness like these somehow made me feel better. The doctor had been dealing with dead and wounded people all day long, and yet he took the time to provide me with something to eat. The person who gave me the chocolate, whose name I never knew, had been running in an attempt to protect his life, and yet, he paused to express gratitude to me. I thought to myself: it is amazing how some human beings can kill indiscriminately and others can give the little they have.

I tried to rest as much as I could, but as usual, I failed. Bombing and skirmishes kept me up for most of the night, along with intense anxiety about the next few days.

12. THE FINAL DAY OF THE SIEGE

Early in the morning, Munther came to Omar Farouq's place and caught me on my way out. I was alone, heading toward the field hospital. Munther was irate.

He said, "How dare you walk alone, Ahmed! The situation in this city is very dangerous, and there are some suspicious-looking gunmen at the field hospital asking about you."

"Gunmen?" I was immediately alarmed. "What did they want?"

Munther answered, "I asked them, but they wouldn't say. I stayed around and watched them just in case you arrived while they were there. I didn't know what they'd do. Eventually they left and said they would return later."

I tried to reassure him. "Try not to worry, Munther. I really have no choice but to go up to the roof. Our equipment is still there and the whole set-up is still functional. I have to participate in the morning news live. I also have to go to the field hospital to get the latest updates." Munther was nervous, and followed me like my shadow. I told him repeatedly that he didn't have to, but he refused to let me walk alone. He just kept saying that he was nervous about the gunmen he had encountered earlier.

When I arrived at the field hospital, it was only a matter of minutes before I was confronted by a strange man.

"I've been waiting for you here since 6:00AM," he said. I didn't recognize him, and I had no idea how to respond to his unconventional greeting. I wasn't worried that he was one of the gunmen—for one thing, he wasn't armed. Secondly, Munther didn't seem to be at all suspicious.

"Don't you recognize me?" the man continued. I searched his face, but came up with nothing. I shook my head.

"I'm the one who attacked you yesterday on the rooftop. I accused you of being a spy for the Americans."

I began to back away in fear, but the man reached out his hand, "Don't be alarmed—I just came to apologize. It was a case of mistaken identity, and I take all the blame. We're in the middle of a war, and either one of us could die any moment. I didn't want to die without your forgiveness."

He then pulled out a piece of paper from his pocket and handed it to me. He continued, "I wrote you this apology in case I was killed during the night. This way I hoped that whoever recovered my body would find this, and deliver it to you."

As I read his apology, the words scrawled out on the paper became blurred by my tears. I hugged him and told him I understood, and that I had understood from the beginning that he had meant me no harm. He wouldn't let go of me, and our embrace lasted for several minutes. He kept crying and asking for forgiveness until we were both crying. I told him we both needed forgiveness for things we might have neglected to do during this chaotic time.

After this emotional encounter, I collected myself and went into the hospital to get the daily update. Once I found the doctors, they told me that the bombing the night before had targeted the Educators', Officers', and Golan Neighborhoods. The doctor also reported that around 1AM a man had come looking for volunteers and an ambulance to retrieve the body of his brother from under the rubble of his home in the Educators' Neighborhood. I jotted down everything and headed to the broadcast location to prepare my report.

The city seemed very tense. All of us were nervous broadcasting from atop such a tall building. Almost everyone we met on the walk from the field hospital to the rooftop warned us not to stay on top of that building, especially after being targeted the night before. Omar Farouq offered to have us broadcast from his house, which was definitely safer than our location. The problem was that we'd be broadcasting from his backyard, which had plenty of space and a good signal, but not a good view of the city. If we were to go up to his roof, which was definitely high enough for all our purposes, we would be taking the same risk we were taking by filming from the rooftop of the clinic. In the end, we made the decision to do the morning broadcast from the rooftop of the clinic, and then move our equipment to Farouq's house, where hopefully the Americans would be unable to find us.

Munther and I climbed the three stories to the rooftop and turned on our equipment. We went live to give our morning update on *Al-Jazeera This Morning*. We filmed as quickly as possible, then descended—we knew we needed to clear the area in a hurry, considering the rumors about the possibility of being targeted by gunmen. Hussain Sameer, Hamed's brother in-law, arrived with his brother Nizar to check on us, and to confirm his invitation for dinner at his place. He also helped us undo our equipment and carry it to Omar Farouq's place.

After we moved our equipment, I headed to the field hospital again, while Abdulazeem Muhammad went to the al-Hadrah al-Muham-madeyah Mosque. At the mosque, a delegation from the Iraqi Governing Council was waiting for him to cover the cease-fire negotiations.

While Abdulazeem was covering the activity at the mosque, I stood outside the field hospital talking to the families of victims, interviewing them, and gathering information from them. I also talked to the paramedics as they wrapped the dead in shrouds for burial. In the middle of all this reportage, I felt a hand touch me lightly from behind. It was one of the doctors. He pulled me from the crowd and led me deeper into the hospital.

I thought this doctor wanted to show me some victims to film or give me an update of the casualty count. Instead, he whispered, "Please don't stay here. The situation is very dangerous for you in particular. We've had numerous reports from Fallujans who have heard information that should concern you. There are many informants and spies around here. We all watched Mark Kimmitt accuse you last night on air of 'changing the truth.' We also watched the Marines target your crew's location yesterday. It's very possible that the Marines or someone working with the American military will try to liquidate you any way they can."

He continued, "You take too many risks to the point of being reckless. You walk alone without any guards, and you don't even know this area very well. It's a recipe for death."

I was puzzled. "What do you think I should do? I don't know what to do differently. I'm just doing my job. I can't stay in a secluded safe place behind closed doors and still report on what is happening in the city and to these people. I have to seek the information myself. We don't have a huge crew, and we're certainly not armed. What protection can I ever have? I have no guards and we didn't bring any vests or helmets with us from Baghdad because we didn't expect to be covering a siege."

The doctor shook his head. I couldn't tell if he was disagreeing with me or just reacting with dismay over the desperate situation.

"Listen," I said, trying to console him. "We've come face to face with death several times since we started our coverage here. I'm not talking about just me—I'm talking about the entire al-Jazeera crew. Despite that danger, no one has died. Hiding will not make it less likely for one of us to be killed. All the children who were butchered yesterday weren't covering news or upsetting the Marines, and yet, somehow they ended up slaughtered. We're not stopping the work of our crew just to seek personal safety. It would do no good to anyone."

The doctor nodded, and seemed to soften slightly. He said, "I understand your obligations. But please come and sit with us inside for a little bit. Maybe the picture will become a little clearer to you then."

The doctor led me to a very small room where Dr. Rafie al-Issawi, the director of the hospital, was sitting along with several other doctors. They greeted me warmly. At the doctor's request, I sat and talked with them for a little bit. The doctors spoke frankly about the situation my crew and I were involved in. Some hinted at the danger facing me alone, while others spoke explicitly about the risk they believed was surrounding the entire al-Jazeera crew. I listened to their objections. When they were finished, I thanked them for their concern, and said my goodbyes.

As I was leaving the room, one of the doctors said in a whisper, "Be really careful, Ahmed. Really careful." I nodded gravely and left the room.

Although none of the doctors quoted any specific American or Iraqi official in this discussion, it seemed to me that they knew something they weren't willing to divulge entirely. It seemed as if they had been told explicitly that a clear threat was made against our lives by some Iraqi or American officials—without naming names, these doctors had spoken of the risks we were running in extremely precise detail. The American demand for our departure hadn't been made official yet, but it had reached both al-Jazeera headquarters and Iraqi officials in Baghdad, including Governing Council representatives. No ordinary citizens should have been aware of the details of such a private threat. As I left the strange meeting, I reasoned that maybe some of those representatives had contacted the doctors because they knew we were spending a lot of time filming at the hospital, and asked them to deliver the threatening message. The doctors knew that Bremer and his Marines were on to us, and that neither was going to let us get away with exposing the crimes committed in Fallujah.

After I left the meeting with the doctors, I finished gathering news from the field hospital and headed back to Omar Farouq's place. Abdulazeem Muhammad returned around the same time I did from his coverage of the negotiations between city leaders and the Governing Council's delegates. He summed up the meeting for me: several Governing Council members were represented at the meeting, even though they didn't personally attend the proceedings. Hachem al-Hassani represented Dr. Mohsen Abdul Hameed, the representative from the Iraqi Islamic Party. There were also representatives for Ghazi al-Yawar and Adnan Pachachi, another couple of Sunni board members. Several people represented the city of Fallujah—two Fallujan men in particular stood out as noteworthy public figures. The first was Dr. Ahmad Hardan, a representative for the Islamic Party in Fallujah. The second was Shaikh Abdallah al-Janabi, who later became the head of the Mujahideen Consultative Council in Fallujah.

Abdulazeem told me of several conditions and demands made by the Governing Council representatives in order for the siege to end and for a cease-fire agreement to be reached. Not all conditions were to be declared to the public. The first condition was that the al-Jazeera crew (me in particular) leave the city, as Wadah Khanfar had told me. As Bremer declared in his memoir, one of the main reasons for this part of the agreement was to get the story of Fallujah off al-Jazeera and thus off the radar of international media.

The conditions that were made public are listed in Bremer's memoir: "The city's sheiks must hand over the killers of our men. We also wanted the names of the foreign fighters there. The insurgents had to lay down arms. If they fired on us, we would react." These were the public conditions Bremer delivered to al-Hassani on Friday, April 9. The delegation didn't actually meet until the next morning, though, because the road had been cut off by the insurgents. Reuters and Agence France-Presse mentioned another undeclared condition, which was submission of a list of Iraqi Police members who had turned their backs on the Marines and joined the insurgents.

It is important to note, however, that with the exception of expelling our crew from Fallujah, the power to meet any of these conditions was not in the hands of Fallujans. The Fallujan people didn't know which insurgents were former policemen. Most Fallujans didn't know who had murdered the four Blackwater USA mercenaries. They didn't know which insurgents were foreign fighters, if any, and they certainly didn't know their names. They had no control over whether insurgents were going to lay down arms or not. Quite simply, Fallujans couldn't accommodate any of the conditions, except for the one that required the expulsion of our crew from the city.

Oddly enough, even this one condition that they could perhaps succeed in fulfilling wasn't entirely within their control, and had come about through no fault on their part. When our crew came to Fallujah to do our coverage, we didn't have anyone in Fallujah sign a permission slip allowing us entry. We didn't even ask those in positions of power to grant us permission. We were authorized by the Coalition Authorities to perform journalistic and press-related activities in Iraq, and we exercised our right and duty. For Bremer to hold our coverage, which he utterly hated, against Fallujans as if it were something for which they were responsible was ridiculous. Civilized people don't hold one group accountable for the deeds of another group.

In exchange for fulfillment of these conditions, Fallujans were guaranteed nothing. They were given the promise of a cease-fire; a promise the Marines had already broken, as acknowledged by Kimmitt and Byrne a day before.

Abdulazeem's summation of the meeting's proceedings was cut short when the newsroom called asking for the noon news segment. It was my colleague Abdussamad Nasser presenting the news. I put Abdulazeem on hold, and began filming the noon news segment. In the midst of my update on the latest developments, AC-130 gunships and F-16s began attacking from the skies.

Over the roar of noise, Abdussamad Nasser asked, "Ahmed, what has become of the cease-fire they've been talking about?"

I shouted in reply, "I'll let these fighter jets and airplanes answer that question."

Abdulazeem was doing the camera work since Hassan and Layth had returned to Baghdad. He tried to maneuver the camera to capture the airplanes in frame, but the fighter jets were much faster than his hand. Also, his view was limited since we were broadcasting from Farouq's yard, not the rooftop. The deafening sound of bombs were very clear to the viewers, though, and provided some clues to what we were experiencing. Massive clouds of black smoke began to rise from every corner of the city, shrouding the entire area in a thick, dark haze.

Soon after this attack began, we got word that world news agencies were quoting an American sergeant serving in Fallujah as saying that the firing at the moment was now as intense as when the siege began. He said that the insurgents didn't believe a cease-fire was even being considered by the Americans, and so they continued to fight, forcing the Marines to fight back in self-defense. Women and children, in the meantime, continued to try to flee the city. Lt. Colonel Brennan Byrne reported that he hadn't received any orders related to a cease-fire, and thus he vowed to continue his operation until he received word to stop. He said he had no information about what went on in the meeting about the cease-fire, and his commanders hadn't ordered him to suspend any hostilities yet. So the fighting continued.

As morning turned into afternoon, insurgency activity increased all over Iraq, even outside the borders of Fallujah. Muqtada al-Sadr's militia continued their rebellion all across the south, retaliating fiercer and stronger because of the Americans' decision to arrest al-Sadr. Residents of Baghdad went on a strike, and protests broke out all over the capital city. Similar protests emerged in many other cities. Battles broke out in just about every major city, and the occupation forces had little time to do anything but fight back in self-defense.

The biggest act of insurgent rebellion on that Saturday afternoon took place in Samarra. Insurgents had gained control of the entire city, including its police stations. The insurgents had gotten their hands on police weapons, communication devices and other hardware, and also gained access to police cars and other vehicles. It wasn't long before American forces were cornered so badly that they had to flee the center of the city and attempt to hide in the outskirts of the city. The insurgents weren't quite strong enough to expel American forces further, so the Americans formed a tight circle around the city, and were able to stand their ground and keep the insurgents inside.

Because of this violence, our day was chaotic from the moment we set out. In between calls to the newsroom, I ran into the streets and gathered information from the people. Hamed Hadeed called his contacts for information in other parts of the city and the country. Abdulazeem was reporting on the Governing Council delegation and the negotiations he had witnessed. Hamed was also making another report on the bombings he had covered and the many violations of the so-called cease-fire. Sayf was monitoring and maintaining the broadcast equipment. We continued in this way for a while, getting the work done as quickly and attentively as we could.

At about 1:30 in the afternoon, a fighter jet passed so close and so fast over our heads that it sounded as though it broke the sound barrier. The jet circled and then dropped a bomb very close by. We ran outside to see if we could tell what the target had been. The smoke spiraled from a building near Farouq's house, but we couldn't get high enough off the ground to have a good view of the entire surrounding area. I decided to run to the field hospital to see if they had more information and to watch for victims if they came in. It was vital that we find out how close the bomb had come to us, so we could find out if we were actually the target.

On my way to the field hospital, a group of people stopped me.

One of them said, "Where do you think you're going, Ahmed? They've just bombed the house where your crew was last night, and the owner is dead! Please, for your sake, stay inside so you don't end up dead as well!"

Shocked by this news, I asked urgently, "Which house? Our crew last night split into three groups and slept the night in three different houses. Which house was hit?" I knew it couldn't have been Omar Farouq's house because I had just come from there.

"Was it Hussain Deli's house or Hussain Sameer's house?" I begged the people for an answer. No one in the group seemed to recognize the names Hussain Deli or Hussain Sameer. They speculated and made all sorts of guesses, but I stopped listening. It was going to be painful for me and the crew to find out either way. My head was spinning in panic. If the house in question was Hussein Deli's house, then we had lost a colleague. If it was Hussain Sameer's house, then we had lost a friend and a relative of one of our colleagues. In either case, the news would be devastating to every single person in our crew.

I ran to the hospital as fast as I could, muttering the names of the two men, knowing that one of them was now in pieces, buried beneath the rubble of his home. I gripped by a kind of hysteria. The crowds and the streets swirled around me as I pushed past the people and made my way to the entrance of the hospital. I prayed for a misunderstanding, a mistake. Maybe it's one of those rumors, I said to myself. This town is full of rumors. Everyone is confused. There's no order to anything. Yes. Yes. I'm sure it's a rumor. I knew I was fooling myself. But I also knew I had to hear the truth about who had died from someone I trusted before I could believe it. I had to get to the field hospital.

I arrived there dazed and out of breath. I grabbed the arm of the first staff member I saw.

But before I could catch my breath and ask who the victim of the last bombing was, I knew the answer. I looked past the emergency medical worker and saw Nizar, Hussain Sameer's brother, standing just beyond the entrance of the hospital.

Nizar was immobile, clutching his arms around his body, consumed by his grief. He released only muffled sobs, but his bloodshot eyes were swimming in tears. As soon as he saw me, he ran to me. He threw his head on my shoulder and released a series of giant, heaving sobs. Although I had had trouble coping with death many times over the course of this siege, this time I couldn't allow myself to collapse. Someone else needed my support; someone who'd just witnessed the murder of his own brother. I tried my best to be a comforting presence for Nizar.

Soon thereafter, the paramedics arrived at the hospital and pulled Hussain Sameer's body out of an ambulance. The paramedics said

Sameer's house had been bombed by a missile and that he had suffered fatal injuries to his head. Two others had been wounded in the attack, but they had survived. I couldn't believe the man with whom we had eaten the night before was gone. Things he had done for us kept running through my mind. He had helped us undo our broadcast equipment. He had made supper for us and let us stay in his home. Since the moment he had come into our lives a few days earlier, he had been a generous and spirited man. We had made plans to have dinner with him again that evening. Now, he was a corpse, a body to be added to the already staggering count of casualties from this bloody conflict.

Outside the doors of the hospital there was a sudden explosion of confusion and hysteria. People began to scurry away from Sameer's house and away from the entrance of the field hospital, where I stood with Nizar.

There was a sudden shout from the middle of the crowd, "Watch out! The Americans are chasing after the al-Jazeera crew! They're bombing the places the crew goes. They had supper at that house last night. The owner is dead now!"

These warnings against associating with us spread through town as fast as fire burns through dry haystacks. It wasn't long before the rumor reached everyone, and Fallujans refused to associate with us. I never knew the identity of that man in the crowd outside the hospital who started the rumors against us, and I never saw him again. But the damage was done. From that point on, we became outlaws in the very city we were trying to protect and defend.

I resisted the urge to find the rest of the crew and go into temporary hiding. Instead, I spent about a half-hour with Nizar, trying to comfort him. When he had collected himself somewhat, I bid him goodbye and headed toward Omar Farouq's house to find the rest of the crew.

When I arrived at Omar Farouq's place, I found the atmosphere inside the house—which had been so welcoming the previous night—unusually tense. As I walked in the front door, I was confronted by the sight of several unfamiliar men sitting in the living room, all with very stern looks on their faces. I felt very uncomfortable. I pulled Abdulazeem to the side and asked him what was going on.

He said, "These are Omar Farouq's uncles. They came here and requested that the crew—and you, in particular—leave the house. A rumor is going around town that the Marines are targeting every place al-Jazeera might be. Omar refused to force us out, but his uncles are insisting. This is a tribal area, and Omar doesn't have the authority to dishonor his uncles' word. He has to do what they say."

I nodded, "Okay. Let's spare the poor man the humiliation. Get our stuff together and we'll leave. Omar has been more than generous already. Good people don't overstay their welcome. We're out of here."

Abdulazeem stopped me, "Not so fast. We'll leave after lunch. The neighbors have made us lunch and they're bringing it over in a few minutes. We can't turn down their offer. I told you—this is a tribal region. These people get offended very easily."

I couldn't believe what I was hearing. I thought to myself, what lunch can one enjoy under circumstances like these? But he was right to say that we had to obey tribal customs, and he was also right that we should accept what generosity was offered to us.

While we ate our lunch, I kept trying to figure out who the man was who had started the rumor about the Marines targeting our crew. I had no idea who would have any interest in spreading such a rumor. The person had to be connected to the same party who wanted us kicked us out of the city. They wanted to scare Fallujans from helping us, and isolate us to the point where we found ourselves alone on the streets. Such isolation would make us very easy targets. Whoever was responsible for this rumor wanted it to appear that Fallujans forced us out of the city on their own accord. This way the international media couldn't say that a world superpower had targeted a group of journalists for simply doing their job. After all, the entire war on this country was waged in the name of freedom of expression and freedom of speech and other things the Bush administration claimed were supported by the American government. This same government couldn't very well be revealed to be stifling the exact values they claimed to hold so dear.

Abdulazeem noticed I was consumed by these troubling musings. He said, "Don't worry about it, pal. We'll find another suitable place to stay, but there is no place for us here." I nodded in agreement and tried to enjoy what was left of my lunch.

Hamed didn't know yet that his brother-in-law had died. He knew that he'd been severely injured, but not that the wounds had been fatal. One of the paramedics very early after the bombing said that Sameer could possibly be saved. This assurance gave Hamed enough peace to keep him away from the hospital for most of the morning. He wanted to work on the news report that was supposed to air on the *Midday News* program. He was planning to go to the hospital as soon as he finished the report, in order to stay with his wounded brother-in-law.

Abdulazeem asked me to deliver the bad news of Sameer's death to Hamed.

I refused. "No. He won't take it very well for obvious reasons, and all his work on the report will go to waste. I'm sure the report has footage of his brother-in-law after he was hit. These images have to go on air today because the best thing we can do for this poor dead man is to let the world know of the brutal crime that was committed against him. I want Hamed to finish the report to the best of his ability. It's only a half-hour segment. Then I'll tell him the bad news."

The first information I had about the bombing at Sameer's house was that Sameer was killed while standing in front of his house, or just inside. I learned from Abdulazeem on the walk to Sameer's place, though, that there were also rumors that a bomb fell on Sameer in the street. He had just finished the noon prayer at the al-Rawi Mosque, which wasn't very far from his house. On his way back from the mosque, he was hit and killed, along with two other men. This was a different story than the version where his actual house was targeted and bombed—a very different story with very different implications. In the new story, we really had no idea if Sameer was intentionally targeted for having sheltered us the night before, or if it was just his fate to be indiscriminately bombed like the hundreds of civilians who had already died.

The rumor that circulated most quickly was that Sameer's actual house was bombed and he was killed inside it. Being bombed in his own home surely meant that he was targeted. The claim that whoever sheltered al-Jazeera's crew would be targeted by the Marines, albeit unverifiable, was very believable to people who had been living in a giant death camp for five days. The version of the story where Sameer's house was blown up with him inside is precisely what urged Omar Farouq's uncles to ask us to leave.

Omar was still traveling around the city with us even after we left his house, but he shied away from me as we did our work. He was a truly polite and sensitive man. He wasn't able to face me after having to ask me to leave his house—it was humiliating and degrading for him. In this tribal culture, it's shameful to ask your guest to leave your house. Omar didn't know that I understood his situation, and that I knew there wasn't really any reason for him to be ashamed of his request. To save him from the humiliation, I hadn't let him physically ask me to leave the house. I just started packing and took my things outside. For the rest of the day, while he was around, I tried to ease his embarrassment as best I could, but I didn't succeed.

As we tried to continue with our work, I puzzled over what we could do to maintain a presence in this city, despite so many obstacles. I reached no satisfactory conclusion. I called Wadah Khanfar, but found his cell phone switched off. I later learned that he'd been on a plane heading to Cairo when I had tried to reach him. So I was left with no advice. I decided to call Shaikh Hamad bin Thamer al-Thani, as I often have when an executive decision has to be made in dire circumstances. I explained the situation to him and outlined the difficulties we had faced in the last two days, which put our work in the city in severe jeopardy.

I asked for his advice.

"The American administration is exerting every form of pressure it can in order to get you out of Fallujah, and they've made their intentions public," he said. "Please, put your safety and that of your colleagues before anything else. You guys and your safety are far more important to us than any piece of exclusive coverage. Even if we were to ignore the media business aspect of it and look at just the humanitarian aspect, we'd still reach the same conclusion. You've performed your duty to the highest professional standards and done a great service to these people. No one is asking you to do more than this. If you stay any longer in Fallujah, you'll become a burden on Fallujans instead of helping their cause. I think it's time to leave, especially considering the fact that the siege is starting to break, even if just partially. There is some improvement in the situation."

I listened to Shaikh Hamad's words carefully and took them into serious consideration, but a part of me still wasn't willing to leave. I believed there was still a chance, albeit a miniscule one, that Hussain Sameer's death wasn't intentional. His death might be chalked up to bad luck or bad timing, not an American attempt to hunt us down. The same logic could be applied to the heavy artillery rockets that were fired at our location the previous night. I knew that my logic wasn't very sound. Yet I held on to the last glimmer of hope that I could stay in the city and keep exposing injustices.

I thanked Shaikh Hamad for his advice. I told him, "Still, I hope you'll let me have one last chance at reaching a unanimous decision with the rest of the crew. I'd like us all to stay or go as one unit. I will meet with them and tell them what you had to say. I'll update you on whatever the crew's final decision is."

Shortly after this phone call, I received another call, this one from

Ahmad Alshaikh, the editor-in-chief at the newsroom. He was very concerned.

He said, "Your mere appearance on al-Jazeera's screen is irritating and agitating the Bush administration. They can't stand the sight of you anymore. Enough is enough, man! Kimmitt mentioned you by name yesterday, and it is clear to us that he's after you and wants your head. Please, please, please stop doing any reports or participating in news segments. Let the rest of the crew do the reports, and stay off the camera."

I agreed to this condition. We were actually considering something like that ourselves, now that rumors had spread all over town and I had become a burden to the civilians I was trying to help. We decided to have Abdulazeem do the 4PM news update. I told Ahmad I had just talked to upper management in Doha, and that I was meeting with the crew to discuss our next action. I promised to keep him posted.

I gathered the entire crew to discuss the situation. Sayf, being a telecommunication engineer and knowing how signals can be tracked, said, "The Marines can easily track us regardless of how well we may hide ourselves. The satellite signals we transmit are easy to follow. I'm sure it registers on their sensors as 'hostile signal' or 'enemy signal' or something like that. This will pose a constant threat to whatever neighborhood within Fallujah we happen to be filming in."

Abdulazeem and Hamed then spoke about having no place to sleep, eat, or rest, but came up with no additional suggestions. From their hesitant talk and reluctance to make a new point, I could tell that they were reluctant to say what was on their minds. So, I said it myself.

I told the crew, "Let's be blunt. You guys are not the problem. After all, this is your city, your home. Even those among you who are not from Fallujah are still Iraqis. You could easily go to any of your relatives' places and stay with them, and you'd be more than welcomed by them in this situation. It's me who has become a burden on everyone. I'm the outsider. I'm the foreigner and the front man here, and I'm the one who is most targeted by the Marines. Kimmitt accused me by name last night; he didn't do the same for the rest of the crew. The Governing Council delegation asked for my expulsion in particular, while they asked that the rest of the crew just stop working."

I paused to make sure they were listening, and to be sure they didn't think I was accusing them of anything. "I came here to show the world the sad reality of civilians being caught between the insurgents and the Marines. We've done a good job showing that. No success is optimal unless it takes place at the right time: not too soon, not too late. Just like there was a time for entering Fallujah, I believe now is the time for me to leave. The last thing I want to do right now is to abandon this mission. However, there is no point in stubbornness. We're journalists, not an army. If remaining in Fallujah means that the city keeps getting bombed, then we're defying the very purpose for being here: to help the people of Fallujah. Also, the siege is almost over, albeit partially, and some people are managing to escape the city or return to it with humanitarian supplies from side roads. So, as far as I'm concerned, I really should leave Fallujah before I overstay my welcome. I have been blessed with the generosity and hospitality of Fallujans, and I will cherish that forever."

There was a palpable lifting of tension in the room. It felt good for me to accept unintentional responsibility for the difficulty we were facing, and our mutual responsibility to leave the city before we caused more damage. These crew members were friends before they were colleagues, and I wanted to make sure I comforted them just as they had comforted me throughout my entire stay in their city.

Sayf said, "If you're leaving, Ahmed, then I am leaving with you. And if you're staying, I will stay too."

"If you leave with me, who would run the satellite equipment?"

He reconsidered. "Okay, I'll return in a few days to do some more work. But first I'll go to Baghdad to see my wife and kids, and then I'll come back here when traveling is a little easier."

Hamed nodded in agreement. "It's good if you leave, because we won't be able to broadcast if you aren't here, and then Fallujans will know if the bombing is linked to al-Jazeera's presence. If the bombing continues after we stop the coverage, then it will be obvious that the Marines didn't need our presence in order to drop the bombs."

We had reached a conclusion that satisfied everyone.

Abdulazeem covered the 4:00PM news segment as I prepared myself to attend Sameer's funeral. Of course, by then Hamed had learned of his brother-in-law's death, and had stopped by to touch base with us before beginning to arrange the funeral. He took the news almost as if he were expecting it. He said he had known that one of the Hadeeds would end up having to pay the price of hosting al-Jazeera's crew and broadcasting images that didn't support Bremer's lies or Kimmitt's propaganda. He said if the immediate Hadeed family were lucky enough to escape death, inevitably a relative, neighbor, or in-law was bound to fall right into its hands.

As he sobbed, he said, "I just wish it wasn't my sister and her kids who had to pay the price for my work. She lost her husband and my nieces and nephews lost their father because I was doing my job. I wish it was me. I wish it was me who was being prepared for burial now."

I stopped him from talking like this and tried to comfort him, "You had no control over this. This is what was meant to be."

He replied as he wiped his tears, "Yes. It's God's destiny. He shall do what He pleases."[34] Hamed then left for the hospital in order to arrange for the funeral and burial.

The day was almost over and time was running out for us to find a place to sleep that night—either in Fallujah or in Baghdad. Abdulazeem went to the hospital to look for an ambulance or a medical aid vehicle that would be leaving that night that might be able to take us to Baghdad. He wanted to try to have Sayf and me out of town by the end of the day. If no cars were leaving, we'd have to figure out a place to crash overnight and find a car leaving for Baghdad very early in the morning.

The ever-helpful Munther was present during the discussion.

"My house is only a few yards from the field hospital, right next to the al-Rawi Mosque. My house is your house," he offered. "Please stay with me overnight." We accepted this generous offer, and the crew members who didn't leave Fallujah that night did indeed stay at Munther's place.

As soon as all these arrangements were made, sadness began to seep into my bones. I hadn't planned on leaving the city with so much unresolved. I wanted to stay until the refugees who'd fled the city were able to return to their homes and until the ones who'd stayed felt safe. But there was nothing I could do to change the situation. I sat and waited as patiently as I could for Abdulazeem to return and tell me my plans for the night.

As I sat, I couldn't stop thinking of Hussain Sameer. I had known the man for only one day, but it had felt like I had known him my whole life. He reminded me of so many men I had known. He was a man in his forties who owned and operated a semi-trailer. He had two daughters and two sons. He was extremely generous and very polite. He was a simple man until the last moment of his life. The supper we'd shared was his last meal, and admirable in its simplicity.

I wanted to make sure that I attended his funeral to pay my respects.

As I was thinking about Sameer, Abdulazeem returned in a frantic state.

"Hurry up, Ahmed!" he yelled. "There is a small pickup truck that was carrying humanitarian aid to Fallujah, and they're leaving now for

Baghdad. An ambulance is taking off tonight as well, but I don't know when. I think the truck is better than risking the smell of blood, so let's take this chance," he tugged my arm and urged me to move.

I protested, "But I want to attend Sameer's funeral—"

"No time. No time. Sameer is dead now, and he'd be happier if you left town safe than if you stayed for his funeral and risked your life. He'd want you to leave now. Stay here. I'll get the truck to come and pick you up. It's not a good idea for you to go to crowded areas. It would be even better if we keep your departure a secret until you're out of here completely."

My time in Fallujah was over. I waited for Abdulazeem to return with the truck. In the meantime, I hoped that what I had been able to do helped, at least in some small measure, bring justice to these people who were suffering so horribly. I hoped that I'd helped make their stories heard.

PART III

POLITICAL BATTLES

"If we don't believe in freedom of expression for people we despise, we don't believe in it at all."
—Noam Chomsky

13. BUSH'S WAR ON AL-JAZEERA

So far, this book has focused on the war the Bush administration waged on the city of Fallujah in April 2004. As became clear during the siege on Fallujah, the US was also waging another war at the same time: against al-Jazeera. This campaign focused on our news team, but the conflict between al-Jazeera and the Bush administration is significant enough for examine beyond the borders of the narrative of that battle alone.

George Bush's concerns about al-Jazeera focused on information being released to international media that exposed the misdeeds of the Bush administration and the American military. Fallujah isn't really of consequence here—Bush and his men would have waged a war on al-Jazeera even if we'd been covering negative American deeds occurring in some area outside of the country of Iraq. As long as the region we covered was a region of political interest to the neoconservatives, Bush and his administration wanted our blood. Fallujah was the battle in which Bush's antagonism toward al-Jazeera was sparked, but it continued to rage long afterward.

As I've discussed, Bush and the American forces began to noticeably resent the presence of al-Jazeera in Fallujah on Friday, April 9. That night, while our crew was resting on the rooftop and awaiting instruction from Wadah, General Kimmitt was briefing members of the press at the command center in Baghdad. This press conference was meant to give world media an update on the situation in Fallujah from the perspective of the Bush administration. Our al-Jazeera crew, on the other hand, was providing the world with an update from the perspective of the Fallujans. In this sense, Kimmitt and I were engaged in an indirect media war from the start.

During this briefing, General Kimmitt repeatedly tried to redirect the attention of journalists to areas in Iraq other than Fallujah—in particular to the confrontations between US forces and Muqtada al-Sadr's militia in Najaf and Karbala. Despite these efforts to divert attention from Fallujah, journalists were still concerned about what they had seen in our coverage. Al-Jazeera's footage of the events in Fallujah gave Operation Vigilant Resolve headline status worldwide. Consequently, reporters at Kimmitt's briefing continually returned the questioning to Fallujah. Had our crew not been able to broadcast live from Fallujah, Kimmitt may have succeeded in downplaying the atrocities committed long enough for the problems to be justified, explained, or simply ignored. In the years since the operation, many observers have speculated that had there been no media coverage of the first battle of Fallujah, it would have remained too vague for any sort of blame to be placed, which is exactly what would happen six months later in Operation Phantom Fury, starting on November 7. (More about that later.)

With journalists scrutinizing Kimmitt's reluctance to speak about the atrocities being committed in Fallujah, Kimmitt had no option but to accuse al-Jazeera of propagating lies. He told reporters to change the channel if they were troubled by what they saw on al-Jazeera, and insinuated that we'd somehow manufactured them. Shocked and awed by this insensitive response, al-Jazeera channel replayed this sound byte repeatedly, even using the clip as part of an ad campaign for its major news segments.

Undoubtedly, the Marines reached a critical moment in Fallujah on Friday. Although they were still holding the city under siege at that point, they were also besieged themselves by insurgents, who had cut off all roads leading in and out of Fallujah. The insurgents controlled highways, attacked Marines without hesitation, and set supply convoys on fire. By Friday, the Marines were no longer willing to put up with the extra stress of seeing what al-Jazeera was broadcasting. The news of their weakened position in the war was detrimental to America's image as a superpower and extremely damaging to the already-deteriorating morale of American forces all across Iraq. By Friday, American forces knew they needed to keep al-Jazeera quiet about the losses Americans were suffering at the hands of the insurgents and the war crimes the Marines were committing against civilians.

Thus the expulsion of al-Jazeera became a condition of the proposed cease-fire. The Americans formed a delegation representing the Governing Council, in order to work out this agreement and express the included condition that al-Jazeera stop broadcasting live from inside the city. The delegation's main task was to get the news off the air and nothing else—the cease-fire and the lives of the Fallujans were quite beside the point. The delegation was so shameless in their objectives that on the morning of Saturday, April 10, when my colleague Muhammad Abdulazeem covered the negotiations, the delegation unashamedly told him that expelling our crew from the city was the sole purpose of implementing a cease-fire.

My colleague Ahmad Samarray, one of al-Jazeera's cameramen who covered Kimmitt's briefings in Baghdad, later told me that Kimmitt complained about me to him several times during this time period.

Ahmad said, "He spoke of you very bitterly. He complained repeatedly about your reports from Fallujah, and became especially angry when journalists roasted him with questions about your coverage."

It seems obvious to me that Kimmitt disliked me so much because I was constantly exposing his misdeeds. My reports weren't random, and many times they focused exactly on what Kimmitt, personally, was doing wrong in Iraq. The standard procedure before doing any of my reports was to call the newsroom in Doha and arrange the broadcast. Then, during these calls, my colleagues in Doha would give me an update on what US military commanders had just said about the situation in Fallujah, without naming any specific names. I didn't know that these reports were mostly feeding me claims made by Kimmitt in particular. My intention was never to irritate Kimmitt himself—I didn't even know he was the person the newsroom staff was referring to whenever they provided claims made by "military commanders."

In any event, after I heard the claims from the Doha office, I would investigate the claims made by American military personnel. The claims were almost never true. I would then film my report and include documented evidence, interviews, and footage that proved the falsity of nearly every single claim Kimmitt, or other American officials, had made to the press. For one thing, they tried to downplay the horrific violence I was witnessing firsthand. It was my duty as the prime source of news in Fallujah to tell about the reality on the ground. I felt that the false claims had to be exposed, along with the misdeeds of the insurgents or anyone else involved in the battle. Unbeknownst to me, my reports made Kimmitt appear to journalists (not to mention the rest of the word) a liar and a buffoon. It was natural that he would accuse me of propagating lies after this kind of humiliation. It was the only way he could save face.

The battle that Kimmitt and I engaged in from the day I entered Fallujah until the day I was forced out was unique because I, personally, didn't know about it until afterward. Because of our dangerous living conditions, I wasn't able to follow his briefings; I didn't know he had placed a target on my back. I simply acted on the updates given to me by the newsroom in Doha. Kimmitt, on the other hand, was following me very closely. He had my reports translated, and scrutinized the text word for word, claim for claim. As Kimmitt and others in the Bush administration were engaged in analyzing my reports, I was walking the streets and alleys of Fallujah and broadcasting what I was seeing firsthand, as directly and clearly as possible.

One of the most obvious lies American officials told during the first battle of Fallujah was that American forces had declared a unilateral cease-fire effective at noon on April 9. Al-Jazeera had undeniable, hard evidence that the cease-fire was not in effect at that time. Several battles broke out in the background as we were doing live reports late in the day on Friday. And their story made no sense: Kimmitt initially denied the existence of a brokered cease-fire agreement; the following morning, April 10, he announced that the cease-fire was already in effect. When journalists embarrassed him with the footage of battles broadcast live on al-Jazeera, he claimed that all of the American fire was justified as "self-defense."

Incidents like these prove that I was not the one who forged evidence or exaggerated stories to expose the Bush administration officials as liars; they were liars on their own. I never told the Marines or the insurgents to break the cease-fire in the background as I went live on camera. I never told them that I needed to expose the fallacy of the cease-fire claim—I didn't even know about the cease-fire at the time this footage was filmed. They exposed their mistakes on their own. It was the inability of Bush administration officials to keep their lies straight that exposed the truth. It had little to do with me.

Apparently, General Kimmitt wasn't the only one angered by our coverage. The highest echelons of power—all the way up to the commander in chief himself—were furious about the images we broadcast live from Fallujah. During his meeting with Tony Blair in Washington, DC, on April 16, Bush told Blair that he planned to bomb al-Jazeera headquarters in Doha and some of its external broadcast bureaus in order to ensure our silence. This was his official plan for revenge. As their hired mercenaries had done earlier in the war, the Bush administration intended to resort to the brutish language of violence to get what they wanted.

Under Fire from All Sides

General Kimmitt's attack on my integrity and credibility was merely a warm-up for more vicious attacks the Bush administration would later wage on me, my crew, and the entire al-Jazeera organization. These attacks were unsurprising; the truth is that the United States had been attacking our organization ever since Saddam's regime was toppled on March 19, 2003 and the Americans seized control of Iraq.

Complaints against al-Jazeera came most frequently from Donald

Rumsfeld and Paul Wolfowitz. Rumsfeld repeatedly accused al-Jazeera of propagating lies, cooperating with insurgents, and supporting Saddam Hussein. Tony Blair also spoke of al-Jazeera as one of Iraq's worst enemies.

These attacks were aimed at hurting al-Jazeera's credibility—not just in the Middle East, but all over the world. Ironically, the more Bush administration officials and Tony Blair attacked al-Jazeera, the more people were drawn to its coverage. Eventually, al-Jazeera was ranked fifth in a list of the "most influential brands of 2004" by BrandChannel.com (after Apple, Google, Ikea, and Starbucks). BrandChannel editor Robin Rusch explained the pick:

> With all the news from Iraq and Afghanistan and the "war on terror," a lot of people are really tuned into the news, and the major news sources have a western bias. I think people are tuning in to al-Jazeera and looking at its website because it does offer another viewpoint. For the global community, it's one of the few points of access we have to news from the region with a different perspective.

Al-Jazeera's spokesman at the time, my colleague Jihad Ballout, fended off many of the accusations leveled against al-Jazeera. He also ignored others, many of which were too ridiculous for any sane person to believe. These reports were incredibly widespread. On November 23, 2005, the *Nation* magazine published an article that detailed one of Rumsfeld's undiplomatic verbal attacks on al-Jazeera. When a reporter asked, "Can you definitively say that hundreds of women and children and innocent civilians have not been killed?" Rumsfeld replied, "I can definitively say that what al-Jazeera is doing is vicious, inaccurate, and inexcusable."

I remember reading this article and my jaw dropping in shock. What did al-Jazeera have to do with any of this? The reporter hadn't asked about al-Jazeera; the question was clearly about the casualty count, and Rumsfeld had instead issued a judgment of our work. I thought to myself: Has this man gone insane? Is he so obsessed with us that he thinks "al-Jazeera is the root of all evil" is a valid response for any questions about American actions in the war? What is wrong with this man?

The inflammatory reports came at all stages of the war. On April 27, shortly after the first battle of Fallujah, Colin Powell held a meeting with Shaikh Hamad bin Jassim bin Jaber al-Thani, deputy prime minister and foreign minister of Qatar. After the two men finished their meeting, Colin Powell told reporters, "The friendship between our two nations is such that we can also talk about difficult issues that intrude in that relationship, such as the issue of the coverage of al-Jazeera. And we had candid discussions about that. When reporters asked him what he expected the government of Qatar to do about al-Jazeera's coverage, he replied, "We're having very intense discussions about this subject, and those discussions will continue over the next couple of days." Obviously, the one thing on Powell's mind was al-Jazeera's coverage, and what it exposed about the American administration.

It wasn't just Powell who was obsessed with al-Jazeera; this hatred was contagious enough to spread to other key figures in the Bush administration. Shaikh Hamad bin Jassim had a meeting with Dick Cheney around this same time period, and again, one of the main topics of discussion was al-Jazeera, and in particular its coverage of Fallujah. Later, on April 27, Richard Boucher, assistant secretary for public affairs and spokesman for the State Department, held a press conference to inform the press of the outcome of the meeting between Powell and Shaikh Hamad bin Jassim. Boucher attacked al-Jazeera in vicious and completely undiplomatic terms. He attacked me by name, which was the second time (after Kimmitt's attack) that I was personally blamed for the aggressive military policies of the Bush administration. Boucher also accused al-Jazeera of broadcasting "inaccurate, false, wrong reports." He said our reports were "designed to be inflammatory" and to "make life—make the situation—more tense, more inflamed and even more dangerous." He also accused me personally of fabricating stories of violence: "Al-Jazeera correspondent Ahmed Mansour reported that children are being killed and women cut to pieces in Fallujah. It's absolutely wrong." Luckily for me, my reports had been supported by live footage, and anyone who reviewed the footage could see the piles of dead children with their own eyes.

Thabit al-Bardisi, a colleague who had covered Boucher's press briefing, prepared a report covering the objections to our work. When the report was aired, our colleague Jameel Azar in the newsroom asked him, "What do they expect us to do? Do they want us to put the caps on our cameras and stop filming what they're doing?"

I was troubled by the fact that I had been mentioned by name, but not because I was worried about my own safety. I still believe that the Bush administration wouldn't dare openly harm a journalist armed with only a microphone and a camera. What troubled me was the "you're with us, or you're with the terrorists" attitude that Bush had adopted since the 9/11 attacks, and the fact that this attitude was becoming disturbingly common in his administration.

I knew my reportage was always aimed at an equal balance between the insurgents and the Marines. The reason my reportage on the Marines appeared to be more damaging was because their violence could often be seen in broad daylight and was therefore easier to capture on film. The insurgents were much more elusive and often worked under the cover of night. How could we be accused of taking sides and aligning with insurgents just because the Americans made it easier for us to catch their misdeeds on film? These images simply represented the aftermath of their violent campaigns in Iraq, and if they didn't like those images, then they should have taken a different approach to warfare. The fact that any government would target a journalist by name and consider him an enemy in a military conflict is very disturbing. The troublesome nature of this issue multiplies when it's a top official in the government of a superpower doing so.

Until the first battle of Fallujah, Bush had avoided mentioning al-Jazeera by name even though members of his administration had done so repeatedly. Bush held a meeting with his top national security aides in Washington to discuss the embarrassment his administration was facing because of our coverage during the first battle, and an April 28 article in the *New York Times*, "The Struggle for Iraq; Test in a Tinderbox," reported simply that Bush said that members of his administration had "voiced concerns that images of fierce fighting in Fallujah will stir uprisings throughout Iraq and outrage throughout the Arab world."

The Bush administration put pressure on me by attempting to drive a wedge between me and the government of Qatar. When I came back from Fallujah, my colleague Ahmad Alshaikh, chief editor of al-Jazeera's newsroom, handed me some papers to look at. These papers were sent by the "Office of Strategic Communications for Coalition Forces in Baghdad, Arab Media Unit." The letter had been sent by American military officials to the government of Qatar, who had forwarded it to al-Jazeera. These pages documented every single report I made from Fallujah, and they were annotated with complaints and protests against my coverage. These reports also included names of several other colleagues who were hosting news segments from the Doha headquarters, but no name was mentioned as often or criticized as strongly as mine. What seemed to make the Americans angrier than anything else was my report about their use of internationally banned weapons and the indiscriminate slaughter of women and children.

While thumbing through the pages, Ahmad Alshaikh told me that the Qatari government was demanding a response to the American accusations.

"I'm not the only one who reported this!" I exclaimed. "There were non-televised media reporters in the city who said the same thing. Besides, everything I reported was supported with footage. I'm not going to let them corner me like I'm guilty of doing something wrong. I don't need to reply to anything. If they don't believe my claims, let them rewind the tapes of my reports and watch them again. They'll see the proof of my claims right on film, just like the rest of the world saw it."

I was safely out of the danger in Fallujah when these reports came to my attention, but I certainly wasn't feeling any better. These accusations made me sick to my stomach. I was deeply disturbed that the Americans were willing to commit war crimes in broad daylight, and then turn around and pin their crimes on someone who was only doing his job. I wondered what kind of upbringing could produce an adult with so little regard for human life and integrity.

This barrage of slander was just the start of the attacks. Many American media outlets wrote about me in their publications, and rarely, if ever, portrayed me in a positive light. I was attacked by Bush-friendly rightwing journalists so many times that it's impossible to list them all. The attacks were the same as those of the Bush administration officials: I was fabricating news, falsifying information, making up scenarios that implicated the Marines in war crimes, taking incidents out of context (the most famous defense in history), and directly or indirectly aiding the insurgents. Some of these journalists went as far as to claim that I was a insurgent disguised as a journalist in order to propagate the insurgent cause.

It was disturbing to me that fellow journalists were willing to make such accusations without doing any research. Didn't these journalists know that they might have to cover something controversial one day themselves, and that it really wasn't in their own best interests to set up a pattern wherein it was acceptable to throw slander at another colleague for doing his job? Didn't they know that they might have to report on a war and expose a truth that bothers one of the sides in the conflict? How would these journalists feel if they were targeted by the governments they exposed and then targeted personally by journalists from that country? Of course, I understand that American journalists were bothered because the image of their country was tarnished by the reckless policies of its administration, but that's no excuse. When you establish a rule that journalists are fair game for any kind of attack during a war, then you, as a journalist, become fair game yourself.

Back in 2003, when American forces bombed al-Jazeera's bureau in

Baghdad and a bureau for another Arab television channel shortly afterward, it was the American journalists who were the most outraged. American journalists attacked American military commanders at United States Central Command in Doha by openly doubting these "accidental" bombings executed by American forces. No one believed that nonsense. American journalists didn't keep their mouths shut simply because it was expected that they line up behind their home government. Instead, these journalists wanted the truth out, even if that meant an embarrassment for the Bush administration. In fact, that's one of the fundamentals any journalism student learns—to have an allegiance only to the truth, regardless of your nationality. This was apparently never part of the training received by the journalists who attacked me. These journalists were not reputable, respectable journalists the international audience could trust and admire. They were Bush-administration journalists, whose only cause was to support the policies of Bush and his cohorts.

Slander and Solidarity

By the end of the first battle in Fallujah, there were already efforts by the Bush administration, through its entourage of well-paid journalists, to indirectly or directly make me a target in the "war on terrorism." I was sure that American intelligence services had dug up everything that they could their hands on: my résumé, the details of my career, my personal relationships, anything that might be used against me. They were looking for any information that would allow for bigger and more direct accusations to be thrown at me or at al-Jazeera.

The Bush administration also tried to get me by using what I call "imported Iraqi journalists"—workers not very different from the imported Iraqi politicians who stocked the temporary Iraqi government. These imported Iraqi journalists launched a massive campaign of personal defamation against me. Bush-friendly Iraqi journalists, who had never existed in Iraq (or the Middle East) prior to the American invasion, were suddenly everywhere, and very obviously working for the Bush administration. These journalists took it upon themselves to tarnish my reputation in any way they could. The attacks waged by these writers were much filthier than the attacks that came from their American-born counterparts. Rightwing American journalists usually took a very minor and very gray detail and turned it into a serious accusation with no substantial backing. Bush-friendly American journalists, in other words, inflamed one small grain of uncertainty and gave it whatever definition they felt served their cause. Bush-friendly Iraqi journalists, on the other hand, didn't even need that grain of uncertainty before they accused me of wrongdoing. They were somehow able to build one fortress of accusations after another without any foundation of truth. These fabricated stories were released in every possible venue: published media, televised forums, political conferences, speeches, and even through old-fashioned social gossip.

All of this slander constituted a well-orchestrated attempt to punish me for my coverage of the Iraq war, and the first battle of Fallujah in particular. Both American-born and native Middle Eastern journalists who supported Bush wanted to destroy my career, my reputation, and my morale. It seemed as though they believed that if they could repeat the fabricated accusations enough times, eventually the public would believe them.

Many international media outlets and networks contacted me to get an interview, a comment, a response, or a statement defending myself against the accusations leveled against me by Bush and his administration. I decided that I wouldn't accept any of these invitations. In one instance, however, the news media contacting me was very assertive in its request for my appearance, and I consented to give a comment.

I told them, "If the Bush administration wants to play the plaintiff, then I will not allow myself to play the defendant part. I won't be part of this play at all. I presented what I saw of the truth, and that was a very small part of the truth because what actually happened in Fallujah was far more extensive and more gruesome than any single TV crew could document. Every piece of information I presented to the public was documented and supported by images, interviews, and footage. I broadcast the reality I witnessed. If you need to interview anyone, maybe you should contact those who have a problem with the reality I presented, not me."

Here I must pay credit to my friend and colleague Lamis Andoni, who was a journalism lecturer at UC Berkeley when all this slander was being published. Lamis called me after I left Fallujah and told me that many independent, anti-war journalists in the US were closely monitoring the massive defamation campaign being waged against me. She said many fair observers were standing in support of me, including the national media watch group known as Fairness & Accuracy in Reporting (FAIR). She asked for material that could help them in their interviews because some of these journalists were activists who were invited to participate in interviews. They needed to know my viewpoint so they could defend me when they spoke in support of me in front of the world.

She said, "I alone get invited to talk about you and your coverage in American media outlets almost every day."

She asked me to participate in some of these interviews. I provided her with the information she needed to supplement her own interviews, but told her of my decision not to reply to any accusations in person.

Lamis suggested that I compose a statement and submit it to a number of human rights organizations concerned with protecting journalists across the world, in order to alert them of the unethical practices of the Bush administration and its entourage of neoconservative journalists. She also suggested that in the letter I ask these organizations to support me in light of this aggressive defamation campaign being waged against me.

Although I hadn't wanted to actively reply to any of the accusations leveled against me, her suggestion to write a letter of this kind made sense. I discussed the idea with Shaikh Hamad bin Thamer al-Thani and Wadah Khanfar. I told them that this would be a statement issued by me personally, not by al-Jazeera, and they would in no way be implicated in anything I said. They were fine with the plan.

I published the statement in both Arabic and English, on April 29, 2004, and distributed it as Lamis suggested. The response was more overwhelming and humbling than I had ever thought possible. My office was flooded with letters of support from American journalists who agreed with my cause and were willing to stand up in my defense. These letters did not only come from American journalists, however. The British Association of Journalists (BAJ), for example, prepared a statement condemning the treatment I was subjected to and demanding an explanation from the American government. This was sent to the US State Department and the Pentagon. American organizations that work to protect journalists did similar things, and American and European human rights organizations also started online petitions in support of me and my work.

However wonderful this show of support was for me, it did not shake the Bush administration's resolve to destroy my reputation and my career. These accusers figured that if repeated lies couldn't tarnish my reputation enough to scare away support from fellow journalists, then maybe they weren't creating lies that were damaging enough. So they changed their game plan and began to aim at my reputation with much bigger guns.

The Mythical Link between al-Qaeda and al-Jazeera

I first heard of this accusation from Clive Adrian Stafford Smith, a British lawyer who specializes in civil rights and the death penalty. Smith visited Doha several times as he prepared to defend my colleague Sami al-Haj after his illegal capture and detention by US officials at the notorious Guantánamo Bay detention camp. Sami worked as a cameraman for al-Jazeera and was assigned to cover Bush's war on Afghanistan. He was illegally detained by American forces on December 15, 2001 while filming in Afghanistan. He was then transferred to Guantánamo on June 12, 2002. He was subsequently treated as though he was a terrorist—or, more accurately, as though he were not a human being—and was held at Guantánamo without charges or trial. Sami's story, of course, is another instance of Bush's war on al-Jazeera.

I met with Clive during one of his visits to Doha in order to arrange an interview with him for my show *Without Limits*. We agreed that he would appear on July 27, 2005 show, after a scheduled visit to Sami in Guantánamo. A few days before the show, I was in London meeting with Clive to discuss final arrangements.

"I have some information that might bother you," he told me.

"What? You're not going to cancel your appearance on my show?"

"No. Of course not. I just want you to know that the Americans have put a lot of pressure on Sami. They want him to admit that you are linked to al-Qaeda. They want him to help fabricate a case against you."

"But I don't know Sami. I don't even think we've met."

Clive replied, "I know. But according to Sami, his interrogators asked about you more than a hundred times. They repeatedly tried to get him to say that you have some relationship with al-Qaeda and that you are propagating its cause through your position at al-Jazeera. Sami says that some of the interrogation sessions are focused entirely on you; all the questions are about you, nothing about him. Sami told them that he doesn't know you personally and that he's only seen you once or twice— one time he said hello to you in one of the hallways at al-Jazeera headquarters, and another time he bumped into you in the cafeteria on the second floor above the newsroom. Still, they're trying everything they can to get him to say you're linked to al-Qaeda."

I paused for a moment, thinking about poor Sami, and, of course, thinking about my own fate. Then I said, "This isn't their first time trying to build unfounded accusations. It's just that this time they've gone lower than ever before. Just when I thought they couldn't possibly get any more inhumane than they already have, they subject a helpless victim—a man who is desperate for anything that would guarantee his release from a hellish prison—to this form of disgusting extortion. I was wrong when I thought that there was a limit to how low the Bush administration would stoop. I was so wrong."

Just to prove how serious the accusations were, Clive showed me a classified document not permitted for use or circulation outside the courtroom—this was spelled out on the document itself. He had composed that document exclusively from the minutes he took during the meeting he had with his client Sami in June 2005.

The document detailed all the charges Sami was being pressured to bring against me. I looked at it in awe. What particularly caught my attention was that the document described the body language of the interrogators. Sami said that it was clear from the facial expressions of the interrogators that they hated me bitterly, and they spoke of me with disgust and repulsion. There were other accusations against me in the document, but they were minor compared to the accusation that I was a member of al-Qaeda.

Eventually, I wasn't the only one privy to Clive's discoveries about Sami's interrogation. In a documentary film about Sami's case that aired on al-Jazeera, Clive disclosed these secrets to the public. He also included the fact that Sami was offered a release on the condition that he'd spy on his colleagues at al-Jazeera for the United States. Sami refused and chose to stay in captivity, even if it meant suffering more interrogations.

Bush Tests the Boundaries

After realizing that fabricating my membership in al-Qaeda wasn't going to completely obliterate my reputation across the globe, Bush knew he had to take more drastic measures. It was at this point that he began to pursue a truly insane objective. He began to consider dropping bombs on a country that was actually supporting the United States during this conflict: Qatar. In response to the worldwide support of my coverage in Fallujah, Bush decided the only way to eliminate my influence on world politics would be to bomb al-Jazeera's headquarters in Doha, Qatar.

This idea was announced in the November 22, 2004 issue of the British tabloid the *Daily Mirror*, with this explosive headline: "EXCLUSIVE: BUSH PLOT TO BOMB HIS ARAB ALLY." The article spilled this plan, and at the same time proved Bush's anger about al-Jazeera's coverage of the war. The *Daily Mirror* included a detailed report of the summit meeting between George Bush and Tony Blair on April 16, 2004. The report included excerpts from a "Top Secret" memo that leaked out of 10 Downing Street in London. The report quoted an inside source saying, "The memo is explosive and hugely damaging to Bush. He made clear he wanted to bomb al-Jazeera in Qatar and elsewhere. Blair replied that this bomb would cause a big problem. There's no doubt what Bush wanted to do—and no doubt Blair didn't want him to do it."

The report also said that, "The No. 10 memo now raises fresh doubts over US claims that previous attacks against al-Jazeera staff were military errors," referring to American bombing of al-Jazeera's offices in Afghanistan in 2001 and the bombing of al-Jazeera's offices in Baghdad in 2003. About how the classified "Top Secret" memo made its way to the public domain, the report said, "The memo, which also included details of troop deployments, turned up in May last year at the Northampton constituency office of then Labour MP Tony Clarke. Cabinet Office civil servant David Keogh, 49, is accused under the Official Secrets Act of passing it to Leo O'Connor, 42, who used to work for Mr. Clarke. Both are bailed to appear at Bow Street court next week."

Following this report, American and British officials immediately denied the presence of such a document. The *Daily Mirror* reported afterward that the White House had dismissed their report as "outlandish." One official even suggested that the threat to bomb al-Jazeera was "humorous." The *Washington Post* that day quoted an unnamed senior Capitol Hill diplomat as saying that the Bush remark as reported by the *Daily Mirror* "sounds like one of the president's one-liners that is meant as a joke."

Of course, these lame justifications didn't hold much water. The global public knew that joking about bombing when you're in a war is a lot like joking about being armed when going through security checks at airports: no one thinks it's funny.

After this scandal broke out and the story was made public, the editor of the *Daily Mirror* met al-Jazeera representatives in a forum held in London. In this meeting, he confirmed that his newspaper had "documented minutes of a meeting that proved that George Bush informed British PM Tony Blair of his intent to bomb al-Jazeera." Oddly, even though American officials denied the presence of the document in question, they still went after David Keogh and Leo O'Connor and pursued legal action against them under the Official Secrets Act. If the memo didn't exist, as these officials claimed, then Keogh and O'Connor shouldn't have been pursued for revealing the plans it contained. The accusation against these men was indeed "outlandish."

The waves caused by the article continued. On November 23, 2005, both the *Daily Mirror* and the *Guardian* published news about Britain's Attorney General Lord Goldsmith ordering the *Daily Mirror* to "cease publishing further details from an allegedly top secret memo revealing that US President George Bush wanted to bomb al-Jazeera." On October 5, 2007, the *Daily Mirror* reported that David Keogh defended his decision to leak the memo by saying that he felt that making the top secret document available to the public would show the world how much of a "madman" Bush was. Keogh also hoped that the document would help the Democratic presidential candidate at the time, John Kerry, defeat Bush in the American presidential elections of 2004. Keogh handed a copy of the memo to O'Connor, a researcher for anti-war Labor MP Anthony Clarke. O'Connor put it among Clarke's papers, and Clarke in turn sent it immediately to Tony Blair's office.

After a long and tiring legal pursuit, on May 10, 2007, the *Independent*, the *Guardian*, and many other British newspapers published news about the sentencing of the men convicted of leaking the document. David Keogh was jailed for six months and Leo O'Connor for three. Justice Aikens described David Keogh's actions as "reckless and irresponsible."

Soon after this fiasco reached a temporary close, hundreds, if not thousands, of articles were published worldwide criticizing the appalling fact that Bush had even considered bombing a television station. As David Keogh had hoped, the leaked memo did indeed show the world how much of a madman Bush had become.

Peter Kilfoyle, a Labour MP, also provided some critical comments that proved the link between this memo and our coverage of the first battle of Fallujah.

In a November 11, 2005 article in the *Daily Telegraph* titled, "Bush plot to bomb al-Jazeera is a conspiracy theory, says Blair," reporter Melissa Kite described Tony Blair losing his cool when he was asked about Bush's intentions to bomb al-Jazeera. "Look, there's a limit to what I can say," Blair said, having difficulty finishing the sentence: "but honestly, I mean, conspiracy theories…"

Peter Kilfoyle, a former Labour defense minister responded, "My concern is that the only conspiracy surrounding this theory was a conspiracy to level the city of Fallujah. He would say 'conspiracy theory.' That's been the American line and now he's adopting it. But if it is so fantastical, why are they prosecuting these two people this week?"

Kilfoyle continued, "I am in no doubt that there was a mention of Fallujah. I was made aware of the contents by Mr. Clarke," and then added, "There was certainly a discussion about Fallujah and attacking Fallujah. They had already had one attack that failed and the next one was a massive one. They used artillery, tanks, jet bombers, white phosphorus. It was a full-scale leveling of a city."

So I wasn't the only one who saw the relationship between Bush's plot to bomb al-Jazeera and his plundering of Fallujah. So much for the "freedom of the press" he used as justification for his invasion of Iraq! Even Saddam Hussein never bombed a newspapers' headquarters; he simply coerced the journalists to "cooperate."

Our director general made a special visit to London to discuss this serious matter with Tony Blair, but the latter "shrugged off" a request for a meeting, as the *Daily Telegraph* reported in the aforementioned article. Wadah wanted an explanation, but he never got close enough to even discuss the issue with Blair. So, as any journalist would, Wadah went to his colleagues in Britain for support, and support they gave him. During my many visits to London, I never met a single British journalist, regardless of political affiliation, who approved of or would even consider approving of bombing al-Jazeera.

In response to the refusal to meet with him, Wadah wrote an article in the *Guardian* on December 1, 2005: "Why did you want to bomb me, Mr Bush and Mr Blair?" The article cited all the harassment al-Jazeera had been subjected to because we did not bend to every single political party that was involved in the conflict being covered. Wadah talked about the previous bombing raids al-Jazeera bureaus had been subjected to in Afghanistan and Iraq. He discussed the persecution of al-Jazeera's Tayseer Allouni at the hands of politically-charged justices in Spain because of his coverage of the war in Afghanistan. He tied this discussion of previous attacks on al-Jazeera to the illegal and inhumane detainment of Sami al-Haj and to the death of Tariq Ayoub, who had been killed covering the Iraq war. At the end of this article, Wadah concluded with his disappointment that Tony Blair was not providing any answers. He writes, "The issue does not only concern al-Jazeera; it concerns the truth for which we have withstood nine years of pressure and harassment, and for which many journalists around the world have endured all forms of intimidation; it is the truth for which Tayseer Allouni is serving a prison sentence in Spain, for which Sami al-Haj continues to be detained in

Guantánamo and for which Tariq Ayoub died in Iraq."

Wadah got it exactly right in this article. Our colleagues had already paid very heavy prices for revealing the truth in this war and others, and journalists all over the world were continuing to risk their lives to reveal the truth. I had the chance to work with many superb and outstanding British journalists during the tense aftermath of the first battle of Fallujah. These professionals were willing to risk their lives every day just to verify a one-line news item. This willingness is indeed the hallmark of a true journalist.

The Impossible Task of Impartial Coverage

"No journalist should try to be a robot and say, 'They've attacked my country, they've killed thousands of people but I don't feel it'…"
—Dan Rather, *Buying the War*, on PBS, 25 April 2007

"There is an inherent bias in the coverage of the American press in general."
—Dan Rather, *Fahrenheit 9/11*

The coverage of the battle of Fallujah and the Bush-driven controversy afterward sparked many heated debates between colleagues within al-Jazeera over the concept of impartial coverage. To be frank, bias-free media is a hoax as far as I'm concerned. Journalists who don't claim to have an agenda usually have a bigger and more dangerous agenda than anybody else. This isn't just my personal conviction. I have discussed this concept with many internationally renowned journalists with undeniable credibility, and I've heard similar views from them. Al-Jazeera held an internal discussion about this topic in the wake of Bush's threats. This forum included staff members from all ranks of the institution—from interns to senior correspondents—and all areas of specialization within the field of journalism. Some of my colleagues criticized my coverage of the Fallujah battle just as Bush had, only they did so with words rather than with bombs and artillery. Some colleagues did indeed feel that I was not impartial enough in my coverage. They thought that their accusations would upset me, but the criticism didn't bother me at all; they are definitely entitled to their opinions and views of my work.

But when it was my turn to speak, I defended myself like this: "When did I claim to be impartial? When did any of you ever hear me say that I don't take sides in my coverage? I am partial toward the truth and aligned with justice, and that will always be my bias. I will always be on the side of humane principles and will always serve humanity. I am always against death and destruction. I am completely, and proudly, biased against injustice and the subjugation of innocent people to military operations. If any journalist in this room or anywhere else in the world demands me to be a machine with no feelings for humanity just so I can be called 'impartial' by their standards, then I'm not interested in the term being bestowed upon me."

After I defended myself, the entire room cheered and applauded in agreement. Truthfully, however, I didn't care about the criticism some of my colleagues directed at me, or the applause that came afterward. When you're on the battlefield, you don't risk your life for applause or criticism. You risk your life for the satisfaction of doing what you believe to be right. Telling the world the truth about the suffering of human beings and working toward its easing was always the goal of any journalistic project I accepted. When I'm asked about objectivity in my reporting, I answer in Neil Cavuto's words: "Am I slanted and biased? You damn well bet I am." Indeed I am slanted and biased—toward humanity and the truth.

I also could care less about the accusations made by the Bush administration or the defamatory lies thrown at me by neoconservative journalists. I certainly didn't see any impartiality from the neocons—politicians, military personnel, or journalists. As far as I'm concerned, they should be the last people on earth to call for impartial and objective coverage. I have never come across any social or political group that more believes it has the only key to the truth.

But I can't in all honesty simply attack the neocons. Were the embedded journalists who ate and slept with Marines and cheered when they fired bombs at the insurgents impartial or objective? When Katie Couric spoke to a Navy SEAL, and applauded him as he went off to fight in Iraq, was that an example of impartiality? Was her on-air statement "I just want you to know I think Navy SEALS rock!" impartial? When Dan Rather, one of America's most respected news anchors admits, "When my country is at war, uh, I want my country to win," is he not admitting that he is aligned with one particular military power? The reporting of these particular news anchors is no more impartial than my own.

These partisan comments by American news personalities appeared everywhere during the early years of the "war on terror." When Dan Rather appeared on *Late Night with David Letterman* on September 17, 2001, with the country still smarting from 9/11, he said, "George Bush is the president. He makes the decisions. And, you know, as just one American, wherever he wants me to line up, just tell me."

When Peter Jennings gloated that "Iraqi opposition has faded in the face of American power," was he reporting the truth at all? When Ted Koppel called the American military "an awesome synchronized killing machine," was he covering the news impartially?

Thanks to Michael Moore and *Fahrenheit 9/11*, we are all aware of the shortage of impartial reporting in mainstream media. Once American reporters become aware of their own obvious biases and abuses of "objectivity," they are more than welcome to demand journalists of other cultures to do the same. For now, at least, the example they are setting suggests that they should probably not lecture others on the subject of impartial reportage.

My dedication to serving oppressed people who cannot defend themselves is why I never found it possible to slant my coverage toward the administration of George W. Bush. I fully, and gladly, accept the accusation that I was on the side of the civilians being killed in Fallujah. I am not, however, willing to accept the accusation that my reporting was done to serve the insurgents' cause. This charge is completely false and unacceptable to me.

The Bush administration started rumors about my sketchy affiliations with the insurgents and with al-Qaeda simply because my reports showed that Marines were guilty of unlawfully killing civilians. The insurgents, it just so happened, may have been committing similar crimes but were doing remarkably little damage in the open. The insurgents were near impossible to locate, and therefore nearly impossible to film. We couldn't document their actions because they moved under cover, fired upward at the Marines from hidden locations, and then disappeared again. There was no way for us to document their violations of human rights or their killings. On the rare instances that we did find insurgents in broad daylight, we tried to get them to talk on camera and did our best to film them. This footage was aired without their permission, just as much of the Marine footage was.

The Bush administration would have the public believe that we chose to ignore the insurgents rather than to seek them out and expose their crimes as well. But if the insurgents used warfare that made it difficult for the thousands of Marines attacking Fallujah to discover them, then how could we, a handful of journalists, detect them any easier? If thousands of soldiers with tracking devices, thermal vision goggles, radars, scanners, and motion detectors failed at finding them, how could we—unarmed and untrained in combat?

The other reason why the Marines looked worse in our reports than the insurgents is simply because of the number of their victims. The Marines were armed with highly sophisticated equipment, and were able to kill far more people than the insurgents ever could. We were in Fallujah to report on the condition of the people. Most often, when we ran to report on a battle scene, eyewitnesses would tell us the Marines bombed from a tank or an airplane and destroyed a house, and a large number of people were dead. These were things that the insurgents didn't have the weaponry to do. The most dangerous weapons the insurgents had were rocket-propelled grenades, which were far too small and reached too short of a distance to do anywhere near the type of damage inflicted by the Marines' weaponry. So, in any given battle, the reports afterward would simply state that the Marines killed "x" number of people with "y" weapon. There was no way the insurgents could match the Marines' numbers with the weaponry they had, and therefore, the insurgents never got the bad press that comes with killing many people.

So, yes, I was indeed aligned with one side during my coverage—the people of Fallujah. Because of that allegiance, I did indeed have an agenda in my reporting. My agenda was to report the inhumane crimes of the insurgents and the Marines. I had the same allegiance to the people of Afghanistan and Bosnia when I covered wars in their countries.

During this time of scandal and personal defamation, I often recalled what I had learned at a seminar on war journalism. David Simon, one of the BBC's finest journalists, spoke about journalistic impartiality in this way:

> These concepts are difficult to apply in a world as troubled as the one we live in. What is objectivity, really, when we as journalists see a weak helpless party being murdered and a strong oppressive party doing the murder? What does it mean to be "impartial" when you're doing journalistic coverage for such oppression and aggression and when you're talking about this magnitude of injustice? Your role in circumstances like these is not just to relay the news about the incident at hand to your audience. Your role is to deliver the truth as much as you can, and that entails more than describing just the incident in question. Showing the truth means showing all aspects of the crime you've just witnessed and making visible oppression and injustice involved in it. This is not easy for many journalists, but this is precisely what they should do. They should have a bias for the truth.

This quest for the truth, unfortunately, comes at a heavy price: inevitably, you're not going to be very popular with certain world leaders or politicians if the truth you tell doesn't show their country in a positive light. I'm not the only journalist who was attacked by Bush after the first battle of Fallujah. Take, for example, the case of Seymour Hersh, one of America's finest investigative reporters.[35] Because Bush and his followers envied Hersh for having what they lack—a functional brain and good foresight—the Bush administration attacked Hersh and his work. In his *Bush at War*, Bob Woodward quoted Bush as blatantly calling Hersh a liar. Donald Rumsfeld likened this well-respected and deeply intelligent man to the Taliban. Richard Perle described Hersh as a terrorist during his appearance on CNN's *Late Night Edition with Wolf Blitzer* on March 9, 2003: "Seymour Hersh is the closest thing American journalism has to a terrorist."

Although I would not downplay the difficulty that Hersh may have encountered with the Bush administration, it was worse to be a targeted al-Jazeera journalist, and know that my own life and the lives of my colleagues were more threatened than our reputations.

Out of Business; Out of Trouble

It was June 28, 2004 when Paul Bremer's failed term as governor of Iraq finally ended. Once he was out of power, he left the fate of Iraq in the hands of several imported Iraqi politicians (IIPs) chosen and planted in the new Iraqi government by the United States. American occupation authorities worked hard to empower these IIPs, in particular those who strengthened the hold of the American occupation. Few of these IIPs helped the American occupation as much as Ayad Allawi, and so when Bremer left, Allawi was given the task of heading the occupation-friendly government. This position put Allawi in charge of any number of difficult and dirty tasks. First and foremost of these was to close the al-Jazeera bureau in Baghdad to eliminate reports like ours from being released to the public.

How can we tell in hindsight that this objective was one of the most pressing tasks Allawi was assigned? The answer is simple: Allawi's first decision as head of the government wasn't to secure the country, end the violence, or provide basic services for Iraqis. It was to assign a special committee the task of "monitoring al-Jazeera." A very strange first decision for someone taking power in a country in which most cities still had little to no access to clean water.

Five weeks into his term, on August 7, 2004, Allawi issued orders for the Baghdad bureau to close. He held a press conference in which he said that the special committee had concluded that al-Jazeera "incites violence and hatred," and that his order to close its bureau was made "to protect the Iraqi people." The bureau was closed first for just a month, but then the closure period was extended, and soon the closure became a permanent rather than temporary ordinance.

Allawi's official orders to close al-Jazeera came after Hoshyar Zebari, the minister of foreign affairs, had prepared the way. In July, Zebari had attacked al-Jazeera by saying that its editorial policy represented "a deviance that complicates events in Iraq." Al-Jazeera issued a statement on June 25, 2004, saying that it considered his attacks a threat to the entire al-Jazeera organization and all of its correspondents.

On the night the order was issued to close us down, Donald Rumsfeld commended Allawi for his action of limiting the freedom of the press in Iraq; for making the press available only to those news sources that were Bush-friendly or didn't mind the presence of the merciless American occupation.

Shortly after the order to shut down al-Jazeera was carried out, Allawi flew to Washington to celebrate his achievements with his boss, George Bush. Prior to this meeting, Bush had just finished completing his plans for one last round of mini-genocidal operations in Fallujah. These plans would commence three months later, in November of 2004.

14. A CONFRONTATION OF WORDS: MY INTERVIEW WITH GENERAL KIMMITT

Four months after I was evicted from Fallujah, all al-Jazeera journalists and staff were evicted from Iraq after a period of constant harassment by IIPs. Kimmitt continued to articulate his anti-al-Jazeera propaganda in his press conferences. Very few other journalists dared to call him on his bogus claims, because many had seen what had happened to al-Jazeera's crew in Fallujah. No one wanted to become the next target for the Bush administration.

In April 2006, I got a call from my colleague Saeed Alshoely, who had been deputy editor-in-chief when we were covering the siege in Fallujah two years earlier. Now Saeed was head of programming, in charge of suggesting ideas for shows and programs.

Saeed asked, "Do you recall General Kimmitt, Ahmed?"

"No, I don't. I've never had any interaction with a General Kimmitt."

Then I had to laugh. "But don't believe me, because I'm a guy whose job is to 'propagate lies and feed viewers with false information.'"

Saeed laughed. "Man, you never forget anything. Well, Kimmitt's going to be in Doha next week, and his media consultant offered us an interview. Your name was the first to pop into my mind when I heard Kimmitt was interested, so I told them if they wanted an interview, there would be no better option than your *Without Limits* show."

I couldn't help but laugh. Saeed wasn't going to let Kimmitt get his propaganda on our screens for free. He was making him pay a steep price for the airtime he wanted. Kimmitt was going to have to deal with the guy he hated most at al-Jazeera: yours truly.

"When they found out you were the host of *Without Limits* they asked for time to think and reconsider, and—"

I had to interrupt Saeed because I was laughing too hard. "Stop, stop! You're an evil man. No need to torture Kimmitt this way. Just give the interview to someone else."

"Man, it was crazy," he said. "They call us to ask to be interviewed, and when they learn you'll be the interviewer, they decide they need time to reconsider. What the heck were they doing in the first place? Weren't they thinking it might be an interview with you? They had to be! I think this guy is developing a love-hate relationship with you."

We laughed a little more, and then I added something serious. "Seriously, man, I don't think he's going to call back. And to tell you the truth, I need time to consider this myself."

Saeed was surprised. "What do you need to think about?"

I said, "Considering how much I know about this particular general, I'm not completely confident I'll be able to do an objective and fair job in the interview. I don't want things to get personal."

Saeed understood, but encouraged me to think about it. "Sleep on it, man. Sleep on it."

My instinct was to decline the offer. I thought I'd get a second opinion, though, so I called Shaikh Hamad bin Thamer al-Thani for advice.

He said, "I disagree with you. You can interview him without letting the whole thing become personal. Just don't discuss what happened between the two of you when you were in Fallujah. That's all you need to do. Besides, everyone knows the history. The viewers saw your coverage and saw Kimmitt's press briefings back then. So it's not like you're coming on with a hidden agenda. We all know there is a history between the two of you, so no one is expecting you to exchange boxes of chocolate or bouquets of roses. We already know it's going to be another battle, just don't let it be personal. It's okay as long as you maintain your professionalism, and I think General Kimmitt will do the same if he ends up deciding to go forward with the interview."

I called Wadah Khanfar for yet a third opinion, and his was identical to Shaikh Hamad bin Thamer's. I decided to take up the challenge.

For me, this interview was largely meant to mark the importance of the third anniversary of the occupation of Iraq and the second anniversary of the first battle of Fallujah. The interview was going to be a battle, just as Shaikh Hamad bin Thamer said. Only this time, General Kimmitt couldn't use his snipers to scare me or his artillery to target me from across the Euphrates. This time, the general had to fight on my turf using weapons I was more familiar with: logic, facts, reason, and patience. I knew Kimmitt would be up to it. He must've had military training on how to deal with journalists. He had stood his ground before hundreds of reporters many times before. His ground may have been shaky when he was confronted with disturbing images of what his troops were doing, but nonetheless, the man stood on it. So, I had to do some studying up on his career and background to prepare myself for the interview.

Although I consented to the interview shortly after Saeed's phone call, Kimmitt's media consultant didn't return with a decision so quickly.

They must have been discussing the advisability of this interview from every angle. The Americans had likely thought originally that they were going to have a good outlet for their propaganda on our screens. When they found out it was going to be me doing the interviewing, they had to think twice. Not because I'm a journalistic Superman by any means, but because they had already blamed me in part for losing their first battle in Fallujah. They didn't want the interview to be another partial contribution to another total loss.

Although it took some time, Kimmitt's people eventually got back to Saeed with a yes. There was one little technical problem, however. *Without Limits* airs live every Wednesday, and Kimmitt was going to be in Doha for only one day, and it wasn't going to be Wednesday. It was suggested that we prerecord the show. At first I refused, because prerecording had the potential to change the open nature of the show, and to increase the possibility that Kimmitt would retract statements later. In the end, however, I had to agree; we had no other options.

General Kimmitt arrived at the al-Jazeera station with three other men, and he was dressed in his military uniform. He greeted me and tried to break the ice.

"You look a lot more elegant than when I saw you on TV during the Fallujah days," he said.

I replied with a thanks. I asked if he wanted to sit down first before the interview.

He replied, "Nope, don't need to sit down. I'm ready for the show."

He then noticed a plaque on the wall. Into it was carved the Charter of Journalistic Integrity known as the Code of Ethics inside al-Jazeera.

"Just let me read this first," he said.

He stood before the plaque (basically a list of principles journalists are expected to adopt and work by in order to provide their service with professionalism and integrity). He began to read the plaque out loud, and during his reading he nodded his head in obvious sarcasm and mockery. I didn't comment on this immature display. I decided to save my energy for the time when I could point out his idiocy on screen.

My colleague Mowafaq Tawfeeq, the man who does live translations for non-Arabic-speaking guests, arrived and introduced himself to Kimmitt. Kimmitt immediately recognized him as the voice that did all the live translations when Americans were interviewed by al-Jazeera. After Kimmitt was introduced to Tawfeeq, we sat in the studio and waited for the director's instructions. The general and I mostly talked about trivial things in the presence of his three friends and my many colleagues who were quickly filling the room. These colleagues were coming to watch the "action," as one of them put it.

Just before the director was about to signal the start of our recording, General Kimmitt said something to me that greatly surprised me.

He leaned in close to me, and said, "I have something to say before we start the interview. I disagree with you, and I disagreed with everything you said during your coverage of the battle of Fallujah. However, please allow me to express my deep respect and admiration for you and your bravery, especially when you were inside the siege of Fallujah."

I wasn't prepared for General Kimmitt to say anything like that, and would never have guessed he would start our interview in such an earnest manner. He didn't have to give me any credit for my work, given our difficult disagreements in the past, but he did. As the old Arab adage goes, "Your true virtues are the ones your adversaries can't deny, and if you're truly worthy of respect, even your vowed enemy would respect you." I did what I considered to be my moral duty in showing the world the horrors of Operation Vigilant Resolve, and this man did everything he could to cover up the war crimes his Marines were committing. My career was threatened by the warmongering administration that this general worked for just because I tried to expose the truth. I didn't pay attention to what he said about me during or after the battle. Colleagues always pointed it out to me—I never sought the information myself.

Still, I never expected him to acknowledge the value of what I did. In fact, I never thought I'd ever see him face to face. And yet, after two years, an adversary who once wanted me dead acknowledged the courage it took to broadcast the truth of the horrors in Fallujah to the world. That was more acknowledgment than I could have imagined. He knew that I had been doing the right thing, even if he had to admit it on his own terms. Hearing his concession was well worth every risk I took with my life and that of the crew in order to cover that hideous military operation.

Although General Kimmitt said this phrase only once, Mowafaq Tawfeeq repeated it in his English-Arabic translation to the audience twice because of how important he felt it was for everyone to hear. Colleagues who strongly disagreed with me about my coverage of the battle of Fallujah acknowledged the integrity of my work after Kimmitt's words. Many of them approached me after the interview and expressed similar sentiments.

"Thank you, General," I said simply. "But this isn't going to change anything in the battle we're about to get into right now. You were just doing your job back then, and so was I. And you're just doing your job right now, and so am I."

Although his face was extremely stern, he smiled lightly and said, "Ask away. I don't mind answering any question you have."

I started the interview by briefly introducing Mark Kimmitt to my audience. I summarized his career as a distinguished US Army General, and then started the questions.

I asked several questions about George Bush's military and political strategy in Iraq. These questions covered the preparedness (or lack thereof) demonstrated by the Iraqi forces—forces that were supposedly trained by the US to eventually take over. I also questioned recent statements made by British and American officials that showed how poorly the war was going for the US.

I was careful to space out my questions evenly, and to give General Kimmitt the time he needed to respond to each question. He appeared not to need this time to think, because his response to every difficult question fit into one pattern. He blamed every negative aspect of the conflict on the insurgents, terrorists, or "foreign fighters" living in Iraq. These groups, he claimed, were the only obstacles standing in the way of Iraqi progress, and these people were the only ones preventing Iraqi citizens from enjoying the "democratic and free system" that had been implemented by the American forces.

In the next phase of the interview, I questioned Kimmitt about his reaction to the chaos engulfing Iraq—by which I meant the deplorable security situation, and the many reports released by NGOs detailing the horrific number of human rights and civil liberties violations in Iraq. Kimmitt dismissed all these claims as being colored by media bias. Or, if the media was not to blame, then the insurgents were. He did not forget to remind viewers that despite all the horror in Iraq, Iraqis still got to vote in three different democratic primaries since the Americans had been in control. I thought to myself, what good is a right to vote if the candidates don't have your best interests in mind? What good do elections do if nothing ever changes to improve your life?

Since Kimmitt's responses were becoming redundant, I figured I had to move to another point not directly related to the insurgency. I posed a question that was dominating the media and the entire American public at that time.

I asked, "Is the Bush administration winning the war?"

Before he had time to respond, I cited previous answers to this question from defense analyst and senior fellow Michael O'Hanlon of the Brookings Institute in Washington, DC. I quoted journalist Robert Fisk. Both noteworthy men had recently written articles arguing that Bush was far from winning the war.

Although my question was about the Bush administration and its performance in Iraq as separate from its dealings with the insurgency problem, General Kimmitt proceeded to ignore the substance of my question and instead spoke of what monsters al-Zarqawi and his gang of insurgents were. In contrast, he painted a glorious picture of how successfully the Americans had brought freedom and democracy for all Iraqis to enjoy.

Seeing that I was getting nowhere, I proceeded to ask about recently published reports detailing the deteriorating mental health of American soldiers and the low morale of US soldiers serving in Iraq. I mentioned the claim that the Department of Defense was covering up its real casualty counts. I cited reports and articles on the subject from *Newsweek*, the *Washington Post*, and the *New York Times*.

Just as expected, General Kimmitt completely ignored the reports I had mentioned from reputable news sources based in the US. Without providing a rebuttal to the claims made by fine American journalists, he once again returned the conversation to the topic of the terrorists, who he claimed were ruining Iraq by killing innocent children. He was also fond of bringing up the captives whose beheadings had been videotaped and broadcast across the globe.

Part of his response was as follows:

> They [American soldiers] cannot be in Iraq without understanding why they went there. There are people being beheaded by terrorists. There are innocent children being murdered by insurgents and terrorists. The stability that coalition forces brought with them [to Iraq] by their continued support of Iraqi forces until they can manage things on their own is probably the biggest factor that may secure the success of this mission. We're very confident that in the future when we look back on this whole thing five years from now, when we see the achievements of the coalition and Iraqi forces, we would conclude that we did the right thing. History will definitely be on our side. I am absolutely convinced that history will be on our side and will judge our joint mission as coalition and Iraqi forces as the right and just thing.

It was disturbing to me that an intelligent man like General Kimmitt, a man with such an impressive military record, was making the absurd argument that American troops went to Iraq because terrorists were beheading people and murdering innocent children. I could not comprehend how a man of his intellect, who was involved in the planning of this war, could look into my eyes and the eyes of my viewers and tell such a bald lie. Kimmitt knew very well that there were no terrorists or insurgents in Iraq when the Americans invaded, let alone terrorists who were beheading hostages and killing children. Yet, he somehow believed the viewer would not see through these lies.

I thought of reminding Kimmitt that the insurgent and terrorist groups formed after American forces occupied Iraq, and also that all evidence suggested that Iraq was far less stable at the time of our interview than it had been during the tyrannical reign of Saddam Hussein. But I held my tongue, figuring he wasn't going to listen. I knew I couldn't cure him of the naive belief that the Americans were a blessed force in Iraq, and that all the actions of the American forces were just and humane. Kimmitt clearly came on the show to convert others to this ridiculous belief, and I figured it was best to let him do that so that viewers could hear his lies and take arms against him on their own.

I decided to let him stand as evidence of his own ignorance and moved to make another point.

"But let's remember that in the recent past, history has not looked on American military pursuits with kindness. Luck hasn't been on the American side in every single conflict. The verdict wasn't in your favor in Lebanon, Somalia, or Vietnam. This may be the case with your invasion of Iraq too. Don't take my word for it. Take the word of former US Marines Staff Sergeant Jimmy Massey. Massey is a twelve-year veteran of the US Marine Corps, and a former Marine recruiter and boot camp drill instructor. He served as staff sergeant in the 3rd Battalion, 7th Marines, Weapons Company during the invasion of Iraq until he was honorably discharged in December 2003. He's written an autobiography entitled *Kill, Kill, Kill*, which is co-authored by Natasha Saulnier, a fellow platoon member. The book was published in France in 2005. In the book Jimmy says that he, along with many of the soldiers sent with him, discovered once they arrived in Iraq that they were sent to kill civilians, not terrorists. He makes these and other very serious claims regarding war crimes and human rights violations committed by the US military. How is history going to be on your side in light of accusations like these?"

With a Bush-like smirk on his face, General Kimmitt answered, "I can get you any number of books written that argue the situation in Iraq to be exactly the opposite of what you're describing."

I thought this weak rebuttal was all General Kimmitt was going to offer, but he continued to speak so that he might have a chance to remind us, once again, that he believed the blame for every problem in Iraq sat squarely on the shoulders of the insurgency.

He continued, "But let's be clear about one thing in regard to the current situation. In addition to the increased sectarian violence, the heart of the matter is the threat from al-Qaeda and those who are associated with it. This threat is a problem not just inside Iraq but across the region in general, which means that it's important for us to stand up against the threat of terrorism not only in Iraq, but across the whole region so that your children and grandchildren can enjoy a prosperous future that's characterized by security, not terror."

I couldn't believe my ears. I was asking him to comment on condemning testimony given by members of US forces—reports accusing the President of the United States and top US officials of supporting policies that violated human rights. The questions were coming entirely from reports given by citizens of the United States, so any reasonable response would have to address American responsibility and American concerns. Yet, somehow, Kimmitt found a way to get terrorists involved in the subject. Somehow, he still found a way to make this argument only about the threat of al-Qaeda.

At this point it became very clear to me that it really didn't matter what questions I asked General Kimmitt. This man wasn't here to give any meaningful answers. He'd come to the studio determined to give the same answer to every question. His clear intention was to defame terrorists in order to subvert blame for the problems in Iraq, and praise the supposed peace and security that the Americans had brought to a country that was actually in shambles.

Once I realized that I wouldn't get anything meaningful out of Kimmitt, I conducted the rest of the interview on a kind of auto-pilot. I covered a variety of subjects and topics related to the war on Iraq, and General Kimmitt gave the same answer every time whatever the substance of the question. In addition to these absurd answers, he frequently made outlandish accusations that everyone involved in the war at the time of the interview knew were fraudulent. He made references to the WMDs hidden by Saddam, a claim that had already been widely dismantled. He also claimed that "most" Iraqis welcomed the US invasion of their country and that they were well-received in most Iraqi communities. Kimmitt also claimed that US soldiers didn't commit any crimes over the course of the war with a few minor exceptions (the fall guys in the Abu Ghraib scandal) and declared that the Bush administration had been entirely truthful about information related to the war at all times.

At this point I had to pause and try to comprehend the multitude and scale of these lies. The discordance between the picture he was creating and the reality in Iraq was impossible for any discerning viewer to take seriously.

I leaned forward and asked, "General, are you saying that the US didn't make any mistakes in Iraq?"

He replied, "Oh, I think any time a war is waged mistakes are made. But we have an internal system within our military establishment that we go back to in order to review our operations… to try to learn from our experiences and enhance our performance."

Of course this vague answer was not satisfactory. I wasn't asking him if mistakes were made in terms of tactics, operations planning and execution, or technical performance. I was asking about mistakes in terms of lapses in human dignity, the committing of horrific war crimes, and the total lack of moral responsibility exhibited by the American forces. I know he knew what I was asking, but he wanted to play dumb. To deprive him of any opportunity to plead ignorance or misunderstanding, I clarified my question to him.

I said, "An article published in the British newspaper the *Independent* on March 18, 2006 spoke of a letter drafted by Mr. Tony Benn,[36] co-signed by more than 1,000 leading figures, and submitted to British Attorney General, Lord Goldsmith, and the UN Secretary-General Kofi Annan. The letter details 28 alleged breaches of the Nuremberg Charter and the Geneva and Hague Conventions. It demands both offices investigate that list of breaches of international law in conjunction with the war on Iraq. Don't you worry that some day you will be accused of committing war crimes?"

At this point, General Kimmitt lost the composure he was trying so desperately to maintain throughout the interview. It was obvious that when I asked this question he realized that he was cornered. He had to stop bringing up insurgents and terrorists and diverting blame to other parties, and he had to answer for deeds committed by the institution of which he was a part.

In a burst of anger, he replied, "Well, maybe we will be questioned about this some day, but the reality on the ground will come through at the end. And I find it plenty interesting that the way you've been conducting this interview and the way your questions are phrased suggests that only coalition forces are killing civilians even though we try to avoid causing civilian casualties. Why don't you talk about al-Zarqawi? Why don't you talk about Saddam's followers and sympathizers? About the insurgents who intentionally target civilians for their terrorist goals and plots? Are you as adamant to get them to reveal the truth as you are with members of the coalition forces? What about the thousands of victims who fell in terrorist attacks? What about the beheadings of innocent civilians? Aren't you also responsible for finding out the truth about those crimes?"

I answered his questions very coldly, "General, I talk to all of my guests in this same way. If my guest was part of one of those groups you mentioned, I would have presented the same questions to him as they pertain to his area of responsibility. Every viewer of al-Jazeera knows my interview style and the format of my show. And I am asking you these questions as a person responsible for the region you're serving in and responsible for setting strategic plans for US involvement in this region. You were in Iraq for several years after the occupation, and you were, and still are, the man who appears in the media to represent the military establishment of the US and defend its deeds. I am talking to you about your responsibility and the responsibility of your forces. I'm talking to you about what your forces are doing in Iraq now. You invaded Iraq, and therefore you're completely responsible for what you're doing there and what's happening in that country. You're the superpower, and you're the country that claimed to bring democracy to Iraq but instead plunged it into a mess of civil war, sectarian violence, and terrorism. You're the ones who got yourselves caught in this quagmire and got this entire region involved in this situation. The insurgents and the terrorists aren't the ones who did this. You did it, and you bear the responsibility for it. Insurgents never claimed to be the beacon of civility, democracy, stability, or security. Insurgents are viewed as rogue organizations of terrorists, while you are supposedly a civilized superpower. I certainly don't hope that you expect me to view the two parties as equal counterparts in this equation!"

My admonishment did not seem to make Kimmitt any more willing to give me honest answers to my questions. I went on with the interview and it was more of the same. Kimmitt provided the same answers to all questions, and instead of talking about the substance of my questions he talked about the evil nature of terrorists and the virtues of the stability and democracy Bush brought to Iraq.

During one of the commercial breaks, General Kimmitt asked me, "Are you always this tough and bold with guests on your show?"

I answered, "Yes, that's my style. Everyone who watches the show knows this is my signature. I play hardball."

To wrap up the interview, I concluded with a general question about American strategies for the future in Iraq.

I asked, "In light of the current foggy situation, the tension, the violence, and the bloodshed all across Iraq, what can you say to viewers who want to see a less gloomy vision than the current vision of Iraq? What is your strategy for the coming period?"

He responded, "Once again, our strategy depends on ensuring stability and peace, allowing for an Iraqi government to form, and building an armed Iraqi force. And more importantly, our strategy is to confront the real danger that threatens this region. To be honest, we're not trying to protect just this region, but the whole world, by attacking and defeating al-Qaeda and the organizations affiliated with it. It's clear to us that al-Qaeda poses a real threat to this region and its interests. We don't want to fight just al-Qaeda; we're also after all other Salafi groups and Islamic organizations that want to take this region back to the days of the caliphs in the 13th century. They are willing and ready to do this in any way they can, even if that means acquiring WMDs and nuclear weapons, and they're not afraid to use them if given the chance. Although Iraq and Afghanistan remain on the top of our priority list as battlegrounds where we hope to defeat al-Qaeda, we're ready to chase and defeat that organization anywhere across the world."

General Kimmitt's closing remarks echoed his obvious purpose in securing an interview with al-Jazeera. He had come to our studio in order to propagate Bush's claims, which he did without subtlety throughout the interview. His closing statement directly outlined Bush's imperial policy, with the ideological zeal of the neoconservative movement. Bush too wants to pursue the ghost-like members of al-Qaeda to the four corners of the Earth. Bush also does not see his power as limited to Iraq and Afghanistan. Bush too has made his crusade religious as well as political in nature.

I didn't know if General Kimmitt realized the highly offensive statement he had made in his closing speech, concerning the Salafis.[37] People other than bin Laden and members of al-Qaeda believe in Salafism. Salafism is a huge school of thought that the entire Gulf region adheres to along with many members of other Arab and Muslim countries. Salafis are the most active Muslim movement in the US and Europe. And Salafis are the dominant school of thought within the Sunni sect. For Kimmitt to close his interview with a statement saying he wanted to go after Salafi groups is not very different from Hitler saying he wanted to go after the Jewish groups. Ironically, one of America's closes allies in the region, Saudi Arabia, follows the Salafi philosophy and reveres it more highly than all others.

15. BESIEGING THE BESIEGER

"No man can put a chain about the ankle of his fellow man without at last finding the other end fastened about his own neck."
                              —Frederick Douglass, in an 1883 speech

When I left Fallujah on the evening of Saturday, April 11, 2004 to comply with the American cease-fire conditions, I didn't come across a single American soldier on the entire route between Fallujah and Baghdad. There were many groups of insurgents clustered around Fallujah and its suburbs, but there were no American soldiers. The insurgents were also spread along the roads that led to Baghdad, even directing the traffic just outside the capital city. Nearly all other alternative roads connecting Fallujah and Baghdad were also controlled by insurgents.

Once I reached Baghdad, I passed the airport, and saw that Airport Street had been razed of all trees and greenery by American bulldozers. American forces were afraid insurgents would use the massive date palm trees as fortification positions. Because of the panoramic view created by the absence of these trees, I could see huge numbers of American military vehicles left abandoned and destroyed in the vicinity of the airport. Some vehicles were still smoldering and others were already cold, charred, and hollowed out. At first I tried to count the abandoned vehicles, but when I realized how high the numbers were going to be, I stopped counting.

Once inside Baghdad city limits, Americans were largely in control, but that control was not existent everywhere. Entire sectors of the city were fast becoming impossible for US forces to manage. The Azamiyah suburb, for instance, was completely controlled by insurgents, who walked the streets entirely unopposed. Very soon people started calling this suburb "liberated Azamiyah." The insurgents were often seen directing traffic in Baghdad; sometimes the insurgents even managed the traffic on the main highways. The ambition of the insurgents here was to track the vehicles as they moved about the city, and attack any vehicle that could possibly be holding American troops. It fairly normal to see American vehicles on fire along the shoulder of the roads controlled by insurgents. Obviously, American trucks and semi-trailers soon stopped going through these streets altogether for fear of ambush.

During my stay in Baghdad, I heard at least five or six explosions a day, and most of them were insurgent attacks on American forces. In the heart of Baghdad was the area known as the Green Zone. This area was originally built by Saddam Hussein as a residential zone, for his own lavish presidential palaces as well as the homes of his ministers and high-ranking officials. When the occupation took over, American forces and diplomats used this zone as their hub as well—the IIPs and newly appointed high-ranking officials set up their offices here. This heavily fortified and constantly guarded area was presumably the safest in all of Iraq. Yet during and after the first battle of Fallujah, it wasn't uncommon for insurgents to attack the Green Zone. Many reports spoke of American officials resorting to sleeping in the "safe rooms" that Saddam had built in the ground beneath his palaces. Eventually, conditions became so dangerous that the safe rooms were occupied all day, not just at bedtime.

Besides constantly monitoring the flow of traffic, the insurgents started to kidnap truckers who were working for US forces. The insurgents used these truck drivers to gain intelligence they could use for their gruesome propaganda, and many times the helpless truckers had no option but to give any information they had to the insurgents, in the hopes that they wouldn't be captured or harmed. The insurgents filmed the truckers as they gave all the information they had, and unfortunately, these filmed reports were often followed by cold-blooded murder right in front of the camera. Murder, however, doesn't adequately describe what happened to these victims—murder can take any shape or form, and can sometimes be quick and painless. This was never the case with these insurgent murderers. The insurgents made sure that truckers working for the Americans were slowly and painfully butchered, and they did this simply to get a point across to the Americans and anyone working on their behalf. The point was this: if we catch you working with the occupation, we will not treat you like a human being, because you aren't one. The tapes of these murders were often released on the internet. This grizzly propaganda was very effective in slowing the recruitment of drivers willing to work in Iraq on behalf of the United States.

Insurgents had also managed to deal a blow to helicopters working for the United States, which Saddam's army and Republican Guard had always failed to do. During one week, ten helicopters were shot down, and that was just in the area around Fallujah. It was these casualties that made the Marines switch to using exclusively F-16s and AC-130 gunships. The Marines then started dropping bombs without discretion and using internationally banned weapons such as cluster bombs. This activity was all reported by eyewitnesses. More than 1,700 civilians were injured in and around Fallujah over the course of the first battle and its aftermath because of this indiscriminate bombing.

This bombing, in turn, outraged people in cities and towns all over Iraq. Average civilians were inspired to join the insurgents. And insurgents flocked from all over the country to join the fight for Fallujah. The American military machine had lost its grip in Fallujah, and the insurgents wanted to take advantage of that. Because of this influx of insurgents, casualties rose in staggering numbers, and cities were destroyed more than at any point since the war had begun. Marines were slaughtering civilians, insurgents were slaughtering Marines and civilian contractors, Marines were retaliating by killing insurgents, and civilians were getting fed up and joining the insurgents to bring death upon the Marines. All of Iraq was caught up in a deadly cycle of violence.

These attacks were, of course, already going on while I was covering the siege in Fallujah. The insurgents' attack that took place on Tuesday, April 6, in Ramadi, 24 miles from Fallujah, resulted in the death of twelve American soldiers. This was the number the Pentagon released, and the same number we aired on al-Jazeera the day before the Pentagon confirmed the news. Other sources, such as Sky News TV, claimed that the Pentagon had lost numbers closer to 150. The source that provided this count said that the high casualty count was from mortar fire that took the soldiers by surprise. Casualty counts were also very high because insurgents had attacked the American base at the heart of the city, where more soldiers were gathering.

Since the high number differed so greatly from the official number given by the Pentagon and we weren't able to confirm its validity, we didn't include it in our broadcast. We did conclude, though, that the number of casualties had to have been higher than the Pentagon had announced. I was in Fallujah when the Americans began to drop bombs in Ramadi in order to avenge the death of the soldiers. I was following the developments of the battle over the phone with my colleague, Hussam Ali. Ali was stuck in downtown Ramadi with his cameraman when the fighting broke out. We hadn't heard the higher casualty number quoted yet, but from what Hussam saw, he could tell the Americans were hurting. He said, "The attack just now was so indiscriminate and so senseless—the Americans couldn't possibly be doing all of this because of twelve dead soldiers. They must've lost a lot more men in order to justify this kind of attack."

The first battle of Fallujah spurred an eruption of battles all over the Anbar province and throughout the Sunni Triangle. Muqtada al-Sadr and his militia also decided to intensify their operations in solidarity with Fallujah, primarily in the Najaf area. During these attacks, the top US commander in Iraq, Lt. General Ricardo Sanchez, had to admit defeat. On April 8, Sanchez told the press that his forces had lost control of Najaf and al-Kut.

This was happening all over Iraq, while we were submerged in the siege in Fallujah. That Friday, American forces were run out of Samarra after losing control of the area to insurgents. Thereafter, the insurgents maintained control within the city limits, and US forces stayed just outside the city. These battles broke out all over Iraq for a single reason: the insurgents were fighting hard in order to show solidarity with the people of Fallujah. This spike in violence resulted in a sudden and over-whelming string of victories for the insurgents across Iraq.

By the time Bush realized his Marines were hemorrhaging in Fallujah, the Marines had already lost many young lives. On April 11, at Fort Hood military base, George Bush acknowledged this: "It was a tough week last week, and my prayers and thoughts are with those who paid the ultimate price for our security."

Later, Bush added that he prayed every day that there would be fewer casualties. When I heard this, I thought to myself, you don't need to pray to have fewer casualties, Mr. President. All you need to do is act to end the war. Without this brutal war, your casualties would be zero. Stop trying to make a place for yourself in human history at the expense of American lives. Stop seeking personal glory. Stop praising this war.

A New Army or a New Burden?

The failure of the American forces during and after this battle was also echoed in the miserable performance of the New Iraqi Army, which Bremer had established to provide Iraqi-born defense against the insurgents. In addition to the US forces and the New Iraqi Army, the Civil Defense Corps and the Iraqi police were also supposed to fight on behalf of the United States. Tens of thousands of policemen were supposed to have grad-uated from the law enforcement academy set up by Bremer's admini-stration. Over 15,000 were also supposed to be trained to join the Civil Defense Corps. The New Iraqi Army, however, had only four major battal-ions when Bremer left his post. The development of all these new military battalions was further hindered by threats from the insurgents against any

Iraqi cooperating with the Americans.

Iraqis who cooperated with the occupation forces were considered fair game to the insurgents. The insurgents didn't care if these people were native Iraqis; if they cooperated with the occupation, they were traitors, worse than the Americans. Within the first year of occupation, insurgents killed more than 700 Iraqis who joined the new Iraqi police. In the early part of the war, the casualty count of new Iraqi soldiers was higher than the count of American casualties.

One of the most active insurgency groups during this time was the 1920 Revolution Brigades, a militant insurgency group that had both a religious and patriotic agenda. This group distributed a flyer in Baghdad on April 10 demanding that new Iraqi police recruits desert their posts within one week or face dire consequences. More radical groups such as Ansar al-Islam and Ansar al-Sunnah didn't warn these new recruits before beginning the slaughter.

Two out of the four major battalions of the New Iraqi Army refused to support the Marines in their operation against Fallujah. One of those battalions refused to even go to Fallujah at all. On April 11, the *Washington Post* reported that "a new army battalion refused to go into combat in Fallujah. Maj. General Paul Eaton explained that they said they had not signed up to fight other Iraqis. General Eaton preferred to refer to this mutiny by the Orwellian moniker 'a command failure.'...." Media sources said that American forces placed this particularly rebellious battalion under siege for a few days when it refused to carry out American military orders. These reports were never verified.

Reports of this defiance explain the whereabouts of the first battalion to abandon the US cause, but what about the second? What became of them?

The second battalion appeared briefly to be supporting the American war effort. The soldiers initially accepted the orders given to them. Once the battle began, however, the drivers took positions in their vehicles, with fellow Iraqi soldiers in the back, and then proceeded to drive as fast as they could in the wrong direction, bailing on their commitments to the United States.

The Iraqi police were the only Iraqi forces that actively participated in the fighting of the first battle of Fallujah. But not on behalf of the Americans. Agence France-Presse reported on April 12 that huge numbers of Iraqi police had not only cooperated with the insurgents, but often joined their ranks and provided them with arms. The report estimated that 25 to 35 percent of the entire organization had joined the insurgents. Occupation forces also reported that they had seen Iraqi policemen aiming their guns at American soldiers.

I didn't need to read this report to know these numbers are accurate. When I was in Fallujah, I witnessed firsthand the arrest of many Iraqi policemen on the charge of cooperating with insurgents. I saw insurgents taking control of Iraqi police vehicles with the permission of the policemen. This cooperation between Iraqi police and the insurgents happened in many places besides Fallujah, including some of Baghdad's suburbs.

The policemen who didn't openly cooperate with insurgents were still not on the side of the Americans. They either didn't want to fight against the insurgents or were physically unable to do so. The result of all these shifting alliances was that Muqtada al-Sadr's militia was able to take control of police stations in the cities of Najaf, Kufa, and Sadr, and was also able to inflict major damage on the forces in Fallujah.

At the time of Paul Bremer's resignation, signs of the American forces' failure to establish a unified, reliable law enforcement agency in Iraq were all over the country—most notably in Fallujah, Abu Ghraib, Samarra, Sadr City, Najaf, Kufa, and al-Kut. Even after a year of repeated attempts, it was obvious that Bush had failed to establish a police force of 85,000 officers strong, and had failed to provide his promised security to the Iraqi people.

Abizaid Pleads for Reinforcements

General John Abizaid held a particular personal grudge against the city of Fallujah even before the first battle began. Fallujan insurgents had tried, and very nearly succeeded, to assassinate him in February 2004. So, when the first battle began, Abizaid had more than enough incentive to take revenge. He found himself neck-deep in trouble, though, when he quickly realized that his troops lacked the power to take down all the insurgents hiding in the city. On April 12, 2004, one week into the siege of Fallujah, Abizaid was forced to request two additional combat brigades in an attempt to control the widespread rebellion not only in Fallujah but all across Iraq. He wanted each brigade to comprise 10,000 troops. This request came after Donald Rumsfeld had already announced the extension of tours of duty for some 20,000 troops because of an earlier request from Abizaid.

When reporters asked Bush about what he thought of Abizaid's request for reinforcements, he replied, "If that's what he wants, that's what he gets."

He then added, "I have directed our military commanders to make every preparation to use decisive force, if necessary, to maintain order and to protect our troops… the consequences of failure in Iraq would be unthinkable."

Abizaid's request for reinforcements was a clear sign that the US forces were experiencing heavy losses. At first, US forces tried to cover up the losses by sealing off the scene of any battles where they had suffered significant casualties. In order to do this, they sent choppers to airlift the victims from the scene and tow away damaged vehicles as close to the end of the battle as possible. After the bodies and damage were cleared away from the scene, they opened the area for journalists, and claimed the losses suffered were very minor.

As I discussed earlier, the attacks became so common and the losses so significant that sometime during the first battle of Fallujah, the Americans were unable to keep up the masquerade. There were just too many damaged vehicles to cover up. Even when burned-out vehicles littered streets and highways, it was still possible to falsify casualty counts, so that it would seem that their forces were in less trouble than they really were. These lies were a way of maintaining morale. Which is precisely why the murder and mutilation of the Blackwater USA security guards outraged the Americans so much. With the murder caught on tape and broadcast around the world, something of the weak position of the American occupation was exposed. Morale among the American forces fighting on the ground was splintering.

The first battle of Fallujah hugely influenced the media, just as the media hugely influenced the battle. Prior to the first battle of Fallujah and the string of insurgent attacks associated with it, American media shied away from showing dead or injured American forces in the media. During and after this battle, however, it became common to see images of body bags stuffed with dead American soldiers broadcast on American news networks. News reports also aired clips of injured soldiers receiving treatment in military medical centers and field hospitals. This trend lasted for a bit, but when the Pentagon realized the damaging effect these broadcasts were having on the morale of American soldiers, the Pentagon condemned the media for showing such images, claiming that it was degrading to US soldiers. Naturally, many US media outlets stopped airing such footage as soon as the Pentagon told them to do so.

A Rise in Brutal Kidnappings

The political situation in Iraq worsened for the Bush administration when they realized that the insurgents subscribed to philosophies not entirely dissimilar from their own. Insurgents were hardened radicals willing to do anything and everything to have their way. They were fanatical in their devotion to their cause and to victory, just like Bush and his cohorts. The Bush administration likely never realized these similarities, but the dedication each side demonstrated to their political cause escalated the violence at an exponential rate.

Kidnappings happen in every war, but usually such incidents aren't particularly widespread. In the war between Iraqi insurgents and the United States, however, the insurgents began to perfect the gruesome and horrific act of kidnapping, often on video. Hostages were forced at gunpoint and on video to denounce the actions of their governments and plead for withdrawal of the American forces and anyone else supporting their cause. When these horrific videos were posted on the internet, leaders around the world were put in very awkward positions. The demands of several small groups of insurgents became top priorities, especially in the native countries of those kidnapped. When the kidnappers' demands weren't met, hostages were butchered in cold blood in front of the cameras, and these images were again broadcast over the internet. Kidnapping was a win-win situation for the insurgents. They either had their demands met, or they killed their hostages, instituting a reign of terror. The kidnapping was never random as in other wars, and the results were always broadcast across the airwaves for the entire world to see. No one was safe. Not even the people in charge of security—intelligence officers—were immune from this brutality. For example, insurgents kidnapped eight Spanish intelligence officers three months before the first battle of Fallujah. This incident was one of the key reasons why former Spanish Prime Minister José María Aznar lost the 2004 elections. The new prime minister, José Luis Rodríguez Zapatero, had made pulling Spanish troops out of Iraq the centerpiece of his campaign. And indeed, one of his first acts when he came to power was to do so, which created a wedge in the Euro-American alliance on the war in Iraq. Of course the Madrid train bombings, for which al-Qaeda was responsible, played an even bigger role in Zapatero's election victory. But without a doubt, the kidnappings were also part of his victory.

Italy found itself in a similar situation during this time, as insurgents began to target Italians serving in Iraq. Prime Minister Silvio Berlusconi already had a tarnished image when the war began, and the scenes of Italian hostages suffering at the hands of kidnappers made his position weaker. He lost the April 2006 elections, and the new prime minister, Romano Prodi, made the withdrawal of Italian troops from Iraq one of his first acts when he came to power.

The political future and career of Junichiro Koizumi, the Japanese prime minister, was also imperiled when Japanese hostages were taken by insurgents in 2004. And after the kidnapping and release of eight Russian citizens on April 13, Russia (who hadn't even participated in Bush's "coalition of the willing") offered to fly home Russians working in Iraq. Clearly, nations all over the world were responding to insurgent demands with impressive submission.

American hostages, of course, were the prize catch for insurgents. Americans were worth a lot more than any other hostages because the propaganda opportunities that came along with butchering an American were the most valuable. The kidnapping of US Army Staff Sergeant Keith Matthew Maupin kicked off a long campaign to kidnap and persecute American soldiers. Maupin was captured on April 9, 2004, and since that kidnapping, images of the young man have circulated throughout the internet and on televised media thousands upon thousands of times.

As any good parents would, Matt's vowed not to rest until their boy was home safe and sound. They called on the Bush administration to save their son's life. This request put the Bush administration in a critical and embarrassing situation, forcing them to break their declared rule of refusing to negotiate with terrorists. Because of the media attention, they were forced to negotiate to secure the release of Maupin and other American hostages. In the midst of these negotiations, the insurgents got the Bush administration to acknowledge that it was holding more than 12,000 Iraqis captive in its detention camps and prisons.

Sadly, the negotiations were ultimately unsuccessful. Eventually a poor-quality video of what was claimed to be Matt's execution was released on the internet by the insurgents; however, no one could verify for sure that that was indeed him who was being killed.

The Shadow of Vietnam

Insurgent kidnappings were not the only aspect of this war that Americans were getting upset about. As soon as the public caught on to the similarities between the war in Iraq and the Vietnam War, there was even more reason to wonder about the wisdom of the American course in

Iraq. Picking up on unrest at home, Bush became desperate to hand over sovereignty to the Iraqis by the June 30 deadline he'd set, even though Iraq was in no state for any peaceful transition of power. Bush knew that handing sovereignty to the Iraqis would make a clear distinction between this war and the one in Vietnam.

Signs of Bush's desperation to hand over power became visible when the Bush administration called upon the United Nations to take an active role in Iraq. Bush had invaded Iraq without the support of the United Nations, and had made it clear that he didn't particularly care about the UN's resolutions or policies. But as the war unfolded, he realized he needed to get other parties to help with the mess. He also sent Deputy Secretary of State Richard Armitage to the Gulf States to ask for help in calming down "our Sunni friends in Iraq." The Bush administration also had the audacity to call on Iran to quell the rioting of "its Shia friends." In short, Bush was asking for help from exactly those he'd alienated since the war began.

On April 13, Bush addressed the American people about the situation in Iraq, and he made it clear that he thought the actions he'd taken to encourage sovereignty would be enough to make a distinction between the Iraq and Vietnam wars. Yet, when it was time for questions, he was still asked about the similarity between the two wars.

One reporter said, "Some people are comparing Iraq to Vietnam and talking about a quagmire. Polls show that support for your policy is declining and that fewer than half Americans now support it."

Bush shrugged off the similarity: "I think the analogy is false." He evaded the rest of the questions by waffling and mumbling, and never actually provided any logical proof that the two were not similar in nature.

Historian Robert Dallek, who specializes in the history of American presidents, heard Bush's address and noted his evasion of the comparison. Dallek commented that Bush's tendency to repeat the same claims over and over without any new evidence only served to weaken his position with the public. A *Newsweek* article published on April 19 reported a statistic that echoed this sentiment: four in ten Americans were very concerned that Iraq would become another Vietnam. It was clear that despite Bush's best efforts to avoid such a problem, the war in Iraq was traveling down the same path the Vietnam War had taken decades before.

As if the fact that the general public was drawing an analogy between this war and Vietnam wasn't bad enough for Bush, the speculation increased as the conflict marched on. It wasn't long before observers and former senior officials admitted that the situation in Iraq was far worse than the situation had ever been in Vietnam. On September 16, Sidney Blumenthal, a former senior adviser to President Bill Clinton, published a piece in the *Guardian* that quoted retired General William Odom, former head of the National Security Agency, as saying, "Bush hasn't found the WMD. Al-Qaeda, it's worse, he's lost on that front. That he's going to achieve a democracy there? That goal is lost, too. It's lost." Odom continued, "Right now, the course we're on, we're achieving bin Laden's ends."

Odom also said, "This is far graver than Vietnam. There wasn't as much at stake strategically, though in both cases we mindlessly went ahead with a war that was not constructive for US aims. But now we're in a region far more volatile, and we're in much worse shape with our allies."

Blumenthal also quoted Jeffrey Record, professor of strategy at the Air War College in Montgomery, Alabama, as saying "I see no ray of light on the horizon at all. The worst case has become true. I see no exit. We've been down that road before. It's called Vietnamization. The idea that we're going to have an Iraqi force trained to defeat an enemy we can't defeat stretches the imagination. They will be tainted by their very association with the foreign occupier. In fact, we had more time and money in state building in Vietnam than in Iraq."

Colin Powell also had his share of Vietnam–Iraq comparisons to respond to. Testifying before a Senate Committee in April 2004, Powell said, "It [Iraq] is not a swamp that is going to devour us."

He then added, "I don't think these types of comparisons are terribly helpful. Vietnam was another part of the world, another time in history, and we ought to see the situation for what it is today and not try to find comparisons that can then be painted in a negative light." Powell seemed agitated and upset at the mere suggestion of similarity between the two wars.

Oddly, the same George Bush who rejected comparisons between Iraq and Vietnam was not above using the comparison when it suited his aims. In August 2007, while speaking to a veterans' organization in Kansas City, he said that "the price of America's withdrawal [in Vietnam] was paid by millions of innocent citizens." Bush spoke of the death toll of Vietnamese citizens as one of the Vietnam War's terrible legacies, and one that would be repeated in Iraq if American troops pulled out.

Following this comment, Dallek called Bush's analogy "an abuse of history." Dallek noted that Bush had "avoided using the Vietnam analogy for a very long time because he didn't want to invoke memories of a failed war." Jonathan Marcus, a fine journalist for the BBC, wrote, "But now he [Bush] was seeking to use Vietnam against critics of the Iraq war by saying that if the US rushed to leave Iraq, the consequences could be similar to the mayhem that afflicted Cambodia and Vietnam."

The more I know of Bush's actions and words, the more I am convinced that he has much in common with the very insurgents he waged war against. In addition to being fueled by religious bigotry and fantasies of global dominance, Bush also shares another characteristic of militant Islamic organizations. They too like to twist words, terms, and events, taking them out of context in order to support their cause.

Congressmen Demand Change

The Iraq–Vietnam analogy urged several senior congressmen to call for an exit strategy. Even as early as April 7, 2004, before the first anniversary of the American occupation of Iraq and the siege of Fallujah, Senator Robert Byrd was already seeing signs of trouble with Bush's policies in Iraq. "America needs a roadmap out of Iraq," he said.

Congressional demands for an exit strategy continued as the violence escalated in Iraq. Long after Byrd spoke out, on January 12, 2005, Senator Edward Kennedy said, "I do not retreat from the view that Iraq is George Bush's Vietnam. At the critical moment in the war on terrorism, the administration turned away from pursuing Osama bin Laden and made the catastrophic choice instead that has bogged down America in an endless quagmire in Iraq," as reported by the *Washington Post*. By November 2005, Congressman Jack Murtha of Pennsylvania was asking for a pullout of the troops within six months. This demand began a filthy battle of curses and insults between the Republicans on the floor of the House. Bill Van Auken of the World Socialist Web Site explored the dynamics of this argument in an interesting and detailed article posted online on November 21, 2005.

Discouraged by the plummeting support for Bush's policy on the American front and abroad, some American conservatives reacted by resorting to insults. Jean Schmidt, the most junior member of the House at the time, commented that a Marine had told her to send a message to Congressman Murtha about the pullout of American troops. The message was, "Cowards cut and run, Marines never do." Schmidt delivered the insulting message without considering that Congressman Murtha had spent 37 years in the Marine Corps before his time in Congress.

Following this, the House went into an uproar. Republicans and Democrats started yelling shouts and insults across the floor to opposite sides of the chamber. *Newsweek* later reported, "The melee was so intense that it brought the soothing presence of Rep. Tom DeLay from his secure undisclosed location."

As for Schmidt, she asked that comment be removed from congressional record, and went into total silence for several weeks. After her refusal to offer Congressman Murtha the public apology he deserved, I must admit that I enjoyed watching Schmidt get nailed on national television by the ever-talented Tina Fey. Fey, the anchorwoman for the satirical news segment on *Saturday Night Live* in 2004, said, "John Murtha was a decorated, 37-year veteran. Jean Schmidt, I'm guessing—judging from her outfit—was a 1970s gymnast." I enjoyed seeing a radical right-wing Republican have to bear the consequences of sticking her foot in her own mouth.

The fury, uproar, taunting, and insults sparked by congressional discussions about an exit strategy or troop withdrawal were themselves signs of how much the crisis was deepening in Iraq. But Bush was not hearing anything about ending the war.

On April 13, 2004, a reporter asked him, "Sir, you've made it very clear tonight that you're committed to continuing the mission in Iraq. Yet, as Terry pointed out, increasing numbers of Americans have qualms about it. And this is an election year. Will it have been worth it, even if you lose your job because of it?"

Bush responded, "I don't plan on losing my job. I plan on telling the American people that I've got a plan to win the war on terror. And I believe they'll stay with me. They understand the stakes…." He seemed to believe that just claiming to have a plan without ever implementing it or even explaining it was enough to calm demands for change.

These calls for a viable exit strategy continued. On January 10, 2007, Bush appointed a team of officers to implement the "new way forward" strategy. This team of officers was playing an advisory role to General David Petraeus in Baghdad. After they did their field research, they concluded that the Americans had six months to win the war in Iraq or they would likely face a Vietnam-style quagmire. On March 1, 2007, Simon Tisdall of the *Guardian* published a detailed story about their findings.

Whether it was 2004 or 2007, whether Bush listened to senators or members of Congress or to his own officers, the Vietnam analogy was chasing Bush's war in Iraq.

The CIA Declares Defeat

On September 16, 2004, Doug Jehl wrote an article in the *New York Times* about the intelligence community's pessimism about the situation in Iraq. An approximately 50-page classified National Intelligence Estimate prepared for Bush in July of that year was laced with "a significant amount of pessimism," according to a government official. The estimate laid out three possible scenarios for Iraq by the end of 2005, with the best case "an Iraq whose stability would remain tenuous in political, economic and security terms," and the worst case an Iraqi civil war. The estimate was initiated by the National Intelligence Council under George Tenet's direction, before he stepped down as director of CIA on July 9, 2004.

This intelligence estimate came as a blow to Bush at a time when he desperately needed support. He was already facing harsh criticism from Republicans and Democrats alike about his decision to shift the spending of funds that were supposed to be used for reconstruction of Iraq to the war effort—Bush had requested $3 billion be diverted to security from the $18.4 billion reconstruction package. Bush's focus on security exposed the fact that the situation really hadn't improved since the start of the occupation. Bush's lack of interest in financing the reconstruction of Iraq also showed his shortsightedness and inability to plan for the future. By then, less than a billion dollars had actually been spent on the reconstruction of Iraq. Republican Senator Chuck Hagel of Nebraska described the lack of spending on reconstruction as "Beyond pitiful. It's beyond embarrassing. It is now in the zone of dangerous."

Republicans on the Senate Foreign Relations Committee issued a warning just a day before this estimate stating that Bush's request for diversion of funds was a sign of real trouble. Senator Richard Lugar, chairman of the committee, said, "The slow pace of reconstruction spending means that we are failing to take full advantage of one of our most potent tools to influence the direction of Iraq." Bush was already under fire from Republicans and Democrats, and now it was the CIA's turn to submit its classified security estimate and further deflate Bush's hope for victory in Iraq. After all this shifting in spending and diversion of funds, security was still a real crisis in Iraq, and the country was at a high risk of being engulfed by civil war.

A Campaign Dogged by Bad Press

After the first battle of Fallujah ended, George Bush went through one setback after another. But October 2004, just before the second and third presidential debates, saw more intense setbacks. Within just a few days before debates, Bush received an onslaught of upsetting reports.

The first came from Paul Bremer, who had completely dropped off the radar after his early departure from Iraq. On October 4, 2004 at a conference held in White Sulfur Springs, West Virginia, he suggested that the lawlessness, looting, and havoc wreaked on Iraq's infrastructure might've been prevented if the US had had more troops on the ground. In essence, he acknowledged that there hadn't been enough troops from the very start of the war, and that Iraq turned into a frenzy of lawlessness almost the minute the US invaded. This press conference did little to improve Bush's image in the international media, which immediately circulated these statements widely across the US and the rest of the world.

Four days later, Bremer wrote a long piece in the *New York Times* retracting what he'd said in White Sulfur Springs and arguing that the media had misinterpreted his remarks. His recanting, however, attracted much less interest than his original remarks, whose vividness was much more believable. That such a key figure in the Bush administration had described the situation in Iraq in such volatile terms was trouble not easily dismissed.

Bremer wasn't the only one to turn on Bush as the election grew near. Donald Rumsfeld also gave Bush a good shove in the wrong direction immediately after Bremer's statement was released. Rumsfeld cast doubt on the very foundations and justification for the war when, just after Bremer's press conference, Rumsfeld told the Council on Foreign Relations that "to my knowledge, I have not seen any strong, hard evidence that links the two [Saddam and al-Qaeda]."

Bush and Rumsfeld had repeatedly accused Saddam Hussein of harboring al-Qaeda members in Iraq and of having an active relationship with this group, and used this as a large justification for this war. Simon Jeffery of the *Guardian* followed up Rumsfeld's remarks with an article that provides an overview of Rumsfeld's early, contradictory statements about al-Qaeda. In August of 2002, Rumsfeld said, "there are al-Qaeda in Iraq" and accused Saddam of "harboring Al-Qaeda operatives who fled the US military dragnet in Afghanistan." The next month, he followed up on this claim by saying, "We do have solid evidence of the presence in Iraq of al-Qaeda members, including some that have been in Baghdad." He also said, "We have what we consider to be very reliable reporting of senior-level contacts going back a decade, and of possible chemical and biological agent training." In October, Rumsfeld said that he was told of "solid evidence of the presence in Iraq of al-Qaeda members." Rumsfeld and Bush continued to maintain that there was a link between Iraq and al-Qaeda far into 2003. In March of that year, "Mr. Rumsfeld says the US-led coalition has solid evidence that senior al-Qaeda operatives had visited Baghdad in the past, and that Saddam had an 'evolving' relationship with the terror network."

How to explain such a radical reversal as Rumsfeld expressed in October 2004? Jeffery reported that "Mr. Rumsfeld claimed he had been 'misunderstood'" about his earlier statements on the relationship between the two organizations. Rumsfeld also said that there were "many differences of opinion [about the link between Saddam and al-Qaeda] in the intelligence community."

The fact is, Rumsfeld had never been the only one trumpeting the Saddam Hussein–al-Qaeda connection. During a June 17, 2004 interview on CNBC's *Capitol Report*, Vice President Dick Cheney said, "There clearly was a relationship [between al-Qaeda and Hussein]. It's been testified to. The evidence is overwhelming. It goes back to the early '90s. It involves a whole series of contacts, high-level contacts with Osama bin Laden and Iraqi intelligence officials."

What happened to all these claims that had been such a huge part of the Bush administration's war-mongering rhetoric? These were the claims on which the war was justified, long before the battle of Fallujah or any other insurgency problems came up. The Americans had invaded Iraq on the basis of two major accusations: an active, strong link to al-Qaeda, and the presence of WMDs. Now, Rumsfeld was exposing the administration's deception to the entire world.

If it was comforting for Bush to know that although the lie about the allegiance between Hussein and al-Qaeda had been exposed, he could still maintain the one about the WMDs, this comfort did not last long. On October 6, just days after Bremer's and Rumsfeld's statements, the Iraq Survey Group (ISG) announced that Iraq possessed no chemical or biological weapons or any stockpiles of weapons of mass destruction. ISG's leader, Charles Duelfer, said, "It is my judgment that retained stocks do not exist. I still do not expect that militarily significant WMD stocks are hidden in Iraq," after presenting the ISG's findings to the US Senate. CNN published a summary of the report on its website saying, "The long-awaited report, authored by Charles Duelfer, who advises the director of central intelligence on Iraqi weapons, says Iraq's WMD program was essentially destroyed in 1991 and Saddam ended Iraq's nuclear program after the 1991 Gulf War."

The release of this information created even more trouble for Bush and his allies. The *Guardian* published an article that day detailing the findings and chastising Tony Blair. Later reports indicated that Sir Menzies Campbell, foreign affairs spokesperson for the Liberal Democrats party in England, said, "Brick by brick, the government's case for going to war is being demolished."

Robin Cook, the former foreign secretary of England who resigned in protest of the war, said, "[this report] comprehensively establishes that Iraq had no stockpile, no biological agents, no chemical feed stocks, no plants to manufacture them and no delivery systems to fire them. Saddam was no threat to us and had no weapons of mass destruction to pass to terrorists. Brushing the UN inspectors aside in order to go to war on false intelligence was a colossal blunder."

Blair finally conceded to the press that the "actual biological and chemical weapons, as opposed to the capability to develop them, has turned out to be wrong." To save his face, he changed his argument slightly. He told reporters, "Just as I have had to accept that the evidence now is there were no stockpiles of actual weapons ready to be deployed, I hope others have the honesty to accept that the report also shows that sanctions weren't working." And he offered one final justification for his country's part in this war: "I can apologize for the information that turned out to be wrong, but I can't, sincerely at least, apologize for removing Saddam. The world is a better place with Saddam in prison."

Blair's spokesperson was all over televised media the next day, trying her best to defend her boss. She acknowledged the findings of the ISG and provided all sorts of excuses for the mistakes, but still didn't give the English or Iraqi people an apology for a war waged on fabricated pretenses.

Surprisingly, none of this bad news appeared to affect Bush's performance in the US presidential debates. Throughout the debates, Bush continued to invoke 9/11 as proof of the need for a global war on terrorism. Bush used these scare tactics all the way into a second term in the Oval Office. Eventually, the scare tactics would wear out. But for the 2004 elections, apparently the fears were fresh enough and the scare tactics were functional enough to propel the Bush administration into a second term.

Looking for a Scapegoat

Perhaps anticipating the truth that would come out about the justifications for war, Bush wanted to convince Americans that at least Allawi, the man he'd appointed as head of the Iraqi government, was making a difference in building a future for Iraq. On September 23, Bush stood in the Rose Garden under the noon sun next to Allawi and spun a web of lies about the successful state of affairs in Iraq.

"Iraqi security forces are taking increasing responsibility for their country's security," he said. "Nearly 100,000 fully trained and equipped Iraqi soldiers, police officers, and other security personnel are working today. And that total will rise to 125,000 by the end of this year. The Iraqi government is on track to build a force of over 200,000 security personnel by the end of next year."

These lies, though, could not cloak the chaotic and deplorable situation in Iraq. Instead, as lies will do, they created more difficulty for Bush. On September 27, 2004, the *Seattle Times* published a report titled "Bush Claim on Training of Iraqis Disputed." The report said, "Pentagon documents show that of the nearly ninety thousand people now in the police force, only 8,169 have had the full eight-week academy training. Another 46,176 are listed as 'untrained,' and it will be July 2006 before the administration reaches its goal of a 135,000-strong, fully trained police force." The report went on to say, "Democrats on the House Appropriations Committee estimated that 22,700 Iraqi personnel have received enough training to make them 'minimally effective at their tasks.'"

Instead of acknowledging the lie exposed by this article, the White House insisted Bush's figures were correct and that "fully trained" was defined as having gone through "initial basic operations training."

The Subtle Language of Defeat

Even though the Bush administration exacted some measure of revenge on Fallujah in Operation Vigilant Resolve, they never quite felt the triumph they were expecting. Officials continued to speak with a tone of defeat long after the first battle was over.

Donald Rumsfeld's distinguishing mien had heretofore been snobbish and self-aggrandizing, an attitude he maintained whenever he spoke of his enemies. He always spoke as if the administration he was part of had the real capacity to sort out the world's problems. On April 27, 2005, however, Rumsfeld dropped this attitude and appeared in public as a defeated commander. When a reporter asked him if he believed the US was winning the war in Iraq, Rumsfeld couldn't possibly answer with a simple "yes" because his forces' inability to win that war was clear to the world by then.

Rumsfeld replied instead, "The United States and the coalition forces, in my personal view, will not be the thing that will defeat the insurgency. So therefore, winning or losing is not the issue for 'we,' in my view, in the traditional conventional context of using the word winning and losing and of war. The people that are going to defeat that insurgency are going to be the Iraqis. And the Iraqis will do it not through military means solely, but by progress on the political side."

These statements were completely unlike those he made in the initial stages of the war. The pre-Fallujah Rumsfeld would've scoffed at the thought of defeat. The post-Fallujah Rumsfeld was entirely too defeated to come across as that arrogant.

Since now "winning" the war was apparently up the Iraqis, Condoleezza Rice made a visit to Iraq to urge leaders to get the political process moving. During her visit to Baghdad, Rice told reporters on May 15, 2005, "The insurgents in Iraq are very violent, but you defeat them not just through military effort. You defeat them by having a political alternative that is strong. Now, Iraqi leaders are going to have to intensify their efforts to demonstrate that in fact the political process is the answer for the Iraqi people."

Between Rumsfeld's comments on April 27 and Rice's comments on May 15, implicit and explicit statements made by other officials expressed concern about the military capacity of the American troops in Iraq. The most notable statement came from General Richard B. Myers, chairman of the Joint Chiefs of Staff, who submitted a classified report to the Congress on May 2, 2005, informing them that, "major combat operations elsewhere in the world, should they be necessary, would probably be more protracted and produce higher American and foreign civilian casualties because of the commitment of Pentagon resources in Iraq and Afghanistan," as Thom Shanker of the *New York Times* reported on May 3, 2005.

This statement, of course, contradicted Bush's statement from a week earlier. In this earlier statement, Bush said he asked General Myers, "Do you feel that we've limited our capacity to deal with other problems because of our troop levels in Iraq?" Bush then continued to claim that Myers had answered, "No, he didn't feel a bit limited. It feels like we got plenty of capacity." The article published in the *New York Times* that exposed this incongruity went on to say, "General Myers cited reduced stockpiles of precision weapons, which were depleted during the invasion of Iraq, and the stress on reserve units, which fulfill the bulk of combat support duties in Iraq, as among the factors that would limit the Pentagon's ability to prevail as quickly as war planners once predicted in other potential conflicts."

In addition to the concerns over the scope of the investment of US resources in the Iraqi war, the Bush administration continued to be concerned about the violence of insurgents. On April 24, 2005, Agence France-Presse published a report quoting a high-ranking official in Washington who requested anonymity. The official said, "The latest wave of violence in Iraq shows that insurgents are better organized than before and their tactics have been enhanced." In another report, Agence France-Presse quotes another official saying that, "the increase in insurgents' attacks is as noticeable as the high level of synchronization [among groups of insurgents] and improved tactics they're adopting." These statements acknowledged increased insurgency activity, and statements by General Myers and others exposed the American difficulties in the war on Iraq. Some statements also exposed that Bush's latest threats against Syria and Iran were no more than hot air. The US couldn't afford to start a war on another military front with Syria or Iran without major losses.

This language of defeat wasn't used simply by officials in the Bush administration. Despite his usual optimism, this language even reached the president himself. In his weekly radio address on June 18, 2005, Bush issued the following statement, "This mission isn't easy, and it will not be accomplished overnight. We're fighting a ruthless enemy that relishes the killing of innocent men, women, and children." He also said that "terrorists have now made Iraq a central front in the war on terror." When compared to other, more confident statements made earlier in the war, these words show the flagging of his confidence.

After this statement was released, Cheney, perhaps worried that Bush was indirectly exposing the administration's defeat, gave an interview on CNN two days later in which he claimed that the insurgency in Iraq was "in the last throes."

Cheney's attempt to cover up for Bush was exposed just a few days later, though. When John Abizaid testified before the Senate Armed Services Committee, on June 23, 2005, he concurred with what Bush had said in his radio address, "I believe there are more foreign fighters coming into Iraq than there were six months ago." The BBC reported that Abizaid also said that "suicide bombers from Algeria, Tunisia, and Morocco were entering Iraq via Syria, joining others from Saudi Arabia and Jordan." Abizaid appeared to be claiming that there was definitely a pattern of terrorism on the rise; nothing was "in the last throes," as Cheney had claimed. The BBC went on to say that Democrat Senator Carl Levin pointed out that Abizaid's comments were at odds with Vice President Cheney's previous indications that the insurgency was in its last stages.

Rumsfeld next jumped to Cheney's assistance, to cover up his obvious mistake with some more obvious propaganda. Testifying before the same committee as Abizaid, Rumsfeld supported Cheney by saying, "[Insurgents] have suffered significant losses in casualties, been denied havens, and suffered weakened popular support." This statement may have been true, but it didn't mean that the insurgency was in its last throes; furthermore, US forces were definitely not winning this war—they too were suffering "significant losses in casualties" and "weakened popular support" (if they'd ever had popular support to begin with).

Rumsfeld's efforts to prove the US was winning the war were those of a man in complete denial. Just because both sides of the war were losing troops did not mean that one side was definitely "winning." At this point in the conflict, no one had enough control to claim any sort of victory—the insurgents or the Americans.

Members of Congress reacted to the inconsistency of these reports with anger. The BBC reported that "Democrat Senator Edward Kennedy said that Mr. Rumsfeld's predictions had been wrong in the past and [he] repeated calls for him to resign."

Despite seemingly unconditional support from both Bush and Cheney, Rumsfeld's lies caught up with him. When Republicans performed poorly in the midterm elections of 2006, Bush had Rumsfeld resign. He might have saved some of his dignity if he had listened to the repeated calls for resignation from Democrats for several months before his forced resignation, but his arrogance got in the way. Rumsfeld was far too confident; it was impossible for him to accept that the Democrats could defeat him and the Bush administration. This arrogance was similar to how he had carried out projects in Iraq—he had been arrogant enough to think that the country of Iraq could be taken with no effort.

The unraveling of Bush's Iraq crusade throughout the election period in late 2004 had started with the failure of the US to secure a total and indisputable victory in the first battle of Fallujah. Fallujah was a wound that festered, and the Bush administration would not leave it alone.

PART IV

NOVEMBER 2004: FALLUJAH DESTROYED

"The pitifulest thing out is a mob; that's what an army is—a mob; they don't fight with courage that's born in them, but with courage that's borrowed from their mass, and from their officers."
—Mark Twain, *The Adventures of Huckleberry Finn*

16. IS THE BATTLE OVER?

When the cease-fire went into effect on April 11, relieved Fallujans began to tend to their wounded and find burial plots for the staggering number of dead. Some of the families who had fled Fallujah amid the violence began returning, even though the cease-fire was still in the fragile early stages. Insurgents had declared victory on the grounds that the Marines hadn't been able to subdue the city.

Agence France-Presse published a story on the first day of the cease-fire, saying that the battle of Fallujah had stripped American forces of the title "undefeated champions," since they had failed to achieve a clear-cut victory over the comparatively few and lightly armed insurgents. If you want to scare a Marine, the story said, the word "Fallujah" would do the trick. The Marines had proved to be no stronger or tougher than any other fighters in the world. As the Marines ducked for cover from simple mortar fire and rocket propelled grenades thrown by insurgents, the idea of "the few and the proud" crumbled.

The insurgents and their sympathizers noted that they had not been the ones to call for a cease-fire. One supporter of the insurgents told me, "The resistance isn't running after the Americans begging them to stop firing. It's the other way around. It's the Americans who were exposed for their crimes and military weakness; it's the Americans who have a superpower image to maintain and an international war crime tribunal to answer for. Aside from the innocent civilians, the only people in Fallujah desperate for a cease-fire were the Marines."

Although I have my reservations about this argument, Paul Bremer himself gave some credence to it when he was interviewed by ABC's George Stephanopoulos later that week.

Bremer said, "What we're trying to do is simply get the [American] forces to stop firing, have the insurgents stop firing on the Marines, and then we'll have a delegation from the [Iraqi] Governing Council go in, and we'll try to find out how we can proceed from there. But at the moment, we're just trying to stabilize the cease-fire." Bremer was indeed desperate for a cease-fire to protect the American image from being tarnished, and to protect the entire political process in Iraq from collapsing on his head.

Immediately after the siege was lifted and the fragile cease-fire went into effect, journalists from across the world poured into Fallujah to report on the aftermath of the battle. This influx of world media was a disaster for the Bush administration. Even after the battle, the world got to see that al-Jazeera had not invented claims about American brutality and American weakness in this battle. World media, American media in particular, verified our claims just by airing footage of the aftermath of the battle. Many international journalists released footage showing the massive numbers of civilian casualties, which demonstrated the Bush administration's disregard for human life. These other journalists also filmed the multitude of destroyed American vehicles and helicopters that proved the American defeat.

Amatzia Baram, Israel's foremost expert on Iraq, was quoted in the April 12, 2004 issue of *Newsweek* as saying, "American honor has been trashed in Fallujah. Now the Americans have to restore their honor in the eyes of the Iraqis."

American military leaders, along with George Bush, knew they had to seek retaliation for the humiliation suffered by the US in the first battle of Fallujah. General Mark Kimmitt vowed, "We will be back in Fallujah. We will hunt down the criminals. We will kill them or we will capture them."

In light of such remarks, newspapers across the US began to publish reports claiming that US military officials were talking about a "prolonged military campaign" against Fallujah. Only one day after the first battle of Fallujah officially ended, it was clear that US forces would one day return for a second battle: the battle of revenge, the battle to restore American honor and glory.

Meanwhile, all over Iraq, music stores were selling out of CDs and tapes of scratchy, low-tech recordings of patriotic music. Behind the melodies, the words to these songs praised Fallujah and its citizens for bravery and lauded the "victory" the insurgents achieved over the "coward Marines."

A Cease-Fire Exploding with Violence

The cease-fire that was established on April 11 was never very secure. In fact, it was repeatedly broken after it was officially accepted as law. On April 16, for example, American warplanes bombed Fallujah, killing fifteen civilians and injuring another twenty. Bremer, unsurprisingly, justified the attack with the standard claim of self-defense. Although we'd seen many suspicious bombings attributed to self-defense, we never did learn whether this particular attack was actually made in self-defense, because by then we were already out of Fallujah.

Richard Jones, deputy administrator for the occupation authority in Iraq, spoke of the fragile cease-fire to the *New York Times* shortly after the deal became official. Jones said, "There has not been a cease-fire. There may have been a diminution of the intensity of the fire, but as of now we don't see a full cease-fire, which is what we asked for and what they committed to try to achieve."

Press reports around the world continued to paint the American occupation as weak in the days and weeks following the cease-fire. The perpetuating of this image fiercely angered the American military and Bush administration. In one article, Agence France-Presse portrayed the soldiers in Fallujah as scared fighters thirsty for revenge for the deaths of their comrades. American forces were clearly not happy with these portrayals. After seeing such reports, it was clear to me that the coming months would bring a plan of gruesome revenge designed especially for Fallujah by George Bush and his administration.

After lengthy negotiations between April 13 and 19, coalition forces announced that they had finally reached a second, more secure cease-fire agreement. Both the political and military wings of the occupation had a part in the negotiations, with Ambassador Richard Jones speaking for Paul Bremer, and the commander of the Marine Corps for the US military. Dr. Ahmad Hardan, a representative for the Islamic Party, described occasions on which Jones agreed to conditions related to humanitarian issues and the Fallujah delegates would be surprised to find out later on that the Marines commander had nixed those agreements because of "security reasons." Hardan said this happened frequently enough for the negotiations to take several days, despite how extreme the humanitarian conditions were at that point.

Dan Senor, senior advisor to the coalition provisional authorities, gave a briefing on the cease-fire agreement on April 19. The conditions specified that the offensive operation would end if insurgents handed over their "heavy weapons," and following that, individual violators would be dealt with on an individual basis. The Marines would allow Fallujans access to the general hospital that was presently being occupied by the Marines. The Marines would also allow for the removal and burial of the dead and the delivery of food and medicine to isolated areas of the city. It was stipulated that a thorough Iraqi investigation must be initiated to find out who murdered and mutilated the Blackwater USA private security guards, the issue that was the cause of the battle in the first place and still had not been resolved. Finally, the parties also agreed on "the pressing need of restoring regular and routine patrols in the city by joint coalition forces and Iraqi security forces."

Press agencies reported further clarifications and items included in the cease-fire agreement. According to Fuad al-Rawi, a member of the political wing of the Islamic Party, these conditions included the re-opening of the Fallujah Bridge so citizens could get to the hospital from across the river. The Marines would move their positions some 250 yards away from the bridge to allow for this easy access. The Marines currently in Fallujah would be replaced by other Marines. The snipers would completely withdraw from the city. The Iraqis and coalition forces would work on forming committees for crisis management, and the Civil Defense Corps and Iraqi police would resume their duties in the city.

The high-level representatives the Bush administration had in these negotiations exposed how troubled they were by the whole situation; they were desperate to put an end to it. But the end created by the cease-fire was to be temporary. The cease-fire agreement was put in place merely to stop the political process in Iraq from completely falling apart, and to allow US forces to regroup. In this recuperation period, the US had time to consider how to go about exacting revenge on Fallujah. Bremer writes of the cease-fire agreement: "The cease-fire in Fallujah gradually took hold. On April 16 Abizaid called, 'I think we've got some breathing space in Fallujah. I've spoken to Conway, and he's satisfied with his situation.'" These are obviously the words of someone who thinks of himself as being at a pause in a battle, not at its end.

A paragraph later, this becomes even more clear:

> On April 21, before an NSC meeting scheduled later in the day, Condi Rice called to ask my opinion about Fallujah. "What if the president orders a full-scale assault?"
>
> "I'm conflicted," I said. "Sooner or later, we've got to go back in there and get those guys. But frankly, the president must assume that if he orders an assault now, it will lead to the collapse of the entire political process." I told her this was the view of all of us at the CPA, including Blackwill, although we needed to be aware that we were merely post-poning action there. But far better that action should occur after there was an Iraqi government in place and, one hoped, with better-trained Iraqi security forces to help with the operation.

So the cease-fire agreement was simply a way to give the defeated Marines time to rearrange its deck of cards—as Bremer said, the American forces were "merely postponing action." These forces wanted an Iraqi puppet government to be in place to approve their dirty politics of revenge, and they also needed Iraqi forces on their side as much as possible. These were Bremer's incentives for accepting a cease-fire. Preserving civilian lives or stopping the spread of war crimes wasn't an incentive for him in the least. Allowing Fallujans to replenish food and water, medicate their wounded, and bury their dead was also not on his mind. In fact, no humanitarian-related issues were on his mind whatsoever. On his mind was the preparation for a grand revenge, which would take the name Operation Phantom Fury. He needed someone to bear the consequences of that vengeful operation. This scapegoat would be Ayad Allawi, who in the few days following the first battle was being actively prepped for this situation by Bush and his team.

Iraqis were not at all ignorant of these plans. Rumors of a second aggressive campaign being planned by American forces began to spread throughout Iraq. In response to these rumors, on April 23, 2004, Shaikh Ahmad Abdulghafour Samarray, head cleric at the Umm-ul-Qurra Mosque in Baghdad, sent a cautionary message to American forces during his Friday sermon. He warned, "You've gone too far already and crossed red lines. Do not dare do it again. Shedding Iraqi blood is not acceptable, and if you attack again, then all of Iraq stretching to all four corners will turn into one big Fallujah for you."

But such threats weren't going to stop US forces. Fallujah was too crucial to be given up simply because of verbal threats from a religious leader.

As Colonel John Coleman said on April 23, the outcome of a second battle in Fallujah could shape the entire future of Iraq. He told reporters, "As Fallujah goes, so goes central Iraq. As central Iraq goes, so goes the nation. Fallujah is the center of gravity."

In response to rumors of a second, more aggressive wave of violence, Fallujan leaders met and drafted a statement voicing their opposition. The flyers, which were distributed by the Islamic Party and AMSI, said that the cease-fire had "allowed the enemy to recuperate from its losses, restart its activity, rebuild its fortifications, and catch a breath of air." Some preachers in Fallujah urged the city residents that same day to "put a stop to the transgression of the Marines because they kill everything that moves in the city, including pets and livestock!"

Fallujans worried about another strike on their city not only because they feared more violence, but because the cease-fire had never even stopped the inflammatory statements vowing revenge from top American military commanders or the skirmishes that were still exploding across the city. Whenever these skirmishes broke out, US forces didn't seem to care whom they killed and didn't hesitate to attribute the casualties to self-defense.

On April 26, Toby Harnden of the *Daily Telegraph* reported,

> at the checkpoint outside the hospital an American military policeman shrugged when asked about the dead and injured of Na'amiya [Naimyah]: "We received some mortar and small arms fire from there and so we said to hell with it, and just went in. We were supposed to wait until today, but we got pissed off and decided to draw a line. We pretty much took out anyone who was in there being stupid."

Eventually, though, the cease-fire was extended indefinitely. It was just that American forces never stopped the "surgical strikes," as Bush called them, even after the cease-fire was implemented. So these "surgical strikes" continued, with soldiers "pretty much [taking] out anyone… stupid." Fallujans were supposed to accept these deplorable conditions as a cease-fire? It was a cease-fire in which only one side was forced to put down its weapons, and thereby become essentially helpless.

The Fallujah Protection Army

On April 29, Lt. Colonel Brennan Byrne, commander of the First Battalion, Fifth Marine Regiment, announced that the Marines would begin their withdrawal to outside Fallujah city limits the next morning. Byrne informed reporters that the Marines leaving the city would be replaced by a newly-formed militia called the Fallujah Protection Army (also known as the Fallujah Brigade), which would consist of 900 to 1,100 Iraqi soldiers who had served in the military during Saddam Hussein's reign. He identified the officer who would lead the FPA as General Jassim Muhammad Saleh, a former division commander under Saddam. The FPA would be subordinate to the Marine First Expeditionary Force.

Bremer was not pleased with this development. In his memoir he describes watching CNN International and seeing General Saleh in his Saddam-era Republican Guard uniform, standing among an ecstatic crowd of cheering Fallujans. Describing his response to General Abizaid's call ("Jerry have you seen the news? I can't tell if we're winning or losing"), he writes, "I was not happy, and told him so." Bremer reports that Ricardo Sanchez was also "chagrined" by the appointment of Saleh. And he quotes Condoleezza Rice as saying, "It looks awful on TV. The guy looks just like Saddam!"

One of Bremer's biggest mistakes in Iraq was the dismantling of the Iraqi Army. His justification was that if Saddam was evicted, so his generals and military people should be. As it turned out, this dismantling of Iraq's military was one of the reasons the country descended into such lawlessness after the invasion. And in April 2004, Bremer found the US occupation needing to beg for help from the very people whom he had stripped of power. As Abizaid said, it was unclear who was winning the war.

The appointment of General Saleh as leader of the Fallujah Brigade sparked protest among many other groups, not just the American occupation. Kurdish and Shia leaders were upset by the choice because it brought back memories of the Saddam Hussein regime—a regime under which they had been oppressed and violated. Bahr al-Ulum, a prominent Shia political and religious leader, called Bremer to protest the choice.

Within two days, in an attempt to quell the protest, General Saleh was replaced by General Mohammed Latif. Still some Kurdish and Shia radicals protested the mere existence of the Fallujah Brigade: the replacement of General Saleh wasn't enough to lift the negative impression his initial appointment had made.

At this point, Bremer had only two months left before sovereignty was supposed to be handed over to the Iraqis. He knew he had to find a way out of the Fallujah crisis, both militarily and politically speaking. He also knew that it would be best for the American occupation if Iraqi forces and politicians did the dirty work for him; he did not want to be visibly responsible for another massive attack on Fallujah. In his memoir, he writes of telling Rumsfeld his concerns in May 2004:

> I explained that in the past two weeks, the new commander of the Fallujah Brigade, General Mohammed Latif, had proven difficult, repeatedly refusing to commit his Fallujah Brigade to combat. The city was one more muddled problem, which would have to be postponed until a sovereign Iraqi government was ready to tackle it.

Bremer was deeply troubled by Fallujah because he knew that the Fallujah Brigades wouldn't serve the purpose he had intended; Iraqis were not about to take out the insurgents in the manner he wished. In fact, the brigade was disbanded in August, after failing to achieve any of its goals. And when commanders of the brigade refused to attack fellow Fallujans, they were accused of corroborating with insurgents.

"We're being salami-sliced out there," he told Dick Jones, in an effort to describe how badly the Marines were hurting in Fallujah.

Bremer sent a private message to Rumsfeld asking for more troops to be sent to Fallujah.

Allawi's Inauguration

Ayad Allawi was the man appointed by Bremer to address the unrest exploding all over Iraq after the first battle of Fallujah. Allawi was supposed to be an Iraqi version of Bremer himself, the ambassador to the newly liberated country.

In the United States, a red carpet of praise and a Hollywood-style reception was set up for Allawi on September 23, 2004. Members of Congress received him with thunderous applause. I remember seeing a television clip of this event, and then changing the channel to something more meaningful: reports on the real situation as it was unfolding in Iraq. As Allawi was being glorified by the US Congress in Washington, other networks were broadcasting images of American soldiers being zipped into body bags. These casualties were averaging about 40 a day at the time of Allawi's inauguration. Other news channels were showing the corpses of Iraqi children and women in Fallujah, Samarra, Baqubah, Ramadi, and throughout the rest of Iraq. A recently kidnapped British hostage pleaded with Tony Blair to rescue him from the same merciless kidnappers who had already butchered two American hostages. Iraqi children dumpster-dived for food and Iraqi housewives stored household items in empty, abandoned nuclear waste drums left behind by the military. These were the kinds of images broadcast in tandem with the happy news of Allawi's inauguration.

Around this time, United Nations Secretary-General Kofi Annan released a damaging statement saying that he believed that "the American-led war on Iraq last year was illegal under the terms of the UN Charter," as reported by the BBC on September 16. The French Minister of Foreign Affairs Michel Barnier declared that his country had never approved of the premises of the war in Iraq and that France wouldn't be sending troops to Iraq "either now or later." Germany stated a similar position.

Bush and his team were naturally unhappy with this. But still these statements made no difference in the miserable lives of Iraqis, who went on being slaughtered in staggering numbers. By then, the number of Iraqi victims who perished in the war had reached 120,000. By the fourth anniversary of the invasion, that count reached 650,000 dead Iraqi civilians, according to *Lancet*, one of Britain's most respected medical journals.

Not surprisingly, the White House dismissed this figure. Other estimates were even higher than *Lancet*'s. These numbers, of course, did not account for the injured or the missing.

There were also the American casualties. On April 23, 2004, the Pentagon announced that 1,040 American soldiers had been killed in action. The number would grow to several times that count by the fourth and fifth anniversaries of the invasion of Iraq.

The classified National Intelligence Estimate reported in the *New York Times* on September 16 further tarnished the public perception of US activity in Iraq at the time of Allawi's inauguration. Speculations about a possible civil war in Iraq didn't help. Rice tried to dismiss the seriousness of these accusations a few days after the public learned of them, but these denials are hard to remember in light of the fact that civil war did end up breaking out in Iraq later on.

The Bush administration was facing criticism not only for their conduct of the war and the political future of Iraq, but also for the financial management of the war. Although the Bush administration repeatedly claimed that the budget allotted for the war was enough to cover its expenses, on September 21, the Pentagon announced that it had resorted to using its $25 billion emergency fund for operations in Iraq. The Pentagon had already spent $2 billion because of the insurgency problem and the rising fuel prices. This news came a few days after it was announced that Bush had used more than $3 billion from reconstruction funds for security and the war.

September 2004 was a very bad time for the Bush administration, and then-presidential candidate John Kerry wasted no time in attacking Bush: "The president misled, miscalculated and mismanaged every aspect of this undertaking and he has made the achievement of our objective—a stable Iraq, secure within its borders, with a representative government—far harder to achieve than it ever should have been," Kerry said in a speech delivered at New York University on September 20.

With all of this negative press coming at the same time, the Bush administration wanted to trumpet the shift in power from Bremer to Allawi. In order to perpetuate the illusion of peace and success in Iraq, Bush needed to appear as though he had made political strides in Iraq by appointing a capable Iraqi military leader. Allawi's illustrious inaugural celebration was designed to cover Bush's tarnished image, not to welcome Allawi. The red carpet, in fact, was rolled out to help Bush win the 2004 election. In fact, by then Allawi hadn't even been in power long enough to achieve much (apart from shutting down al-Jazeera's bureau in Baghdad) so any celebration in his honor would have been fairly meaningless.

Bush put on a good show to market his man to the American people. Allawi, in two-month's time, would be responsible for the implementation of Bush's vision: a near-complete annihilation of the city of Fallujah.

Rumblings of a Second Slaughter

On September 10, 2004, the front page of most Arab newspapers pictured an Iraqi infant who had been killed during one of Bush's surgical strikes on Fallujah. US surgical strikes were supposedly conducted with near-perfect accuracy—the shooters were supposed to avoid civilian targets like women and children. In the picture, Fallujans hold the body of the dead infant high in the air, proving either that there is really no such thing as such surgical strikes, or that children were actually targets. Spokespersons for US forces maintained that their troops only targeted and fired on insurgents, and would continue to do so. The fact was, though, these attacks were not conducted with enough accuracy to spare the lives of babies and children.

Toby Harnden of the *Daily Telegraph* reported on September 14, that Lt. General James Conway, who was relinquishing his command, criticized Bush's strategy in Fallujah, saying "I think we certainly increased the level of animosity that existed." Conway was speaking about the management of the Fallujah situation from the start. He agreed with the Fallujans' claims that they were being collectively punished to avenge the killing of the four private security guards. He had spoken of his uneasiness with Operation Vigilant Resolve from the very beginning; before the operation began, he had released a statement saying, "We ought to probably let the situation settle before we appear to be attacking out of revenge."

By the time Conway was relinquishing his command, US forces had controlled and desecrated cities throughout Iraq. Cities such as Najaf, Karbala, and al-Kut—all sacred to Shiites—had seen massive destruction, at the cost of high casualty counts among US forces. Because of this, residents of predominantly Shia areas reported hearing American troops vowing revenge.

As summer turned into fall, Iraqi leaders worried about how events were unfolding. First, US forces had worked out a compromise that resulted in the creation of the Fallujah Brigades. Next US forces began accusing these very brigades of collaborating with insurgents, giving them radios, weapons, and vehicles. In August, US forces attacked the Fallujah Brigades by air, and a few days later announced the decision to disband the entire force.

The Fallujah Brigades lasted less than four months. During this entire time, the Marines never paused in their indiscriminate bombing of the city of Fallujah. It was clear that US forces wanted Fallujah to continue to suffer, and when it appeared that the brigades weren't fulfilling the wishes of US forces, American warplanes took to the skies to fulfill those wishes themselves. Many of those killed in these bombings were children, who were obviously unaffiliated with insurgent groups. No one ever believed the insurgents had the power to recruit infants and small children to their militias, so no one believed that the target of these bombings was the insurgents alone. It was evident throughout even this period between the two fierce battles that the US was not actually letting up on its aim to punish Fallujah.

By then, American troops had achieved some success in breaking the city of Samarra, a symbol of Sunni defiance, and in controlling Karbala, Najaf, and Sadr City. All of these cities were Muqtada-friendly cities and had once raised Muqtada's anti-occupation banners in defiance of the occupation. The only city left in Iraq with a reputation for being defiant was Fallujah. It stands to reason, then, that the US forces would target it.

Abdulsalam Kubaisy, a prominent member of AMSI, concluded early on that American forces were eventually going to escalate their violence in Fallujah to something much greater than a scattering of indiscriminate bombings. On September 16, Kubaisy exhibited remarkable foresight when he told the London-based *Al-Hayat* newspaper, "American forces are preparing to invade Fallujah." This prediction came almost two months before November's Operation Phantom Fury.

Despite the obvious negative consequences of invading Fallujah a second time, US forces were determined to do it. Those who had a desire for revenge were single-minded about seeking that revenge. Even others who didn't have the same desire still felt an obligation to fight. Conway, who had criticized the handling of Fallujah, believed in that kind of commitment: "When you order elements of a Marine division to attack a city, you need to understand what the consequences will be and not perhaps vacillate in the middle of something like that. Once you commit you have to stay committed."

After Allawi's return from his ceremonial visit to the US Congress, his first assignment was to set the stage for the second battle of Fallujah—Operation Phantom Fury. Allawi was to appear as the Iraqi leader, and therefore bear the largest part of the shameful responsibility for what would commence during that operation. In accordance with this plan, on October 13, Allawi told Fallujans that if they didn't hand over insurgent leader al-Zarqawi and his men (whom the Bush administration had begun to claim had orchestrated the murder of the four mercenaries), they'd open their city to the possibility of another, even more aggressive, military campaign.

Ironically, it was never proven (or even claimed before this point) that al-Zarqawi or his organization, a branch of al-Qaeda called al-Qaeda in Mesopotamia, had been behind the killing of the four private security guards back in March of 2004. Even if al-Zarqawi was in Fallujah when Operation Phantom Fury began, he had not been a suspect behind the attack in March. Threatening the city with war over someone who had not been proven guilty (and might not even be present in the city) seems to me a desperate and pitiful attempt to justify a revenge operation against the Fallujah. But this was the justification offered to explain the destruction that would eventually take place in mid-November.

Of course Allawi knew that demanding al-Zarqawi was futile. American forces—with all their spy satellites, global positioning systems, thermal detection, night vision, heat sensors, and sophisticated warplanes—were unable to locate al-Zarqawi in Fallujah. How could Fallujans, with no technological resources whatsoever, do something the Americans could not?

In any case, Fallujans adamantly denied that al-Zarqawi was in their city. Fallujan insurgents repeatedly and proudly announced to the world that there weren't foreign fighters in Fallujah, and that all the insurgents were Iraqi-born. The insurgents fighting in Fallujah were native Fallujans, not Jordanians or Saudis as al-Zarqawi's men might be. Quite simply, the repeated indiscriminate bombing from the American forces over the past year had outraged enough Fallujans to make ordinary people want to join the local insurgency—it was unnecessary to go beyond even Fallujah's borders to recruit fighters. The biggest supporter of insurgents in town, Shaikh Abdallah al-Janabi, head of the Mujahideen Consultative Council in Fallujah, declared that his fighters were local Fallujans who knew nothing of al-Zarqawi.

To make sure Allawi didn't get away with these fabricated accusations, Fallujans responded to his threat by sending a letter to UN Secretary-General Kofi Annan. The letter contested the claim that al-Zarqawi even existed, let alone resided in Fallujah. At the time, rumors were being spread that al-Zarqawi was a mythical figure: No one seemed to have seen him, despite the many recordings of his voice that had been released to the public. To Fallujans, it didn't really matter whether al-Zarqawi existed or not, because they were certain he wasn't in Fallujah. The exact wording of the letter of October 14 is as follows:

> The people of Fallujah assure you that this person, if he exists, is not in Fallujah and is probably not anywhere in Iraq. The people of Fallujah have announced many times that any person who sees al-Zarqawi should kill him.

Not only were the Fallujans claiming this man was not in their city, but they were also allowing that if he were, they would comply with the American wishes to eliminate him. The letter went on to say:

> We know that we are living in world of double standards. In Fallujah, they [US forces] have created a new vague target: Al-Zarqawi. This is a new pretext to justify their crimes: killing and daily bombardment of civilians. Almost a year has lapsed since they created this new pretext, and whenever they destroy houses, mosques, restaurants, and kill children and women they said "we have launched a successful operation against al-Zarqawi." They will never say that they have killed him, because there is no such a person. And that means the killing of civilians and the daily genocide will continue.

The hunt for al-Zarqawi began an endless cycle in Fallujah: American forces would bomb a civilian house and declare they'd just bombed an al-Zarqawi hideout; reporters would snap pictures and shoot footage of dead civilians; and the phantom al-Zarqawi would not be found. The bombings intensified in July and reached their peak in mid-October, immediately after Allawi threatened Fallujans to hand over the enemy. Despite claims that these bombings were targeting "al-Zarqawi hideouts," it was obvious there were never set targets for the bombings. No neighborhood in Fallujah was bombed more often than another, because the US forces were putting little thought into who might be affected by their bombs. Despite appeals from the Fallujans to the UN, bombings continued all over the city, and naturally, Fallujans felt unsafe virtually everywhere. Even Haj Hussain's Kabob Place, the most popular kabob joint in town, suffered a bombing on October 12. Of course spokespersons for US forces claimed that the restaurant had become a rat hole for insurgents. Afterwards these insurgents, naturally, remained elusively on the prowl.

This intensified bombing caused some Fallujan families to flee the city again, only six short months after they had returned in the aftermath of the first battle. These families considered the escape to be temporary. Since family ties are very strong in that region, they had no problem finding relatives outside Fallujah to stay with. But many Fallujans had trouble getting to those relatives safely because migrating convoys of civilians were often bombed. On October 12, one entire family (including young children) was bombed on the way out of Fallujah, and images of the bombed car were broadcast by news networks across the world.

One of the more gruesome crimes US forces committed while "looking for al-Zarqawi" took place on October 8. American forces claimed to have directed an accurate surgical strike on an important al-Zarqawi hideout. Iraqi doctors who treated the wounded later revealed the target to have been a civilian house where a wedding had just taken place. The bride was injured, along with nine other women and six children. The groom was killed along with ten other people. Out of the eleven killed there were eight from the same family: a father and his seven children. Dancing, rejoicing, and celebrating a wedding were suspicious enough to call for a bombing that would kill eleven people and injure seventeen others. Despite the fact that doctors exposed this horrendous story and Reuters reported the news internationally, American forces maintained the position that they hadn't done anything wrong—they continued to claim that they had bombed an al-Zarqawi hideout with "surgical accuracy."

The slaughter of this wedding party wasn't the only war crime committed in October. In another case, a family who had left the city to escape the wrath of the bombs, decided to return home to pick up some things. On that night of October 19, their house was bombed by two massive rockets and killed them all. Reuters correspondent Yasser Faisal confirmed that he'd seen all six members of the doomed family—two parents and four children—being pulled from the rubble. Neighbors told the same story. But spokespersons for American forces once again claimed that the strike targeted, with surgical accuracy, a house that sheltered al-Zarqawi's men.

American forces continued to bomb Fallujah even after a public admission by US forces that perhaps al-Zarqawi was not in the city at all. On October 31, Kim Sengupta of the *Independent* wrote,

> The US military now says that al-Zarqawi may no longer be in Fallujah. This makes nonsense of the demand by Ayad Allawi, Washing-

ton's client Prime Minister in Baghdad, for people of the town to hand over the Jordanian militant leader if they want to avoid the onslaught.

Sengupta also reported that the day before eight Marines had been killed and nine injured, "in the bloodiest attack on US forces for seven months," adding, "US military vehicles were burning on the roadside to the east of the city, and there were prolonged firefights. But it was unclear last night whether this was the start of the long-awaited offensive to storm Fallujah."

To this same report, General Dennis Hejlik added, "We're gearing up to do an operation and when we're told to go, we'll go. When we do go, we'll whack them." And despite no proof that al-Zarqawi was in Fallujah (and many rumors to the contrary), Allawi continued to demand that Fallujans turn al-Zarqawi in to the US forces or suffer the consequences.

Bush knew that a successful operation in Fallujah would bring him much-needed positive publicity for the upcoming presidential elections. The *Independent* reported that "there has been intense speculation that the Fallujah offensive would be timed to coincide with the US presidential election on Tuesday, allowing President Bush to boost his image as a war leader." Bush needed a victory in Fallujah to burnish both his and Allawi's image. Of course no polishing of Allawi's image would ever help him among Iraqis. But the better he looked to Americans, the better Bush's chances for reelection.

From the start of the occupation in April 2003 until November 2004, according to a report by Quds Press quoting medical sources in Fallujah, there were 2,825 dead civilians, 11 of whom were journalists. This does not account for dead insurgents, of course. Another statistic reported by the Fallujah Civil Defense Corps mentioned that at one point 345 bombs and rockets had been dropped on the city within a single week, and that overall 3,211 houses were destroyed along with 18 mosques, 1,600 stores and workshops, 8 gas stations, 19 schools, and a college. Over 538,195 square feet of farming land was also destroyed.

These statistics are appalling. And yet they represent only a warm-up for the second battle of Fallujah, whose destruction was unparalleled by any earlier part of the war.

17. PREPARING FOR ANNIHILATION

On November 3, Tony Blair demanded that Fallujans drop their weapons and adhere to the orders of the interim Iraqi government. That demand, delivered on the floor of the House of Commons, was Blair's response to Labour Party politician Alice Mahon. Mahon had demanded earlier that Blair not engage British troops in a collective punishment that would lead to the indiscriminate slaughter of innocent civilians in Fallujah. She did not want British troops to play a role in Operation Phantom Fury. Blair did not listen to a democratically elected politician who sat in the same House of Commons building as him. Instead, he chose to listen to George Bush. It's clear that Blair should have paused to get his political priorities straight, but he did not.

On November 6, Dexter Filkins and James Glanz of the *New York Times* reported that American military commanders and Bush administration officials were doing final reviews of battle plans for Operation Phantom Fury: "At the presidential retreat at Camp David, Maryland, President Bush was briefed Friday morning on the battle plans in a videoconference with his top national security advisers." This direct supervision by Bush was a clear indication that the administration was in the final countdown for the assault. Filkins and Glanz reported that the "Americans were setting up military checkpoints to choke off access roads." It was the preparatory step for the mayhem to come.

On the same day, Fallujans began to leave in a mass exodus. Those who couldn't took refuge in schools, auditoriums, gyms—any public facility where they could gather in numbers and hope this guaranteed safety. The thought was that if they made it abundantly clear to American troops that these locations were strictly shelters for civilians, the troops wouldn't attack, or at least would be reluctant to attack, in fear of being accused of war crimes.

On November 6, UN Secretary-General Kofi Annan sent a letter to Bush, Blair, and Allawi formally warning the three parties of the consequences of a planned assault on Fallujah. Among many things, Annan wrote,

> I wish to express to you my particular concern about the safety and protection of civilians. Fighting is likely to take place mostly in densely populated urban areas, with an obvious risk of civilian casualties... the threat or actual use of force not only risks deepening the sense of alien-

ation of certain communities, but would also reinforce perceptions among the Iraqi population of a continued military occupation.

The US did not heed this warning. By November 7, all roads leading to Fallujah were sealed. US forces patrolled the city, threatening to arrest anyone under 45 attempting to leave the city. Agence France-Presse reported that Colonel Michael Shupp of the Marines told his troops to shoot any Iraqi civilian who approached them with raised hands, because he or she might be a "suicide bomber." This openly declared intent to target civilians was also reflected in the thoughts and words of lower rank soldiers. On this same day, Lance Corporal Joseph Bowman told the Associated Press, "I want to go and kill people so we can go home. Kill them and go home—that's all we can do now." Of course, one cannot expect moral behavior from troops being commanded by officers like Michael Shupp.

The official American count of forces participating in the operation was more than 10,000 troops: two Marine battalions along with one battalion from the Army's First Infantry Division. Other reports at the time suggested a count approaching 20,000 soldiers, with two thirds from the Marines and one third from the US Army. These numbers of course did not account for mercenaries from firms such as Blackwater USA. The number also did not include American-trained Iraqi security forces, most of whom were Kurdish or Shia and, according to some sources, were in the struggle simply to fight against the Sunnis.

The bulk of the insurgency force, as before, was made up of local Fallujans. Not all of these participants were hardened insurgents, and none of them, according to insurgent leaders, had anything to do with al-Qaeda or al-Zarqawi or any other "al." The new recruits didn't seem to have affiliations with organized insurgent groups or connections with political or ideological currents outside Fallujah—the bombing of the city was enough justification for their involvement. Even Fallujans who had once resented the insurgents picked up pistols and shotguns and anything they could find to form their own resistance. Between hardened insurgents, freshly-recruited civilians, and locals with shotguns, the total count of fighters defending the city still did not crest 2,000, according to the highest estimates at the time.

Although these Fallujan fighters weren't all hardened insurgents, they were definitely hardened Fallujans, with indelible spirit. By the start of Operation Phantom Fury, it was widely understood that the retaliation would be extreme, which drove Fallujans to react with similar extremism. The fighters decided that they were not going to let Fallujah go easily.

Fallujans knew many people would die and that their city might be destroyed, so they wanted to make the cost of the death and destruction as high as possible for the American who were attacking them—in casualty counts, material losses, and political standing.

The motley but determined mix of Fallujan fighters wasn't an image that Bush or Blair wanted the world to see. Nor did they want the true image of the assault—the mass slaughter of civilians—to become public. Bush and Blair wanted the world to believe that the US was only targeting insurgents—al-Zarqawi's men.

Not surprisingly, Bush and Blair cleared the city of nearly all media before the operation began. Allawi had already shut down al-Jazeera's Baghdad bureau in August. We felt that because of this shutdown, we had little chance of covering Phantom Fury, but we hoped that other media crews would be able to provide the necessary coverage. Naturally, many media outlets sent TV crews to Fallujah when it became very clear that an assault was going to take place. I hoped that with so many journalists covering the story, no reporter would be singled out as the enemy, as had happened to me. Reporters from different news outlets would show the images, and the Americans wouldn't be able to claim that footage from so many different sources was all distorted. The promise of this journalistic presence satisfied me that the battle would receive good coverage.

Of course, my satisfaction did not last long. Just before Phantom Fury began, American forces went into Fallujah with the express purpose of rooting out all televised media crews, especially those with mobile broadcast vehicles. The only media personnel who refused to leave the city (and were allowed to stay) were those journalists from Fallujah—local Fallujah residents who were correspondents for international news agencies. Among these journalists were Dr. Fadhel al-Badrani, a correspondent for Reuters and BBC Radio, and al-Jazeera's very own Hussain Deli. These journalists played a significant role in exposing war crimes in the aftermath of this battle, but no one could show live video coverage during the conflict. The war crimes during this battle were exposed mostly by newspapers, magazines, and radio stations.

The other journalists officially allowed to stay in Fallujah were those working with US forces. These embedded journalists played an integral role in Bush's war because they helped the US spread its propaganda after the battle. There were also photographers working for US forces. Other than these US-friendly news sources, no single journalist was allowed to keep a camera in Fallujah during Operation Phantom Fury. For televised news stations, the orders were to leave the city altogether. For journalists working for printed media and newspapers, they were ordered to surrender their cameras to US forces.

Despite Bush's extreme attempts to control the information flow from Fallujah during the operation, some still leaked out. Eyewitnesses narrated their accounts to other news organizations when they were able to. One couldn't rely, though, on these eyewitnesses to cover the war during the actual operation. Communication was very difficult, and no one could predict where their next hiding place would be. There were no safe places, and consequently no places from which journalists could report what was happening. Eyewitnesses spoke when they could, and the flow of information was sporadic.

The eyewitnesses who occasionally gave information about what was happening in the city were sometimes journalists, sometimes private citizens, and sometimes journalists who'd become private citizens because they were forced out of their jobs as journalists. Although they were in the midst of the battle as private citizens, whenever they were able to, they delivered their accounts to news sources. Other information came from journalists who managed to get into the city immediately after the operation had ended and spoke to survivors and documented the wreckage. All in all, these eyewitnesses played a significant role in exposing at least some of the war crimes, as we will see later. A cover-up is never complete.

Holy Day, Unholy Deed

"The FO I relieved for Bravo Company told me… he was proud of destroying a good portion of Hue City…"
— Lance Corporal Kenneth Campbell, Vietnam War crimes hearings, April 28, 1971 in Washington, DC

Early in the morning of November 7, Ayad Allawi declared a state of emergency—basically martial law—effective for 60 days across the entire country of Iraq (except the Kurdish-controlled northern regions). He ordered the closure of the Baghdad International Airport and sealed off the borders with Syria and Jordan. These actions could be called the official start of Operation Phantom Fury, which was described by Fox News as "the biggest Marine-led urban assault since Vietnam."

The date was noteworthy because according to the Muslim calendar,

November 7, 2004 fell on Ramadan 25, 1425. The month of Ramadan is the holiest time of the year for Muslims. And the last ten days of Ramadan are particularly holy, and the odd-numbered dates within those last ten days the most sacred. In essence, Ramadan 21, 23, 25, 27, and 29 are the holiest days in a Muslim's year. Allawi could not have picked a more offensive day for the start of Phantom Fury—indeed an unholy course of action.

There are two possible explanations (if one assumes that Allawi had any power in the matter whatsoever). The first is that Allawi didn't know the significance of that date and therefore didn't really realize how disturbing his choice was. This would indicate a sincere lack of understanding, knowledge, and appreciation of the culture of the people he claimed to be representing. This wouldn't surprise many Iraqis, because they viewed him as an imported Iraqi politician anyway; they knew he represented Bush and his ideology, not Iraqis and their culture.

The second possibility is that Allawi knew exactly what he was doing. This explanation, of course is the most highly offensive one. To attack Fallujans during Ramadan would be an intentional attempt to outrage Fallujans, who have a reputation for being deeply religious. If Allawi made this choice knowingly, it would prove that he did indeed have a special vengeance and hatred for Fallujans, because they had resisted the occupation that he supported. This isn't an outlandish assumption by any means—planning the operation during Ramadan would be a recommendation that came from the Bush administration; the same administration that later chose to execute Saddam Hussein on Eid al-'Adha, another holy day in the Muslim calendar.

As Iraqis heard the news of the state of emergency from their imported leader, Marines in Iraq stood before their exported leaders ready for instruction. More than 2,500 Marines were standing around Lt. General John Sattler, the commanding general of the First Marine Expeditionary Force, as he declared, "This is America's fight. What we've added to our force are Iraqi partners. They want to go in and liberate Fallujah. They feel this town's being held hostage by mugs, thugs, murderers and terrorists."

In this pre-combat speech Sattler encouraged his troops with these words: "God bless you, each and every one. You know what your mission is. Go out there and get it done."

Sattler wasn't the only commander trying to boost his Marines' morale. Sgt. Major Carlton W. Kent told his troops, "You're all in the process of making history. This is another Hue City in the making. I have no doubt that if we do get the word each and every one of you is going to do what you have always done: kick some butt."

I remember reading these statements and thinking, Yes, Fallujah is another Hue City in the making—just like Iraq is another Vietnam in the making. And you, Carlton Kent, are another Kenneth Campbell in the making.

Lt. Colonel Mike Ramos defamed Fallujans to boost his troops' morale: "If I see someone who looks like a martyr driving at high speed toward my unit, I'll send him to Allah before he gets close." To this statement Kent added, "This is a whole can of whoop-butt all combined here."

What caught my attention most after reading these statements was the invocation of God. Marine commanders had no problem openly telling their troops to target and kill civilians, and then following that command by bestowing God's blessing on those deeds. These leaders saw a problem with suicide bombers who killed indiscriminately in the name of Allah, but none with American bombers doing the same in the name of their God.

Not to be outdone, Iraqi Defense Minister Hazem Shaalan tried to lift the morale of Iraqi forces taking part in the operation by saying, "When we came to Iraq with the coalition forces, our decision was to build Iraq through its sons. Today is your day, and jihad is for you—not for those rats."

When I was reading these statements from outside the walls of the battle, I lost track of whom the Americans believed God would support, and whether that support was a good or bad thing. Was God on the side of the American-trained Iraqi forces, most of whom weren't Christian, who had a reputation for running from battles in fear? Or was God on the side of the US forces with their reputation for indiscriminate slaughter and senseless bombing? Or was God an evil force, named Allah, fighting on the side of hardcore insurgents with a reputation for kidnappings, beheadings, and suicide bombings?

I must admit, at this point the insurgents seemed to me the lesser of three evils. Insurgents, quite simply, believed God was on their side and they were not ashamed to declare it. It was well known to everyone that these men were fighting strictly out of religious devotion. In other words, their religious extremism was clear to the entire world. In contrast, those who claimed to be secular yet strained to add some sentiment of holiness to their fight (while constantly putting down other groups for using religion as a tool for fighting) were much more troublesome to me. The American forces claimed that the enemy was radical and extremist because they believed their cause to be holy. But these were the same American forces that represented a presumably democratic and secular regime and yet still claimed that God was on their side.

Perhaps God was on the side of the innocent Fallujans—the women and children and elderly who had committed no crime but living in a city they called home.

18. OPERATION PHANTOM FURY

Robert Worth and Richard A. Oppel, Jr. of the *New York Times* reported that troops began moving toward hospitals and other strategic bridges in Fallujah at 9PM local time on November 7. That advance was the only preparation needed for the big assault the following day.

Within two hours, the American forces were able to control the Fallujah General Hospital on the western side of the Euphrates. My colleague Hussain Deli (who had remained inside the city) tried to contact Dr. Rafie al-Issawi at the hospital for updates. Deli found he was out of the country on a visit to Mecca. Dr. Salih al-Issawi had temporarily replaced him as acting director of the hospital, so Hussein spoke with him instead.

"Marines accompanied by Iraqi National Guard forces broke into the hospital and started kicking, beating, punching, striking, and smacking just about everything they could see in the hospital," Dr. al-Issawi told Hussein. "It didn't even matter to them what was human being and what was object. They broke hospital bedposts for no apparent reason. They kicked many patients out of their rooms and even out of the hospital altogether. Then they started kicking and beating the medical staff and the patients."

Other sources quoted other members of the medical staff who summarized the break-in thus: "An overzealous, thuggish band of Iraqi troops stormed a place where there were no rebels and only terrified, ill, and injured patients." An ambulance driver at the hospital said that the Iraqi forces stole his money and cell phone before beating him up.

The Saudi-based *al-Sharq al-Awssat* newspaper interviewed the Fallujah Central Clinic's director Dr. Ahmad Ghanem. Ghanem said that he was having a problem coping with casualties at his modest clinic because the Marines and the Iraqi National Guard had arrested the entire medical staff and all employees at the Fallujah General Hospital, hence cutting off a major source of the already limited medical resources in the city. The staff was later released, but the arrests caused urgent problems in the early hours of the operation.

Although shockingly inhumane, attacking the hospital was clearly a strategy for the Americans in this operation, just as it had been in the first battle. Hospitals are the main source of information on casualty counts and victims. The troops needed to show the Fallujan doctors early in the battle what would happen to them if the information they released did not please US forces. As the *New York Times* reported, "The hospital was selected as an early target because the American military believed that it was the source of rumors about heavy casualties. 'It's a center of propaganda,' a senior American officer said Sunday."

The hideous start of this battle—making a hospital an open target—took place with full approval from Donald Rumsfeld and Richard Myers. The *New York Times* reported, "In Washington, Pentagon officials said Secretary of Defense Donald H. Rumsfeld and General Richard B. Myers, the chairman of the Joint Chiefs of Staff, were monitoring the preparations and updated combat reports." This was the battle of revenge, and Rumsfeld wanted to make sure to avoid the bad publicity his troops had received in April.

Day Two: The Battle Thickens

The insurgents resisted American forces fiercely, giving the battle all they had. The fighting continued through the night of November 7 and into the morning. US forces were able to achieve their initial objectives very effectively: they cut off bridges, trapping insurgents (and others) in the city, and attacked the hospital, warning doctors to be invasion-friendly. US Army General George Casey, commander of the Multinational Force in Iraq, acknowledged that insurgents had put out a good fight during the night and mounted a resistance fierce enough to set the stage to make the second battle of Fallujah "a tough fight."

When ground advances stopped on the morning of November 8, pilots began to litter the city with indiscriminate aerial bombardment.

Lt. Colonel Todd Desgrosseilliers spoke of the bombardment saying, "We probably had 20 to 30 air strikes in the Golan [Neighborhood] and probably two to three times that in artillery missions." The bombing was so intense and indiscriminate that scorched human flesh was scattered nearly everywhere in the doomed area. Rumsfeld's promises of "precise and carefully targeted munitions" were clearly not being upheld. Agence France-Presse also noted that "at least four 900-kilogram bombs were dropped" and "more than 500 rounds of 155-millimetre Howitzer cannon shells have been fired." The result for November 8 alone was the complete leveling of ten percent of the buildings in the Golan Neighborhood. Many structures that remained standing also sustained very serious damage.

Fallujan mosques were targeted from day one, as reported by the *Washington Post*. The *Post* commented that when asked to justify these illegal acts against sacred religious spaces, "Military commanders said insurgents had been seen moving weapons into the mosques." Of course, no evidence was presented for this accusation—not even suspect satellite images like the ones Colin Powell presented to the UN when he accused Saddam Hussein of amassing weapons of mass destruction.

The fact that the Iraqi forces participating in the operation against Fallujah, a mostly Sunni Arab city, were made up of Shiites and Kurds was also suspicious. This element of the conflict further inflamed the already palpable tension between Arabs and Kurds as well as between Shiites and Sunnis. This situation was just another example of George Bush's attempts to play ethnic and sectarian animosities to his advantage, and it was a cruel choice.

To combat this explosive clash, AMSI wanted to remind Shiites, Sunnis, and Kurds (who are mostly Sunnis, but not Arabs) that they were all Muslims and therefore shouldn't fight with one another. On November 8, AMSI issued a fatwa on the participation of Iraqi soldiers in Operation Phantom Fury. As reported by Agence France-Presse, it included the following: "The participation of Iraqi forces in an assault on Fallujah under the banner of invading foreign forces that are known to be heathen is strongly prohibited and is considered one of the bigger violations that make participants in this assault deserve the wrath of God." Shaikh Muhammed al-Faydhee spoke on behalf of the association saying, "Those who kill Iraqis are not Iraqis... be careful not to repeat this experience because the occupier will leave one day, but the people will stay. They shouldn't be tools in the hands of the occupiers. An assault against Fallujah is an assault against all Iraqis." This fatwa was the association's way of fighting against the threat of ethnic and sectarian war that Bush's divide-and-conquer tactics exacerbated.

In addition to the fatwa, other Fallujans and local clergy took a far less diplomatic approach to the Iraqis fighting with the Americans. These threats amounted to, "We swear by God that we will stand against you in the streets, we will enter your houses and we will slaughter you like sheep."

This statement was frightening enough to scare a good number of Iraqi soldiers away from fulfilling their commitment to the US forces. It was not unlike the start of the April battle, when Iraqi forces deserted their posts. The Associated Press reported that "US military and Iraqi commanders estimated that up to 200 Iraqi troops had resigned, with another 200 'on leave.'"

With televised media out of the city and doctors warned against revealing the truth about casualty counts, Rumsfeld took the opportunity to tell reporters that he did not expect high casualty counts among Fallujan civilians at any point in the conflict because the soldiers participating in the operation were skilled in urban combat and using precise and carefully targeted munitions.

Ground assaults in Fallujah resumed at 7PM on November 8 with a round of indiscriminate artillery firing. The fiercest resistance against US forces came from the insurgents standing guard in the Golan Neighborhood.

Day Three: Continuing Chaos

On November 9, American forces responded to the resistance in the Golan Neighborhood with the power of six battalions. These troops pounded the area in a joint effort called "The Wedge," a maneuver in which the six battalions approached the neighborhood from several different angles and joined forces as they approached the center.

As US forces advanced, insurgents hit back harder with mortar fire and shoulder-held missiles, and managed to shoot down a US helicopter, as reported by the Associated Press. The report stated, "Witnesses said the helicopter burst into a ball of flame. The number of casualties was not clear." US forces denied the incident. They didn't deny, though, the fierceness of the resistance. Associated Press quoted Captain Robert Bodisch as saying, "They are putting up a strong fight and I saw many of them on the street I was on."

The Associated Press also reported two American tanks and several Humvee vehicles seen smoldering after they'd been attacked by insurgents. AP also reported that a Kiowa helicopter had been struck by ground fire, "appearing to wound the pilot, who nonetheless managed to return to an American base." Of course, publicly, the US forces maintained their position that no helicopters had been shot down and that the US was standing strong in this fierce battle.

On this third day of the operation, Reuters reported some of the casualties American forces suffered so far. An American soldier who was awaiting medical evacuation because of his wounds was quoted as saying, "A buddy of mine and another soldier were killed and I have seen about 50 other wounded [US] soldiers." The soldier refused to give his name to Reuters. The *New York Times* also reported that American officials in Baghdad had counted at least ten dead in the fighting.

The day before these reports were released, American forces had sent a clear message to Fallujan doctors not to release damaging information about casualties unless they wanted to suffer the consequences. After these reports came out, Americans made their message clearer by bombing and destroying a clinic inside the city, thus further limiting the medical service available to the city residents. Reuters quoted Sami al-Jumayli, a doctor who had escaped the General Hospital just before his colleagues were beaten and arrested, as saying: "There is not a single surgeon in Fallujah. We had one ambulance hit by US fire and a doctor wounded. There are scores of injured civilians in their homes whom we can't move. A thirteen-year-old child just died in my hands."

In response to this chaos and the dwindling health resources in the city, Dr. Hashem al-Issawi turned his clinic into a field hospital. "Medical conditions in Fallujah are extremely difficult," al-Issawi said. "There are tens of wounded people in need of surgeries and amputations, but we have no surgeons, no medicine, no electricity or water, no fuel, and the clinic has been in total darkness all night. We are pleading with international organizations to intervene or else a human catastrophe will fall on this city."

Because of the obvious suffering in Fallujah, Iraq's Islamic Party once again found itself in the embarrassing situation of being linked to a foreign country that was intentionally hurting its people. As a result, the Islamic Party threatened to withdraw from the Iraqi government if the harassment in Fallujah continued. The Associated Press reported, "Iraq's official Sunni Muslim political party has threatened to quit the US-backed government unless the attack is halted, a spokesman said today."

The threat from the Islamic Party did nothing to curb the attack. Just before the sun set on November 9, US forces began cutting off the electricity in Fallujah. By 5PM, the entire city was without power. After the American forces finished cutting off the power supply, they moved to cut water and phone lines. By nightfall, Fallujah was pitch dark and out of touch with the rest of the world.

Because of Fallujah's forced isolation from the rest of the world, the al-Jazeera crew and I were cut off from the experience there as well. As I read a BBC correspondent's report of the water being cut off, I thought that there had to be an international law incriminating such appalling behavior. In fact, there is, and it didn't take much looking to find it: Article 14 under Protocol II of the Geneva Conventions. "Starvation of civilians as a method of combat is prohibited. It is therefore prohibited to attack, destroy, remove or render useless for that purpose, objects indispensable to the survival of the civilian population such as food-stuffs, agricultural areas for the production of food-stuffs, crops, livestock, drinking water installations and supplies and irrigation works."

Cutting off Fallujan access to essential services such as water and electricity was not the only way in which the Americans violated the code of conduct required by the Geneva Conventions. As I've alluded to, mosques were a frequent targets in this battle, just as they had been during the first battle. Mosques were under constant and direct fire, and the US always defended this by claiming that insurgents were hiding inside. Agence France-Presse reported that one of its correspondents in the city received a call from Abdulhamid Farhan, head cleric at the Abdulaziz Mosque in the center of Fallujah. Farhan told the reporter that he was trapped with other civilians inside a mosque, and that there were even more civilians trapped at two other mosques in the city—the Abi Obaida Mosque and the al-Furqan Mosque. He said no one was able to stand up because of the intensity of the firing around them. Clearly, those hiding in the Mosques were not dangerous insurgents—they were civilians praying for their lives to be spared.

Day Four: The Myth of al-Zarqawi Continues

While Fallujah's Golan Neighborhood was being subjected to these atrocities, the mythical figure used as an excuse for the entire operation, al-Zarqawi, was apparently operating somewhere else. About 45 people were killed in attacks at police stations in the city of Baqubah, and al-Zarqawi boasted responsibility for these attacks soon after on the internet. Oddly, al-Zarqawi's immediate statement of responsibility for the attacks in Baqubah did not seem to catch the attention of US forces, who continued to use his presence in Fallujah as an excuse to blanket the city with bombs.

US forces continued their attacks on November 10, despite the fact that al-Zarqawi was reportedly working elsewhere. According to ABC News, the Americans were "knocking down walls," "spraying rounds of machine gun fire at buildings," after they had "ploughed through fields" and "smashed through a railway line" with their heavy military equipment.

Edward Wong and Eric Schmidt of the *New York Times* reported that al-Zarqawi "[had] almost certainly fled, military officials believe" adding, "some military officials said Mr. Zarqawi could be operating out of Falluja, but his precise whereabouts have not been known."

The article quoted Lt. General Thomas F. Metz, commander of the multinational forces in Iraq, as saying, "I personally believe some of the senior leaders probably have fled." But US forces didn't pause to question why they were still in Fallujah if the targeted man was working elsewhere. The senseless pounding of the city continued without question.

Because al-Zarqawi had proven his active and lethal presence well outside Fallujah, American officials had to change the official mission of their operation as declared to the public. Prior to the start of the operation, Americans and the imported Iraqi officials in Allawi's government had been saying the official target was "al-Zarqawi and his foreign fighters." Now, they had to cover up for the embarrassment of an exposed false front to this battle. They couldn't possibly tell the public that their objective all along had been to exact revenge on Fallujah for its defiance of the occupation, so they had to alter the objective of the entire mission to make it suitable for the new facts. So, many officials were quoted with new justifications for the battle on this fourth day. The *New York Times* quoted a senior American official who closely followed the battle as saying, "The important idea to consider is that this is not an operation against al-Zarqawi or his network. It is just one of many steps that need to be taken in order to defeat a complex and diverse insurgency in which the Zarqawi network is but one element." This statement clearly contradicts earlier mission statements released by the United States.

I remember meeting several Fallujans prior to the battle and discussing this particular point with them—the idea that al-Zarqawi and his men might have left town before the operation even began. Almost all of them said, "Al-Zarqawi was never in Fallujah to begin with. We have no knowledge of his presence at all." They did believe, however, that although al-Zarqawi himself was never in the city, his men were indeed present at some point; though they thought most of them had left with other groups of insurgents. As one insurgent leader put it, "What would be the point of staying to engage in an impossible battle when we could leave and attack Americans from somewhere else? We're light, small, and mobile. We could use our size to maneuver. We could tell the civilians to leave, and this way all the Americans would have for targets would be empty houses."

This solution appealed to insurgents and civilians alike. Indeed, 75 to 90 percent of the civilian population had left the city before Operation Phantom Fury. More than half of the insurgents left town, and that statistic was acknowledged by American officials and reported in the media. What remained, then, were no more than 1,000 to 2,000 insurgents and 10 to 25 percent of the civilian population. The small number of insurgents that remained was almost 100 percent Fallujan.

On al-Jazeera's *Iraqi Scene* program, hosted by Abdulazeem Muhammad, Shaikh Abdallah al-Janabi, head of the Mujahideen Consultative Council in Fallujah, was asked about this. He said, "The truth is that we gave everyone the option to leave. The fighters who remained did so entirely by their personal choice. This was particularly the case of fighters who were native Fallujans and other Fallujans who had just joined the resistance. They felt that they were better off dying in their own land than living as refugees anywhere else. Their slogan was, 'It's better to die standing than to live on your knees.' As for fellow Arab fighters, almost all of them had left. If there were any of them still in the city, we certainly didn't know about them. They had to have been just a handful. When we said we have no foreign fighters in Fallujah, we meant it. We knew of none."

When asked why the insurgents were not instructed to leave the city instead of being given an option to stay, Shaikh al-Janabi responded, "Unlike the image portrayed by occupation forces, the reality of the resistance is far more diverse and democratic than American officials are willing to acknowledge. Not all fighters are of the same background, ideology, or philosophy. You can't just impose your view on such a diverse group, especially when we're talking about an issue of life and death. You can't expect people to make such a critical decision based on your personal view while disregarding their own. So, we had to leave the option to each individual."

Abdulazeem asked Shaikh al-Janabi about the presence of al-Zarqawi in Fallujah. He replied, "Americans can lie all they want. They know that al-Zarqawi isn't here. They know the people who fought them and humiliated their massive army were native Fallujans, not al-Zarqawi's men. It was native Fallujans who negotiated with Americans between the two battles of Fallujah. It was native Fallujans who allowed Americans to run joint patrols with the establishment of the Fallujah Brigades. Americans did not deal with al-Zarqawi or his men during any of these steps. They dealt with us. They can lie about the presence of al-Zarqawi, but at the end of the day, they know very well whom they've been dealing with all along here in Fallujah."

On November 16, after the most intense days of Operation Phantom Fury, Andrew Buncombe of the *Independent* published a report quoting Colonel Michael Regner, operations officer for the First Marine Expeditionary Force at Fallujah: "at least 1,052 prisoners had been captured in the battle. No more than about two dozen of them were 'foreign fighters.'" Two dozen people termed as "foreign fighters" out of 1,052 amounts to no more than 2.3 percent. Shaikh al-Janabi was right. They were indeed a handful at most. The 97.7 percent of local fighters did not catch the attention of Bush and his men; it was the scary numbers of "foreign fighters" led by al-Zarqawi. Those were the ones the operation was allegedly waged against.

Bush's original objectives—to install a democratic government in Iraq, remove weapons of mass destruction, and dismantle a suspected relationship between Saddam and al-Qaeda had already been proven false. When al-Zarqawi turned up in Baqubah, not Fallujah, and the number of foreign fighters in Fallujah turned out to be marginal, the rationale for Phantom Fury was also proven false. To remedy this embarrassment, the official objective of Phantom Fury became not simply to target al-Zarqawi himself, but also to break down the insurgency network of which al-Zarqawi and his "foreign fighters" were only a small part. It is important to note that over the course of two years, the official reasoning for the actions of the Bush administration in this war changed a dizzying number of times. These changes followed the same pattern as all of Bush's justifications for every offensive and brutal action he committed in Iraq: first he made a case for self-defense, and later when the case was exposed as fraud, the objective became to somehow generously improve the life of an oppressed people.

Early on during the combat operations that took place on November 10, the US forces reported that they had control of 70 percent of the city—including the mayor's office, several mosques, a commercial center, and several other major civic landmarks. Later on in the chaos of November 10, American forces announced that they were expecting to have the entire city of Fallujah under control within 48 hours. They also said it would take about ten days to completely clear the city of insurgents. These predictions proved to be baseless. A Reuters correspondent working with US forces reported that insurgents weren't showing any signs of surrender. They were instead taking fortified positions along Main Street and firing from automatic rifles and mortar fire launchers.

Despite the claim that the city would be under American control in 48 hours, the heavy bombardment continued. American commanders said US troops and Iraqi security forces secured the Golan Neighborhood with very little resistance, but US forces in the southwestern neighborhoods of Resala and Nazzal reportedly encountered more defiance.

Reporters working with the US spoke of bodies and concrete rubble littering the streets of Fallujah—streets that were empty of all human activity save battles. With no unbiased televised media in town, it was difficult to get a census of the casualty counts on either side. The little contact that Fallujans had with the outside world gave them the chance just to plead for help for the countless victims in the city. Ahmad al-Rawi, a spokesperson for the Red Crescent issued this bleak portrait of Fallujah to the world: "There are thousands of people, including women, children, and the elderly, trapped in the city and in need of shelter, medical supplies, food, and water."

The fighting continued, and the pleas for humanitarian aid remained unheard. Much of the fighting in the middle days of the battle was sparked by the Iraqi insurgents' supposed use of mosques as arms fortifications. According to US forces, Fallujan rebels were using mosques as weaponries/operation bases (similar accusations had come in the first battle of Fallujah, and resulted in many casualties and the destruction of many city mosques) and therefore the US forces accused Fallujans of violating international law. After these claims were made, the US insists that only Iraqi security forces were used to search and secure the mosques because of their high cultural importance to the Iraqi people. That American forces never entered the mosques is something that's hard to prove without witnesses, though, and it seems out of sync with the actions carried out during the first battle of Fallujah.

Based on the accusation that armed Fallujans were hiding in mosques, US forces captured several mosques during the heat of this second battle, including the al-Hadrah al-Muhammadeyah Mosque. The *New York Times* reported the al-Muhammadeyah Mosque as strategically significant to the battle because the US believed that insurgents were using it as a command center and bunker. A convention center and two other buildings in close vicinity to the mosque were also captured on the basis that they held dangerous weapons and the capacity to manufacture more dangerous material. As in similar incidents in the first battle of Fallujah, it was difficult for these claims to be substantiated without the presence of the press or the words of other eyewitnesses for verification.

According to a report released from the al-Jazeera newsroom in Doha on November 10, half of the mosques in Fallujah had been destroyed or damaged by US artillery and warplanes at this point in the operation. Because these buildings represent a sacred connection to the religion and culture of these people, this destruction was undoubtedly one of the most damaging and devastating parts of the war for the city of Fallujah, the "city of mosques."

A View from inside the Battle: November 7–10

"Attacks against civilian drinking water installation and irrigation works are prohibited."
— Protocol I, Section 2, Article 54, Geneva Conventions

"In an occupied territory, the occupying power has the responsibility of assuring adequate medical supplies for the population."
— Article 55, Fourth Geneva Convention

"If there is a lack of medical supplies, the occupying power must agree to and support relief efforts by states or humanitarian organizations."
— Article 59, Fourth Geneva Convention

We at al-Jazeera had no access to Fallujah, and although our colleague Hussain Deli was living in the city, his movement was very limited due to the indiscriminate bombing. Desperate for information, on November 10 I called Dr. Fadhel al-Badrani to see if he had any updates. Al-Badrani was the correspondent for Reuters and BBC Radio in Fallujah, and I asked him to give us an eyewitness account of what he'd seen from the start of the operation.

Al-Badrani spoke of a serious food shortage in the city. During the intense bombardment just before the official start of the operation, no storekeepers dared to open their shops for people to buy groceries. Shops were closed for at least six days before the operation began and continued throughout. People were already short on food even before the active fighting commenced. As do many populations throughout the world, Fallujans rely primarily on fresh produce and meat for sustenance. Canned goods aren't commonplace. So the closure of grocery stores and produce stands was quite dangerous. With the electricity out, refrigerators didn't work, so the chance of keeping meat and produce fresh for any length of time was very low. Within the first couple of days, the little food people had in their refrigerators had rotted. Dates were the only food that kept well and ended up playing a major role in preventing mass starvation. Of course, only those lucky enough to have bought a large supply of dates just before the operation had the advantage of their long shelf life.

Water was also in dangerously short supply. From the start of the operation, American forces had targeted the water tanks on the rooftops of Fallujan houses. Very few people had water tanks that weren't damaged by gunfire. And then American forces cut off the water supply to the entire city by bombing the plumbing infrastructure of the city. There was a deliberate attempt to cut off the water supply at every level of the water delivery process. These two actions combined worked to slowly and intentionally dehydrate the entire population of Fallujah.

When the Fallujans became desperately dehydrated, they started digging for water. Of course, they knew the water that came out of the ground (if they found any) would not be clean enough to drink, but they didn't have much choice. An adult—a lucky and very healthy adult—could possibly get away with drinking untreated ground water for a couple of days, maybe a week, before developing a chronic stomach disease or other severe illness. But what about infants? Babies wouldn't last two days on such filthy water. But Fallujans had to take this risk in order to avoid death or severe illness due to dehydration.

The only time to dig and recover ground water without being caught by the Americans was under the cover of night. Volunteers willing to risk their lives dug for this water, and then moved very carefully in a limited parameter to deliver the water and any surplus dates to people in need.

Dr. Fadhel al-Badrani was one of these volunteers, and he provided al-Jazeera with an eyewitness account of his experience. While on these basic supply delivery trips, he ran into mothers who desperately begged for formula for their babies. Fadhel had no answer for these women. Even if he could risk the life of the baby and give the mother untreated groundwater to make some milk, where would he get the formula to begin with? There were no answers.

Elderly people weren't any better off than the infants—although the largest problem for the elderly was the short supply of medication needed to control conditions from diabetes to colon cancer and anything in between. On one of his trips to deliver water to those in need, Fadhel entered a house where a very ill elderly woman sat with her children and grandchildren. She was crying in pain.

She pleaded with her family, "Let me go out in the street to be shot dead by the Americans. It would be a lot easier than dealing with the pain I am in." Her sons and daughters naturally tried to comfort her and dismiss the insanity she was uttering.

Her son patted her head as he said, "You can't think of that kind of suicide, mother. Aren't you afraid of God's wrath for even thinking of that?"

She then begged Fadhel, "Please tell the world about my health. Blood pressure and diabetes are killing me a thousand times a day. Tell them I don't need food or water. I can drink the groundwater. How long do I have left to live anyway? Dirty groundwater won't kill me. The only thing I ask is that what little time I have left not be as painful as it is now."

Fadhel promised her he'd help her as best he could. He wrote a statement explaining the conditions in Fallujah, and sent it to all the news agencies he was working with along with a number of humanitarian and international human rights organizations. He sent the same statement with updates for three days, and every day one of the lady's sons would sneak to Fadhel's house to ask if he'd received any word of further assistance.

Every day the woman's son got the same answer: "I'm doing the best I can, but no answer so far."

On the fourth day, a representative of the Iraqi Red Crescent called Fadhel with good news, "We're here with supplies. We're just outside Fallujah. We came to take care of people's medical needs, but American troops aren't letting us in."

Fadhel was happy to receive the call even though he knew it would be difficult to get the medicine in his hands. He asked the Red Crescent representative to try to negotiate his way into the city. In the meantime, he ran out to the old lady's house to tell her about the call. He figured the news might give her the strength to live a little longer until the representative made it into the city to deliver her medicine.

By the time he reached her house, the elderly woman had been dead for two hours.

Another story Fadhel told detailed the experience of three brothers who lived in a house right in the middle of the city. The three were sitting in their home as Marines were doing house-to-house searches. The Marines entered their house very politely and calmly, and talked with the men for a few minutes. They asked them a few questions, and the men answered. Then the Marines told the brothers they were finished with their questions, and got up to leave.

On their way out, the last Marine to exit the house turned to the three brothers, wiggled his fingers in a sarcastic wave, and said, "Buh-bye." He then pulled out a hand grenade. He took off the spoon, let it cook off,[38] and hurled the weapon at the three men. The Marines ran from the house, laughing. As a parting insult, one them yelled, "Fire in the hole, bastards...fire in the hole!"

The three brothers tried to scatter quickly enough to avoid being killed by the grenade, but could not get out of the way. Two were severely injured in this attack and the third one suffered less critical injuries. As the two severely injured brothers lay bleeding and whimpering in pain, the third brother began to rip his clothes into bandages in order to repair his brothers' wounds. He was bleeding heavily too, but his injuries were much less substantial than his brothers'.

Fifteen minutes passed as one brother tried to keep the other two alive. Suddenly, the three heard sounds of the Marines coming back to the house. The brother with the fewest injuries dropped to the floor and did not move, playing dead. The other two brothers were too badly injured to hide their moaning or stop their bodies from shivering.

One Marine busted through the door. He kicked at the brother who was playing dead. He saw no response and assumed he had been taken care of. The other two Marines looked at the brothers who were still breathing. One of the Marines pulled out his gun and fired a bullet into the head of each one. The Marines left then, and didn't return a third time.

After some time, volunteers came to check on the house because they'd heard the explosion and the gunshots. They found the third brother still alive and playing dead. They rescued him and he lived to tell the story.

These were the kinds of gruesome tales that came from eyewitnesses.

Bush, of course, had a different perspective on how the operation was going in Fallujah. While innocent civilians were dying of starvation, dehydration, and gunfire, George Bush was holding talks with NATO Secretary General Jaap de Hoop Scheffer. After the talks, he briefed reporters on the situation in Fallujah. He said he'd just met with General Casey that day.

Bush summarized, "Things are going well in Fallujah and they're making very good progress in securing that country."

Now, when slaughter of civilians comes with a smile and a "buh-bye," and that is considered "progress," then the aggressor officially has a problem diagnosing how to go about winning a battle. When you laugh as you take the lives of innocent civilians, the only progress being made is progress in losing your humanity. Not even the most repulsive and radical of insurgents laughed as they butchered their victims.

Bush was featured again in the news later the same day when talks with Tony Blair were reported by Agence France-Presse. Just as the first battle of Fallujah had been urgent enough to require a summit between the two allies in April, the second battle required a similar summit on November 12. Given the grave circumstances in Fallujah and the exposed lies of the Bush administration, Blair and Bush needed to chalk out a new set of plans. Agence France-Presse reported that Fallujah was at the top of the agenda for that meeting.

On this same day, Tony Blair announced before the House of Commons that American and Iraqi forces deserved a salute of respect for what they were doing in Fallujah. When I read that piece of news, I thought to myself: Way to go, Tony. Send them a salute of respect for how easily they're murdering innocent people, and for the enjoyment they get from blowing up civilians and depriving the elderly of medicine long enough for them to die. Reading Blair's words was infuriating to me, and to many others. Robin Cook, Blair's former secretary of defense who had resigned in protest over the war, didn't let Blair get away with his statement.

The *Times* quoted Robin Cook as saying, "What has happened in Fallujah is in many ways an example of what has happened across Iraq. The resistance has escalated with the heavy-handed military tactics." Cook was criticizing the whole operation, not just specific hideous incidents. At the time, with the limited media access, Cook had no way of knowing these horrific stories.

He continued, "This operation will increase the resistance again and decrease the support for our presence within Iraq. This really has got to be the end of the strategy of trying to pacify Iraq by bombing it."

Another official infuriated me even more than Blair. It was US State Department spokesperson Richard Boucher. Boucher informed reporters that day that the US government had sponsored 99 reconstruction projects in Fallujah with a value over $89 million. Boucher said the projects included, "cleanup projects, improving connections to the power grid, restoring water treatment plants, constructing new housing, and repairing roads." He also mentioned that "the Iraqi Government has identified, as well, $50 million for Fallujah reconstruction." In the midst of the destruction being rained on Fallujah that very day, I could not believe the audacity the State Department had to boast about its plans for reconstruction.

Stephen Zunes, the chair of the Peace & Justice Studies Program at the University of San Francisco, called the promises of rebuilding Fallujah after leveling it "ludicrous." "They're trying to tell Fallujans 'we've just destroyed your city, but we're building it right back up.' I don't think Fallujans will fall for that."

Day Five: America Strengthens its Grip

There was a brief, unofficial cease-fire agreement between the insurgents and the US forces in the overnight hours between November 10 and 11, but artillery fighting began once again in the early morning hours. The fire from the US Marines was centered mostly on the northwest side of the city. Later in the afternoon, two helicopters were shot down by rockets in separate incidents and forced to make emergency landings. Although both crews were unharmed and brought to relative safety, there was still much obvious danger in the city for both sides of this battle.

Much of the activity on November 11 related to the discovery of locations where the insurgents had been keeping hostages—places that were later called "slaughterhouses" by the Iraqi forces commander Major General Abdul Qader Mohammed Jassim Mohan. Inside these specific buildings, US forces reportedly found black clothing and hoods that resembled the widely distributed video footage of US hostages at the mercy of insurgent captors, and in some cases also uncovered the banners and flags seen in the background of these videos. There were times when actual hostages were found in these buildings as well—including one incident in which three extremely malnourished and severely injured hostages were found in a Fallujah basement. There were also incidents in which Iraqi people were the victims of cruel detainments—US troops found an Iraqi man chained to the wall on the northeast side of town. The man showed evidence of a severe beating, and was shackled at the hands and feet in order to ensure he would not escape. The man was an Iraqi taxi driver, who said he had been abducted before the operation began and beaten with cables by his captors.

Discovery of the places where hostages were detained represented a victory of sorts for the Americans—these discoveries moved the Americans a step closer to abolishing the terrorist hold on Fallujah. At this point in this fierce second battle for Fallujah, the US reported that it was in control of at least 75 percent of Fallujah, and meeting very little defiance from the insurgent or rebel fighters. The US forces had quelled the resistance in the Golan Neighborhood and were able to turn control of the district to Iraqi security forces. This act was significant because that particular neighborhood had once been the strongest symbol of Fallujan resistance to the US occupation. The US was also able to finally maintain control throughout the northwest part of the city, due to operations carried out under the command of Captain Robert Bodisch. According to General Richard B. Myers, who was chairman of the joint chiefs of staff during this operation, hundreds of rebels were killed in the successful completion of this operation. Myers coined the operation a "big success" because of the relative calm established in the Golan Neighborhood and other parts of the city.

Following these military gains, US forces began to direct their efforts toward rooting out what remained of insurgent power in the city. Iraqi security forces and US troops continued house-to-house searches in order to subvert any suspicious activity and confiscate any weapons or remaining insurgent fighters. The US forces issued a statement predicting that full control of Fallujah by US forces was near, but also cautioned that more time would be needed to ensure the city was absolutely free of rebel forces and secure enough for the withdrawal of US troops.

This cautiously optimistic report from the US did not mean, however, that fighting had been eliminated in the city or that the loss of life was not significant throughout the five days of the battle. In the afternoon of November 11, a crushing and destructive fireball ripped through the northwest part of the city, serving as a clear demonstration that the fighting was far from over. Reuters released an article entitled "Human Disaster Looms in Encircled Fallujah," which lamented the massive humanitarian crisis that was unfolding in the city. Among the devastation discussed in the article is the obvious plight of people suffering without food and water, but also young children dying from conditions that would have been curable with medical care, or suffering injuries from shrapnel or bullets meant for the insurgents or the US forces. Although the US forces repeatedly assured the global public that there were few women and children left in the city, and that more than half the city population had fled to other cities, the longer the fighting persisted the more obvious it became that there was deplorable, massive devastation in the city.

The Americans were suffering from the loss of life as well. The Pentagon reported on November 11 that thirteen soldiers had been killed in Fallujah since the start of Operation Phantom Fury, and eyewitnesses from military hospitals elsewhere in the world reported a rise in wounded soldiers being transferred in order to receive medical attention. Later reports from the US military indicated even higher numbers of US soldiers killed—18 rather than 13—and that another 164 troops (both Iraqi and American) were wounded over the course of this first five days of this battle. Iraqi troops fighting on behalf of the US also counted 5 dead among their soldiers.

US military also reported that as many as 600 insurgents and rebels met their end during Operation Phantom Fury—a staggering number compared to the numbers lost on the opposing side.

It should also be noted that on November 11 in New York City, hundreds of protesters demonstrated against the war in Iraq and the US offensive against Fallujah. An organization called United for Peace and Justice organized the demonstration, and its size was a clear indication of the American people's discontent with the actions of their President and military.

Day Six: An Official End in Sight?

Although there seems to be no agreement about the official end of the second battle of Fallujah—and many contend that the battle has never ended and persists to the present moment—many sources acknowledge November 12 as the last day of volatile, active fighting. In the early hours of that morning, the US military reported that all rebels and insurgents were trapped in the southern region of the city and entirely surrounded by US forces. The US estimated control of approximately 80 percent of the city.

Later in the morning, a battle broke out near a mosque in the Golan Neighborhood. But despite this small squabble, the US military maintained that resistance in Fallujah was being contained at a manageable level. Captain Robert Bodisch announced that in addition to the dozens of insurgents captured that day alone, 300 individuals had also surrendered after the battle near the mosque, and 151 additional individuals were being held by the US forces until they could be cleared of suspicious activity. Clearly the Americans had a case for making the declaration of a nearing victory in this second battle, even if the final stages of the cleanup loomed very far in the distance.

Official claims of victory in Operation Phantom Fury varied widely by date and content, sometimes contradicting each other and often contradicting the state of affairs on the ground in Fallujah. The first declaration of victory on November 12 came from Prime Minister Allawi, who announced from Baghdad in the early afternoon that "the assault on Fallujah would not last [much longer]." Reports from Washington confirmed this announcement a short time later by declaring the assault to be "terminated." Later, Kassem Daud, Iraqi minister for national security, "reported that the Fallujah offensive had ended successfully."

Although it may seem that these statements represent a fair and clear assessment of victory and success in the battle of Fallujah, they do contradict many of the earlier statements made by the US forces, including the rationale that the battle was initiated primarily to capture al-Zarqawi. In the midst of these declarations of victory from Baghdad and Washington, DC, US troops actually failed to capture al-Zarqawi outside Baghdad, and also missed the capture of his senior aide, Abdallah al-Janabi. Because this man, identified earlier as the main target of the operation, successfully evaded US forces after the close of the second battle, it might be argued that this operation was not a success in the terms of its original objective.

And the battle wasn't over for the insurgents. Following the announcements of victory from the US forces, the insurgents publicly announced that the battle was not over, and in fact, that they had been successful in killing 150 US troops and wounding 270 more. Although Donald Rumsfeld denied this, November 14 saw a rise in combat again in Fallujah, in which 80 insurgents resisted US forces within city limits, and forced the US into brief combat. Although this resistance continued for the next few days, Washington continued to report that the "entire city of Fallujah" was occupied by US forces.

The point here is not that the US was intentionally reporting false information or that the insurgent forces were truly dominating the US forces in the late days of the battle. The point about this lack of clarity on the official end is that without an official victor, an official withdrawal date, and an official agreement by both sides that fighting be considered over, the besieged city remains to this day in a state of uncertainty. To this day all parties involved admit this operation to be one that never had a firm ending. Sources investigating this operation were very scant on the specifics of the military movements on and after November 12, and that elusiveness carried through the weeks, months, and years following the decline of combat in the city.

The insurgents of course, paint an extreme portrait of the terror the US is still inflicting on the citizens of the city, and the US talks about the success in rebuilding that is encouraged by the presence of American forces. Because of this discordance, it's difficult to find reliable sources that present an unbiased account of the happenings in this city any time after November 12, 2004. As I'll discuss, this lack of certainty about the end of this battle led to a continuation of the US presence in Fallujah, and a continuation of the crimes committed therein. This operation, in essence, is still going on. More than four years later.

19. "CLEANING UP": WAR CRIMES, MASS GRAVES, AND AN EMPTY CITY

"Relief consignments, equipment and personnel must be able to pass rapidly and freely if the assistance is meant for the civilian population of the opposing side. This includes medicines, religious items, food and clothing."
—Protocol I, Article 70, Geneva Conventions

"Warring parties must allow the free passage of medicine, food and clothing intended for children under 15."
—Article 4, Section 23, Geneva Conventions

Because of the deplorable number of wounded and injured Fallujans, not to mention the critical lack of water and food and highly unsanitary conditions, the Iraqi Red Crescent requested to be allowed inside the city in order to deliver much needed supplies. These supplies included an emergency medical staff for the main hospital. The Red Crescent was slow, however, in getting a response from the Iraqi government, who claimed they had already sent for fourteen trucks filled with medical supplies and humanitarian aid, along with reconstruction crews and medical emergency teams, to the affected area. The Red Crescent was denied entrance in the assurance that these supplies would reach the needy by the following day, November 13. This promise was not upheld, and the Fallujans trapped inside the city remained with minimal amounts of water, food, and medical supplies in the weeks following the operation. Further worried by this situation, the Iraqi Red Crescent attempted to send more convoys into the city on November 13, 14, and 15, and were denied entrance by the Marines each time. Although the convoys were able to deliver supplies and relief materials to some of the squatters living on the outskirts of the city, those in the most desperate situations inside remained without help. The US forces maintained that these convoys were kept out of the city because continued fighting made it unsafe to allow anyone to enter city limits. This reasoning doesn't mesh with the official statements released between November 13 and 15, claiming that the operation and the violence were over.

Signaling an unofficial end to the active combat of this battle, statistics began to emerge. Not surprisingly, the numbers changed dramatically as the fighting subsided and more victims were discovered. On November 12, allied US and Iraqi forces gave the official number of Fallujan civilian casualties as 22, in addition to 170 wounded or injured. Additionally, Prime Minister Allawi announced that 15 foreigners were arrested by US forces: ten Iranians, one Saudi, one Egyptian, one Syrian, one Jordanian, and one Frenchman. On November 12, counts of insurgents killed during the operations were estimated as high as 1,000, compared to 30 to 40 Marines. Reports released in the weeks, months, and years following the operation disagree the most on the number of civilians killed or wounded in the midst of this battle. In an article published on the one-year anniversary of Operation Phantom Fury in the *Guardian*, Mike Marqusee states that troops who were working in Fallujah following the attack estimated between 4–6,000 dead, most of them civilians, which contradicts with the US claims that 1,000 insurgents were found dead.

In the days following the decline of active violence, Fallujans discovered a gruesome mosaic of death in their cities: bodies of decapitated soldiers littered the streets; a woman's body was found half-devoured by dogs; another mutilated woman's body was discovered missing arms and legs; couples were discovered shot dead in the middle of a loving embrace. Death was as omnipresent in Fallujah as the American soldiers themselves, and this constant sight undoubtedly made life in post-battle Fallujah a terrifying and devastating ordeal.

Although the obvious loss of human life in the city of Fallujah was an emotionally wrenching ordeal for its citizens, Fallujans were also faced with another daunting task: rebuilding the physical structure of their city. The most pressing and immediate problems were lack of electricity, water, and phone service in most of the homes. In a report released by NBC on April 14, 2005, five months after the operation had subsided, only half of the homes not entirely destroyed by the battle had electricity, and phone service was still nearly non-existent. A lack of electricity meant an inability to pump water for the city's water supply. The existing water system had been so heavily damaged by US bombing that 60 percent of the city relied on storing water in tanks. This was problematic because the tanks themselves had been damaged by artillery fire over the course of the battle, and there was still the marked difficulty of obtaining water in the first place.

In the article investigating the first anniversary of Operation Phantom Fury, the *Guardian* reported that Fallujah's compensation commissioner announced that "36,000 of the 50,000 homes in Fallujah were destroyed, along with 60 schools and 65 mosques and shrines." Although numbers were lower immediately following the battle, still the number of Fallujans needing to drastically rebuild their homes was staggering. Several sources say that 32,000 Fallujans filed for compensation from the Iraqi government to rebuild their homes. In an article in the *Washington Post* on April 19, 2005, it was reported that projects to rebuild the city would cost upwards of $100 million, and would include rebuilding the sewer and electrical systems, schools, police stations, clinics, and wastewater treatment plants.

The US government defended their use of damaging techniques, saying that houses could only be searched after tanks had brought the walls to the ground and explosives had been used to otherwise unravel the houses—US forces claimed these things had to be done in order to ensure that the houses were not wired with booby-traps or hiding dangerous explosives or weapons caches. This kind of house-by-house searching caused undeniable widespread destruction of Iraqi homes, and it stands to reason that a portion of those homes revealed none of the elements mentioned above despite the reasoning for the precaution.

Destroyed homes were obviously of first concern to the citizens of Fallujah, many of whom were left with no place to stay after the battle's violence had deflated. And very quickly a new concern emerged: finding employment for those who were left within the city limits. According to *Time* magazine, in the midst of Operation Phantom Fury, "at least 900 shops and factories were destroyed or seriously damaged." Green Left reports that 70 percent of Fallujah's residents were employed by factories or workshops just like these, which left a large majority of the city without income. In an article by Ann Scott Tyson in the *Washington Post* in April 2005, an Iraqi construction engineer stated that in his experience working with reconstruction crews, he'd estimate that 85 percent of the Fallujan population was out of work.

The largest problem with reconstructing Fallujah came with the slowness of the recovery efforts. These efforts lagged because US forces were unwilling to loosen security in and around the city. Shops and factories, for example, were not rebuilt because of fears that they would become secret manufacturing facilities for bombs. In Tyson's April *Post* article, the Iraqi engineer laments the fact that many of his hired men were taken away on false arrest, which set his work schedule back by weeks. Similar problems existed with the extra security at checkpoints in and out of the city, which led to delays in supplies and equipment being delivered. Ultimately, the American security grip on Fallujah worked to perpetuate the problems—with no supplies and no workers, recovery could not begin and civilians could not be given jobs. Without jobs and income, there was very little to keep Fallujans from accepting money to join insurgent forces. With no recovery of the city's resources, food, water, and shelter could not be given back to the Fallujans; and without all of those things, the city could not heal from the human suffering they had been through in the midst of the battle. These problems were further compounded by the lack of a central government or ruling authority in Fallujah that could speak on behalf of its citizens, which left the city entirely at the mercy of the occupying forces. In the months following the attack, such groups were set up, but the general disorganization and lack of communication between authorities in the city ultimately did not lead to a solution in this crisis.

In order to survive during this dismal time of lean employment options, Fallujans had only inadequate solutions to poverty to fall back on. Although 32,000 Fallujans registered with the government for compensation for the destruction to their homes (in amounts that totaled just twenty percent of the value of the homes), as of April 2005, NBC reported that only 2,500 had actually received their payments. Those who weren't so lucky were often subsisting on one-time payments issued by the Iraqi or American governments ($100 from the Iraqi government and $200 from the Americans). This compensation was not nearly enough to keep most Fallujans afloat until employment became more stable. Many resorted to selling personal items or borrowing money from neighbors or relatives.

In short, Operation Phantom Fury was not only successful in killing an overwhelming number of rebel insurgents, but also in leaving the city of Fallujah in a desperate, terrible state.

A City in Limbo

Although no one seems to be able to clarify an actual, official end to Operation Phantom Fury, it's important to note both the absence of the media during the event and in the wake of its aftermath. Prior to November 12, when there was a more equal balance of power between the insurgents and the Marines, a relatively decent amount of trustworthy information somehow made it out of Fallujah to be released to the global audience. But after November 12, when the Marines gained primary control of the city, that balance was shattered and it became difficult, if not impossible, to receive accurate, unbiased, and detailed accounts of what was going on within the city walls.

Part of this difficulty came from actions taken by the Iraqi government shortly after the second battle. On November 12, Iraqi authorities in Baghdad reminded all Iraqi reporters that they were required to support the version of events as told by the Iraqi government and not to deviate from that story. If reporters refused to support the government-mandated version of truth, reporters would risk being sent to prison. This harsh ruling came out of Paul Bremer's Iraqi Media Commission, which demanded that media organizations in Iraq refrain from publishing any material that could be viewed as supporting the insurgents or any form of terrorist activity (this included blaming the Americans for anything that occurred during any specific battle). This ruling was possible because the 60-day state of emergency Allawi had declared allowed a suspension of habeas corpus, and because Bremer's free-of-government charter insisted its motive was to prevent government control over media. The other part of the difficulty came simply from the conflict itself—in the last days of the battle, information leaking out of the city was more in the form of verbal attack from one side or the other rather than an accurate, straightforward account of military action. The actions of the government, however, did little to help the situation.

The control that the American and Iraqi authorities demonstrated over the media after the second battle was part of the total picture of occupation. Residents of Fallujah had little control over their own lives; in fact, many described the city as "a giant prison." Fallujans who had fled the war-torn city were allowed reentry only if wearing government-issued IDs. When these cards were issued to city residents, Marines took retina scans and prints of all ten fingers. These fingerprints and retina scans were eventually to be used to build a database of potential insurgents in order to provide additional security. Extra security measures aimed at preventing any insurgent uprisings continued far after the assault was over. NBC reported as late as April of 2005 that an overnight curfew remained in effect, and that the passengers of every single vehicle entering the city were still being strip-searched before being allowed entrance.

US troops justified this heavy security by reasoning that without it, the insurgents would begin to retaliate. Although some residents of the city reported feeling safer with the extra security measures, the prison-like atmosphere was not denied: residents were unable to attend religious services because of the curfew, were not allowed to own their own weapons, and were in many cases not allowed to visit hospitals except in the case of an emergency, and even then only with a government official.

Because of the government gag rule on journalists who were present during or received information about the events that took place during Phantom Fury and the virtual lockdown of the city that has existed from the end of the operation until the present, a certain amount of suspicious mystery surrounds what goes on within city limits. Many TV stations centered in the Middle East that have attempted to get information from those coming from or going to Fallujah have been largely unsuccessful. The residents from the city who do travel outside city limits are very close-lipped about what's happening in the city, and instead make general references to the negative implications of the US occupation of Iraq as a whole. Most people who have spoken to these residents agree that they are quiet not because they have nothing to say, but because they fear not being allowed reentry to the city, and therefore risk losing contact with their families and losing their homes.

The people in Fallujah are denied personal freedoms, which they had always enjoyed and they have a right to, and without journalistic coverage of they city, we as the global audience have lost the privilege of hearing about the crimes that are possibly being committed there, and trying to stop them.

The Debate over White Phosphorous

One of the most heated debates that emerged after the second battle of Fallujah was the controversy over whether or not the US had engaged in the unlawful use of white phosphorous (WP), a deadly chemical weapon. Because of its extremely harmful and sometimes deadly effects on human beings, use of WP during battle (when specifically aimed at "civilians or civilian objects") has been banned by the UN since 1980. The harmful side affects caused by incendiary devices like WP are listed in Article 2, Protocol III of the United Nations Convention on Certain Conventional Weapons: "death, harm or temporary incapacitation to humans or animals through their chemical action on life processes."

It's obvious why rumors of the use of a chemical known to cause this kind of human suffering sparked a worldwide clamor for investigation. In response to the allegations in the aftermath of the second battle, Iraq's acting human rights minister, Narmin Othman, put together a group of investigators to determine whether the US indeed used these materials in a manner intentionally harmful to Fallujan civilians, or whether the use of WP was simply military in nature. The largest part of the investigation was to include a close examination of civilians injured or killed in the battle, in order to ascertain the cause of the injuries and deaths. If any civilian deaths or injuries were attributed to WP or other internationally banned weapons such as napalm, there would be cause for further action.

It is important to note, however, that WP is not disallowed from being used for strictly military purposes in wartime. WP is still commonly used as a tool of self-defense: many military groups use it to make it harder for the enemy to see the movements of their soldiers while in combat. The question was whether the US had been within the scope of allowable use or had used it with the intent to harm civilians.

The controversy over WP and its possible use in the second battle of Fallujah was put into motion by a documentary entitled *Fallujah: The Hidden Massacre*, which was produced by the Italian state broadcasting service, RAI. The documentary accuses the US of using chemical weapons such as WP with the deliberate intent of hurting the civilians living inside Fallujah, including women and children. This claim was based on eyewitness accounts, along with the documentation of physical burns and other skin damage on the bodies both of those who had survived and those who had died. The footage in the documentary included testimony from Jeff Englehart, a former Marine who had been in Fallujah during Operation Phantom Fury.

Englehart said, "I heard the order to pay attention because they were going to use white phosphorus on Fallujah. In military jargon it's known as Willy Pete. Phosphorus burns bodies. In fact, it melts the flesh all the way down to the bone... I saw the burned bodies of women and children."

The documentary was full of such damning testimony. After it was released, the global outrage was so strong that it ignited investigations and the US government was forced to explain its behavior. Although the US adamantly denied the use of WP for the purpose of killing civilians, the US freely admitted to using WP during Operation Phantom Fury to confront the enemy. US forces admitted that some artillery guns fired white phosphorous rounds to create a screen of fire that could not be extinguished with water. Even the Pentagon admitted to the use of WP for military purposes. According to Lt. Colonel Barry Venables, WP was used to obscure troop deployments and also to "fire at the enemy." At the same time, the US denied any use of WP outside of self-defense and enemy fire. The US State Department initially claimed that WP shells were used "very sparingly in Fallujah, for illumination purposes. They were fired into the air to illuminate enemy positions at night, not at enemy fighters."

This report was later recanted when firsthand accounts given by soldiers who fought on the ground in the second battle contradicted these claims. The corrected statement read that "White phosphorous shells, which produce smoke, were used in Fallujah not for illumination but for screening purposes, i.e., obscuring troop movements and [according to first-hand accounts published elsewhere]... to flush out enemy fighters so that they could then be killed with high explosive rounds." This correction came as a reaction to firsthand accounts published in a 2005 issue of *Field Artillery* magazine.

Despite these admissions of using WP in finding and defeating the insurgents, the US refused to acknowledge any direct responsibility for using outlawed or banned weapons to intentionally kill or injure civilians. After the above correction was published, the State Department also released a statement reaffirming that "the facts are that US forces are not using any illegal weapons in Fallujah or anywhere else in Iraq." This statement was repeated in a letter written by the American ambassador to London, Robert Tuttle, to the British newspaper the *Independent*. Tuttle emphatically stated: "US forces do not use napalm or white phosphorus as weapons."

Eyewitness accounts suggesting the opposite began to multiply. These accounts came from soldiers who had participated in the battle, reporters who were investigating the claims, residents of the city, and health care workers. The three soldiers responsible for the article in *Field Artillery* magazine offered a detailed account of their experience with WP while fighting this battle.

In the March–April edition of the magazine, the men reported that "WP proved to be an effective and versatile munition. We used it for screening missions... and, later in the fight, as a potent psychological weapon against insurgents in trench lines and spider holes. We fired 'shake and bake' missions at the insurgents using WP to flush them out and high explosive shells (HE) to take them out." This fairly straightforward admission to using WP certainly implicates the US in using the weapon against military targets, but doesn't necessarily implicate US forces for using the chemical against civilians. Critics, however, have contended that US forces could not avoid hitting civilians in an urban setting like Fallujah.

Reporter Darrin Mortensen, working for *North County News*, worked as an embedded journalist during the second battle of Fallujah, and offered another first-hand account of the action. Mortensen told of soldiers being directed to fire WP into areas that were not certifiably cleared of civilian occupation, and he also added that the US forces seemed unconcerned about the possibility of injuring or killing civilians using this particular weapon.

The most compelling evidence pointing to the use of WP by the Americans, however, came from the residents of Fallujah themselves. Much of this evidence was physical: the damage to the bodies of the dead and of the injured. Workers at hospitals in Fallujah reported that during and after the second battle, patients came to the hospital with burned skin, and that some corpses that entered the hospital were entirely melted—injuries that are consistent with the harm caused by WP. Some of those injured or dead with these wounds were insurgents, of course, but there were civilians as well. According to an article published by the *Guardian* on November 15, 2005, many of the doctors who remained in the city amid the fighting reported that civilians came to the hospitals presenting unusual burns. These civilians reported that these burns came from "weird bombs that put up smoke like a mushroom cloud" and they said they watched "pieces of these bombs explode into large fires that continued to burn on the skin even after people dumped water on the burns." One doctor said he had "treated people who had their skin melted." An article published in the *Washington Post* confirmed this reality: "Kamal Hadeethi, a physician at a regional hospital, said, 'The corpses of the Mujahideen which we received were burned, and some corpses were melted.'"

Despite the mounting evidence from eyewitness accounts, the debate over whether the US forces had committed unlawful acts continued. The US went on emphatically denying breaking the international treaty against the use of WP on civilian targets, and called rumors of the US using these weapons "myths." The official statement released by the State Department after the initial accusations reads as follows: "The United States categorically denies the use of chemical weapons at anytime in Iraq, which includes the ongoing Fallujah operation. Furthermore, the United States does not under any circumstance support or condone the development, production, acquisition, transfer or use of chemical weapons by any country. All chemical weapons currently possessed by the United States have been declared to the Organisation for the Prohibition of Chemical Weapons (OPCW) and are being destroyed in the United States in accordance with our obligations under the Chemical Weapons Convention."

Much of the denial from the US stemmed from the fact that WP shells are not "outlawed" in a broad context, and that the accusations came from a misunderstanding that the public had of the limitations of the weapons' use. Peter Kaiser, a spokesman for the Organisation for the Prohibition of Chemical Weapons (OPCW), supported the idea that the WP used by the United States in certain parts of Phantom Fury was not a violation of the international treaty that banned such weapons. Kaiser stated that the burns caused by WP were thermal rather than chemical and as such are not prohibited by the treaty. There was also some contention on the point of the wounds sustained by Fallujans that appeared to be caused by WP—those skeptical of the footage shown in *Fallujah: The Hidden Massacre* argued that exposure to the environment of the battle was bad enough to cause the kinds of wounds seen on the dead bodies, and that WP should not be seen as the undisputed cause.

The US also claimed that the general public was confusing Operation Phantom Fury with other operations that used chemicals similar to WP and napalm, and claimed that several websites were continually publishing erroneous accounts of proceedings in Fallujah during Operation Phantom Fury. On the whole, the US blamed the rumors on miscommunication. This accusation had some truth to it—and the US forces themselves were partly to blame. Initially, the US had made very emphatic denials about using WP as anything other than a device to illuminate the enemy's location. These denials came from the US Embassy in Rome, from the State Department, and from American ambassador to London Richard Tuttle, who in his letter to the *Independent* claimed WP was not used as a weapon against "human targets," including insurgents (though that would be lawful).

The story was changed following the published eyewitness reports in *Field Artillery* magazine. After the published article, the State Department was forced to admit that WP was used to target insurgents in certain situations. This constant changing of the facts did not help American credibility. Instead, this miscommunication made it much more difficult for the global audience to trust American denials on the use of WP to harm civilians inside the city.

The Aftermath of Deceit

"The essence of Government is power; and power, lodged as it must be in human hands, will ever be liable to abuse."

—James Madison

Once the dust had settled from the second battle of Fallujah, many truths came to light about the intentions of the US government in launching the campaign, and about the practices of the troops while engaged in the battle. American objectives were fairly solidified by November 10: American forces were in control of most of the city. The insurgents were holding their ground pretty well, but the resistance was indeed trapped in small, isolated pockets. Insurgent movement had been hindered significantly by the American forces, and their maneuverability was almost completely lost. "There are groups numbering from five to thirty," General Natonski reported. American forces claimed to be merely "cleaning up" by November 10.

Because the American objective was close to being achieved, military leaders felt relaxed enough to reveal their plans for the future and their original intentions for the city of Fallujah. Bush administration civilian and military leaders seem to think that one needs excuses and justifications only to start something horrific, but once started, it needs no logic other than momentum. As James Madison reminds us, if those in power fall privy to human emotions such as the need for revenge, the ultimate result is the abuse and oppression of others. Power in the hands of an administration that put no stock in following through on its promises had devastating effects on the citizens of Fallujah.

The Bush administration showed that they believed the original justifications for armed combat did not matter many times. The invasion of Iraq is the most notable of such instances. Once the justifications for invading Iraq were exposed as hoaxes, the Bush administration was even more obligated to stay in the region; a sudden pullout would be clear humiliation. That kind of twisted reasoning seemed perfectly acceptable to Bush and his supporters. Fallujah was no exception to this logic. Once Fallujah was about 70 percent under American control, Major General Richard Natonski felt comfortable enough to let some of the truth out, confident that the troops would stay in place.

On November 11, in the middle of the battle, the *Michigan Daily* published an interview with Natonski. The article began by reminding the reader of the earlier failure of US forces: "In April, 2,000 Marines fought for three weeks and failed to take Fallujah from its insurgent defenders." Then the *Daily* quoted Natonski as saying, "Maybe we learned from April; we learned we can't do it piecemeal. When we go in, we go all the way through." What US military commanders apparently learned was to send six times the number of troops. They learned they needed more than twenty different types of swarm aircrafts to pound the city before and during the assault. They learned that they needed unconditional permission to commit any atrocity in order to completely subdue the city. War crimes couldn't be committed "piecemeal." Committing these crimes in a piecemeal fashion would mean reporters would stick their cameras, microphones, and noses in every time a horrendous act was committed by US forces. Natonski said, "We had the green light this time and we went all the way." "All the way," indeed.

Natonski's statements suggested that throughout the Bush administration, there was tacit approval of the crimes against humanity that were committed in Phantom Fury. As mentioned earlier, Bush and other officials did "final review of battle plans." Rumsfeld and General Myers reportedly "monitor[ed] the preparations and updated combat reports." At least these three men, and likely many others, were directly and personally responsible for the war crimes committed in Phantom Fury. Everything was done according to the plans that the three men supervised. The *Michigan Daily* went on to say, "Battle planning began in September [2004]… hundreds of other US military and civilian planners designed the overall effort."

And what did Natonski think of his troops' atrocities and the senseless bombardment of the city during Phantom Fury? He called it a "flawless execution of the plan we drew up. We [were] actually ahead of schedule."

What about the excuse to invade the city? What about the presence of al-Zarqawi, Omar Hadid, Abdallah al-Janabi, and other "foreign fighters"? When asked about them, Natonski replied, "We never expected them to be there. We're not after Zarqawi. We're after insurgents in general."

I remember reading the article and thinking that I had never seen people in such high power lie so obviously and so boldly, and then have the audacity to tell those lies to the global public—a global public that neither cared for nor endorsed its policies.

The Dangers of Bush's Ethno-Sectarian Game

Allawi would have to pay a high price for playing such a big part in Bush's game, including supporting his pitting Iraqi sects and ethnicities against one another. Bush, as discussed earlier, felt it was perfectly fine to have a force made up of Shiites and Kurds attacking Sunni Arab Fallujans. If Bush was too shallow to educate himself about the delicate and dangerous balance between Iraq's ethnicities and sects, Allawi might have tried to advise him. To some extent, it's understandable that Bush didn't see what a gross mistake he was making. Allawi, however, is an Iraqi; he had no excuse for not understanding that the make-up of Iraqi troops was bound to inflame sectarian and ethnic animosities.

The London-based *Al-Hayat* newspaper interviewed Shaikh Mahdi al-Sumaiday on November 11, 2004 regarding these cultural conflicts. Shaikh al-Sumaiday is one of the leading figures of the Salafi movement in Iraq.[2] The article quoted the shaikh as saying, "I am absolutely certain that Ayad Allawi has declared war on Sunnis." He also accused Ali Sistani, an influential Iranian religious Shia leader who has been residing in Iraq for decades, of playing along with Allawi. He said, "Sistani's silence in regard to what's happening in Fallujah is a reflection of his support for this operation."

Shaikh al-Sumaiday called upon religious Shia leaders in Hawza, the main educational and religious institution in the Shia hierarchy, to issue an Islamic edict that prohibited Shiite soldiers from fighting against Fallujans. He revealed that talks between Sunni and Shia religious leaders had been held to formulate a common stand against crises that could bring the two sides closer. Al-Sumaiday also accused Allawi of having had no interest in negotiating with Fallujans to begin with and wanting to start the operation to, "use the same methods Saddam Hussein used to oppress Iraqis," as he put it.

Shortly after al-Sumaiday's statements were published, US forces encircled the Ibn Taymiyyah[39] Mosque in Baghdad. The siege lasted several hours, and the end result was that al-Sumaiday, several of his supporters, and the mosque guards were arrested. That was the second time al-Sumaiday was arrested by the Americans (the first was several months earlier).

US forces issued a statement the following day, November 12, saying Iraqi National Guards supported by US forces had detained 3 imams and 23 suspects during a search operation for weapons at a mosque in western Baghdad. It is noteworthy to mention that in a war-plagued country, virtually everyone has a weapon of some kind, mostly pistols and sometimes more. War-torn countries are nearly completely lawless, and every political or religious institution with any weight has several armed guards keeping a perpetual eye on the institution. The Ibn Taymiyyah Mosque was not alone in this. The entire country was like that. The search, then, seemed less about weapons and more about limiting al-Sumaiday's freedom of speech.

Al-Sumaiday was not the only one arrested. Several Sunni scholars and religious leaders who openly opposed the assault on Fallujah and opposed Allawi's traitorous actions were also arrested. US forces raided the house of Dr. Harith Aldhary, the secretary general of AMSI the same day they arrested al-Sumaiday. Aldhary had openly denounced the American assault on Fallujah and called for boycotting the upcoming Iraqi elections. Other Sunni religious leaders were arrested for their denunciations of the assault on Fallujah. The excuse was almost always the same: carrying weapons. In a country where everyone carried weapons.

Meanwhile, Shia religious leaders, most notably Ali Sistani, were left unharmed. Their guards had weapons of a caliber far beyond what's needed for self-defense, but Allawi left them alone: they supported the operation against Fallujah. The only exception was Muqtada al-Sadr. As a young, inexperienced Shiite leader with a rebellious mindset, he didn't know how to play the game as elders such as Sistani played it. He fought against the occupation as hard as he could. He didn't, in the beginning at least, get involved in the sectarian game. He wasn't helping Bush with his divide-and-conquer plan. He wasn't trying to instill sectarian hatred in Iraqi society. So, he too was a target for the crackdown.

For many Sunni leaders, both religious and political, the ethnic-sectarian Kurdish–Shia make-up of the Iraqi force that attacked Fallujah was a sign of sectarian and ethnic power-mongering. The fact that not a single Shiite preacher, clergyman, imam, or scholar issued an Islamic edict to prohibit, or at least discourage, his followers from participating in attacking Fallujah, was a sign of sectarianism as far as Sunni leaders were concerned. Shia leaders simply went mute about the assault. It was as though it were taking place in Timbuktu. That was the last straw, breaking any trust between Shia and Sunni leaders. Shia leaders appeared to be condoning the slaughter of Sunni Arab Fallujans. Thanks to the Bush–Allawi coalition, sectarian tension was brewing again.

War Crimes

"Persons taking no active part in the hostilities, including members of armed forces who have laid down their arms and those placed hors de combat (out of combat) by sickness, wounds, detention, or any other cause, shall in all circumstances be treated humanely…"

—Common Article 3, Geneva Conventions

Compared to the war crimes committed during Operation Vigilant Resolve, the atrocities committed by American forces during Operation

Phantom Fury were much worse. A complete cover-up of the crimes committed in the second battle was impossible given their scale, but the Bush administration came up with a workable solution: pass the blame to any of the other parties involved in the conflict.

A deliberate attempt was also made by American authorities to make these atrocities appear to be isolated incidents rather than a pattern of many equally reprehensible crimes. This approach had been already employed in the Abu Ghraib scandal. In this situation, a few soldiers were used as scapegoats by the Department of Defense to cover up for the abusive treatment of prisoners that occurred on a much larger scale.

In the case of Fallujah, an incident that took place on November 13 was isolated as the single demonstration of human rights violations during the conflict. In this episode, a soldier was caught on film shooting a wounded, unarmed Iraqi who was taking shelter in a mosque. *USA Today* reported on November 16 that the "dramatic footage was taken Saturday by pool correspondent Kevin Sites of NBC television, whose report said the man who was killed didn't appear to be armed or threatening in any way, with no weapons visible in the mosque."

In the footage, a Marine enters the mosque and examines an unarmed, wounded man.

"He's fucking faking he's dead!" the Marine shouts as he looks at the defenseless man.

Other Marines join the examination and concur, "Yeah, he's breathing."

The first Marine responds with another shout, "He's faking he's fucking dead!"

The Marines fire at the wounded man, killing him instantly.

One of them is heard saying, "He's dead now."

Sites was also quoted in this article as saying that three other wounded Iraqis were killed in the same fashion at the same mosque.

Of course corporate mercenaries were the first to defend the crime after it was received with public contempt. Charles Heyman, a senior defense analyst with Jane's Consultancy Group in Britain, defended the Marines' actions. Heyman maintained that the wounded man could have been concealing a firearm or grenade. "In a combat infantry soldier's training, he is always taught that his enemy is at his most dangerous when he is severely wounded. If the injured man makes even the slightest move, in my estimation they would be justified in shooting him."

Fellow Marines also justified their partner's crime. It was claimed that this incident was a result of "combat stress," an intense mental pressure that forced the Marines to murder the wounded man in cold blood.

When interviewed about the murder, Lance Corporal Christopher Hanson of the Marines said, "I can see why he would do it. He was probably running around being shot at for days on end in Fallujah."

Other Marines showed their true colors with racist statements that painted Iraqis or Fallujans with a wide brush: "I would have shot the insurgent too. Two shots to the head," said Sergeant Nicholas Graham. "You can't trust these people."

The footage of the incident sparked violent outrage across Iraq. Iraqis described the incident as an indisputable example of the war crimes routinely committed by US forces during this conflict.

"If they are capable of doing this in front of the camera, then imagine what they have done behind it," said Niran Mohammed, an Iraqi woman who was quoted by the *Los Angeles Times* on November 17. Mohammed added, "It goes to show that [Marines] are not any better than the so-called terrorists. Their true intentions are getting clearer by the day."

Alistair Hodgett, an Amnesty International spokesperson, declared that, "If indeed this was a deliberate shooting," then it undeniably fit the definition of a war crime.

This particular episode was the only one that hit the headlines all across the world. Without a real, free televised media presence in the city, the bulk of the war crimes committed during the second battle of Fallujah went unreported. The United States was thus allowed the luxury of claiming this episode was one that occurred in isolation and could thus be easily dismissed.

Crimes against Medical Staff

Operation Phantom Fury began as an attack on the Fallujah General Hospital, as mentioned earlier. In and of itself, an attack of this sort is a massive violation of human rights, and goes against the rules of the Geneva Conventions as well as the rules of human decency. But this attack on the Fallujah General Hospital was not the end of the American crimes against medical facilities. In fact, throughout the operation, the targeting of hospitals, medical staff, and the wounded seemed to be central to the planning and execution of the mission. The purpose of attacking hospitals and clinics was to "hide the true numbers of casualties amongst Iraqi civilians and American combatants," the British journalist Steve Nicolas wrote in the *al-Watan* newspaper on November 15, 2004.[40]

Quds Press News Agency, which broadcasts from London, published a report on November 9 that detailed the attack on the General Hospital that took place on the first day of the operation and the subsequent complications that followed. The correspondent responsible for this report quoted Dr. Muhammad al-Jomayli, a doctor at the Fallujah General Hospital, as saying, "American forces and the Iraqi National Guard attacked the General Hospital and arrested all surgeons who work there. There is not a single surgeon now left in the city. They're all locked up. No one can perform urgent ER duties here that require any surgery, and most cases require surgery!"

Dr. al-Jomayli added, "They kicked the patients out of their beds and hauled them in military pickup trucks. They ravaged and destroyed just about everything in the hospital, and they even shot one of the doctors for no reason at all. The American forces went at it attacking and beating over 20 wounded people and arrested them while a gang of Iraqi National Guard thugs mugged the hospital personnel. It was a blatant armed robbery, and they took some of the hospital's assets and all of its money."

Dr. al-Jomayli also reported that there was no electricity or water available at the hospital, a factor that complicated the job of the doctors even more. Medical supplies and medicine were also very limited. He said doctors were using pillowcases in place of gauze. These pillowcases fell seriously short of medical sanitation standards because of the lack of water. He pleaded to humanitarian organizations and the Iraqi government to secure the bare minimum needed for the operation of at least one hospital in the city.

Some of the crimes against the medical staff and facilities of Fallujah were recorded by Fares al-Dulaimi, an Agence France-Presse reporter. Al-Dulaimi had refused to heed the orders of the Marines to leave the city before the onslaught of Operation Phantom Fury. Al-Dulaimi managed to stay in Fallujah until November 15. When he eventually left the city, he barely escaped with his life. When he reached safety, he wrote an extensive report, "The Diaries of a Journalist under Fire in Fallujah," which AFP published on November 16. In this report, al-Dulaimi writes about an incident he witnessed on Wednesday, November 10:

> In the Educators' Neighborhood, the bombing didn't spare a single house. Holes in the ground were all over the sidewalks… Even the medical centers were targeted. The General Clinic[41] had been bombed a few hours before, and the wounded were left bleeding to death.

At al-Jazeera, we had our own eyewitness report. On November 12, al-Jazeera managed to contact a doctor named Ali Abbas, the only survivor of yet another medical care center bombing in Fallujah. Dr. Abbas provided a phone interview for our news bulletin.

"We as doctors can't do our job if we're targeted at the workplace," Dr. Abbas said. "Bombing people in their own houses doesn't seem to be enough for these forces. No, they're... bombing the hospitals. I am the only survivor in our clinic. All of my staff has perished. It is no longer necessary for the wounded to come to clinics because they know they're going to get bombed there too along with doctors and nurses. The wounded are now being left to bleed to death because they can get bombed in their vehicles or ambulances on the way. Even if they make it alive, once they're in a hospital then their chances of being bombed are even higher. There are mounds of corpses littering the streets, and we can't do a single thing about it as doctors."

How is it possible to carry out deliberate attacks on hospitals, clinics, medical facilities, and medical personnel and claim to have committed no war crimes? These acts were not singular war crimes, and they were not committed just by one or two random members of the US forces. These were crimes planned with a specific purpose, approved by powers very high up in the US chain of command, and systematically carried out for the sole purpose of taking human lives.

Civilians Murdered in Cold Blood

Fares al-Dulaimi's report also speaks of corpses littering the streets of Fallujah during the worst days of Operation Phantom Fury. Fares writes:

> The smell of death was everywhere. I could see a countless number of dogs and cats feasting on decomposing corpses in the street. I returned Thursday night to the Andalus Neighborhood and stayed in an open house several families used for hiding because their houses had been bombed. I couldn't sleep a wink because there were wounded and hungry children crying all night and mothers crying and wailing over their dead children.

Fares recounts his journey attempting to leave the next day:

> I moved from one house to another hoping to find a way out of the city. In one of the houses, I found corpses of four men who'd been shot in the head. So I ran away trying to get away from the bloody scene as fast as possible, but a woman's cry stopped me. A woman cried from an

adjacent house. I followed the cries and the weeping to the source. I found a mother with her twelve-year-old daughter and a ten-year-old son who'd been wounded in the shin. Next to them, three adult and teenage male family members lay dead. The woman told me the Marines barged in quick, killed the three men, shot at the boy, and ran out as quick as they'd come in. They didn't bother talk to anyone or ask about anything. They just killed any adult male they could see.

On November 15, the Associated Press cameraman in Fallujah, Bilal Hassan, reported that all over Fallujah he had seen dead and wounded bodies in the streets, laying side by side, and with no one to bring assistance, the wounded were left to bleed to death.

Hassan said that civilians who tried to flee the city were turned back by the Marines. "The Marines started firing randomly at civilians' houses, so I figured I'd better run out of my own," Hassan reported. Hassan's house was indeed fired at and bombed after he fled. He described the Golan Neighborhood where he once lived, "It is now the Rubble, Debris & Death Neighborhood. It's not the Golan Neighborhood anymore."

He concluded his narrative, "The most gruesome thing I had seen there was the death of an entire family of five individuals. That family was trying to cross the Euphrates to run out of the city, and choppers just mowed them down with a shower of bullets from the air."

Of course children were fair game for the Marines. In other reports, a twelve-year-old boy named Alaá Barham, his brother, and his two-year old cousin were also killed by bombs.

Journalists reported that Alaá's mother was holding her little nephew's bandaged arm, asking, "Is this two-year old toddler also a follower of al-Zarqawi? Is he a foreign fighter too?"

Fares al-Dulaimi, Bilal Hassan, and other journalists continued with their description of the bloody scenes they witnessed in the doomed city.

We must pause and ask ourselves: if intentionally detaining, wounding, and killing all adult-age males, senselessly slaughtering an entire family in broad daylight, and widely denying medical treatment to a population in need doesn't count as genocide, what does? If these acts are not defined as genocide, then I have to wonder who in their sane minds would strip them of the title of "war crimes."

Mass Graves for Mass Murder

US forces estimated the casualty count of Iraqis in the Golan Neighborhood alone to reach at least 600. Because so many civilians had been killed and the Marines wished to cover up the massive slaughter, the Marines found themselves resorting to digging mass graves—something that had been common practice during Saddam's reign. Countless eyewitness reports came into the al-Jazeera office from survivors who managed to make it out of the city later on. Eyewitnesses reported the use of bulldozers for the purpose of digging mass graves and for transporting the corpses to the gravesites.

Reports of this kind of behavior were not al-Jazeera exclusives by any means. World news agencies aired reports on November 21 about the use of mass graves not only in Fallujah but throughout Iraq. Some graves were dug in the adjacent town of Saqlawiyah in order to hide the dead.

Of course Marine officials didn't refer to these sites as mass graves. They referred to the digging of mass graves and any other war crimes committed after Operation Phantom Fury as "clean up." Indeed: a massive clean up for a massive crime.

When one official was asked about how long it would take to finish the "clean up," he responded, "It'll take some time. Just think of how long it took us to clean up Ground Zero after September 11th." Just like George Bush, this Marine knew that when caught committing a nasty crime, reminding people of 9/11 frightened them just enough to distract them from the truth.

Mass Displacement

In the period preceding Operation Phantom Fury, all Fallujans were forcefully urged to leave their homes and their city in order to save their lives. US forces maintained that this forced evacuation would work in favor of Fallujans by severely reducing their chances of getting caught in gunfire between insurgents and American forces, and also maintained that those who adamantly demanded to stay behind in Fallujah could be logically accused of working with the insurgent forces. This put those who did not leave the city upon the urging of the Americans at great risk of being shot and killed. The official story from the American forces, then, was that this strongly encouraged evacuation was meant to save the lives of the Fallujan people.

This evacuation, however, did not always work to the advantage of the Fallujans fleeing for safety. Although this urging came from the mouths of the American forces and at face value was an effort to secure the safety of Fallujan civilians, the warning rendered thousands upon thousands of Fallujans refugees. Contrary to what often happens in international conflicts, these refugees did not usually seek shelter in another country, but in other areas of Iraq. The massive number of displaced people created an entirely new humanitarian and political crisis in this war.

Many of the Fallujans who heard the warning to flee their homes before the annihilation of Phantom Fury did so, but the results were often not good. The luckiest of the refugees found homes with relatives on the outskirts of Fallujah or elsewhere in Iraq. This was not unusual, because Fallujah is a close-knit city and family ties are very important to its people; nearby relatives were always willing to open their doors if they could. But some Fallujans had relatives that lived too far away, or had already been killed in conflict, or had otherwise been displaced by the war. Those who were not able to find shelter with family or friends were often thrown to the unsettled landscape beyond the outskirts of Fallujah. This countryside was rough and often nearly uninhabitable, and daily difficulties included finding clean water and edible food. Eventually the Red Crescent, the UN, and other relief organizations set up small camps aimed at helping these refugees, but these groups did not always have enough resources to help everyone in need.

Agence France-Presse reported that on November 12, some of the few Fallujans who chose not to flee the city were ordered to gather in the al-Ferdawos and al-Furqan Mosques. Despite their wish to stay within city limits, all women and children among this group of people were then mercilessly expelled anyway. The males among the group that had gathered in the mosques were detained by US forces and not allowed to flee the city or return to their homes.

One of the refugees forced out of the city, a woman named Saeyah Abdulkarim Obais, fled to Baghdad. Saeyah ended up living in a tent in the Exhibition Grounds, an empty lot normally used for shows, carnivals, and exhibitions. She told a Reuters correspondent about the journey that had taken her from her home in the Golan Neighborhood to the mosques, and finally to the Exhibition Grounds in Baghdad. Reuters quoted her saying, "We were rendered refugees without any mercy [from US forces]. They forced us to the mosque first and then shipped us off to this refugee camp."

Saeyah's story was certainly not atypical of what was occurring in and around Fallujah in the time surrounding the launch of both operations. The Global Policy Forum, which monitors the proceedings of the United Nations, and reports published by the United Nations Assistance Mission to Iraq confirm that of Fallujah's 300,000 people, between 200,000 and 220,000 were displaced by the military operations. The bulk of these Fallujans became refugees after Operation Phantom Fury, which left some observers calling the city "a ghost town."

These estimated 200,000 refugees fanned throughout Iraq seeking shelter in the brutal winter months that followed Phantom Fury. A report compiled by the Emergency Working Group estimated that following this operation, these people spread throughout the following smaller Iraqi cities: Karma, Habbaniya, Amiriyah, Saqlawiyah, Naimyah, Heet, Aana, Rawa, and Hadeetha. Many people also sought refuge in the capital city of Baghdad. Once there, these refugees found shelter in the buildings of Baghdad University, and sometimes in tents on poorly-maintained fairgrounds.

In all of these refugee situations, people found themselves in dire need of humanitarian aid and assistance. In each of these cities, Fallujan escapees were in need of basic human necessities like non-perishable food, baby food and formula, soap, and detergents. Refugees also found themselves without enough blankets, mattresses, or proper winter clothing to keep them from being further injured by the elements while staying in makeshift houses. Even if food was delivered, most of these refugees did not have the means to cook anything. Those organizations who sought to bring relief to these refugees were called on to not only bring food and warm clothing, but also cooking materials. As of December 2004, the city of Amiriyah alone registered 10,970 internally displaced families in need of canned food, detergents, mattresses, and heaters. Another 5,620 families registered need for vegetable oil, cooking stoves, and cooking sets.

In response to the development of this massive humanitarian crisis following Operation Phantom Fury, many different global organizations attempted to remedy the situation. The United Nations Assistance Mission to Iraq reported that as of December 31, the United Nations Higher Commissioner for Refugees (UNHCR) and International Organisation for Migration (IOM) had "begun emergency distributions of food and non-food items to over 36,000 internally displaced families." The non-food items being distributed to those in distress included "3,800 blankets, 2,000 mattresses, 300 tents and 300 cooking stoves for immediate distribution, and made available 30,000 blankets and 2,500 cooking stoves to meet emerging needs." Knowing that these supplies would not possibly provide relief to the overwhelming number of refugees, these groups also planned for the future: "UNHCR is presently replenishing its

Baghdad warehouses by drawing upon the stocks in the region. In the coming days over 80,000 blankets, 11,000 stoves, 8,000 mattresses and 1,000 tents will be transported to Iraq." This report also states that UNICEF provided water, blankets, and boots to these refugees.

Although humanitarian aid was planned for these massive refugee camps, and some refugees did see the benefits of the shipments sent by these generous non-profit organizations, getting this aid to all the people in need proved difficult. The largest roadblock to assistance was set up by the American forces still present in Fallujah and the surrounding areas. Many of the non-governmental workers who asked permission to deliver aid to the affected areas ran into problems with security that either delayed delivery or prevented delivery altogether. This difficulty persisted throughout December, when the refugees were most desperate. Those just outside the city of Fallujah were also often exposed to the same conditions as those inside—including no access to water, electricity, and widespread sanitation problems.

Because of the massive number of refugees evicted from Fallujah prior to Operation Phantom Fury, debate began to focus on how to repopulate the city as well. The American forces had already established their security checkpoints and required Fallujans to be fingerprinted, get a retina scan, and wear a photo ID in order to be let inside city limits. But these measures did not help repopulate the city. In an effort to try to gauge how many people planned to return to Fallujah, the UNHCR contacted 70,000 of those who had fled the city to determine how many planned to return, and what they would need for protection. The UN remained involved in the planning for reentry by working with the Interim Government to try to keep resources moving into the city in anticipation of a large-scale repopulation. Organizations like the Emergency Working Group attempted to monitor this progress within city limits, and continued to encourage humanitarian parties from around the world to get involved in order to ensure that the US follow all stipulations of the Geneva Conventions and any other international laws.

This kind of general inquiry was just the beginning of the process of repopulating the city, however. The dedication these organizations exhibited to preserving the human rights of these refugees did not necessarily guarantee that the American forces on the ground would cooperate. The American forces demanded that before the Fallujans be allowed back into the city, the entire city must be cleared of booby traps and other weapons that could have been planted by the insurgents. Then, the refugees would only be allowed back inside city limits in small groups, and only on a limited basis, to make first assessments of their homes before moving back on a permanent basis. It was clear that the road back home for these refugees would be long, hard, and full of red tape.

Even if these refugees were able to find their way back into Fallujah with the approval of the American government, returning to the city still did not solve their problems. Many refugees would return to homes that were damaged or destroyed entirely, and would thus have no place to live for an undetermined amount of time. Even those who found their houses intact returned to a city without schools or adequate hospitals, and lived in fear of finding unexploded bombs.

AFTERWORD

On May 2, 2008, I found myself standing on the streets of Khartoum, Sudan's capital city. Tens of thousands of people filled the streets along with me, and all of us were eagerly awaiting the release of Sami al-Haj. Sami was the al-Jazeera cameraman who was illegally captured and detained at the infamous Guantánamo Bay prison. Not surprisingly, one of the first conditions the Americans made for the release of Sami was that al-Jazeera would not be present at the airport to film his return. I watched Sami's actual release on television, since I wasn't allowed to get anywhere near the airport that day.

Sami was released just as he was detained: without charges, without a trial or due process, and with very little attention to his basic human rights. No one knew what charges brought Sami into Guantánamo Bay, and the same mystery surrounded his release. Sami had been on a hunger strike for the last 480 days of his detention. He was force-fed by tubes shoved through his nose down his stomach, but he never consumed food intentionally. The trip aboard the US military aircraft from Guantánamo to Khartoum took 20 hours, during which Sami was blindfolded, chained to his seat, and handcuffed. Naturally, he was unable to walk when he was let out of the aircraft. His hands and feet were still cuffed and tied as he was carried by three American servicemen. It seemed as though they regarded him as dangerous despite his extremely fragile condition. They wouldn't undo his chains and cuffs until he was officially handed to the Sudanese authorities.

Although al-Jazeera wasn't present when Sami was released at the airport, other world journalists did their job and the global audience still got to see the incredibly inhumane way Sami was treated during his release. This treatment also demonstrated an obvious display of the severe insecurity the Bush administration was experiencing, even this late in George W. Bush's term as president. They were still afraid of what this man—a man who was half dead anyway, and had never posed a real threat to anyone—might do as they released him. Several Sudanese dignitaries who attended Sami's release told me that the envoys from the American Embassy at Khartoum were clearly embarrassed by Sami's treatment and had to repeatedly turn their eyes to the ground. They expressed how painful it was to watch America's image being tarnished, live, on so many international news networks. The Bush administration had some major cleaning up (and covering up) to do regarding Guantánamo Bay if the Republican candidate in the upcoming 2008 presidential elections was to have any success. Illegal and inhumane detainment of prisoners outside the parameters of the Geneva Conventions was one of the ways George W. Bush had managed to inflict serious damage to the reputation of the US around the world. Now the damage seemed to have caught up with his Republican Party at home.

After Sami was released, he got to see his family and hug his 7-year-old son, who had been only a few months old when Sami was taken to Guantánamo. The scene of their reunion brought all audiences—those who watched in person and those who viewed it on television—to tears.

Sami is finally free, but what will become of our world—which is still not free from war and injustice? How long do we need to remain so enslaved to our love for material goods and power that we allow it to justify wars over possession of oil, land, and other natural resources? How long will we continue to raise our children with the notion that one race, nationality, or religion is superior to another? How long will we perpetuate the idea that this superiority justifies the crimes we commit against each other? What do we need to do to make sure we are not raising children who end up like Saddam Hussein—who forced his power over Kuwait—and like George W. Bush—who wanted to force his power over the entire country of Iraq? How long must we be enslaved by the blind, excessive, and extreme forms of patriotism that enflame our need for revenge—enflame this need enough for us to attack nations that don't pose a viable threat to our security? How long will we drive gas-guzzling SUVs and thus feel justified in doing whatever it takes to secure a constant supply of cheap oil? How long must we remain slaves to our toys, our material possessions, our egotism, our blind forms of patriotism?

If we are to leave this world a better place when we pass from it, these are questions we need to ponder, and ponder seriously. Resolving these problems will not be an effort of one person, one nation, or one political party—rather the resolution will come when all individuals, nations, and politicians come together and rise to the challenge of improving our world for the benefit of all who inhabit it.

NOTES

PROLOGUE

1 The last battle for Baghdad in particular is rumored to have many secrets such as the appearance of Saddam Hussein leading a group of soldiers and participating in combat operations himself, the supposed use of controlled nuclear bombs by the US, the sudden disappearance of the Iraqi army along with their heavy weapons, the use of some unknown weapons with bizarre effects, and other wild claims.

2 Governing Council created by the United States and set in place in Iraq during July of 2003, after the collapse of Baghdad and the capture of Saddam Hussein. The Council lasted until June 1, 2004, and consisted of a group of Iraqi leaders of varying backgrounds commissioned to advise and lead the country until transfer of power to the Iraqi Interim Government.

CHAPTER 1: IRAQ AFTER A YEAR OF OCCUPATION

3 Located in northern Iraq, Mosul is the capital of the Ninawa province and is situated about 250 miles northwest of Baghdad. The city is situated on both banks of the Tigris River, with five bridges linking the two sides.

4 Iraqi political party founded in 1940 as a resistance to occupation and rule by Western countries. The Ba'ath party has roots in Arab socialism. Originally part of the Arab nationalist movement, the Ba'ath party was the ruling party in control of Iraq in 1963, and again from 1968–2003. The party is strongly associated with the reign of Saddam Hussein, and lost control of Iraq when Hussein was ousted from power in the spring of 2003. The US occupation forces banned the Ba'ath party from Iraq in June of 2003.

5 The Arabic edition of Paul Bremer's memoir, *My Year in Iraq: The Struggle to Build a Future of Hope* (New York: Simon & Schuster, 2006) was published by Dar Alkitab al-Arabi in Beirut in 2006.

6 An association of religious leaders representing Sunnis in Iraq formed on April 14, 2003, only 5 days after the fall of Baghdad, during the invasion of Iraq. Known as AMSI for short, the association is not a political party but does have significant political influence due to the high status its members have in religious, academic, and tribal circles. AMSI was founded mostly to unite Sunnis against the occupation and in light of Islamic teachings as Sunni scholars see them. AMSI adopts an anti-occupation, anti-terrorism, and anti-sectarian violence policy. The first policy caused it to come under attack by US forces and the US-installed New Iraqi Government, and the latter got it into trouble with Sunni insurgency groups such as al-Qaeda and Shia militant groups such as Muqtada al-Sadr's militia. AMSI has proven to be extremely instrumental in quieting the Sunni street during crises and equally influential in mobilizing Sunnis against the occupation and terrorism. AMSI maintains that it is not a political party and that one of its main goals is to look after religious institutions and mosques, in addition to saving Iraq from civil war and other ill results of the occupation.

7 The Islamic Party was founded on April 26, 1960, by a group of Iraqi religious patriots who believed in both country-bound nationalism and a religiously based broader brotherhood with the rest of the Muslim world. The party practiced its activities openly at times and secretly at others when the political climate in Iraq didn't tolerate the presence of a religiously based political party. Saddam's regime executed, deported, tortured, and imprisoned several of its leaders. The party moved its activity outside Iraq until the occupation of the country by the US. Although the party is made up of primarily Sunnis, it is known for good relations with other Muslim sects, namely Shia. The party's ideology is fairly relaxed and does not condone extremism in any way, but this also means it sometimes appears a little too pragmatic, perhaps opportunistic, to the general public.

CHAPTER 2: THE CITY OF FALLUJAH

8 Marouf Alrassafi is an Iraqi poet and writer (1875–1945) who contributed to Iraqi and Arab literature a great wealth of sophisticated writing and colorful poetry. In 1933, he moved from Baghdad to Fallujah to flee the capital's clutter and have a more peaceful writing environment. He worked on several books while in Fallujah including some of his masterpieces. He eventually left Fallujah in 1941 when the revolution against the British in Fallujah got too fierce for any peace to remain.

9 Anbar province in Western Iraq shares borders with Syria, Jordan, and Saudi Arabia. Anbar province is Iraq's largest in terms of landmass. Its population is primarily Sunni Muslim.

10 Noor al-Deen al-Zawba'ie was a young construction worker from Fallujah who joined the insurgency and in no time became one of its leaders. He planned, led, and executed numerous operations against US targets. Stories of absolutely mythical proportions circulate Iraq about the accuracy of his planning, the flawlessness of his execution, and the fearlessness of his character. He is believed, by residents of the so-called "Sunni Triangle," to be the man who put their area on the map of insurgency. His death exposed some of these urban legends, as he died while booby-trapping a vehicle to be used to attack American forces. The charges went off prematurely.

11 My book, *Qisat Soqoot Baghdad* (The story of Baghdad's fall) was published in 2004 by Dar Ibn Hazm Publishers, a subsidiary of the Arab Scientific Publishers, Inc., in Beirut, Lebanon.

12 The Chinook is one of the fastest attack helicopters used by the American military today. Chinooks can fly up to 196 miles per hour, and are frequently used to transport troops and replenish supplies.

13 The Black Hawk is another type of assault helicopter put in use by the American military after the 1960s. Unlike the Chinook, the Black Hawk is a medium-lift helicopter that can fly at speeds as high as 220 miles per hour.

14 A movement in Somalia led by warlord Mohamed Farrah Aidid, in response to the American-launched Operation Gothic Serpent, and the US support of the United Nations Operation in Somalia II. Known as UNOSOM II, this UN operation consisted of a military presence meant to increase security in Somalia in order to allow humanitarian aid to be delivered to people experiencing famine and poverty.

CHAPTER 3: MERCENARIES IN THE IRAQI–AMERICAN CONFLICT

15 Based in England, War on Want is an organization that seeks to remedy the problems faced by nations stricken with poverty or experiencing other forms of economic or social difficulty. War on Want seeks to encourage global awareness of the problems facing these countries, and encourages global organizations, as well as the individuals living in these countries, to pursue active solutions to these social problems.

CHAPTER 4: RUMBLINGS OF REVENGE

16 Peter Pace, the US Army general appointed by George W. Bush as the 16th chairman of the Joint Chiefs of Staff, holds the distinction of being the first Marine to be selected for this elite position. He followed US Air Force General Richard Myers.

17 Abu Spinoza is a pseudonym for an economist who is an occasional columnist for Press Action. His essays have appeared in Counterpunch.org and Zmag.org. Based in Arlington, Virginia, and launched in November 2002, Press Action is an online publication of news analysis and commentary [www.pressaction.com].

CHAPTER 5: THE ROAD TO SAMARRA

18 Located in central Iraq, Ramadi is about 70 miles west of Baghdad. The capital of the Anbar province, Ramadi has often been the focus of the US occupation in Iraq because it is

one of the strong corners of Iraq's "Sunni Triangle," otherwise known as the "Triangle of Death." Ramadi is also the location of a railroad connection to Syria. Therefore, the US has long suspected this particular city to be a hotbed of terrorist and insurgent activity moving in and out of the country.

19 The Diyala region of Iraq runs along the Iraq–Iran border. Primarily a farming region, this area is known for its proximity to the Tigris and Diyala rivers, and its production of oranges and dates. Nevertheless, half the province's population resides in cities.

20 The Abbasids were a powerful dynasty of Muslim rulers that started in the year 750 with the Prophet Muhammad's youngest uncle, Abbas ibn Abdulmuttalib. It thrived for several centuries and had a distinctively rich culture. Its contributions to the arts and sciences remain unique among world cultures to this day, especially in architecture, interior design, literature, and translations. After supporting a high culture and a great civilization, it eventually ended in 1258 when Hulagu Khan ravaged Baghdad.

21 Al-Mu'tasim was a Muslim ruler born in 794, who assumed the throne in 833. He was a ruler of the Muslim state during the Abbasid era. He was known to be a very proud ruler who did not tolerate the rights of the citizens of his country to be violated. His reign was characterized by several rebellions against the Abbasid rule, all of which were crushed and their perpetrators put on display in a fabulous way befitting the political propaganda rules at the time. He is most famous for the impolite and threatening letter he sent to Theophilos, the Byzantine emperor. Theophilos had just captured a Muslim village on the outskirts of al-Mu'tasim's territory. Theophilos tortured and disfigured several of the village citizens, particularly women, according to Muslim historians. One of these women cried, "Oh, our Mu'tasim" in a desperate plea for help. When news of the woman's words made it to al-Mu'tasim, he sent Theophilos a letter that said, "From al-Mu'tasim, the commander of the faithful, to the dog of the Europeans, let the lady go free or else I will send you an army [that when stretched] would start where I am and end where you are." Al-Mu'tasim then amassed a huge army, defeated Theophilos, and conquered Amorium, which was one of the last sites the Byzantines were trying to hold on to in Asia Minor. Al-Mu'tasim died on January 5, 842, but to this day, his name invokes sentiments of national pride and sovereignty in Iraqis and most other Muslims.

22 Atwar Bahjat was an Iraqi journalist who worked for al-Jazeera as one of its Baghdad correspondents, then moved on to work for the Saudi-based al-Arabiya satellite channel. Because of her cutting-edge reporting, Atwar became one of the most familiar and popular faces on Arab news networks after the occupation of Iraq. Because of her style and popularity, she, her technician, and her cameraman were kidnapped in Samarra and murdered on February 22, 2006, in the aftermath of the explosion that took out the dome of the Shia shrine.

23 The *Thousand and One Nights* is a collection of tales based on myths and folk stories, and often passed down orally between generations, set in a variety of ancient Middle Eastern and Asian countries including India, Persia, Pakistan, Afghanistan, and Egypt. These tales are estimated to have been originated between 800 and 900 CE.

Chapter 6: Dawn Breaks

24 The Soviet–Afghan conflict is considered the last episode of Cold War confrontations between the US and the Soviet Union. The war was waged between the Soviet Union and the Marxist Afghan government on one end and Islamic insurgents backed up by the US, the six Gulf States, and a few other Arab regimes on another end. The war lasted from December 1979 until February 1989 and resulted in the defeat of the Soviets, the destruction of most of Afghanistan, and the creation of numerous militant leaders and organizations, one of which was al-Qaeda, with bin Laden as its leader.

The Bosnian war took place between Croatia and Bosnia & Herzegovina on one side and Serbia, Republic of Srpska, and what is called now Serbia & Montenegro on the other.

The war lasted from March 1992 until November 1995. The parties involved in the war changed their declared goals and alliances repeatedly during the war. It resulted in mass rapes, ethnic cleansing, torture, and attempts at genocide against Muslims in Bosnia.

25 Born in 1950 in Khost, Afghanistan, Shahnawaz Tanai is a communist general who became the minister of defense and chief of army staff in the Soviet-backed Afghan government. He is currently the leader of the Afghanistan Peace Movement and takes an active, but not very popular, role in Afghan politics.

Chapter 7: Day One

26 Cluster bombs, large bombs that can be dropped from the air or launched from the ground, release a cluster of smaller bombs on the target area. The explosion of these smaller bombs can be delayed, which means the people on the ground can fall victim to the bombs long after fighting has ceased. Cluster bombs were made illegal in May of 2008, during the Convention on Cluster Mutions, held in Dublin, Ireland. The international treaty banning the use of these weapons was signed in December of 2008 (but notably, not by the United States, Russia, or China).

27 The city of Kufa about 105 miles south of Baghdad and 7 miles northeast of Najaf. It was founded in 638 as a garrison town by Omar bin Khattab, the second caliph. The city lies on the Hindiyah branch of the Euphrates. It is one of the four Iraqi cities with particular religious significance to Shia, along with Najaf, Karbala, and Samarra. The population of Kufa is about 110,000.

Chapter 8: Day Two

28 Tariq Ayoub, an outstanding Kuwaiti-born Palestinian journalist, was born on June 29, 1968. After graduating from high school in Kuwait, he obtained a B.A. in literature from the University of Calcutta, India in 1990. He then got a master's degree in English literature and journalism. He worked for the French WTN and the APTN. He joined al-Jazeera in 1998 and was killed by a direct missile attack by American forces on al-Jazeera's Baghdad bureau on April 9, 2003. His killing was condemned by international media because it did not seem like an isolated or unintentional incident. He was not the only journalist that the American forces murdered on their way to conquering Baghdad.

29 Saqlawiyah is a town about eight miles northwest of Fallujah on the highway that connects Fallujah to Ramadi. Students going to college in Fallujah often live in a dormitory in Saqlawiyah. The Marines called it "Saq" for short.

Chapter 9: Day Three

30 The AC-130 gunship is a heavily armed airplane used primarily by the US Air Force since its start during the Vietnam War. This airplane is armed with side-firing power and equipped with sensors that allow the pilot to detect the difference between benign ground forces and the enemy target. The US Army uses the AC-130 gunship to support groups on the ground and perform premeditated operations against specific targets and also to defend US Army facilities.

31 Captain Christopher J. Sullivan, 29, of Princeton, Massachusetts, died January 18, 2005, in Baghdad, Iraq, when an improvised explosive device detonated near his parked vehicle. Sullivan was assigned to the First Battalion, 5th Cavalry Regiment, 1st Cavalry Division, Fort Hood, Texas.

32 The F-16 Fighting Falcon is a versatile, lightweight attack plane developed to give the pilot better visibility, the ability to sustain higher winds, and the power to make greater turns. The F-16 was developed for long-range fighting, and has the advantage of large radar systems and the capacity to attain high speeds. The Fighting Falcon is set to be replaced by

the US Army in 2011, but for now remains a common plane for the armies of the US and 25 other countries around the world.

CHAPTER 10: DAY FOUR

33 William Kristol (born December 23, 1952 in New York City) is a Republican pundit and strategist. He is the son of Irving Kristol, one of the founders of the neoconservative movement, and Gertrude Himmelfarb, a scholar of Victorian literature.

CHAPTER 12: THE FINAL DAY OF THE SIEGE

34 In Islam, believing in one's fate and destiny is the last of the six pillars of faith: Believing in God, the angels, all the prophets of mankind, all the Holy Scriptures and testaments, judgment day, and fate and destiny, ill or well. Believing in fate and destiny implies that when an uncontrollable external act of fate happens in one's life, one should accept it regardless of it being positive or negative. Despairing when one is struck by a tragedy, questioning fate, uttering the wishes to avoid one's fate is prohibited. Therefore, when a Muslim is hit with a calamity out of his control, aside from working on alleviating it as much as possible, he or she is supposed to say, "*It's God's destiny, and He shall do what He pleases.*" This supplication is intended to end negative thoughts and instill the idea that God knew of this calamity and knew that it may hold some good in the future. In Islam, accepting one's fate is a sign of accepting God's infinite wisdom.

CHAPTER 13: BUSH'S WAR ON AL-JAZEERA

35 Seymour Hersh, the Pulitzer prize-winning investigative journalist and author, was born on April 8, 1937. He is credited with exposing such important political scandals as the cover up of the My Lai massacre during the Vietnam War and mistreatment of prisoners at the Abu Ghraib prison during the Iraq war. Hersh has also been the five-time recipient of the George Polk Award for Magazine Reporting and received the National Book Critics Circle award for his 1983 exposé, *The Price of Power: Kissinger in the Nixon White House.*

CHAPTER 14: A CONFRONTATION OF WORDS

36 The British politician Anthony Neil Wedgwood Benn (b. April 3, 1925) is the Labour Party's second longest serving member of parliament. He served as minister of technology, secretary of state for industry, and secretary of state for energy. He's a distinguished writer, and has published eight volumes of his diaries in addition to other books and essays. He's a peace activist and was voted twelfth in the list of "Heroes of Our Time" compiled by the *New Statement* magazine in 2006.

37 Salafism, a school of thought within Islam, is a leading school among Sunnis and the official school of the Kingdom of Saudi Arabia. Salafis are known in Western literature as "Wahabis" and their school of thought is known as "Wahabism," but these terms are considered derogatory and defamatory by Salafis. They never refer to themselves as "Wahabis." Instead, their adversaries use this term against them—intentionally in the case of some other Muslim sects, or out of ignorance, in the case of many Westerners. The Salafi school is characterized by a refusal to compromise on principles, which can make it appear radical to observers even though there is nothing in Salafism itself that constitutes radical beliefs.

CHAPTER 18: OPERATION PHANTOM FURY

38 " Cooking off" refers to the time a hand grenade is held on to after it's been armed in order to reduce the time it will take to detonate. This is done to keep your enemy from having enough time to run away.

CHAPTER 19: "CLEANING UP"

39 Ibn Taymiyyah (1263–1328) was a Muslim scholar of Kurdish descent who lived in what is now Turkey. His prolific output of over 600 books on a variety of subjects made him stand out as a distinguished intellectual as his opponents sank into anonymity. He is highly respected in all Sunni schools of thought while bitterly opposed by nearly all Shia. The Salafis derive many principles from Ibn Taymiyyah's books, which is why Shia are more likely to clash with Salafis than with other Sunnis. The mosque named after Ibn Taymiyyah in Baghdad is a Salafi center.

40 *Al-Watan* is a Qatari newspaper that publishes articles contributed by journalists from all over the world.

41 The Fallujah General Clinic is to be distinguished from the Fallujah General Hospital, which is located on the other side of the Euphrates. The Fallujah General Hospital was attacked on the first day of the operation; the Fallujah General Clinic was targeted three days into the operation.

INDEX

A

Aana, 337
Abbas, Ali, 333
Abbasids, 60, 344n20
ABC, 23, 37, 49, 127, 186, 275
Abdul Hameed, Mohsen, 16–17
Abdulaziz Samarray Mosque, 44, 142–144, 145, 147, 160, 302
Abi Ayoub al-Ansari Mosque, 161
Abi Obaida Mosque, 302
Abizaid, General John, 13, 57, 150, 186, 194, 256–257, 270–271, 278, 280
Abo Jamal, Mahmoud Khodar, 188–189
Abo Omar, 70, 81, 82, 83–84, 100, 101, 126, 127, 152–153, 166, 178, 196
Abraham, Abdulaziz. See Abo Omar.
Abu Ghraib, 16, 58–60, 75, 247, 256, 330
Abu Ghraib–Fallujah Road, 185
Abu Hanifa Mosque, 18
Abu Hatem, 157
Abu Spinoza, 53, 343n17
AC-130 gunships, 138, 203, 252, 345n30.
    See also F-16 Falcon Fighting jets;
    helicopters; warplanes.
AD Rendón, 11
Advertising Federation of Lincoln, 11
Afghanistan, 11, 228, 232, 249, 265, 269
Agence France-Presse, 18, 33, 159, 181, 182, 185, 202, 255, 270, 275, 277, 291, 298, 299, 302, 310–311, 332, 336
Ahmad, Imam Sheikh Khaled, 44
Ahmad, Omar Ali, 163
Aikens, Justice, 231
Airport Street, 251
Albo Eesa, 23
Aldhary, Dr. Harith, 14, 179, 329
Algeria, 271
Ali, Hussam, 116, 253
Alilah, Crown Prince Abd, 43
Allawi, Ayad,
    closing al-Jazeera Baghdad bureau, 237–238, 292
    government of, 17–18, 48, 185, 268, 285–286, 288, 327–328, 329
    inauguration, 282–284
    and second battle of Fallujah, 279, 290, 293–294, 314, 317, 320
Allouni, Tayseer, 232
Alrassafi, Marouf, 19, 343n8
Alshaikh, Ahmad, 101, 210, 223
Alshoely, Saeed, 42, 146, 239–240
Amara, 157
Ambush Street. See Baghdad–Samarra freeway.

American troops. See US Armed Forces.
American occupation. See occupation.
Amiriyah, 337
Amnesty International, 331
Amreyat al-Fallujah, 95
Amreyat al-Fallujah Road, 155
AMSI. See Association of Muslim Scholars in Iraq.
Anbar province, 19, 91, 94, 97, 116, 120, 156, 157, 177, 254, 343n9
Anbar School, 154
Andalus Neighborhood, 333
Andoni, Lamis, 226
al-Ani, Dr. Abdulmalik, 189
al-Ani, Dr. Wathiq, 163
Annan, Kofi, 247, 282, 286, 290
Ansar al-Islam, 255
Ansar al-Sunnah, 255
Arbeel, xii
Armed Iraqi Force, 249
Armitage, Richard, 260
Associated Press, 291, 299, 300, 301, 334
Association of Iraqi Journalists, 10
Association of Muslim Scholars in Iraq (AMSI), 14, 44, 116, 142, 146, 150, 151, 158, 179, 279, 285, 299, 329, 342n6
At the Center of the Storm, 156–157
Ayadh, Abdulqader, xii, 178
Ayatollah Khomeini, 64
Ayoub, Tariq, 111, 232, 345n28
Azamiyah, 116, 251
Azar, Jameel, 93, 114, 222
Aznar, Prime Minister José María, 258

B

Ba'ath Party, 9, 12, 14, 154, 342n4
Badran, Nouri, 157
al-Badrani, Dr. Fadhel, 292, 307–309
Baghdad, 70, 91, 141, 188, 314, 337
    bombings in, 191, 192
    Exhibition Grounds, 336
    fall of, xii, 21, 63, 148–149, 342n1
    fighting in, 251–253
    media in, 56, 178
    1958 coup, 43
    protests in, 151, 158, 204
    under occupation, 9, 10, 18, 116, 150
Baghdad–Fallujah highway, 155
Baghdad International Airport, 293
Baghdad–Samarra freeway, 57
Baghdad University, 337
Baha al-Din, Saladin, 12, 15, 17, 25
Bahjat, Atwar, 62, 93, 344n22
Bahjat, Imad, 148
Bahrain, 61
Balad, 54, 56
Balloutt, Jiha, 221

348

Baqubah, 54, 116, 156, 282, 302, 305
Baram, Amatzia, 276
al-Bardisi, Thabit, 222
Barham, Alaá, 334
Barnier, Michel, 282
Barwana, 97
Batalona, Wesley John Kealoha, 40–41
BBC, 186, 236, 261, 270, 271, 282, 292, 301
Benn, Tony, 247, 346n36
Berlusconi, Prime Minister Silvio, 258–259
bin Jassim bin Jaber al-Thani, Shaikh Hamad, 221, 222
bin Jeddo, Ghassan, xii
bin Laden, Osama, 250, 261, 262, 266
bin Thamer al-Thani, Shaikh Hamad, 196, 209, 227, 240
Blackwater USA, 30, 33, 35, 38, 40–41, 202, 257, 277. See also mercenaries.
Blackwill, Bob, 150, 194, 278
Blair, Tony, 145, 149, 156, 220, 221, 230, 232, 267, 282, 290, 292, 310–311
Blumenthal, Sidney, 261
Bodisch, Captain Robert, 300, 312, 314
Bosnian war, 83, 94, 102, 138, 236, 344n24
Boucher, Richard, 222, 311
Bowman, Lance Corporal Joseph, 291
Brahimi, Lakhdar, 150–151
BrandChannel, 221
Bremer, Paul, 13, 33, 265
    account of Mar. 31 mercenary attack, 26, 38, 46
    and cease-fire, 181–183, 202, 278–279
    criticism of, 145, 156
    as governor of Iraq, 17, 48, 144, 150–151, 157–158, 237, 254, 320
    and Fallujah, 21, 93, 115, 117, 141, 143, 275, 276, 280–282
    and al-Jazeera, 144, 185–187, 194, 201
    resignation of, 256
British Association of Journalists (BAJ), 227
Brookings Institute, 244
Buhayrat al-Tharthar (Lake Chatterbox), 6–7
Buncombe, Andrew, 304
Burns, John F., 47
Bush administration, 29, 183, 258, 294, 340–341
    call for cease-fire, 181–182, 206–213
    criticism of, 156–157, 220, 242, 262, 283
    and hostage negotiation, 259
    and Iraq war, 268–271, 326–327
    and al-Jazeera, 184, 217–238
    and media coverage in Fallujah, 36, 38, 42, 276, 277
    military and political goals of, 10–11, 207, 243
    and United Nations, 260
    and war crimes, 60, 330

Bush, George W., 340–341
    and Ayad Allawi, 268
    criticism of, 45–46, 48, 145, 156, 265, 284
    and Fallujah, 28, 149–150, 194, 254, 271, 290, 292, 310–311
    and Iraq war, vii, 256–257, 260–262, 263, 264–271, 282, 299, 305, 327–328
    and al-Jazeera, 184, 194, 220, 229–232
    vows to bring mercenaries' killers to justice, xii, 39, 45, 53
Bush at War, 237
Byrd, Robert, 262
Byrne, Lt. Colonel Brennan, 143, 146, 182, 203, 280

C

Caliph al-Mu'tasim, 60, 65, 344n21
Caliph al-Mu'tasim Mosque, 61, 65
Cambodia, 262
Campbell, Sir Menzies, 267
Capitol Report, 266
Casey, General George, 298, 310
casualties. See first battle of Fallujah; US Armed Forces; US–Iraq war.
CBS, 37, 156, 186
cease-fire. See under first battle of Fallujah; Mansour, Ahmed.
Central Intelligence Agency (CIA), 10, 18, 51, 156, 264
Chalabi, Ahmed, 17
checkpoints. See military checkpoints.
Cheney, Dick, 150, 156, 222, 266, 270, 271
Chomsky, Noam, 52
CIA. See Central Intelligence Agency.
Civil Defense Corps, 254, 278
civil war (Iraq), 264, 283
Clarke, Anthony, 230, 231
Clinton, Bill, 261
cluster bombs, 90, 92, 253, 345n26
CNBC, 266
CNN, 37, 49, 186, 237, 266, 270, 280
coalition forces. See US Armed Forces.
"coalition of the willing," 259
Coalition Provisional Authority, 16, 39, 202, 277, 278. See also occupation.
Coleman, Colonel John, 279
Combined Press Information Center, 71
Control Risks, 35
Conway, Lt. General James, 278, 284, 285
Cook, Robin, 145, 267, 311
Corporate Mercenaries: The Threat of Private Military and Security Companies, 34–35
Council on Foreign Relations, 265
Couric, Katie, 234
CPA. See Coalition Provisional Authority.
crimes against humanity, 55, 327. See also Geneva

Conventions; human rights; war crimes.
curfew. *See under* Fallujah; first battle of Fallujah;
US Armed Forces.

D

Daily Mirror, 149, 229–231
Daily Telegraph, 231, 232, 280, 284
Dallek, Robert, 260
Dam Street (Fallujah), 91, 101, 108, 114, 126, 138,
    139, 152. *See also* Hadeed family, house of.
Darley, Colonel William, 23
Daud, Kassem, 314
Day's Harvest, 42, 43, 96, 97, 123, 146
de Hoop Scheffer, Jaap, 310
DeLay, Tom, 263
Deli, Hussain, xi, xiii, 27, 69
    and first battle of Fallujah, 100, 122, 123,
    126, 147, 153, 160, 162, 166, 177, 195, 196,
    205
    and second battle of Fallujah, 292, 297, 307
Democrats, 45, 46, 262–263, 264, 268, 271
Dempsey, Judy, 39
Department of Defense. *See* US Department of
    Defense.
Desgrosseilliers, Lt. Colonel Todd, 298
detention. *See* Abu Ghraib; Guantánamo Bay;
    occupation.
Dhloeya, 56
al-Din, Sayf, 105, 106, 111, 113, 169, 177, 187,
    196, 204, 210, 211, 212
Director of Central Intelligence (DCI), 117
Diyala province, 54, 56, 116, 156, 344n19
Diyala River, 32, 33
Dobbs, Lou, 13
Doha. *See under* al-Jazeera.
Downing Street memo, 230–231
Duelfer, Charles, 266
al-Duhlaimi, Fares, 332, 333, 334

E

Eaton, Maj. General Paul, 255
Educators' Neighborhood, 96, 163, 199, 332
Eid al-'Adha, 294
Eleventh Imam. *See* tomb of Imam al Hassan
    al-Askari.
Emergency Working Group, 337, 338
Englehart, Jeff, 322
Ereli, Adam, 38
Euphrates River, 7, 75, 97, 148, 161, 192, 297

F

Fahrenheit 9/11, 235
Fairness and Accuracy in Reporting (FAIR), 226
Faisal, Yasser, 288

Fallujah,
    bombing of, 276, 289
    cemeteries, 130, 161, 163
    city of, 19–29, 80, 99, 231, 232, 285, 289
    and curfew, 320
    destruction of, police department, 23
    and farming, 289
    history of, 19–20
    humanitarian conditions in, 277, 319
    insurgent operations in, 20, 21, 49–50, 55,
    115, 286
    mass graves in, 334–335
    media coverage of. *See* media
    old market, 87, 88, 107, 113
    people of, 55, 279–280, 286–287, 294, 317–
    319, 320–321
        leaving city, 288, 290, 303
        as refugees, 335–339
    reconstruction of, 311, 316–319, 338–339
    resistance to US occupation, 20–21, 22–23,
    28–29, 46, 53, 89–90, 114
    schools, 100, 104, 154, 289, 318
    security in, 256, 320–321
    tension in, xii, 42–44, 101
    and tribal community (family importance),
    79, 81, 131, 207, 336
    troops surround, xi, xiii, 69, 70, 76, 93, 102,
    290–291
    under Saddam Hussein, 19–20, 82
    and water system, 317
    and al-Zarqawi, 286–289, 302–305
    See also first and second battles of Fallujah.
Fallujah Bridge, 278
Fallujah Brigade, 280–281, 284–285, 304
Fallujah Central Clinic, 297
Fallujah General Clinic, 332, 348n41
Fallujah General Hospital, 92, 93, 99, 122, 301,
    331–332, 348n41
    occupation of, 103, 277, 297, 332
    See also first battle of Fallujah, hospitals.
Fallujah Protection Army. *See* Fallujah Brigade.
Fallujah: The Hidden Massacre, 322, 325
Farhan, Abdulhamid, 302
Farouq, Omar, 196–197, 198, 199, 203, 205, 206–209
Farqad (driver), 70, 82, 110
al-Faydhee, Shaikh Muhammed, 299
al-Ferdawos, 336
Fey, Tina, 263
Field Artillery, 323, 325
field hospitals. *See* first battle of Fallujah, hospitals.
Filkins, Dexter, 290
Financial Times, 39
first battle of Fallujah, vii, viii, 268, 271
    bombing of houses during, 90, 96, 97, 122,
    123, 163, 236
    bombing of neighborhoods during, 92 102,

111, 129, 139, 144, 147
and burial of dead, 123, 129–132, 134, 161–165, 182, 190, 275, 277
casualties, 102, 114, 122–124, 129, 142, 147, 163, 173–176, 187
cease-fire, 158, 181–182, 187, 275, 276–280
   conditions of, 181, 189, 191, 193, 202, 206–213, 218
and curfew, 92, 93, 96, 103, 123, 146
destruction of mosques during, 141–147, 151
fuel crisis during, 123, 152
and hospitals, 92, 99, 103–104, 122–123, 128, 160, 163–164, 175–177, 188, 195, 199–201
and house searches, 113, 138
humanitarian aid, 159, 170, 181, 182, 183, 277, 279
importance of media coverage in, 85, 146, 148, 151, 162, 166–167, 185–187, 257, 276
industrial area, 101–102, 126, 139, 147, 160
and Iraqi anger toward US, 130–134, 154, 253
medical care during, 99, 103, 122–123, 159
and people of Fallujah, 50, 89–90, 108, 130–134, 154, 188–189, 196, 197, 202
   attempts to escape, 168–175, 188
   interviews with, 88–90, 108, 134, 187
   support for, 159, 179
protests against, 151, 158–159
repeal of gun permits during, 97
religious community response to, 144–145, 179
second anniversary of, 240
start of, xi–xiii, 88–98
store/shop closures during, 88, 101, 105, 113
unidentified bodies, 164
utilities during, 94, 152
withdrawal of Marines, 280
Fisk, Robert, 244
Foreign Affairs, 156
foreign fighters. *See* insurgents.
Fort Bragg, 11
Fort Hood, 254
Fox News, 23, 35, 186, 293
Frame, Captain Bruce, 143
From Washington, 148
F-16 Fighting Falcon jets, 52, 140, 143, 147–148, 182, 187, 203, 252, 345n32
   See also AC-130 gunships; helicopters; warplanes.
al-Furqan Mosque, 302, 336

G
Geneva Conventions, 143, 146, 247, 301–302, 331, 338, 341. *See also* human rights.
Ghanem, Dr. Ahmad, 297
Glanz, James, 290
Global Policy Forum, 336

Golan Neighborhood, 107, 126, 188, 302, 305, 312, 334, 336
   bombing of, 90–92, 97, 99, 122, 123, 147, 199, 298
   fighting in, 108, 148, 154, 184, 187, 314
Goldsmith, Attorney General Lord, 231, 247
Gonzales, Juan, 52
Goodman, Amy, 52–53
Gordon, Michael, 21
Governing Council. *See* Iraqi Governing Council.
Graham, Sargeant Nicholas, 331
Great Disappearance. *See* al-Muntathar.
Green Left, 318
Green Zone, 12–13, 38, 71, 252
   See also al-Qadisya.
Guantánamo Bay, 228, 340–341
Guardian, 33, 38, 156, 230, 261, 263, 265, 267, 317
Guided Caliphs' Mosque, 91, 108, 112, 113, 142, 160
Gulf States, 17, 73, 260
Gulf War. *See* 1991 Gulf War.
gun permits, 97

H
Habbaniya, 337
Hadeed family, 79, 91, 168, 211
   house of, 86, 97, 108–109, 139, 144, 152
   under sniper threat, 139–140, 145, 151–153, 165
Hadeed, Hamed, xi–xiii, 70, 75, 78–79, 100, 153
   and broken satellite transmitter in Fallujah, 105–107, 109
   and first battle of Fallujah, 80–81, 84, 86, 94, 126, 135, 139, 145–146, 166, 169, 176–179, 189, 210, 211
   and news reports, 100–101, 113
   and relatives and acquaintances in Fallujah, 99, 118–119, 167, 196, 204, 207–208
Hadeed, Sami, 167
Hadeed, Zeyad, 167
Hadeetha, 94, 97, 337
Hadeethi, Kamal, 324
Hadid, Omar, 327
al-Hadrah al-Muhammadeyah Mosque, 199, 306
Hagel, Chuck, 264
Hague Conventions, 247
Haj Hussein's Kabob Place, 88, 287
al-Haj, Sami, 228–229, 232, 340–341
Hamas, 51
Hameed, Dr. Mohsen Abdul, 183, 201
Hanson, Lance Corporal Christopher, 331
Hardan, Dr. Ahmad, 201, 277
Hart Group, 35
Hashimi, Aqila, 17
Hassan, Bilal, 334
Hassan, Hamdi Kamel, 163

Hassan, Muhammad Kamel, 163
al-Hassani, Hachem, 158, 181, 183, 185, 201, 202
Harnden, Toby, 280, 284
Hawza, 328. *See also* Shiites.
Al-Hayat, 184, 285, 328
Heet, 337
Hejlik, General Dennis, 289
helicopters, 75, 84, 96, 118, 135–136, 138, 147,
   182, 257, 276, 343nn12, 13
   bombs dropped from, 111, 187
   downed, 94–95, 107, 140, 154, 252, 300, 312
   See also AC-130 gunships; F-16 Falcon
   Fighting jets; warplanes.
Helvenston, Scott, 40
Hersch, Seymour, 237, 346n35
Heyman, Chalres, 330
Hilary, John, 34
Hiran Valley, 33
Hizbullah, 64
Hodgett, Alistair, 331
hospitals. *See under* first and second battles of
   Fallujah.
hostages. *See under* insurgents.
House Appropriations Committee, 268
House Armed Services Committee, 49
House of Commons, 290, 311
house searches. *See under* first and second battles
   of Fallujah; US Armed Forces.
Howaydi, Muhammad, 104
Hue City, viii, 294–295
human rights, 24, 237, 243, 245, 279, 287, 288,
   313, 330, 331
   and children, 128, 164, 168, 169, 171–176,
   222, 285
   and the elderly, 142, 168, 170, 171, 172,
   174, 308
   medical staff, 331–333
   organizations, 227, 309, 337–338
   women, 168, 169, 171, 308
   See also crimes against humanity; Geneva
   Conventions; war crimes.
humanitarian aid, 337, 338. *See also* first and
   second battles of Fallujah.
Hunter, Duncan Lee, 49
Hussein, Saddam, 220–221, 248
   compared with US occupation, 3, 22, 28,
   232, 245, 328, 335
   connection to al-Qaeda, 265–266, 305
   execution of, 294
   invasion of Kuwait, 1990, 94, 138, 341
   reign in Iraq, 4, 9, 32, 82, 148, 192, 280, 281
   treatment of Fallujah, 20
   and weapons of mass destruction, 246, 267,
   299

I

Ibn Taymiyyah Mosque, 328, 347n39
Ibrahim, Abdulkarim Ashour, 163
Imported Iraqi Politicians (IIPS), 183, 185, 237,
   239, 252, 303
Independent (UK), 145, 247, 288–289, 304, 323, 325
industrial area. *See under* first battle of Fallujah.
insurgents, 90, 93, 275, 281, 295, 326
   blamed for chaos in Iraq, 243–246, 248,
   270–271
   casualties, 313, 317
   control of neighborhoods and roads, 251–
   252, 300
   cooperation of civilians with, 50, 117, 154,
   253, 286, 291, 319, 335
   defeat of, 269, 314
   and destruction of mosques, 143, 145–146,
   298–299, 306
   differences of, 154, 304
   filming of, 108–109, 138, 148, 184, 235
   and first battle of Fallujah, 96, 107, 118–119,
   135–136, 155–156, 165, 180, 182, 188, 218
   and foreign fighters, 202, 243, 270, 286,
   304–305, 317
   and Iraqi police and soldiers, 255–256, 284
   kidnapping/hostage taking, 252, 258–259,
   282, 312
   killing civilians, 248
   response to first battle of Fallujah, outside
   of Fallujah, 116–117, 203–204, 254
   revenge operations, 20, 23–24, 49–50,
   54–56, 57
   and second battle of Fallujah, 291–292,
   298–299, 300, 303–304, 305, 315
   submitting photographs to al-Jazeera, 58
   use of snipers, 154–155
International Organisation for Migration (IOM),
   337
International Republican Institute, 11
Iran, 61, 64, 65, 157, 260, 270
Iraq–Iran border, 32
Iraq–Iran war, 32
Iraq Survey Group (ISG), 266, 267
Iraqi Army, 4, 32, 252, 281, 342n1
   leaders of, xii, 148–149
   See also National Defense Agency,
   Republican Guard.
Iraqi Broadcast & Television building, 12
Iraqi Civil Defense Corps, 13, 93, 141
Iraqi Governing Council, xiii, 7, 12, 15–18, 134,
   158, 181, 183, 185, 187, 193, 342n2
   and cease-fire, 199, 201–203, 210, 218, 275
   opposition to Fallujah attacks, 144, 157–158
Iraqi Interim Government, 268, 290, 301, 311,
   318, 319, 320, 338
Iraqi Islamic Party, 158, 176, 181, 183–184, 185,

192, 201, 277, 278, 279, 301, 342n7
Iraqi Media Commission, 320
Iraqi National Guard, 297, 328, 332
Iraqi National Museum, 5
Iraqi police, 6, 141, 157, 202, 254–255, 268, 278
Iraqi political parties, 12–13
Iraqi resources, 3–8. *See also* occupation, oil.
Iraqi Scene, 303
Iraqi security forces, 268, 278, 291, 295, 305, 306, 312, 313
Iraqi Red Crescent, 159, 176, 206, 309, 316, 336
Iraqi Union of Oil Experts, 3
Iraqi Women's Association, 12
Irrigation Project Road, 75, 82
ISG. *See* Iraq Survey Group.
Islam, 44, 346n34
Islamic Army of Iraq, 32
Islamic law, 44
Islamic Revolution (1979), 64
al-Issawi, Dr. Hashem, 301
al-Issawi, Dr. Rafie, 122–123, 160, 162, 177, 187, 201, 297
al-Issawi, Salih, 129
al-Issawi, Dr. Salih, 297

J

Jackson, Gary, 33
Jalalabad, 83
al-Janabi, Shaikh Abdallah, 202, 286, 303–304, 314, 327
al-Janabi, Dr. Taleb, 99, 103–104, 114 , 128
    hospital of, 100, 101, 122, 126, 127
Jane's Consultancy Group, 330
Jarf al-Sakhr, 33
al-Jazeera, vii, 43, 44, 80, 88, 162, 221
    and Ahmed Mansour, 3, 70–71, 76, 136
    bombing of, 220, 224–225, 229–232
    coverage of first battle of Fallujah, 92, 93, 96–97, 101, 114, 120, 123, 128, 129, 136, 139, 144, 146, 148, 155, 163, 173–174, 219–220, 222
    and broken satellite transmitter during first battle of Fallujah, 105–107
    Baghdad bureau, xi–xiii, 56–58, 70, 109, 196, 224
        closing of, 237–238, 239, 292
    casualties in US–Iraq war, 62, 111, 232
    coverage of Ramadi, 116, 253
    crew covering first battle of Fallujah, 70, 79, 159, 194, 202, 206–213
    criticism of, by American officials, 57, 143, 144, 185–187, 217, 221
    Doha newsroom, 129, 178, 191, 195, 219
    and first anniversary coverage of US occupation, xii, 165, 177, 178
    and George W. Bush, 149–150, 217–238

interviews with General Mark Kimmitt, 146, 239–250
linked to al-Qaeda, 228–229, 235
and March 31 mercenary attack, 25–26, 27
and second battle of Fallujah, 306, 307, 333
use of freelance photographers, 56–58
Al-Jazeera This Morning, 100, 199
Jeffery, Simon, 265–266
Jehl, Doug, 264
Jennings, Peter, 235
jihad, 44
Jomaylat tribe, 79, 81
al-Jomayli, Dr. Muhammad, 332
Jones, Richard, 16, 277, 281
Jordan, 70, 73, 110, 155, 271, 293
journalists, 146, 237, 257, 275–276, 334
    deaths of, during US–Iraq war, 62, 111, 127, 232, 289
    difficulties reporting on Fallujah, 319–321
    embedded, 243, 292, 323–324
    and impartial coverage, 233–235, 236
    Iraqi journalists, 9–12, 225–226, 320
    rightwing/neoconservative, 224–226, 227, 234
    role in covering war, 100, 170, 186, 224–225, 241, 293, 340
    support for Ahmed Mansour, 226–227
    See also Mansour, Ahmed; media.
Jubail area, 163
al-Jumayli, Sami, 301

K

Kabul, 83
Kagan, Robert, 156
al-Kahky, Amro, 97, 98
Kaiser, Peter, 325
Karbala, xii, 111, 154, 284, 285
Karma, 337
Kazimeyah, 116
Kennedy, Edward, 262, 271
Keogh, David, 230, 231
Kerry, John, 46, 231, 283
Kent, Sgt. Major Carlton W., 294–295
Khaldiya, 97
Khanfar, Wadah, xi, xiii, 42, 62, 69, 179–180, 191–192, 193, 195, 202, 209, 227, 232–233, 240
Khuddam al-Hussain Hotel, 111
kidnappings. *See under* insurgents.
Kilfoyle, Peter, 231–232
Kill, Kill, Kill, 245
Kimmitt, General Mark, 13, 39–40, 41, 129, 276
    and Ahmed Mansour, 191–192, 200, 210, 219–220, 239–250
    and cease-fire, 181, 203
    interviews with, 114–115, 146, 184, 217–220

vows to bring mercenaries' killers to justice, 47–48, 53
Kite, Melissa, 231
Koizumi, Prime Minister Junichiro, 259
Koppel, Ted, 235
Kraishan, Muhammad, xii, 174–175, 178, 184, 191
Kristol, William, 156, 346n33
Kubaisy, Abdulsalam, 285
Kubaisy, Sheikh Makky, 44, 145
Kufa, 93, 154, 256, 345n27
Kunduz province, 83
Kurds, 281, 291, 299, 327, 329
Al-Kut, 154, 254, 256, 284
Kuwait, 94, 138, 341

L

Lake Chatterbox. *See* Buhayrat al-Tharthar.
Lake Habbaniya, 19
Lancet, 282–283
Late Night with David Letterman, 234
Late Night Edition with Wolf Blitzer, 237
Latif, General Mohammed, 281
Lautenberg, Frank, 46
Lebanon, 18, 61, 64–65, 245
Levin, Carl, 271
Los Angeles Times, 331
Lugar, Richard, 264

M

al-Ma'adeedy cemetery, 163
Madrid train bombings, 258
Mahdi Army, 64, 93, 154 *See also* al-Sadr, Muqtada.
Mahon, Alice, 290
Main Street (Fallujah), 101, 102, 108, 126, 127, 139, 160, 305
Mansour, Ahmed,
    appearance on *Democracy Now!*, 52
    and broken satellite transmitter in Fallujah, 98, 100, 105, 109–110
    and cease-fire, 181–187, 193, 202, 203, 206–213, 218
    criticism of, 223, 226, 235
    coverage of March 31 mercenary attacks, 42–43
    coverage of first battle of Fallujah, 96–97, 89–93, 103–104, 126, 128, 136, 139, 148, 168–181, 187–188, 222
    coverage of other wars, 83, 94, 102, 175, 236
    emotional reactions to war, 88, 104, 114, 162, 163, 164, 173–176
    entering Fallujah to cover the first battle, 70–85, 89
    and General Mark Kimmitt, 191–192, 200, 210, 219–220, 239–250
    filming of insurgents, 108–109, 138, 148, 184, 235
    filming of US troops, 91, 92–93, 100, 101, 140, 151, 184
    and insomnia, 69, 99, 124, 165, 197
    interactions with US soldiers, 6, 71–72, 73–74, 76–77, 78
    interviews with civilians, 3–9, 12, 27–28, 42, 43, 88–90, 104, 108, 112, 128–129, 133, 303
    interview with John Hilary, 34
    interview with Ibrahim al-Shimari, 32–33
    and al-Jazeera crew in Fallujah, 70, 82, 87–88, 136, 166–168, 176, 177, 193, 194, 200–202, 209–211
    journalistic intentions, 133–134, 136, 186, 200, 210–211, 213, 222–223, 241
    leaving Fallujah, 209–213
    live news reports during first battle, 91–93, 105, 114, 123, 135–136, 153, 187
    and other journalists, 224–227
    and Sami al-Haj, 228–229, 340–341
    and second battle of Fallujah, 301
    security of, 190, 198–201, 204
    and start of the first battle, xi–xiii, 69–70, 85
    under sniper threat, 139–140, 145, 151–153, 165, 168
    and verification of reported news, 94–96, 118, 219, 226
    visit to Diyala River, 32–33
    visit to Samarra, 3, 54–56, 60–65
    wife and family of, 130, 137–138, 171–172
    See also al-Jazeera, *Without Limits.*
Marcus, Jonathan, 261
Marines. *See under* US Armed Forces.
Marqusee, Mike, 317
Martyrs' Neighborhood, 75, 84, 86
Mash-hadany, Dr. Ali, 3–5
Massey, Jimmy, 245
al-Matloub, Muhammad Jasim, 163
Maupin, Keith Matthew, 259
McCarthy, Rory, 38
McClellan, Scott, 38, 46–47,
media,
    and advertising, 11
    American, 36–37, 48, 52–53, 235, 257, 276
    Arab, 36, 284
    coverage of March 31 mercenary attacks, 26–27, 36–37
    coverage of Fallujah, vii, 38, 52–53, 69, 223, 288, 303, 320–321, 331, 335
    coverage of Iraq war, 54, 56, 120, 221, 243, 265–267, 277
    death of journalists during war coverage, 62, 111, 127, 232, 289
    and first battle of Fallujah, 97, 114, 146, 155, 185–187, 202, 207, 217–218, 222, 257, 276

Iraqi paparazzi, 56–58
internet, 37
and second battle of Fallujah, 292, 305, 319–320
under the occupation, 9–12, 225–226
See also specific media outlets.
medical care. See under first battle of Fallujah.
mercenaries, 21–22, 29, 30–41, 330
    attack on, March 31, vii, xii, 25–26, 40, 43–44, 49, 113, 202, 277, 286
    Arab, 90
    Chilean, 33
    deaths of, 53
    descriptions of, 31, 60, 72–73, 74–75
    Iraqi, 90
    legal responsibilities of, 35
    mass graves for, 32
    mistreatment of civilians, 22, 31
    number of, in Iraq, 34, 291
    responsibilities of, 30
    salaries of, 33–34
    war crimes committed by, 36
Merle, Renae, 34
Metz, Lt. General Thomas F., 302
Michigan Daily, 326–327
Midday News, 207
Middle East magazine, 34
military checkpoints, 71–73, 76–77, 86, 91–92, 118, 290, 318
Military Neighborhood, 99, 100, 101, 104, 126, 142, 147, 160
Ministry of Defense of Iraq, 43
"Mission Accomplished" proclamation, 20
Mogadishu. See Somalia.
Mohammed, Niran, 331
Mohan, Abdul Qader Mohammed Jassim, 312
Moore, Michael, 235
Morocco, 271
Mortensen, Darrin, 323–324
mosques, 19, 44, 51, 61, 99, 132, 141–142, 179, 287, 289, 330
    destruction of, during first battle of Fallujah, 141–147, 151
    destruction of, during second battle of Fallujah, 147, 298–299
Mossad, 51
Mosul, 6, 53, 156 342n3
Msalmy clan, 81
Msalmy (guide into Fallujah), 82, 84–85
Muhammad, Abdulazeem, 27, 42–43, 111, 303
    and first battle of Fallujah, 159, 177, 192–194, 196, 199–203, 210, 211, 212, 218
Muhammad, Burhan, 127
Muhammad, Sayfuldeen, 70, 82, 91, 98, 100, 105, 110
Mujahideen Consultative Council, 202, 286, 303
al-Mukhtar, Ghazwan, 52–53

al-Muntathar, 63
Muqdadiyah, 54
Murtha, Jack, 262–263
Mushtaq, Layth, 70, 109, 126, 136, 139, 187
    appearance on Democracy Now!, 52
    death of Rasheed Wally, 111
    and filming first battle of Fallujah, 71, 88–89, 91, 92–93, 100, 101, 103, 106, 107, 113, 119, 135, 138, 153, 169, 170, 172–173, 176, 178
    filming March 31 attack, 27
    leaving Fallujah, 192, 196, 203
    smoking habit, 112
Myers, Richard B., 150, 269–270, 298, 312, 327

N

Naimyah, 106, 280, 337
Naimyah Desert Patch, 79, 81
Naimyah Road, 75, 76, 118–120, 122, 124, 187, 188
    civilian deaths on, 168–174, 180
Najaf, xii, 116, 150, 154, 254, 256, 284, 285
Nammour, Jumana, 42
Nantz, Lt. Colonel Eric, 25
Nasariya, 150
Nasser, Abdussamad, 77–78, 89, 203
Nasser, Katia, 146
Nation, 221
National Defense Agency, 8
National Guard. See under US Armed Forces.
National Institute for Democracy, 11
National Intelligence Council, 264
National Intelligence Estimate, 264, 283
National Security Agency, 261
National Security Council (NSC), 149–150, 182, 194, 278
NATO, 39
Natonski, General Richard, 326–327
Nazzal Neighborhood, 86, 91, 113, 135, 139, 142, 144, 147, 160, 162, 176, 305
NBC, 23, 37, 186, 317, 319, 330
neoconservatives, 156, 217, 249
New Iraqi Army, 93, 139, 141, 254–255
New York Times, 10–11, 18, 21, 37–38, 47, 156, 223, 244, 264, 265, 269, 277, 283, 293, 297, 298, 300, 302, 303, 306
newspapers, 9–12. See also journalists, media.
Newsweek, 244, 260, 263, 276
Nicolas, Steve, 331
Nimrawi, Khamis, 123, 128–129, 161
9/11. See September 11, 2001
1958 coup, 43–44
1991 Gulf War, 267
1920 Revolution Brigades, 51, 255
North Atlantic Treaty Organization. See NATO.
North County News, 323
NSC. See National Security Council.
Nuremberg Charter, 247

O

Oakland Tribune, 25
Obaid, Munther Muhammad, 189–190, 198, 212
al-Obaidy, Brigadier General Muzher, 149
Obais, Saeyah Abdulkarim, 336
occupation, 9, 117
    authorities, xiii, 97, 237, 277
    brutality of, 52, 53, 89, 247, 276, 282, 287
    calls to end, 45, 48, 51, 262–263, 314
    criticism of, 182, 277
    and detention of civilians, 16, 52, 54, 58–60,
      63, 259. *See also* Abu Ghraib.
    four year anniversary of, 156, 282–283
    gun permits issued under, 97
    Iraqi response to, 23, 29, 154, 247, 285, 286,
      291, 321. *See also* Fallujah.
    journalism during, 9–12, 130, 202, 225–
      226, 238
    plundering of Iraqi resources, 3–8
    rights of people living under, 44, 321
    security problems, 13–14, 243, 256, 264,
      281, 283
    treatment of women, children, and the
      elderly under, 22, 24, 28
    and unemployment, 8–9, 318–319
    one year anniversary of, 3–18, 156, 157,
      165, 168–181, 262
    three year anniversary of, 52, 240
    See also Bremer, Paul.
O'Connor, Leo, 230, 231
Odom, William, 261
Office of Strategic Communications for
    Coalition Forces in Baghdad, 223–224
Officers' Neighborhood, 113, 126, 142, 147, 160,
    199
Official Secrets Act, 230
O'Hanlon, Michael, 244
oil, 3–5, 341
Oil for Food program, 5
old market. *See under* Fallujah.
OPCW. *See* Organisation for the Prohibition of
    Chemical Weapons.
Operation Phantom Fury. *See* the second battle
    of Fallujah.
Operation Vigilant Resolve. *See* the first battle of
    Fallujah.
Oppel, Jr., Richard A., 297
Organisation for the Prohibition of Chemical
    Weapons, 324–325
Othman, Mahmood, 17
Othman, Narmin, 321

P

Pace, General Peter, 49, 343n16
Pachachi, Adnan, 17, 157, 201

Palestine, 51
Party of God's Revenge, 12
Pelley, Scott, 156
Pelosi, Nancy, 45
Pentagon, 10, 33, 140, 227, 253, 257, 268, 269–
    270, 283, 298, 313, 322
Perle, Richard, 156, 237
Petraus, General David, 263
Philip, Catherine, 24
Pinochet, Augusto, 33
PNAC. *See* Project for the New American
    Century.
Police Neighborhood, 160
Powell, Colin, 39, 150, 194, 221–222, 261, 299
Press Action, 53
prisons. *See* Abu Ghraib; Guantánamo Bay.
private security contractors. *See* mercenaries.
Prodi, Prime Minister Romano, 259
Project for the New American Century, 156
Prophet Muhammad, 62–63, 64

Q

al-Qadisya, 13, 15. *See also* Green Zone.
Qa'em, 94, 97
al-Qaeda, vii, 228–229, 246, 249–250, 258, 261,
    291
    connection to Saddam Hussein, 265–266, 305
    and al-Zarqawi, 286
al-Qaisy, Shaikh Abdulwahab, 134
Qatar, 221–222, 223, 229
Quds Press, 289, 332
Quran, 58–59

R

Ramadan, 294
Ramadi, 54, 56, 91, 94, 97, 116, 253, 282, 343n18
Ramos, Lt. Colonel Mike, 295
Rather, Dan, 234–235
Rawa, 337
al-Rawi, Ahmad, 306
al-Rawi, Fuad, 278
al-Rawi Mosque, 208, 212
Red Crescent. *See* Iraqi Red Crescent.
reconstruction (of Iraq), 264, 283, 311, 315
    See also US–Iraq war, cost of.
Record, Jeffrey, 261
Regner, Colonel Michael, 304
religious community responses to Fallujah,
    43–44, 144–145, 179, 279, 299, 328–329
Republic Neighborhood, 100
Republican Guard, 8, 32, 149, 252, 280
Republicans, 262–263, 264, 271, 341
Resala Neighborhood, 305
Reuters, 202, 288, 292, 300, 301, 305, 313, 336
revenge operations. *See* insurgents.

Revolution City. *See* Sadr City.
Rice, Condoleezza, 150, 156, 194, 269, 278, 280, 283
Rodríguez Zapatero, Prime Minister José Luis, 258
Royal Air Force (RAF) Station at Habbaniya, 19, 25
Rumsfeld, Donald, 14, 23, 221, 237, 238, 256, 265–266, 268–269, 271, 281, 282, 298, 299–300, 315, 327
Rusch, Robin, 221
Russia, 259

S

Sadr City, 93, 116, 141, 154, 256, 285
al-Sadr, Muqtada, 64, 115, 150, 154, 156, 158, 185, 285, 329
    attacks on US Forces, 93, 154, 203–204, 254, 256
    See also Mahdi army.
Saladin, 6
Salafis, 249–250, 328, 346n37
Saleh, General Jassim Muhammad, 280–281
Salem, Ali, 105
Salim, Ezzedine, 17
al-Said, Prime Minister Nuri, 43
Samarra, 3, 43, 55–56, 116, 156, 256, 282, 285
    history of, 6, 54, 60–63
    religion in, 61
    under occupation 60–61, 62–63, 204, 254
Samarray, Sheikh Ahmad, 18, 159, 218–219, 279
Samarray, Iyad, 181, 183, 185
Samarray, Sheikh Nahedh, 3, 62, 63
Samarray, Suhayb Albaaz, 56–60
Sameer, Hussain, 195–196, 199, 211–213
    death of, 204–206, 208
Sameer, Nizar, 196, 199, 205
San Francisco Chronicle, 45
Sanchez, Lt. General Ricardo, 16, 57, 93, 144, 194, 254, 280
Saqlawiyah, 116, 335, 337, 345n29
Sarajevo, 83
Sattler, Lt. General John, 294
Saturday Night Live, 263
Saudi Arabia, 250, 271
Saulnier, Natasha, 245
Schmidt, Eric, 302
Schmidt, Jean, 262–263
Scott Tyson, Ann, 318
Seattle Times, 268
second battle of Fallujah, viii, 140, 218,
    bombing of neighborhoods, 298, 313
    casualty counts, 297–298, 299–301, 305, 331
    and cease-fire, 311
    civilian casualties, 290, 317, 334
    destruction of mosques, 147, 298–299, 302, 306, 318
    end of, 314–315

and food shortage, 307
and hospitals, 297–298, 300–301, 331–333
and house searches, 309, 313
and humanitarian aid, 306, 309, 316
humanitarian crisis during, 313, 336, 337
importance of, 279
lead up to, 284–289, 290–296
media coverage of, 292–293, 299–300, 319–320
official start of, 293–296
people of Fallujah during, 333–334, 335–339
protests of, 313
role of mercenaries in, 35
utilities during, 301–302, 317
and water supply, 307–308, 317
and white phosphorous, 321–325
and al-Zarqawi, 302–305, 314, 327
sectarianism, 61–62, 154, 179, 246, 248, 299, 327–329. *See also* Kurds, Shiite, Sunni.
Senate Armed Services Committee, 270
Senate Foreign Relations Committee, 264
Sengupta, Kim, 288–289
Senor, Dan, 277
September 11, 2001, 222, 234, 267, 335
Shaalan, Hazem, 295
Shanker, Thom, 269
al-Sharq al-Aswat, 21, 50, 297
Shayeb, Layla, 114
Sheehan, Cindy, 52
Sheikh Ahmad Yasin Brigades, 51–52
Shiites, 158, 179, 182, 260, 281, 284, 291, 299, 327–329
    beliefs of, 61, 63–65
al-Shimari, Ibrahim, 32–33
Shola, 116
Shupp, Colonel Michael, 291
Simon, David, 236
Sistani, Ali, 328, 329
Sites, Kevin, 330
60 Minutes, 156
Sky News TV, 253
snipers. *See under* insurgents; US Armed Forces.
Somalia, 18, 27, 37–39, 245, 343n14
South America, 18, 33
sovereignty. *See* transfer of formal sovereignty.
Soviet–Afghan war, 83, 94, 102, 137, 236, 344n24
Stafford Smith, Clove Adrian, 228–229
Stephanopoulos, George, 275
Story of Baghdad's Fall, The, 21, 343n11
Sudan, 340
suicide bombers, 271, 291, 295
Sullivan, Captain Christopher J., 139, 345n31
al-Sumaidy, Shaikh Mahdi, 328
Sumidaee, Sameer, 17
Sunnis, 158, 179, 182, 260, 285, 291, 299, 327–329
    beliefs of, 61, 65

maintenance of tomb of Imam al-Hadi, 61
  political parties, 301
Sunni Triangle, 6, 254
Supporters of Truth, 31–32
Supreme Defense Academy, 8
surgical strikes, 280, 284, 288
Swan Lake Hotel. *See* al-Jazeera.
Swannack, General Charles, 13
Sydney Morning Herald, 143
Syria, 70, 73, 155, 270, 271, 293

T

Taji, 56
Taliban, 237
Tanai, Lt. General Shahnawaz, 83, 345n25
tanks, 15, 76, 102, 126, 138, 300
Tarmeya, 56
Tawfeeq, Mowafaq, 241, 242
Teague, Michael, 40
Tenet, George, 156–157, 264
Tenth Imam. *See* tomb of Imam Ali al-Hadi.
Tet Offensive, viii
Thra'a Dijla, 185
Al-Thawra City. *See* Sadr City.
thermal detection, 153, 235
A Thousand and One Nights, 65, 344n23
Tigris River, 7, 342n3
Tikrit, 6, 54, 56, 116, 156
Time magazine, 318
Times (London), 24, 25, 37, 311
Tisdall, Simon, 263
tomb of Imam Ali al-Hadi, 61–62, 63
tomb of Imam al Hassan al-Askari, 63
Toolan, Colonel John, 135
trailers (transporting resources and supplies), 6, 159
transfer of formal sovereignty, 45, 46, 48, 114,
  158, 260, 281. *See also* Allawi, Ayad;
  Bremer, Paul
Transitional National Assembly, 185
Tribune (India), 49
Triple Canopy, 35
Tunisia, 271
Turkey, 6
Turki, Abdel Basit, 157
Tuttle, Robert, 323, 325
Twelfth Imam, 63–65

U

al-Ulum, Bahr, 17, 281
Umm-ul-Qurra Mosque, 159, 179, 279
unemployment, 8–9
UNICEF, 338
United for Peace and Justice, 314
United Nations, 113, 150, 151, 260, 267, 299,
  321, 336, 338

Assistance Mission to Iraq, 336–337
  Charter, 282
  Higher Commission for Refugees
    (UNHCR), 337, 338
  Security Council, 18, 150
US Armed Forces,
  behavior toward civilians, 52–53, 54, 112,
    117, 248, 280, 287, 288, 291, 333–334
  bombing of civilians, 102, 117, 129, 182
  blocking humanitarian aid, 159, 277, 309,
    316, 338
  breaking Geneva Conventions, 143, 146
  confrontations with insurgents, 20, 23–24,
    54–56, 57, 118–121, 135–136, 165, 180,
    188, 251
  casualties, 23, 55, 116, 120, 141, 253, 282,
    283, 300, 313, 315,
  criticism of, 146
  defeat of, viii, 89, 150–151, 155–156, 254,
    275–276
  descriptions of, 31, 60, 71–72, 73–75
  descriptions of, during first battle of
    Fallujah, 101, 103, 121, 126,
  and destruction of mosques, 141–147, 287
  enforcement of curfew, 92, 93, 96, 103, 146
  extended tours in Iraq, 140, 256
  fighting during first battle of Fallujah, 96,
    107, 108, 109, 114, 118–120, 135–136,
    139–140, 184
  filming of, during first battle of Fallujah, 91,
    92–93, 100, 101, 140, 151, 184
  and Green Zone security, 13, 15, 38
  guarding trailers, 6
  and house searches, 22, 25, 28, 113, 138,
    309, 313, 318
  and Iraqi forces, 141, 202, 244, 255–256,
    299, 312
  Marines, 116, 151, 176, 194, 200, 242, 262,
    275, 326
    and cease-fire, 203, 277–280
    fighting tactics of, 252–253
    and first battle of Fallujah, 93, 135,
      138–141, 160, 161–165
    and Naimyah Road rumor, 168, 180
    and second battle of Fallujah, 294–295,
      309–310, 312, 316, 319
    treatment of civilians, 235, 330–331,
  morale of, 89, 121, 122, 218, 244, 257, 294–
    295
  and Muqtada al-Sadr, 93, 154, 203–204,
    254, 256
  National Guard, 139
  numbers of, in Fallujah, 19, 34, 93, 138–139,
    140, 291
  occupation of hospitals, 103, 277, 297, 332
  and propaganda, 11

protocol following an attack, 55, 57, 257
reputation of, 186, 218, 223, 236, 275, 295, 298
and Samarra, 3, 63, 156, 204, 254, 285
and second battle of Fallujah, 297–315, 326, 335
snipers, 107, 111, 114, 139, 140, 142, 151–153, 160, 182, 194, 278
statements made to media, during first battle, 92, 139, 143, 146, 203
and supplies, 155–156, 165, 182, 185, 218
surrounding Fallujah, xi, xiii, 69, 70, 76, 93, 102, 290–291
and white phosphorous, 321–325
See also first and second battles of Fallujah.
US Army Psychological Warfare Unit, 11
US Central Command (Doha), 225
US Congress, 46, 50, 262–263, 269, 271, 282, 285
US Department of Defense, 18, 244, 330
US Department of State, 18, 50, 227, 311, 322, 323, 325
US–Iraq war, 150, 246
 calls to end, 45, 48, 51, 262–263, 314
 casualties
  civilian, 25, 102, 114, 122–124, 129, 142, 147, 163, 173–176, 187, 276, 282–283, 289
  media, 62, 111, 127, 232, 289
  US Armed Forces, 25, 55, 116, 120, 127, 141, 253, 282, 283, 300, 313, 315
 comparisons to Vietnam War, viii, 15, 259–262, 263, 295
 cost of, 4–5, 270, 283, 311, 318
 criticism of, 45–46, 48, 244, 311
 and European allies, 258
 and fall of Baghdad (2003), xii, 21, 63, 148–149, 342n1
 and humanitarian crises, 336
 illegality of, 282
 justifications for, vii, 114–115, 134, 207, 232, 244, 249, 266, 305
 role of paparazzi in, 56–58
 US strategy for, 45, 140, 243, 249, 263, 284
US puppet regimes, 18, 279
US Senate, 261, 266 See also Senate Foreign Relations Committee.
USA Today, 140, 330
USS Abraham Lincoln, 20

V

Van Auken, Bill, 262
Venables, Lt. Colonel Barry, 322
Vietnam, 18, 245, 293
 and comparisons to Iraq war, viii, 15, 259–262, 263, 295

W

Walid, Hassan, 70, 88–89, 100, 103, 126, 127, 130, 131–132, 136, 170, 176, 178, 191, 196, 203
Wally, Rasheed, 109–111
war crimes, 36, 60, 117, 242, 245, 247, 279, 288, 293, 327, 329–331, 333, 334. See also crimes against humanity; Geneva Conventions; human rights.
war on Iraq. See US–Iraq war.
war on terror, 225, 262, 267, 270
War on Want, 34–35, 343n15
warplanes, 15, 90, 92, 122, 140, 276, 285, 306
 See also AC-130 gunships; F-16 Falcon Fighters; helicopters.
Washington, DC, 145, 314
Washington Post, 30, 34, 48, 143, 230, 244, 255, 262, 298, 318, 324
al-Watan, 331, 347n40
Weapons of Mass Destruction (WMDs), vii, 246, 249, 261, 266–267, 299, 305
Weekly Standard, 156
Wefaq Junior High School, 104
White House, 50, 156, 268, 283
white phosphorus, 232, 321–325
Without Limits, xii, 12, 25, 35, 148–149, 228, 239, 241
Witness for an Era, A, xiii
Wolfowitz, Paul, 49, 221
Wong, Edward, 302
Woodward, Bob, 237
World Bank, 49
World Socialist Web Site, 262
Worth, Robert, 297

Y

Yasin, Sheikh Ahmad, 51
al-Yawar, Ghazi, 17, 158, 201

Z

Za'atra, Yasser, 184–185
Zahr Eldin, Lina, 129
al-Zaki, Jaffar, 63
al-Zarqawi, Abu Musab, 244, 248, 286–289, 291, 292, 302–305, 314, 327
al-Zawba'ie, Noor al-Deen, 20, 23, 343n10
Zebari, Hoshyar, 238
Zovko, Jerry "Jerko", 40
Zunes, Stephen, 311